WHAT IT TAKES
WISDOM FROM PEER SUPPORT SPECIALISTS AND SUPERVISORS

Edited by
Rita Cronise
Jonathan P. Edwards
Gita Enders
Joanne Forbes

With major contributions by
Lori Ashcraft
Dana Foglesong
Kelsey Knowles
Ian Winter

Contents

PART 4: SUCCESSFUL SUPERVISION OF PEER SUPPORT

PART 5: SPECIAL INTERESTS

APPENDIX A: BIOGRAPHIES

APPENDIX B: HISTORY OF N.A.P.S.

APPENDIX C: TRIBUTES TO FALLEN LEADERS

DEDICATION

This book is dedicated to the memory of Steve Harrington, founder of the National Association of Peer Supporters (N.A.P.S.). Steve was a Renaissance man; highly intelligent and deeply compassionate. He was a scholar, a lawyer, a biologist, a social scientist, an artist, a humorist, and a thought leader. He saw the need for peer support specialists to connect and form community with one another. This book is the result of the contributions from members of the community that he started, and his spirit lives on in the community of peer support that continues to evolve.

Acknowledgments

The editors of the book wish to thank the Board members of the National Association of Peer Supporters (N.A.P.S.) for their support and encouragement during the development of this book. We also want to thank the following contributors:

Amey Dettmer, Anna Rockhill, Ashley Sproul, Carina Teixeira, Celia Brown, Cheryl Gagne, Chris Martin, Clarence Jordan, Dan Berstein, Dana Foglesong, Debbie Nicolellis, Diann Schutter, Elizabeth Thomas, Jonathan P. Edwards, E. Sally Rogers, Gayle Bluebird, Gita Enders, George Braucht, Hayley Peek, Ian Winter, Jason Robison, Jessica Wolf, Joanne Forbes, Kim Sunderland, Larry Davidson, Lori Ashcraft, Laysha Ostrow, Linda May Wacker, Lisa Kugler, Lyn Legere, Michelle Love, Morgan Pelot, Mark Salzer, Mx. Yaffa, Nicole MacAskill-Kylie, Patty Blum, Phyllis Foxworth, Rita Cronise, Ruth Hollman, Scott Palluck, Tammi Sue Paul, Thomasina Borkman, Vic Welle, Wallis Adams, and Yumi Ikuta

We also want to thank Dana Foglesong for acting as the liaison to the N.A.P.S. Board during the initial stages of the book's development and for her ongoing involvement as the book started to take shape. We thank Lori Ashcraft for taking on the task of writing a whole chapter when we found we didn't have enough narratives to cover the topic, Ian Winter for bringing the perspective of the youth peer specialist to meetings as the book evolved, Mae Murray and her team for preparing the book for publication and special thanks to Kelsey Knowles for her willingness to pick up tasks that needed to be accomplished along the way and to share her knowledge of the publication process, contacts, and guidance, which were invaluable at many points throughout the development of the book.

FOREWORD
WHAT IT TAKES: WISDOM FROM PEER SPECIALISTS AND SUPERVISORS

Foreword by Celia Brown

Stories have shaped the field of peer support since the very beginning and this book is filled with contemporary stories by and for peer support specialists and supervisors. I have been friends with the editors and many of the authors included in this volume for many years and offer gratitude for the care with which they have researched, captured, and included meaningful stories from practitioners as they were told at the National Peer Support Conference in the past five years. It represents a snapshot in time in the evolution of the field of peer support and I believe it will be referenced well into the future.

As one of the first peer support practitioners in the 1990's, and the first civil service peer specialist title in the country, I have seen the promise and problems associated with including peer support within mental health settings. Having experienced peer specialists involved in the design of programs and the supervision of peer support staff makes a difference in the quality and effectiveness of any program that is providing peer support services.

As the peer support field continues to spread into new and varied settings, it is important for the peer specialist voice to be strong and to lead the inclusion efforts in settings where they will be working alongside clinical practitioners that do not have the same values or scope of practice. Too often, peer specialists are seen as an "entry level" position without the same level of academic credentials as their counterparts. However, the value that peer specialists bring is the shared stories that create connection, a shared worldview, and the trust that comes with seeing someone who has been there and done that and has been successful in overcoming the very same kinds of challenges as the person is currently facing.

What this book offers are chapters by and for practitioner of peer support on recovery, the history of peer support, the values and standards of practice, and the inclusion of peer support in behavioral health care settings. There are also chapters on what helps and what hinders, advice from communities of practice. From the perspective of supervisors of peer support specialists, there are voices of peer support supervisors, research and resources, and practice standards for supervisors. Finally, there is a chapter on inclusion and collaboration that includes peer support during the pandemic, research questions from the perspective of peers, youth in residential treatment facilities and transforming lives with the arts.

I encourage you to find those chapters that are most meaningful for you on your own journey into peer support and/or supervision and to share this book with other practitioners you know.

Foreword by Larry Davidson

The editors and authors of this timely and invaluable resource are well-justified in tying the birth of mental health peer support to the contemporary mental health consumer/survivor movement. They have in many ways grown up in tandem. There have, however, been earlier efforts to deploy persons in recovery as mental health staff in hospitals which did not turn out so well and which offer us a cautionary note which makes this new volume all the more important.

The first record of such a practice can be found in Pinel's *Treatise on Insanity* from the 1790s, in which he credits the superintendent of the Bicetre asylum, Jean Baptiste Pussin (who had himself been a patient at the hospital) with deploying former inpatients to stay on the wards to take care of the other patients, just as he had done himself. A similar strategy was employed by the American psychiatrist Harry Stack Sullivan (who was thought to have had a serious mental illness himself), who hired his recovering patients to work on his inpatient ward. Who better, thought Sullivan, to be able to reach and mentor his young patients than those who had recently been through psychosis and treatment themselves?

Neither of these practices lasted, however, and at least one main reason for this was the lack of a supportive infrastructure that included such resources and supports as training, supervision, and a ladder of opportunities for advancement. The contemporary form of peer support, while growing, is at risk of traveling down this same old road unless and until the kinds of resources available in this volume become widely assessable. For mental health peer support to survive as it has been created and envisioned—as a unique peer-to-peer practice separate from, and not subordinate to, clinical practice—this kind of supportive infrastructure will be essential. This volume goes a long way toward arguing and advocating for, and toward showing what this essential peer-driven infrastructure looks like in practice. It offers a most welcome inoculation against the kinds of watering down and betrayal of the essential tasks, aspirations, and values of true peer support which currently pose the risk of going the same way as Pussin and Sullivan innovations that began centuries and decades ago. The book offers us the tools to get it right this time around.

INTRODUCTION

What It Takes: The Wisdom of Peer Support and Supervision arose from a workgroup that had been meeting regularly to revise the National Practice Guidelines for Peer Specialists and Supervisors (launched in 2019) and a Supervision Learning Collaborative (held in 2020 and 2021). The next project the group decided would be of benefit to the workforce was an application-oriented book on peer support and supervision, in which practitioners could share their practical knowledge of peer support through stories that could resonate with individual practitioners and their supervisors.

This book covers a wide range of topics-all of them are submissions from presentations at national peer conferences over the last five years. In so doing, the editors wish to reflect some core tenets: Nothing about us without us! and Each one, Teach one!

Although there has been progress in research about peer support and even recognition of peer support as an evidence based practice, the practice of peer support is being shaped on the ground by courageous peer supporters joining the ranks of mental health teams often more closely aligned with a medical model of care. These peer support workers are figuring out how to bring peer values like mutuality into workplaces that have historically operated within a power differential paradigm. This is no easy task!

Given the barriers and challenges faced within these evolving workplaces, this book is intended to give peer support workers, their allies and co-workers, an opportunity to hear from those who are contributing to the effort of bringing the peer voice to those places that intersect with peers in need of help with mental health conditions. The first section considers the role of peer support in behavioral health. While *What it Takes: The Wisdom of Peer Support and Supervision* is not a book about recovery per se, recovery is a central concept that drives the work of peer supporters and allies everywhere. So it is with a nod to the importance of the concept of recovery that this book begins. Following that is a discussion about peer support and its history. If it were not for the pioneers who offered another world view in challenge to the pessimism of a mental health delivery system, the recognition and subsequent professionalization of peer support would not have taken place.

The second part of this book discusses peer support values and standards. Peer support values and how they are expressed are what set the act of peer support apart from traditional professional roles in mental health. The chapters in this section talk explicitly about those values and also take the reader into some of the effort needed to reach consensus and bring those values into peer support practice. Although the peer support profession is built on the foundation of those values, it is often a challenge to express and represent those values in mental health systems that are not yet practicing a recovery oriented practice. Within this part of the book therefore are chapters on the efforts to include peer support into existing behavioral health systems.

The third part of *What it Takes*, is dedicated to the actual practice of peer support. It is within the daily effort to bring peer support to those peers experiencing mental health challenges that the tenet, Each One Teach One finds expression. One chapter in this section represents advice taken directly from communities of practice. The apprenticeship model of learning is alive and well within this chapter as peer support workers report out on issues that are common in peer support work, like facing our fears, handling conflict and creating human resource practices that support this growing profession. Early on in the self help/consumer/survivor/ex-patient movement, it was the voice of peers that brought to the attention of the mental health system those common practices or attitudes that got in the way of a person's journey to recovery. To illustrate the strengths based focus of peer values, this same group also took the time to identify those attitudes and practices that were helpful. There is the continued effort by peer supporters to identify practices that help and support personal growth and recovery and to point to and shout out those practices that hinder those efforts.

Part IV of this book is essential to the ongoing success of peer support: Successful Supervision. Within these chapters are the voices of those peers providing supervision, researching peer supervision and identifying practice standards that can successfully guide peer supervision. Peer drift is a real and constant threat to the practice of peer support. As currently constructed through the guidance of CMS, many peer support workers are supervised by non-peers. This is unheard of in other professions and is a constant source of concern within the ranks of peer supporters. These chapters are meant to provide guidance about peer supervision from both those who are providing supervision but also from research.

Finally, in the last part of this book, the reader will get a sampler of some of the special interest issues that are emerging from the peer workforce. Diversity, equity and inclusion are important guiding principles of peer support. Although not the focus of this book, issues that impact diversity,equity and inclusion always need to be brought forward. Given the impact of COVID on workforce issues, it is not at all surprising to see interest in this topic reflected in the national discussions peers are having. Youth, families, spirituality and thoughts on needed research tease the reader with a look at the issues coming to the forefront.

Appendixes to the book contain tributes to leaders and allies of the peer support workforce that have passed within the past five years (the same time-frame as the contributions from conference presentations for this book were drawn from). While it is impossible to recognize every person who has passed that has made major contributions to the peer support movement, the editors of this book were personally connected to those mentioned in the appendix. They wanted to use the book as an opportunity to remember their mentors and friends. Also included in the appendixes is a brief history of the National Association of Peer Supporters (N.A.P.S.) by several of the founding members.

This book is meant to reflect just some of the interests and issues important to the growing peer support workforce. It is also meant to keep the discussions and needed guidance squarely in the hands of peer supporters and those they walk alongside. "Nothing about us without us!" remains as important today as it was those long decades ago when courageous folks stood up to a mental health system that needed to do better.

PART 1:
UNDERSTANDING PEER SUPPORT IN BEHAVIORAL HEALTH

Chapter 1: An Overview of Recovery

- Chapter Introduction by the Editors
- Section 1: What is Recovery?

Chapter 2: What is Peer Support?

- Chapter Introduction by the Editors
- Section 1: Reflections on Peer Support
- Section 2: What is a Peer Specialist?
- Section 3: The Peer Workforce, Results of a National Survey
- Section 4: Sharing Your Wellness and Recovery Story

Chapter 3: The History of Peer Support

- Chapter Introduction by the Editors
- Section 1: History of the Consumer/Survivor Movement
- Section 2: Challenging the Status Quo: Breaking the Mold in the 21st Century
- Section 3: Mental Health Peer Support Workforce Designline

CHAPTER 1
AN OVERVIEW OF RECOVERY

CHAPTER INTRODUCTION BY THE EDITORS

RECOVERY IS A CENTRAL CONCEPT IN SUBSTANCE USE PROGRAMS, BUT ONLY recently has it been thought possible for people with mental health conditions. All peer support workers and their allies should be familiar with the longitudinal research studies reported by Courtenay Harding and other researchers on the long-term outcome studies of people diagnosed with schizophrenia and the most severe mental conditions. These studies were among the first research that demonstrated recovery was possible while highlighting the benefits of mental health supports and services. If you are not familiar with this pioneering research read, the online excerpt from *Recovery from Severe Mental Illnesses: Research Evidence and Implications for Practice, available from Boston University Center for Psychiatric Rehabilitation*.

Prior to these studies, the prevailing wisdom in mental health systems of care was that persons diagnosed with mental illness did not and could not recover. Such "knowledge" drove treatments that were often paternalistic and shrouded in hopelessness and despair. Courtney Harding's research "proved" what so many psychiatric survivors had been saying for years - that the very systems set up to "help" were frequently doing more harm. For an inspirational article by Courtenay Harding about her research and those who stood by her and supported her during the years of scrutiny by a system that tried to discredit her findings read, *The doctor who saw through psychiatric labels to find the real person underneath*, American Journal of Psychiatric Rehabilitation, 2016, Vol 19(1), 17-22.

The President's New Freedom Commission report is also worth reading. It represents the work of experts assembled by U.S. PresidentGeorge W. Bush in 2002 to conduct a comprehensive study of the U.S. mental health service delivery system and make recommendations based on its findings. People with lived experience were invited to sit on the panel of experts. The Commission's findings helped begin the transformation of the mental health system in the United States. The final report can be found by searching for *"President's New Freedom Commission."* The Substance Abuse and Mental Health Services Administration (SAMHSA) later issued a working definition of recovery from mental disorders and/or substance use conditions, which is:

A process of change through which individuals improve their health and wellness, live a self-directed life, and strive to reach their full potential.

The full description with four dimensions and ten guiding principles can be found in the article in this chapter and the SAMHSA website. These concepts are foundational to understanding recovery and the work of peer support providers in both substance use and mental health settings.

For an even deeper understanding of recovery-oriented practices, be sure to read the works of William Anthony, who is known as the father of psychiatric rehabilitation and credited with being a guiding force in the paradigm shift towards recovery. Two of William Anthony's articles (Anthony, 1993a; Anthony, 1993b) are referenced at the end of this chapter and excerpts may be found through Boston University's Center for Psychiatric Rehabilitation website by searching for *"William Anthony and recovery."*

While *What it Takes: The Wisdom of Peer Support and Supervision* is not a book about recovery per se, recovery is a central concept that drives the work of peer supporters and allies everywhere. And the voice of people with lived experience on the topic of recovery should be central to any discussion about recovery. With that in mind, we have included in this chapter, with permission, the following excerpt from the N.A.P.S. founder, Steve Harrington's, 2011 Peer Specialist Training Manual, Fourth Edition, National Association of Peer Specialists.

Section 1: What is Recovery

Steve Harrington, M.P.A., J.D., CPS
Founder, National Association of Peer Specialists (N.A.P.S.)

Excerpt from the 2011 Peer Specialist Training Manual, Fourth Edition,
National Association of Peer Specialists
Used with Permission

"Life is a grindstone, and whether it grinds a man down or polishes him up
depends on the stuff he's made of."

— JOSH BILLINGS

Defining Recovery

TWO PEOPLE MAY SHARE the same diagnosis but their experiences with that
illness are likely to be much different. This is true whether it be a medical or
psychiatric illness. The same is true of recovery. The recovery path for one
person, even if they share the same diagnosis, is likely to be different for
another person.

This is because each person brings with them their set of values, attitudes,
understanding and life experiences. Also, people have different types of
supports in the lives that can have a profound effect on their recovery journey. This uniqueness must be recognized by all those who work in the mental
health profession.

Just as each recovery path is different, so is each person's definition of
recovery. This ambiguity sometimes makes it difficult to implement recovery
endeavors and it is equally difficult to measure recovery progress.

What is Recovery Anyway?

Consider the following essay on recovery from one person's perspective:

I was sitting in a workshop at a "recovery" conference as a presenter
detailed eleven stages of recovery. The presenter had impressive credentials.
He had a Ph.D. and has performed extensive research on the topic. One thing
he didn't have, however, was personal experience as a person with a mental
illness.

For each stage, the presenter identified a series of interventions he
promised would be effective in helping a person move forward. While I was
heartened that he included "setbacks" as part of the final stage, he failed to

account for the dynamic nature of recovery. For him, recovery was a linear, orderly process and he supported this position with a mountain of surveys, data, and professional literature.

While he concluded his presentation, I thought back to my own experience. I was very sick for a long time. For five years, I languished on a sofa and sobbed at soap operas and commercials. If a clinician had placed me in a recovery stage, I wouldn't have cared. It simply wouldn't have mattered to me. All I knew was that I was feeling badly and wanted to get better.

Several months later, I had an opportunity to talk with another recovery researcher who made more sense. "There are only two recovery stages," he explained. "Either you are doing it, or you're not. If you're not, let's explore the barriers and go from there."

Discussion

That approach made much more sense to me but it caused me to re-examine my thoughts about recovery. What is it—really? I searched a host of databases looking for professional literature that would provide me with a meaningful definition. Most mental health professionals relied on various government reports that defined recovery in technical or bureaucratic words.

Seeking simplicity, I decided—on my own—that recovery is being happy. But my simple definition begged another question: What is happy? What does that mean? I went back to the literature but found no real guidance. Finally, I stumbled across guidelines for peer specialist services in Michigan's Medicaid waiver rules. The guidelines required peer specialist services to address "medical necessity," which was defined as: community inclusion and participation, independence, and/or productivity.

My first thought was, "Oh, great! More bureaucratic words that are clearly out of touch with recovery." But, then, I started thinking again about happiness and those medical necessity rules. Who doesn't want to belong? Being part of a community—be it a church group, bowling league, poker club, or other organization—is important. It is certainly part of the happiness picture.

Encouraged by this revelation, I thought about independence. Who doesn't want to be independent? From the time we learn to walk we try to distance ourselves from our dependence on our parents. Yes, I decided, independence is another part of being happy.

Finally, I thought about productivity. Who doesn't want to get up in the morning and feel they have something meaningful to do that day? Holy smokes! The bureaucrats got it right!

Does recovery mean freedom from medications? Maybe, but often this is not the case. Certainly, one can be happy even though medications continue to be involved. Does recovery mean complete independence? Maybe, but one can be happy in a supported-living arrangement, if it is really necessary (of course, no one says such living arrangements must be permanent). Does recovery mean freedom from relapses? Maybe, but one can falter and learn from the experience and make their recovery all that stronger.

I still am not sold on the stages-of-recovery approach and fear the "cookbook" approach it can mean to mental health treatment. Each person's mental illness is unique. No one feels exactly alike, even though they may share the same diagnosis. Recovery, too, is unique to the individual. But there are commonalities.

Hope and courage are fundamental to recovery and must be addressed throughout the process. Peer support can be especially helpful. For friends and family of persons with a mental illness, the experience can be especially difficult because no one likes to see a loved one go through the pain such illnesses bring. Frustration, worry, and desperation can drive friends and family to search for a remedy.

While such advocacy can be extremely useful, friends and family can offer very beneficial supports. A listening ear may be the most useful. A supporter doesn't have to have answers, very often it is enough to just listen. Friends and family can also help by including the person affected by including them in even routine activities. Ask the loved one to accompany you on errands, to a movie, a dinner, or any other event that gets them out of the house and into the community.

Perhaps the most difficult task for friends and family is being patient. Understand it may take a long time with different types of medications and psychotherapy for results to be seen. Hang in there, though, persons with a mental illness need the special kind of support and understanding only friends and family can provide.

Models that explain different stages of recovery are called "developmental" models. This means a person progresses from one stage to another. While such models are sometimes helpful in explaining what a person may be experiencing at a given time, most such models do not account for the dynamic nature of recovery. A person may jump one or more stages forward in their progress or they may go the other way.

One danger of adopting rigid recovery models is that it could lead to "cookie cutter" approaches to treatment. Clearly, one size does not fit all. Each person is an individual and every contact must approach that reality with flexibility and understanding.

Apparent lack of progress toward recovery may be frustrating for those in the helping professions, but even though a person may appear to be stagnant in their recovery process, they may be processing information. As a result, a person may suddenly "get in gear" and make significant progress in a relatively short period. This processing can take a very long time—even years, but patience and a positive attitude on the part of the peer specialist is vital.

Peer specialists have an important place in the recovery model of treatment. The mere presence of peer specialists may reflect an organization's recovery orientation. When working with peers, peer specialists can inspire the hope and courage necessary for a person to move forward. Personal recovery stories, appropriately told, can reverse a downward slide and help a peer overcome even life's most difficult challenges.

It is all about the shared experience. Some mental health administrators—and even some peer specialists themselves—believe people with a criminal history should not be allowed to become peer specialists. While there may be some exceptions, the incarceration experience can be a valuable asset when it comes to relating to and inspiring others in those same circumstances. The same is true of substance abuse experiences and family issues.

There is increasing pressure to measure recovery. Mental health administrators, responding to the need to account to taxpayers, seek ways to show progress. There are nearly a dozen surveys that may help administrators measure such progress. One way peer specialists are helping in this endeavor is by designing and implementing surveys and conducting focus groups (small groups designed to obtain information about issues). Many times, mental health administrators seek the help of peer specialists because of the bond and trust that can rapidly form between them and peers.

Consider the following essay on two approaches to mental health treatment:

There are generally two ways to approach mental health treatment; the medical and recovery models. Each aims to alleviate the pain of mental illness but the approaches are far different. Which model that is selected can have profound effects on way treatment is delivered and the nature of that treatment.

The medical model has long been used for mental health treatment. Those who subscribe to this treatment speak in terms of diagnoses, symptoms, and medications. They tend to rely heavily on the effects of psychotropic medications and little else.

The recovery model, on the other hand, is more holistic. It focuses on strengths, individual courage, self-esteem, problem-solving skills, coping mechanisms, therapy, and hope. It is true enough that medications are part of the recovery model—an important part—but medications do not rule treatment options as they do with the medical model. Instead, the recovery model accepts pharmacological intervention as a step in the road to recovery and places greater responsibility for wellness on the individual.

The recovery model, which has been embraced by most contemporary mental health systems, also relies heavily on the strengths perspective. This means that mental health clinicians must focus on an individual's unique gifts, talents, and capabilities. This approach may also mean a new role for clinicians. Instead of benefactors, where much is done for those they serve, clinicians must become partners in the mental health healing process. In this role, they must offer access to resources and encouragement. But the decision to act must remain with the individual served.

One social work author compared the models and came to the conclusion that persons with a mental illness respond more quickly and enduringly when the clinician "lives and breathes the recovery model."

Hope is an important component of the recovery model for one must have hope in order to believe he/she has the power within themselves to overcome the devastation mental illness can bring. What is hope and where does it come from? These are difficult questions. Hope, it seems, is the presence of aspirations as in plans for the future. Hope can come from many sources. Some find hope through spirituality. Others find hope through friends and family who offer effective support.

When it comes to hope, peer specialists are in a unique position—perhaps the most envied position in social work because peer specialists can instill hope in otherwise hopeless peers. In many cases, the process begins with validation. Peer specialists can easily relate to peers because they have "been there." Through expressions of empathy, they can help others understand their often-confusing feelings.

Another way peer specialists can instill hope is through modeling. Peers can see others who have recovered to the point where they can help others. Others can learn they can manage or even be cured of mental illnesses. It is a powerful position.

Most mental health systems that employ peer specialists have embraced the recovery model. Peer specialists are a natural extension of that philosophy. Take pride in what you do. It is important work and you are helping more people than you may think!

Definition of Recovery

The Substance Abuse and Mental Health Services Administration has devised a working definition of recovery:

A process of change through which individuals improve their health and wellness, live a self-directed life, and strive to reach their full potential.

This section of the guide is from the brochure: SAMHSA'S Working Definition of Recovery and Ten Guiding Principles, which can be found on the SAMHSA website.

Dimensions of Recovery

Through the Recovery Support Strategic Initiative, SAMHSA delineated four major dimensions that support a life in recovery:

Health

Overcoming or managing one's disease(s) or symptoms—for example, abstaining from use of alcohol, illicit drugs, and non-prescribed medications if one has an addiction problem— and for everyone in recovery, making informed, healthy choices that support physical and emotional wellbeing.

Home

A stable and safe place to live.

Purpose

Meaningful daily activities, such as a job, school, volunteerism, family caretaking, or creative endeavors, and the independence, income and resources to participate in society.

Community

Relationships and social networks that provide support, friendship, love, and hope.

Principles of Recovery

In addition to the working definition, and dimensions, SAMHSA identified ten principles of recovery:

Recovery emerges from hope

The belief that recovery is real provides the essential and motivating message of a better future—that people can and do overcome the internal and external challenges, barriers, and obstacles that confront them. Hope is internalized and can be fostered by peers, families, providers, allies, and others. Hope is the catalyst of the recovery process.

Recovery is person-driven

Self-determination and self-direction are the foundations for recovery as individuals define their own life goals and design their unique path(s) towards those goals. Individuals optimize their autonomy and independence to the greatest extent possible by leading, controlling, and exercising choice over the services and supports that assist their recovery and resilience. In so doing, they are empowered and provided the resources to make informed decisions, initiate recovery, build on their strengths, and gain or regain control over their lives.

Recovery occurs via many pathways

Individuals are unique with distinct needs, strengths, preferences, goals, culture, and backgrounds— including trauma experience — that affect and determine their pathway(s) to recovery. Recovery is built on the multiple capacities, strengths, talents, coping abilities, resources, and inherent value of each individual. Recovery pathways are highly personalized. They may include professional clinical treatment; use of medications; support from families and in schools; faith-based approaches; peer support; and other approaches. Recovery is non-linear, characterized by continual growth and improved functioning that may involve setbacks. Because setbacks are a natural, though not inevitable, part of the recovery process, it is essential to foster resilience for all individuals and families. Abstinence from the use of alcohol, illicit drugs, and non-prescribed medications is the goal for those with addictions. Use of tobacco and nonprescribed or illicit drugs is not safe for anyone. In some cases, recovery pathways can be enabled by creating a supportive environment. This is especially true for children, who may not have the legal or developmental capacity to set their own course

Recovery is holistic

Recovery encompasses an individual's whole life, including mind, body, spirit, and community. This includes addressing: self-care practices, family, housing, employment, transportation, education, clinical treatment for mental disorders and substance use disorders, services and supports, primary healthcare, dental care, complementary and alternative services, faith, spirituality, creativity, social networks, and community participation. The array of services and supports available should be integrated and coordinated.

Recovery is supported by peers and allies

Mutual support and mutual aid groups, including the sharing of experiential knowledge and skills, as well as social learning, play an invaluable role in recovery. Peers encourage and engage other peers and provide each other with a vital sense of belonging, supportive relationships, valued roles, and community. Through helping others and giving back to the community, one helps one's self. Peer operated supports and services provide important resources to assist people along their journeys of recovery and wellness. Professionals can also play an important role in the recovery process by providing clinical treatment and other services that support individuals in their chosen recovery paths. While peers and allies play an important role for many in recovery, their role for children and youth may be slightly different. Peer supports for families are very important for children with behavioral health problems and can also play a supportive role for youth in recovery.

Recovery is supported through relationship and social networks

An important factor in the recovery process is the presence and involvement of people who believe in the person's ability to recover; who offer hope, support, and encouragement; and who also suggest strategies and resources for change. Family members, peers, providers, faith groups, community members, and other allies form vital support networks. Through these relationships, people leave unhealthy and/or unfulfilling life roles behind and engage in new roles (e.g., partner, caregiver, friend, student, employee) that lead to a greater sense of belonging, personhood, empowerment, autonomy, social inclusion, and community participation.

Recovery is culturally-based and influenced

Culture and cultural background in all of its diverse representations— including values, traditions, and beliefs—are keys in determining a person's journey and unique pathway to recovery. Services should be culturally grounded, attuned, sensitive, congruent, and competent, as well as personalized to meet each individual's unique needs.

Recovery is supported by addressing trauma

The experience of trauma (such as physical or sexual abuse, domestic violence, war, disaster, and others) is often a precursor to or associated with alcohol and drug use, mental health problems, and related issues. Services and supports should be trauma-informed to foster safety (physical and emotional) and trust, as well as promote choice, empowerment, and collaboration.

Recovery involves individual, family, and community strengths and responsibility

Individuals, families, and communities have strengths and resources that serve as a foundation for recovery. In addition, individuals have a personal responsibility for their own self-care and journeys of recovery. Individuals should be supported in speaking for themselves. Families and significant others have responsibilities to support their loved ones, especially for children and youth in recovery. Communities have responsibilities to provide opportunities and resources to address discrimination and to foster social inclusion and recovery. Individuals in recovery also have a social responsibility and should have the ability to join with peers to speak collectively about their strengths, needs, wants, desires, and aspirations.

Recovery is based on respect

Community, systems, and societal acceptance and appreciation for people affected by mental health and substance use problems— including protecting their rights and eliminating discrimination—are crucial in achieving recovery. There is a need to acknowledge that taking steps towards recovery may require great courage. Self-acceptance, developing a positive and meaningful sense of identity, and regaining belief in one's self are particularly important.

Conclusion

Ask yourself: Do all these components apply to me? Would all these components apply in the same way or would some be more important to you than others? How would this affect the way you convey recovery principles to persons you serve? Would you add other components? Would it be "okay" for another person to develop their own recovery components even if they are different from those illustrated above?

As you can tell by reading thus far, a great deal of the value of peer specialists lies in the ability to inspire hope and courage. This is a theme that will be repeated throughout your career. Consider it carefully because it is vital to the success you will have as a peer specialist. Be aware, however, that your behavior—your conduct, words, and attitudes—will play an important role in your ability to be a successful peer specialist.

You should start asking yourself again and again: Why do I want to be a peer specialist? If you have a good grasp on your own feelings and values in this regard, you are halfway there!

References

(From the Chapter Introduction by the Editors)

Anthony, W. (1993a). Recovery from mental illness: The guiding vision of the mental health service system in the 1990's. Psychosocial Rehabilitation Journal, 16(4), 11-23. https://doi.org/10.1037/h0095655

Anthony, W. (1993b). The decade of recovery. Psychosocial Rehabilitation Journal, 16(4), 1.https://doi.org/10.1037/h0095657

Ashcraft, L. (2021). Tributes to Bill Anthony, compiled by Lori Ashcraft. https://aps-community.org/2020/09/17/tributes-to-bill-anthony-compiled-by-lori-ashcraft/

Davidson, L. Harding, C. & Spaniol, L. (2005). Excerpt from Recovery from Severe Mental Illnesses: Research Evidence and Implications for Practice, available from Boston University Center for Psychiatric Rehabilitation.

Center for Psychiatric Rehabilitation. Available online https://cpr.bu.edu/
wp-content/uploads/2011/11/Preview-Recovery-from-Severe-Mental-
Illnesses-Research-Evidence-and-Implications-for-Practice-Volume-1.pdf

Harding, C. (2016). The doctor who saw through psychiatric labels to find the
real person underneath, American Journal of Psychiatric Rehabilitation, 2016,
Vol 19(1), 17-22. https://www.tandfonline.com/doi/full/10.1080/15487768.
2016.1136175

Harrington, S. (2011). Peer Specialist Training Manual, Fourth Edition,
National Association of Peer Specialists. (Out of print.) Used with Permission.

Harrington, S. (2012). Organizational Culture Change Can Help Mental
Health Organizations Thrive. National Association of Peer Specialists Newsletter. Used with Permission.

SAMHSA (2012). SAMHSA's Working Definition of Recovery. Substance
Abuse and Mental Health Services Administration. https://store.samhsa.gov/
sites/default/files/d7/priv/pep12-recdef.pdf

The President's New Freedom Commission on Mental Health: Achieving the
Promise. https://govinfo.library.unt.edu/mentalhealthcommission/reports/
FinalReport/FullReport.htm

CHAPTER 2
WHAT IS PEER SUPPORT?

CHAPTER INTRODUCTION BY THE EDITORS

PEER SUPPORT IS AN EVOLVING FIELD IN BEHAVIORAL HEALTH CARE, BUT IT 'shows up' as a natural human response whenever one person is able to comfort and provide the wisdom of experience to another person who is going through a shared personal challenge. In later chapters this volume traces the origins of mutual self-help, which is the tap root of all authentic peer support and the essence of what makes peer support effective. Experiential knowledge or the "experiential credential" allows people who have gone through a particular challenge to have the credibility to offer hope and a source of inspiration to those who are currently in the midst of similar challenges in their lives.

This chapter offers insight into peer support and what makes it effective. It begins includes another reprint (with permission) from the Peer Specialist Training Manual Fourth Edition (2011) by Steve Harrington, founder of the National Association of Peer Supporters (N.A.P.S.). His definition of peer support and description of peer specialist practices is as relevant today as it was when he last updated the manual in 2011.

In 2015, Steve Harrington had a career ending stroke, which caused him to re-evaluate what peer support meant to him. The chapter also includes a brief essay of his experience with the stroke and reflections on peer support titled, On Peer Support. Following Steve's essay is a narrative by Amey Dettmer on sharing your recovery story to motivate, educate, and inspire and the results of a national survey of the peer support workforce that was conducted by the National Association of Peer Specialists and reported by Rita Cronise, Carina Teixeira, Sally Rogers, and Steve Harrington in the Psychiatric Rehabilitation Journal.

SECTION 1: REFLECTIONS ON PEER SUPPORT

Steve Harrington, M.P.A., J.D., CPS
Founder, National Association of Peer Supporters (N.A.P.S.)

When I looked out my window one morning several months ago, I saw a man and his young daughter in my vegetable garden picking weeds. I stumbled out the door to ask them why they were tending my garden.

"I heard you had a stroke and it looked like you were falling behind in your gardening. Hope you don't mind."

I was flabbergasted! I had recently moved to a rural area and my large garden seemed to be a community project.

Yes, I had a stroke and had fallen a little behind in its care. Other neighbors (again, some of whom I had never met) were knocking on my door with canned goods, cooked meals, cookies, muffins and offers of help.

"We all live out here in the country," one neighbor explained as she handed me a fresh batch of brownies. "We're all in this together."

These helpful neighbors were peers; bonded by where and how we live in the same country neighborhood. This was a form of support I thought was long past.

But is it peer support?

I think so. Simply put, peer support occurs when people in a particular circumstance reach out to help others in the same or a very similar circumstance. It is the act of a person or persons reaching out to others to help them deal with life challenges. Peer support can be organized through formal groups or it can occur informally. The key aspect is that people are able to help others in the same or similar circumstances through what they have learned from those experiences.

This help can take many forms and we are seeing it grow daily as humans throughout the world experience a myriad of challenges and reach out for help. And it is not new. A generation or two ago, neighbors commonly helped neighbors during times of distress. It wasn't unusual for neighbors to seek out others in their neighborhoods to offer support.

When I was a child, my brother was stricken with a serious illness. Although it was many years ago, a steady stream of neighbors stopping by our rural home. They brought meals, babysat my sisters and I and sometimes just sat with my parents as my brother teetered between life and death. And the support continued through my brother's eventual recovery.

My mother reciprocated throughout her life. Pies were baked, pets were fed, and neighbors were driven to wherever they had to go.

Our society has changed as many people now live their lives without ever meeting their neighbors. Peer support, in many ways, is a return to the days when people cared about the welfare of their neighbors and did what they could to help.

Peer support, as a result, is more important than ever. And it is more organized than ever before with support organizations for those with cancer, diabetes, heart disease, raising children, addictions, learning disabilities, epilepsy, and strokes to name just a few.

For peer supporters, there is a link of empathy and caring resulting from a bond of common experience. For me, most recently, that common experience was simply living in the same rural neighborhood.

Although we are often isolated by our own lifestyles, we remain linked through the common trials of the human experience.

We have, to a considerable extent, become more isolated as humans. Very often, we have little or no contact with neighbors and are immediately suspicious of kind acts by strangers. We relate to others, too often, via computer screens instead of friendly conversations in our neighborhoods.

But peer support has evolved in a way that compensates for changes in how we relate to one another. Support groups are found online and e-mails and social media keep people connected. Just the method has changed.

When it comes to mental health support, the reality is that support rarely involves a single issue. Substance abuse, poverty, incarceration, housing, employment, physical ailments, and a host of other issues make the original and more simple notions of peer support too narrow for relevance in our society. Peer support is too broad—and valuable—to be viewed as only relating to mental health.

This broader view of peer support is not a threat to NAPS but, rather, an opportunity. The values that drive peer support apply to a broad range of human experiences and embracing this broader definition of peer support welcomes vastly more people and enriches our perspectives about life challenges. In accepting a broader definition of peer support, we create far greater opportunities for reciprocal sharing of experiences and lessons learned.

Instead of attempting to carve out a narrow niche based on what peer support was, or is, or should be in only mental health, let's be inclusive of the larger segments of society that can—and should—contribute to the value of the human experience.

A broader view of peer support—what it is and how it is delivered—may at first be uncomfortable for those who have defined "peer" only in terms of mental health but opening up to new possibilities can be exciting. Broadly defining peer support and recognizing its value in all contexts can help to integrate it as a "normal and expected" part of the human experience.

SECTION 2: WHAT IS A PEER SPECIALIST?

Steve Harrington, M.P.A., J.D., CPS
Founder, National Association of Peer Supporters (NAPS)

What you can do, or dream you can do, begin it; boldness has genius, power and magic in it.

— *JOHANN VON GOETHE*

Definitions

Because peer specialists are relatively new to mental health systems, definitions vary. For some organizations, definitions are very narrow and relate to specific tasks, such as support group facilitation and education.

For many other organizations, a peer specialist can be broadly defined as a person with a mental health experience (past or current) who helps others diagnosed with mental health conditions. This broad definition is often useful because it is inclusive. Under this definition, one may be a volunteer. Also, agency administrators often discover varied roles for peer specialists as the peer specialists themselves explore new skills, knowledge, and abilities.

Virtually all definitions, however, incorporate the peer specialist's recovery experience as a means of inspiring hope in those they serve. You may wish to think about what a peer specialist is to you.

As the value of peer specialists in the mental health system is recognized, the term is used to include others. Substance abuse and developmentally disabled programs are increasingly using the term to describe persons with a shared experience who help others.

Roles/Tasks

The role of a peer specialist can be quite variable. While some peer specialists focus on issues such as housing, transportation, and employment, others work one-on-one with others to offer counseling and support. Some help others create person-centered plans, psychiatric advance directives, or educate them on issues and/or recovery strategies.

Some believe certain tasks are not "true" peer specialist functions. For example, some administrators believe transportation or gathering intake information can be accomplished by a person without a recovery experience. And while that may true in many respects, one must examine what a peer specialist can bring to such tasks.

A good example can be found in transportation assistance. While anyone with a drivers' license can drive another to and from appointments, pharmacies, or grocery stores, a peer specialist can use transportation as an opportunity to inspire hope in others and encourage them to create a meaningful life. The ancillary communication can promote engagement and be an important link between mental health systems and the people they serve.

We all bring certain skills, abilities, ideas, enthusiasm, education, and gifts to a job. There is one basic interest we all share. That is the desire to help others. Peer specialists, like no other class of mental health workers, offer the advantages of shared experiences. We have been there, done that. We know the journey to recovery is real and attainable because we have traveled that path.

Through contacts with others struggling with mental health conditions, we can share our experiences and instill hope. That is a common theme throughout this manual. We hope you take this important function seriously because instilling hope is not only useful to those we serve; it is a positive remnant of our mental health experience.

Although there is a continuum of the range of duties peer specialists perform, there are some basic attributes of peer specialists. These include:

- Willingness to listen.
- True caring for others struggling to find or proceed on their recovery journey.
- Enthusiasm for the job.
- Flexibility.
- Knowledge.
- Creativity.
- Problem-solving ability.
- Compassion.
- Empathy.
- Ability to communicate effectively.

There are some basic assumptions of peer specialists in mental health settings. Those assumptions include:

- Peer specialists have similar backgrounds as their peers.
- Peer specialists may have suffered difficulty and hardship due to the nature of their own mental health experience.
- Peer specialists have demonstrated the ability to cope with their mental health challenges.
- Peer specialists have a desire to help others.
- Peer specialists have received some training for their role.

ALTHOUGH ROLES MAY VARY among and even within mental health agencies, it is generally recognized that peer specialists will provide the following services:

- Provide information to their peers.
- Act as a referral source (to clinicians and other mental health professionals) in their agency.
- Provide support and understanding to their peers.
- Help peers in problem solving, decision making, and setting goals through a partnership, not a benefactor role.

THE PEER SPECIALIST-PEER relationship can be extremely complicated. Often, a closeness develops, particularly when the relationship is positive. The relationship is further complicated by the fact that the peer specialist is also receiving mental health services (often from the same agency). Very often, the peer specialist acts as a counselor and the same qualities in a counselor-consumer relationship holds true for the peer specialist in the counselor role. The peer specialist will also use his or her past experience as a means of developing a positive relationship. Listening, sharing, and caring may develop more naturally for a peer specialist due to the shared mental health experience. Use that to your advantage but beware of potential problems!

Honesty is a constant theme in this manual. Peer specialists and the people they serve develop a mutual respect when both are genuine. Honesty can involve confrontation, conflict, making uncomfortable statements or hearing uncomfortable statements. Dealing with these issues develops a real relationship. A real relationship will cause a variety of feelings. Some are suspicious of a peer specialist-person served relationship when the peer specialist or the person served are never angry at each other. If they can talk constructively about their feelings in the interest of resolving their differences, their relationship will strengthen.

The relationship will also strengthen if they are able to listen to each other. Listening is a skill that many people take for granted. Listening is an important basis for understanding. It is difficult to understand if you are not listening. If you are not listening, you are not trying to understand.

Sharing also helps build a positive peer specialist-person served relationship. The relationship will strengthen if the peer specialist and person served create an atmosphere in which sharing is encouraged. While appropriate ways for peer specialists to share their experiences will be covered later, the fundamental basis for such sharing is honesty.

Honest sharing is called "self-disclosure" but not everything will be shared due to the nature of the relationship. That is to be expected. When a peer specialist or person served does not feel comfortable sharing, they should state just that, rather than lie or evade the issue.

Caring is also an important aspect of the peer specialist-person served relationship. A caring peer specialist will listen, share, and promote honesty. He or she will also try to create an atmosphere of warmth and genuineness. Caring for others whom a peer specialist serves might mean stating something the other person does not want to hear. Responding with empathy demonstrates an effective peer specialist.

Difficult or resistive persons will often test a pear specialist by entering a session with a negative attitude, silence, being late, or threatening behavior. Often, these persons have not been cared for (or about) or have been hurt in close relationships and feel they have no reason to communicate honestly and openly. In these difficult situations, the peer specialist is encouraged to understand the problem, respond with empathy, and be patient. Also, talk to peers and supervisors about the stress of dealing with a difficult person. (This is an extreme set of circumstances, so don't panic!) The expectation is that the person will want the help.

As a person who has also experienced the mental health struggle, the peer specialist may be able to relate through their own experiences. They may recognize fear and frustration more quickly than others.

Everything covered thus far will lead to trust in a peer specialist-person served relationship. Trust develops with time. It generally needs to be built. Often, trust is broken by lack of honesty or caring. It is hard to re-establish trust, but it can be done. A positive relationship will have a high degree of trust.

As stated earlier, the peer specialist-person served relationship is often extremely complicated. This is a professional relationship. There is a boundary between the two parties. That boundary can be difficult to maintain, particularly as the parties develop a positive relationship.

We have already examined some functions of the peer specialist role. Let us now examine some guidelines for the peer specialist:

- The peer specialist will maintain counselor/person served confidentiality.
- The peer specialist will demonstrate appropriate language.
- The peer specialist will demonstrate appropriate hygiene and clothing in the workplace.
- The peer specialist will always work in the interest of helping those they serve.
- The peer specialist will demonstrate the ability to ask for help and receive feedback from the persons they serve, colleagues, and supervisors.
- The peer specialist will maintain boundaries appropriate to the peer role.

JUST A WORD about the last guideline. Maintaining boundaries can be difficult, particularly when parties have known each other, or if they receive mental health services in the same area. It can become confusing (and detrimental) for a peer specialist to counsel a friend (in his or her working role). The peer specialist might have a disagreement with his or her friend that would affect the counseling relationship. Conversely, there might be a disagreement in the counseling session that would affect the friendship. It is best to maintain a clear boundary. Peer specialists are NOT friends. They are role models, counselors, teachers and a variety of other roles.

Remember that peer specialists have a unique position when it comes to relationships. The best advice is to keep it professional.

What Do Peer Specialists Do?

What do peer specialists do? This is a question often asked by friends, family, clinicians, other mental health professionals, and even the people they serve. If there is one thing, we have learned by talking to peer specialists across the country, it is that there is no single job description that adequately defines the peer specialist position in all circumstances. It seems to be as variable as the number of mental health provider agencies employing persons with a mental health experience to help others.

Another interesting aspect of the peer specialist movement is labeling. What are peer specialists called? We have heard them referred to as "consumer advocates," "peer supporters," "peer counselors," "peer advocates," "recovery specialists" and "peer support specialists."

The truth is labels mean little. What matters is the actual work accomplished by peer specialists. On one end of the spectrum, we have peer specialists who have relatively little contact with others with mental health conditions. These peer specialists may provide transportation, clerical work, or other services. Some peer specialists in this category even perform security duties. On the other end of the spectrum, we find peer specialists who have almost continual direct contact with peers. Very often, they serve others through one-on-one support sessions. This is very useful because peer specialists can share their experiences with peers and, in the process, inspire others to begin or continue their recovery journey.

Again, what is important, regardless of the position, is for the peer specialist to use his or her own recovery experience as a means of inspiring hope in others they serve.

Tokens are for arcades. Too often, peer specialists are hired for ambiguous roles that are relatively meaningless. Some states require the hiring of persons with a mental health recovery experience and do so only to comply with such requirements. This is unfortunate and the relationship between peer specialists and the people the work with and for will be explored later.

In conversations with peer specialists across the country, we have found a link between acceptance (even embracement) of the recovery model and the hiring of peer specialists. And while some peer specialists have relatively little contact with others with a mental health condition, the vast majority are involved in direct, one-on-one peer support. This appears to be the best use of their experiences and skills.

There is a variety of interventions used by peer specialists during support sessions. Very often, peer specialists can "reach" even very difficult people because of their shared mental health experience. This readily developed empathy means peer specialists can play a special role in engaging others in needed services.

In some sessions, peer specialists help guide others on the recovery road by teaching coping skills the peer specialists learned on their own journey down that road. They may also monitor the mental health status of others and report changes that require attention from clinicians and others.

And perhaps one of the most important services peer specialists provide is accessing community resources. This may mean resources as diverse as free meal programs or volunteer opportunities.

One surprising role many peer specialists play involves their relationships with case managers or support coordinators. Many times, peer specialists become the treatment team's "expert" on relations with those served and are asked how a peer may react to a particular intervention. Or, in consultation with others on the treatment team, peer specialists may suggest interventions that worked particularly well for them. It is this unique ability to place oneself in the position of the person served that makes peer specialists especially valuable.

Regardless of your role, remember that your mental health experience is valuable and is now seen as an asset. Many agencies—and even some psychiatric hospitals—actually advertise they have peer specialists on staff.

As peer specialists continue to demonstrate their value to mental health systems, the occupation is certain to grow. Peer specialists' skills and knowledge are likely to grow and result in an increasing number of traditional "professionals" using their mental health experience to deliver the most effective services.

Therapy vs. Counseling

While some states have progressed to the point where they have entirely peer-run and operated case management services, clubhouses and drop-in centers, it is important to remember that peer specialists are NOT therapists.

Therapists are highly trained and educated clinicians. The role of the peer specialist is to help peers access and use therapy in the most effective manner. But engaging in true therapy is beyond the scope of peer specialist employment.

Some clinicians are threatened by peer specialists because they do not understand roles. Peer specialists may find themselves educating therapists and other clinicians about how roles differ. This can lead to greater acceptance, conflict resolution and expansion of peer specialist services and duties.

Again, the primary role of the peer specialist is inspiring hope among a group of people who need it most. Those served by mental health systems often lack self-esteem and the courage to create a recovery plan and then act on it. These are key areas that can use peer specialists' skills most effectively.

Why Do Peer Specialists Do What They Do?

The results of a recent survey of peer specialists across the U.S. revealed the vast majority of peer specialists find their greatest reward by helping others. They report it not only helps peers, but themselves as well.

Many people, especially those in technical or business occupations, may find this an unusual if not bewildering reason to perform one's work. Later in this manual, we will explore values. But to spark your thinking on this topic, consider the following story adapted from *The Star Thrower*, by Loren Eiseley:

One day, a man was walking on a beach when he noticed a figure in the distance. As he got closer, he realized the figure was that of a boy picking something up and gently throwing it into the ocean.

Approaching the boy, he asked, "What are you doing?"

The youth replied, "Throwing starfish into the ocean. The sun is up and the tide is going out. If I don't throw them back, they'll die."

"Son," the man said, "don't you realize there are miles and miles of beach and hundreds of starfish? You can't possibly make a difference!"

After listening politely, the boy bent down, picked up another starfish and threw it into the surf. Then, smiling at the man, said, "I made a difference for that one."

References

Eisley, L. (1969). The Star Thrower. Essay published in the Unexpected Universe. Harcourt, Brace and World ISBN 0-15-692850-7

The Star Thrower (1978, Times Books (Random House) hardcover: ISBN 0-8129-0746-9, 1979 Harvest/HBJ paperback: ISBN 0-15-684909-7.

Harrington, S. (2011). Peer Specialist Training Manual, Fourth Edition. Recover Resources, Ada, Michigan.

SECTION 3: THE PEER WORKFORCE, RESULTS OF A NATIONAL SURVEY

Rita Cronise, MS, ALWF,

Faculty, Rutgers University
Carina Teixeira, PhD,
Center for Psychiatric Rehabilitation, Boston University

E. Sally Rogers, ScD,
Center for Psychiatric Rehabilitation, Boston University
Steve Harrington, MA, JD, Founder,
National Association of Peer Supporters (N.A.P.S.)

This article provides an overview of the findings from a national survey of the education, compensation, and satisfaction of peer support workers (PSW) conducted in 2014 by the National Association of Peer Supporters (N.A.P.S.)[1], which was also published in 2016 in a special edition of the *Psychiatric Rehabilitation Journal* on Peer Support Services. For more details on the survey methods and findings, please see the journal article in the Reference section.

The National Association of Peer Supporters (N.A.P.S.) is a membership organization, founded in 2004 by a group of working peer specialists, to provide education, support, and advocacy for the peer support workforce. The organization has hosted an annual national conference since 2006, which is the oldest continuously running annual conference devoted specifically to the peer support profession in the U.S.

In 2007, N.A.P.S. conducted a membership survey of compensation and satisfaction. Seven years later, the association repeated the survey, with added questions about education and training. The purpose for the second survey was to compare data to the previous survey, looking for trends, and to consider ways to better serve and grow the membership.

Discussion

The *Peer Support Provider Education, Compensation, and Satisfaction Survey* was conducted online using SurveyMonkey between July and December 2014. An invitation to participate with a link was provided on the N.A.P.S. website and in the member newsletter. A copy of the survey was mailed to members who indicated that they could not receive email or go to the website to complete the survey. (At that time, there were still several members who were receiving printed copies of the newsletter through the mail.) The invitation to participate in the survey was also disseminated by the National Mental Health Consumers' Self-Help Clearinghouse and the Directors of Offices of Consumer Affairs in many states.

No compensation was offered, but there was a place in the survey for respondents to provide their contact information if they were interested in getting a copy of the results. More than half provided their names and wanted to be more involved.

Sally Rogers and Carina Teixeira from Boston University Center for Psychiatric Rehabilitation worked with Rita Cronise and Steve Harrington of N.A.P.S. on the analysis and reporting on results.

A total of 608 people from 44 states responded to the online survey. Five surveys were missing data and six surveys were eliminated because respondents resided outside of the United States. A total of 597 responses were used in the data analysis.

Demographics

As seen in Table 1, a proportionally high percentage of those who responded were female, middle-aged, Caucasian, and fairly well educated.

Table 1: Demographics

Gender	N	Percent
Female	380	65
Male	203	34.6
Transgender	3	0.5
Age	N	Percent
18-24	13	2.2
25-35	69	11.7
35-44	111	18.8
45-54	185	31.4
More than 55 years	211	35.8
Race/Ethnicity	N	Percent
White/Caucasian	437	74.4
Black/African American	91	15.5
Hispanic/Latino	57	9.7
Native America/American Indian/Alaska Native	27	4.6
Asian	4	0.7
Mixed	22	3.7
Education	N	Percent
Bachelor's degree or beyond	233	39.4
Some college/Associate's degree	272	46.0
High school or equivalent, or trade/technical school	83	14.0
Some high school	3	0.5

Location

Responses came from 44 states. There were no responses from Arkansas, Hawaii, Montana, New Mexico, North Dakota, and South Dakota. The largest percent was located in large urban/urban areas (64%), suburban (23.2%), rural/frontier (24.5%) and tribal (0.9%).

Job Training

More than half (57.4%) of those who responded to this question (N=521) completed between 20 and 80 hours of training to qualify in their state as a PSW. Table 2 shows the main categories of topics included in their training to become a PSW.

Table 2. Training Topics

Training Topics	N	Percent
Peer Relationship	531	97
Direct Peer Support/Telling Your Story	525	96
Advocacy and Rights Protection	520	95
Recovery Concepts	512	93
Traditional Mental Health Services	505	92
Administrative, Supervision, Workplace-Related	490	89
Alternative Healing and Wellness	419	76
Pre-crisis and Crisis Support	362	66

Job Titles

While the majority had job titles of peer specialist, the survey was not limited to those who were certified peer specialists. The invitation to participate was open to anyone with a role as a PSW. Table 3 provides the percentages of job titles held by respondents.

Table 3: Job Titles

Job Titles	N	Percent
Peer Specialist/Peer Support Specialist	367	62
Recovery Support Specialist	142	24
Peer Advocate	82	14
Recovery Coach	71	12
Recovery Educator/Recovery Trainer	54	9
Peer Coach	50	8
Peer Bridger	17	3
Other Job Titles*	40	7

*Other job titles include administrative job titles and titles related to pre-crisis and crisis peer support

Work Tasks

During the analysis, a large number of work tasks were placed into categories according to the type of work being performed. Respondents were able to choose all of the work tasks that they regularly performed. Direct peer support (94%) was reported as the most frequent work task. Table 4 shows the percentages of work tasks reported by the respondents.

Table 4. Work Tasks

Work Tasks	N	Percent
Direct Peer Support Tasks	481	94
Clinical or Administrative Tasks	456	89
Teaching/Skill Development Tasks	441	86
Ancillary Tasks	389	76
Advocacy Tasks	323	63
Housing, Educational, and Vocational Assistance	232	45
Other Supportive Tasks	74	15

Work Settings

The work settings were categorized according to the level of restrictedness (i.e., locked inpatient units vs. open community-based support programs). As seen in Table 5, peer support was found in many different program types, the most common was community and/or peer-run programs.

Table 5. Work Settings

Work Settings	N	Percent
Community and/or Peer-Run Program Settings	388	66.3
Less Restrictive Mental Health or Substance Abuse Treatment Settings	226	38.6
Restrictive Mental Health or Substance Abuse Treatment Settings	160	27.4
Less Restrictive Residential Settings and Programs	139	23.8
Pre-Crisis or Crisis Settings	127	21.7
Restrictive Residential Settings and Program	82	14
Employment or Educational Settings	75	12.8
Criminal Justice Settings	85	14
Other Setting	81	13.8

Years on the Job

As shown in Table 6, one third of the respondents had been working between 2-5 years. Those that had been working less than two years or more than five years were evenly distributed.

44

Table 6. Years on the Job

Years on the Job	N	Percent
Less than 1 year	90	18
1-2	118	23
2-5	167	33
5-7	61	12
More than 7	78	15

Full-Time vs. Part-Time

As shown in Table 7, the majority of respondents (61%) were working full-time, (39%) were working less than 32 hour per week. The reasons given among those working part-time or volunteered (N=161) for not working more hours or seeking financial compensation were that they enjoyed working part-time (39.8%), the lack of full-time work (39.8), or the fear of losing cash benefits (31.1%).

Table 7. Full-Time vs. Part-Time

Hours Worked per Week	N	Percent
Less than 20 hours/week	134	23
20-36 hours/week	94	16
More than 36 hours/week	362	61

Compensation

There are complicating factors in the analysis of compensation, including calculations involving annual salary vs. hourly wages, calculating compensation for those holding multiple positions or working as a volunteer, and several other factors. To account for different methods of compensation, those reporting annual salaries had their amounts transformed to an hourly wage for an average 40-hour week.

Table 8 shows the reported compensation only for those who provide direct peer support and excludes those who indicated providing other functions such as program director or employment specialist. Also excluded were those performing unpaid work.

Table 8. Compensation

Compensation of Peer Specialists						
	Full Time Workers (N=96)		Part-Time Workers (N=61)		Total (N=162)	
	N	Per cent	N	Per cent	N	Per cent
$5-10 per hour	11	11.5	7	11.5	20	12.2
$10-15 per hour	47	49.0	48	78.7	98	60.5
$15-20 per hour	26	27.1	6	9.8	32	19.8
$20-25 per hour	10	6.2	0	0	10	6.2
More than $25/hour	2	1.2	0	0	2	1.2

Job Satisfaction

Overall, PSW rated their satisfaction with the job as: 56% Very Satisfied, 33% Somewhat Satisfied, 4% Neither Satisfied nor Dissatisfied, 5% Somewhat Dissatisfied, and 2% Very Dissatisfied

Out of 517 respondents, the greatest reward from working as a PSW was helping others (85.5%). The second most frequently cited reward was helping in their own recovery (10.4%).

Out of 375 respondents, 64.3% reported seeing or feeling stigma or discrimination from non-peer co-workers such as licensed professionals. Almost 30% also reported seeing or feeling stigma or discrimination by leadership (administrators, executives, and management) and by other members of the agency staff (such as Human Resources, security, etc.) Another 22.1% reported seeing or feeling stigma from those they provided support to, which may speak to a lack of orientation provided to people receiving support about the role of the PSW from the organizations that provide peer support services.

Out of 242 respondents, the most frequent forms of discrimination cited were unequal compensation practices and policies (62%), unequal job advancement practice and policies (58%), and unequal hiring practices and policies (44%). In addition, out of 498 respondents, the majority (74.3%) reported feeling supported by their supervisor and (68.9%) by their peer colleagues.

The majority of respondents who replied to these questions (N=516; or 94%) agreed or strongly agreed that they feel respected by the peers they support, whereas (80%) agreed or strongly agreed that they feel respected as an equal member of the team (and not a patient or client) by their supervisors and colleagues. A significant number (40%) reported being "not satisfied" with their compensation and (23%) were "not satisfied" with the level of recognition in their job (out of 508 respondents).

The things that predicted satisfaction included:

- Responsibility that reflects the level of training and lived experience
- Feeling respected by supervisors and colleagues
- Feeling respected by the peers who receive the service
- Perception of having sufficient training to do the job
- Working in community settings and/or peer-run programs
- More hours of training to qualify as a PSW
- Perception that their peer support skills are utilized

Secondary source of satisfaction: Helping others helps in their own recovery
Primary source of dissatisfaction: Wages
Other Findings
Some of the key findings from this survey include:

- 38% report being supervised by a peer
- 22-30% report feeling stigmatized or discriminated against by other professionals or the individuals with whom them worked
- About half of those who responded had other credentials (e.g., nursing)
- There were differences in wages by geography and by gender, even when controlling for factors such as education

Limitations
The survey was not a random sample of peer support specialists. No random sampling from a large database of known peer specialists was available. Thus, purposive sampling was used with survey invitations distributed

to the N.A.P.S. membership and further disseminated by state mental health officials and affiliated peer organizations. Therefore, it is difficult to know how representative these data are of the entire workforce of peer providers/specialists

All questions were developed for the membership survey itself—there were no standardized questions

Significant recoding was needed to report on complex question/answers, particularly those related to compensation; thus, those findings should be interpreted cautiously.

Conclusion

The purpose of this survey was to gather information about work roles, tasks, settings, training, compensation and satisfaction of peer support workers. It provides a snapshot of the peer workforce based on responses to the survey given in 2014. Some key finding from this survey include:

Peer support workers are employed in a wide range of settings and perform a wide variety of tasks

Peer support workers receive training in many areas, but training time and supervision time is not high

On average, salaries for peer support workers remains quite low

Important drivers of satisfaction include being respected by colleagues and others

As the workforce continues to grow and evolve, it will be important to regularly gather data on roles, tasks, training, compensation, and satisfaction to inform policy makers to help meet the needs of this unique workforce.

References

Cronise, R., Teixeira, C., Rogers, E. S., & Harrington, S. (2016) The Peer Support Workforce: Results of a National Survey. *Psychiatric Rehabilitation Journal, 39*(3), 211-221. DOI: 10.1037/prj0000222

SECTION 4: SHARING YOUR WELLNESS AND RECOVERY STORY

Amey Dettmer, CPS,
The Copeland Center for Wellness and Recovery

During training to become a peer support specialist, it is taught that sharing our lived experience is part of our role as peer supporters. Being able to share our life experiences with mental health, substance use or other wide-ranging experiences is key to creating mutuality, connection, and building direct and honest relationships. Choosing what stories to tell and skillfully telling them in a way that motivates, educates, and inspires takes practice and sometimes additional education.

Through my work with the Copeland Center for Wellness and Recovery, I've had the chance to take the Sharing your Wellness and Recovery Story Training as a participant, as well as to shadow facilitators, eventually working my way up to co-facilitating and training others to co-facilitate this particular curriculum. I have also presented on the topic in a few different states at peer support conferences.

This training was first developed by Gina Calhoun and Scott Heller, two inspiring peer leaders who have been involved in the peer support workforce for decades. In 2012, I heard Gina's story for the first time at a conference keynote. Her story has left the most memorable impact on the possibilities for people and the impact of peer support in one's life that I can ever recall hearing. Learning the skills that I witnessed first-hand from Gina's story has been life-changing in my career and pursuance in expanding the peer support workforce.

Discussion

Most often as peer specialists, we share our stories one on one with others, or in group settings as peer group facilitators. Usually, in these places, we share short stories of self-disclosure. However, there are many other spaces and places where our stories of lived experience would be beneficial to be shared with an audience. Often these stories are longer and have a specific structure to the story layout.

The education I received in this training gave me the confidence and self-efficacy to share stories of my own life experiences as the keynote speaker at conferences, in Public Service Announcements, in written form for newspaper articles, and to many other larger audiences. Wellness and Recovery Stories in settings like these share a few purposes; to educate, to inform, to highlight a key message, and to call an audience to action. A core value of peer support is to facilitate change. Sharing my story to larger audiences has allowed me to participate in the facilitation of change; away from injustice, for the advocacy of human rights, and to increase access to peer support.

There are important questions to ask ourselves about our story: What do we want to do without story? What change will our story facilitate? Is our story supporting a status quo or is it moving people to see new hopes and possibilities? How will we use it to inspire an audience and facilitate the changes that so many of us believe are desperately needed within the systems that serve our communities? These are all important questions to ask ourselves when we pull together a story of wellness and recovery.

Story Sample:

March 2020 will likely be an unforgettable event for every citizen of the United States and for people all around the world. In the USA, our schools shut down, we were told to stay home, isolate, and avoid others as concerns of COVID-19 struck the Nation. I was 8 months pregnant, 36 weeks into my pregnancy. I had routine doctor's appointments scheduled for myself and my soon-to-be newborn baby. I tried to go to one in-person appointment, but I was denied access to even enter the medical center upon arrival. After that, all of my appointments were canceled by the medical provider. I recall crying in the parking lot, feeling at a remarkable loss for how to provide myself and my baby with the standard preparations and medical expectations that expecting mothers typically go through during pregnancy.

With the onset of COVID-19, I found myself fear-stricken and unable to stop reading about the disease and its implications all over the news. I watched inmates be released from prisons based on safety concerns of COVID-19 impacting confined spaces. I was told not to go to a grocery store, to wipe down anything that was brought to my home, and to not go near anyone other than my immediate family. I deeply feared going into the hospital, where my mind told me that I would be placing my baby in danger going to the same place that anyone sick with COVID-19 would be going to.

I thought to myself that arranging a home birth would be the best way to keep me and my baby safe. But that wasn't an option, as all midwives were booked, and no one could take me last minute. I engulfed myself in articles that addressed the sudden changes to hospital policies for anyone using hospital services, specifically focusing on what was happening in labor and delivery units. These policies included mask-wearing (even during labor), the strictest visitation policies I've ever heard of, and even potential separation of mother and baby upon birth.

My reality in March 2020 was that I could go into labor at any moment and have no choice but to go to the place that I wanted to avoid the most, the hospital. Anxiety has been something that I have lived with most of my life, but I was never as scared and plagued by anxiety, as I was in the first weeks of the COVID-19 pandemic. My anxiety was so bad in the last weeks of my pregnancy that I was having three to five panic attacks a day.

As the uncertainty of my upcoming hospital stay came closer, I kicked into action the tools and concepts my recovery journey taught me about. I self-advocated (over the phone) for what I needed while preparing for the hospital. I ensured that the hospital would provide me with a tablet and zoom line so that I could at least have my supporters join me via zoom before, during, and after the labor and delivery experience. I educated myself on the best protections I could take to protect me and my newborn, which even included packing my own food to eat while in the hospital and bringing my new baby's car seat and belongings into the hospital covered in plastic bags to protect the items from exposure to unwanted germs. I even advocated to be induced at the earliest time possible and to verify that my hospital stay, given all went smoothly, would be as quick as possible.

Before the onset of the pandemic, I arranged for a doula to be present. A doula is a non-clinical trained person who accompanies a mother through the labor and birthing process. Evidence-based doula support includes physical and emotional support through the process of bringing new life into the world. It has been found that doula support significantly lessens the impact of anxiety for mothers. Luckily, this Doula was able to be physically present during my birth, but I needed to advocate to make that possible. Having the support of a doula during this time was hugely helpful in decreasing my stress and positively impacting my overall experience.

Hope is crucial for my mental health wellness, and even amongst the massive anxiety I faced, I was still able to hang tight to moments of hope that showed up for me. One way hope presented itself was through the thoughtfulness of one community member who volunteered to do all my grocery shopping for me. I did not leave my home for the last 3 weeks of my pregnancy other than the time I tried attending a doctor's appointment. There was no way I could go into a grocery store without having massive panic caused by the concern that I was risking harm to my baby. This community volunteer's act of kindness was hope-filled for me and allowed me to see the good in the world during a time when I was consumed by fear and anxiety.

The second way I recall hope finding its way into my view was through the presence of wildlife crossing my path. On the night before I was scheduled to get induced, I witnessed my first moose sighting. Wildlife viewing is an all-time favorite wellness tool of mine, and to witness my first moose on this particular evening still to this day nearly gives me a sense of spiritual hope that everything is going to be okay and a higher power as I understand it is looking out for me.

In early April 2020, I gave birth to a beautiful and healthy baby girl. I drove myself to the hospital and I drove us both home. Upon our arrival at our home, many fears lifted and anxiety subsided. I share this story today to demonstrate that even in the most trying of times the recovery concepts of hope, support, and self-advocacy continuously support me in my recovery journey, no matter where that journey takes me in life. So many people claim that recovery is a journey, not a destination, and this is true for me. Life is filled with really good times, and rough times, but in all times, I *can reflect and learn from the experience while always catching a glimpse of hope to hang on to.*

Conclusion

Now that you have read this story of mine, I encourage you to think about what stood out for you. Did you learn anything? What parts of this story did you connect with? Do you feel touched to look at your own life in any new ways as a result of what you read?

My hope for sharing my experience through this story was to invite you to a place of relatability during a confusing onset of a pandemic while providing examples and encouraging ideas for continuously hanging on to wellness even in the most difficult of times. Another element of the story, from my perspective as the writer, was to educate others about doulas. More recently in 2021, I accepted an invitation to be interviewed by doula researchers looking to grow access to doula support, and ever since that involvement my gratitude for doulas has grown. I have learned that there are a lot of parallels between doula services and peer support.

I love that Sharing your Wellness and Recovery Story is about sharing in a way that honors those things that we are passionate about and gives us the chance to creatively design and build a message through storytelling that others can hear and relate to.

Sharing our wellness and recovery story matters as it gets our messages of recovery, hope, wellness, etc. out to our world in ways that are beyond just the stories we tell in our mutual relationships. These larger audience stories give us the chance for new ways of decreasing stigmas and standing up for the causes we may each deeply believe in. As a peer supporter, learning this skill has supported me in the development of my career and paved a path towards leadership in the peer support profession.

More Information

Sharing Your Wellness Recovery Story - This course is about sharing stories to inspire, inform and motivate others toward hope and action. Your life journey is a gift and how you share that gift through story can make a difference. Although this training primarily focuses on learning techniques and story development for a Peer Empowered Presentation (PEP), it offers easily transferable skills for a variety of storytelling opportunities. Stories are a way of sharing values, ideas, and life lessons to individuals, organizations, and communities. Intentional stories hold power. Research tells us that stories have an impact on how data and information are received. This course will focus on the benefits of storytelling as well as provide a step-by-step guide for developing your wellness/recovery story in a way that can be shared verbally at conferences and events.

https://copelandcenter.com/
https://www.doorstowellbeing.org/copeland-center-trainings

References

Calhoun, G. (n.d.) Storytelling Training. The Copeland Center for Wellness and Recovery. https://copelandcenter.com/news/telling-your-recovery-story

Dekker, R. (2019, May 4). *Evidence on: Doulas*. Evidenced Based Birth. Retrieved February 7, 2022, from https://evidencebasedbirth.com/the-evidence-for-doulas/

National Association of Peer Supporters (2019). National Practice Guidelines for Peer Specialists and Supervisors. N.A.P.S, Washington, DC. https://www.peersupportworks.org/wp-content/uploads/2021/07/National-Practice-Guidelines-for-Peer-Specialists-and-Supervisors-1.pdf

---

1. The National Association of Peer Supporters (N.A.P.S.) was known from 2013 to 2020 as the International Association of Peer Supporters (iNAPS). It was iNAPS at the time the survey was conducted in 2014. In 2020, the organization changed its name back to the "National Association" to return its focus to U.S. efforts.

CHAPTER 3
THE HISTORY OF PEER SUPPORT

CHAPTER INTRODUCTION BY THE EDITORS

GAYLE BLUEBIRD BEGINS THIS CHAPTER WITH A MEMORABLE QUOTE: "HISTORY connects us with our past, with those who have gone before us and those who have earned remembrance." The rich history of what came to be known as the consumer/survivor movement remembers those who fought for humane treatment of people with "mental illness" and worked toward alternatives to the mental health system where people could gain acceptance and work toward recovery. While many in the consumer/survivor movement were challenging the system, others were working from inside the system toward change for kinder and more recovery focused care. The history continues to play out and this is but one chapter in what can be expected to be a long story on how peer support evolves into one that remains founded in the wisdom of experience.

Gayle Bluebird, known to most simply as "Bluebird," shares an account of the history from her own personal relationship with leaders in the consumer/survivor movement. Gayle Bluebird is well known for her work in the arts and she has a separate contribution in the chapter on inclusion and collaboration. This chapter also includes a narrative titled Challenging the Status Quo: Breaking the Mold in the 21st Century by Lisa Kugler and Clarence Jordan that traces the evolution of peer support services and the need for addressing stigma through a Managed Care lens. Finally, the chapter ends with the Mental Health Peer Support Workforce Design line, by Jessica Wolf, which offers key events in the history of the peer support workforce from 1900 – 2020.

SECTION 1: HISTORY OF THE CONSUMER/SURVIVOR MOVEMENT

Gayle Bluebird, RN
Consumer/Survivor

History connects us with our past, with those who have gone before us and those who have earned remembrance. Persons currently working as peer supporters may not be aware of the rich history to which they now belong. The purpose of this account is to review the early history of the "Consumer/Survivor Movement" so that peers can learn about their roots, where they came from, as it applies to their work today. It is time to pay tribute and to honor those early pioneers who created the path so that we would someday benefit from their work and continue the journey.

The history of the consumer movement began in the 1970s, although there were many earlier pioneers. Among these, probably best known is Clifford Beers who wrote *"A Mind that Found Itself"* (1908), a book which ultimately led to the establishment of the American Mental Health Association. But the history that most directly relates to the activities of consumers/survivors today began at a time when the organized efforts of other civil rights groups were taking place, such as the Black/African American Civil Rights Movement, the Women's Movement for the right to vote, and less visible, the Physical Disabilities Movement and the Gay Movement, were in full force.

Discussion

De-institutionalization of large state mental hospitals had begun in the late 1960s consequent with laws established to limit involuntary commitment. It was at this time that ex-patients began to find each other, form in small groups and organize in different cities all over the country, though initially they would not know about each other's activities. They met in living rooms, church basements or community centers, expressing outrage and anger at a system that had caused them harm. Many had been forcibly subjected to shock treatments or insulin therapy. Seclusion Rooms and use of restraints (spread eagled, tied down) were a common practice, as it still is in some hospitals today. People knew about or were witness to many patients who had died and were still dying in institutions. Mental patients were used as unpaid labor at state hospitals and in some hospitals sheeting in cold packs were used as methods for behavioral control.

Homosexuals or others thought to be deviant were also being diagnosed and hospitalized as "mentally ill." It was not until 1974 that the politically active gay community in the United States led the Board of Directors of the American Psychiatric Association to remove *homosexuality* from the *Diagnostic and Statistical Manual of Mental Disorders* (DSM). The consumer/survivor movement began to include persons who had been harmed by the system for being gay. Mark Davis, a leader of this sub-movement, later used humor with his performance he called "Drag with a Tag."

These ex-patients with whatever diagnosis given, felt de-humanized and degraded. Indeed, many of them had been told they had life-long mental illnesses and would never recover. Fully denying any belief in "mental illness", their initial goals were to create a Liberation Movement--not to reform the mental health system-- but to close it down. The term they most used to define them was "ex-inmate."

The politics of these groups were considered radical and their protests were often militant, but while this stronger, more vocal arm of the movement was being organized, there were equally strong voices among the protesters who began to focus on self-help (defined as both personal and interpersonal help). They began to recognize people's needs for support. The concepts of ex-patient- run alternatives that we are familiar with today, was conceived during this same period.

Among the first groups to form as an organization was the *Insane Liberation Front*, in Portland, OR (1970), followed by the *Mental Patients Liberation Project* in New York City and the *Mental Patients Liberation Front* in Boston (both in 1971), and in San Francisco, the *Network Against Psychiatric Assault* formed in 1972. (Chamberlin, 1990). The activities of these groups often included demonstrations at psychiatric hospitals and at conferences of the American Psychiatric Association; once forming a human chain that prevented conference attendees from entering. Another demonstration involved a month-long "sleep-in" at then Governor Jerry Brown's office in California. Approximately 30 people occupied the office and remained there until their demands were heard. The primary issues were patients used as forced labor, un-investigated deaths, and abusive treatment. This demonstration brought attention to the issues and resulted in some changes particularly deaths of patients that were occurring in institutions. During this same period there were other protests held at psychiatric hospitals that used ECT. Marches took place in many cities hosting anti-psychiatry conferences, always featuring songs, chants and homemade signs with anti-psychiatry slogans.

Early protestors began to communicate with each other by means of a national newsletter and an annual conference. *Madness Network News*, (which featured the byline "all the fits that's news to print"), was published in San Francisco for over ten years, with subscribers both nationally and internationally. The newsletter provided an outlet for people to find each other, share their stories, and political strategies for social change. Poetry and artwork was prominently included in every issue, much of it stark with depictions directly relevant to the political issues presented.

An annual Conference called Human *Rights against Psychiatric Oppression* was held in different parts of the country most often on campgrounds or college campuses. The first of these conferences was in Detroit in 1972. People came by bus, by hitchhiking, and in cars packed full. Although most people were surviving on social security disability checks, and with no other income, they found a way to get to these conferences which were among the few opportunities that people had to network and share political views and strategies. One early and significant product emerging from one of these conferences was the development of a Bill of Rights, not too dissimilar from Patients' Rights today. Meetings often lasted into the late hours while people debated issues and values and strategies. They tackled difficult subjects such as whether to take money from the government, whether to allow membership to persons who had not been hospitalized and whether to open their meetings to "sympathetic" professionals.

Judi Chamberlin, one of the early organizers, explains it this way, comparing our movement with other civil rights movements: "Among the major organizing principles of these movements were self-definition and self-determination. Black people felt that white people could not understand their experiences; women felt similarly about men; homosexuals similarly about heterosexuals. As these groups evolved, they moved from defining themselves to setting their own priorities. To mental patients who began to organize, these principles seemed equally valid. Their own perceptions about "mental illness" were diametrically opposed to those of the general public, and even more so to those of mental health professionals. It seemed sensible, therefore, to not let non-patients into ex-patient organizations or to permit them to dictate an organization's goals." (Chamberlin, 1990).

Though the movement believed in egalitarianism, leaders did emerge. Names still familiar, such as Judi Chamberlin, though deceased in 2010, will always be remembered as the *Mother of our Movement*. Sally Zinman, deceased in 2022 continues to be well known for her activism in California today. Howie the Harp, (now deceased) started organizing in New York City but later moved to the West Coast. Su and Dennis Budd are still active in Kansas. George Ebert continues to be active with *Mental Patients Alliance* in Syracuse, New York.

As the movement grew and changed, many leaders would eventually decide to sit at policy-making tables in order to have a voice, and to get funding for consumer-operated drop-in centers and other types of consumer-run programs. Some of the activists maintained their position of separatism and never participated in the evolving changes. Leonard Frank, one of the founders of the *Network Against Psychiatric Assault* in San Francisco, is an example. He chose instead to write a book, *The History of Shock Treatment* and has continued writing on different subjects, although always available for consultation.

In 1978 a landmark book was published: *On Our Own: Patient Controlled Alternatives to the Mental Health System*. This book, written by Judi Chamberlin, has been widely read, reprinted several times and is still considered an authority on the development of ex-patient-controlled alternatives. One of the key principles she recommended is that alternatives be autonomous and in control of the hands of the users.

The 1980s was a transition time. The Federal Government began to take notice that ex-patients were organized and that they were operating successful programs independently without funds or outside support. The Community Support Program at the National Institute of Mental Health began to provide funding for these alternative programs.

In 1983 *On Our Own of Maryland* was the first to be funded with state funding: In 1985, the Berkeley Drop-In Center; the Ruby Rogers Drop-In Center, 1985, in Cambridge, MA; and in 1986, the Oakland Independence Support Center in Oakland California. The Berkeley Drop-in Center is still in operation and On Our Own of Maryland has transformed into a large statewide organization with many different programs.

In 1986, Sally Zinman, Howie the Harp, and Su and Dennis Budd, wrote the first manual with funds from the Federal Government; SAMHSA (Substance Abuse Mental Health Services Administration). *Reaching Across* provided information about self-help and how to operate a self-help support group. In a chapter on Support Groups, Howie the Harp describes how peers and professionals provide support differently. "Support is not therapy", he wrote. "In support, the goal is to comfort, to be available as a caring friend, to listen, and to share the knowledge of common experiences....[while] In a therapeutic relationship the client is requested to change the way he/she thinks or acts."

The first Alternatives Conference was held in 1985, in Baltimore with funding from the Community Support Program at the National Institute of Mental Health, again, with funding from NIMH. By this time there were a variety of different voices with different perspectives on mental illness, some with more moderate views that, while opposed to forced treatment, were not entirely against the medical model.

The conference with over 300 persons attending was challenged by a need to come up with a name to call them. The term "consumer" was eventually selected and it was meant to signify "patient choice" of services and treatment. Many people still add the word "survivor" which usually means having survived the mental health system more than having survived an illness. Issues around self-referential terms continue to baffle; no one really likes "consumer", but another commonly acceptable term has not yet been found to replace it.

1985 was also the year when the final edition of the *Madness Network News* was published and thus marked the decline of radical militant groups. The conference on Human Rights and Against Oppression was also discontinued that year, and a more moderate tone began to reflect the movement.

In 1986, following numerous reports and investigations of abuse and neglect in state psychiatric hospital and findings of inadequate safeguards of patient rights, Congress passed the Protection and Advocacy Act for Individuals with Mental Illnesses (PAIMI) Act. This act provided funding to existing disability advocacy groups in each state to investigate complaints of abuse, neglect or the denial of legal rights to all people in mental health facilities and to some living in the community. Many of the activist consumers sat on advisory committees to the state PAIMI program and continue to do so.

In 1988 funds were provided by SAMHSA for 13 self-help demonstration programs. Though these may have been successful most of these programs did not survive when the federal funding ran out.

More clients or consumers began to sit on decision making bodies. Language had changed from negative to positive. The activities of the militant groups changed to activists voicing strong opinions for change rather than organizing demonstrations to protest.

By the 1990s many new consumer groups formed. Two national technical assistance centers were formed, The Self-Help Clearinghouse in Pennsylvania under the direction of Joe Rogers, and the National Empowerment Center under the direction of Dr. Dan Fisher. Offices of Consumer Affairs were established at the state level in Departments of Mental Health and there was big growth in consumer- run alternative programs. Bill Anthony, Director of Psychiatric Rehabilitation, in Boston, in 1991, described it as the "decade of recovery."

In the 2000s we saw an increase in gains for peer involvement in all areas of the mental health system. The most dramatic change is the development of roles for peer specialists in community settings and in inpatient settings. Peers are being trained to become peer specialists with a special peer-developed curriculum covering subjects such as "how to tell their story," "WRAP" training, combating negative self-talk, stigma and discrimination and how to work with difficult clients, among others. Many specialized positions are being created for peers to work in emergency departments, in homeless programs, forensic facilities, and crisis alternatives. An increasing number of peer-run alternatives are beginning to be developed including wellness programs and specialized drop-in centers and with job training programs and a variety of services. Peer Specialists are being trained in all parts of the country and following certification are working in community as well as inpatient settings. Crisis alternatives are being established with one of the first ones, the "Living Room", created in Phoenix, Arizona. Training is being provided by internet and in extensive hands-on training programs. The Alternatives Conference is in its 25th year and has changed from an advocacy/activist focus towards goals of skills building and promoting wellness and peer support.

Unmarked cemetery and gravesites are being restored in many states with a national memorial planned at Saint Elizabeth's Hospital in Washington, D.C. with Larry Fricks and Pat Deegan leading the effort. The memorial will honor psychiatric patients whose graves were abandoned and forgotten.

A national organization was formed, The National Mental Health Coalition that is bringing statewide organizations and individuals together for advocacy and federal policy development with Lauren Spiro serving as national director. Five consumer and family led technical assistance centers have been federally funded to provide assistance to consumers throughout the country.

Conclusion

The list of our successes is endless. What we can expect in the future is up to the visionaries of today; fulfilling and implementing new strategies for involving persons with psychiatric histories in every level of decision making and employment at all levels in mental health agencies and facilities. We envision a time when persons with psychiatric disabilities are welcomed into society, integrated into jobs and living on their own or in assisted housing in communities. With all of us working together institutions may yet become obsolete. There is still work to be done. As our movement continues to unfold our membership might well include all of us working together in partnership, persons receiving services, family members, providers, consumer/survivors and friends!

More information

Bluebird, G. (2019). Gayle Bluebird interview in The Historical Roots of Peer Support Services. Academy of Peer Services https://www.academyofpeerservices.org/

Bluebird, G. (2019). Gallery of History, photos by Gayle Bluebird. https://aps-community.org/gallery-of-history/

Bluebird, G. (2008). Paving New Ground. Peers Working in In-Patient Settings. National Association of State Mental Health Program Directors. https://www.nasmhpd.org/content/paving-new-ground-peers-working-patient-settings

MindFreedom, International: www.mindfreedom.org

National Empowerment Centre: http://power2u.org/
Zinman, S. & Bluebird, G. (2015) History of the Consumer/Survivor Movement with Sally Zinman and Gayle Bluebird, Webinar 22, National Association of Peer Supporters. https://youtu.be/OzjYi8Ag6fQ

References

Beers, C. (1953). A mind that found itself. Garden City, New York;
Doubleday.

Chamberlin, J. (1979). On our own: Patient –controlled alternatives to the
mental health system. New York; McGraw-Hill

Chamberlin, J. (1990). The Ex-Patients' Movement: Where We've Been and
Where We're Going. The Journal of Mind and Behavior. Accessible at the
National Empowerment Center Website: http://power2u.org/articles/
hisotry-project/ex-patients.html

The Gardens at Saint Elizabeth's: A National Memorial of Recovered Dignity:
www.memorialofrecovereddignity.org

Zinman, S., Bluebird, G., & Budd, S. (2009). History of the Mental Health
Consumer Movement https://web.archive.org/web/20150308024719/http://
promoteacceptance.samhsa.gov/teleconferences/archive/training/
teleconference12172009.aspx

SECTION 2: CHALLENGING THE STATUS QUO: BREAKING THE MOLD
IN THE 21ST CENTURY

Dr. Lisa Kugler
Beacon Cares
Clarence Jordan, MBA
Beacon Health Options

This narrative looks at our increasing understanding of how illness impacts
those affected. It also reviews the evolving competencies of peers that have
enabled them to more effectively support those in need. Peer support services

have enjoyed a tremendous boom with the development of certification programs. Protocols have enabled organizations and policy makers to gather relevant impact data demonstrating powerful outcomes for those supported by these services.

How does one use their own lived experience to become a peer specialist? I begin with my own story by taking into full account what that lived experience has been for me, is now, and what I aspire for it to be in the future. I never knew I had a mental illness until I was told I had one. Most of my life leading up to the moment of diagnosis was, in the words of those who knew me best, that I was a wild child.

Before I became a peer support worker, I was a designated subject matter expert in the field of lived experience. A familiar line of inquiry at the time was, "which do you treat first, the addiction or the mental illness?" I personally had not a clue as I found it difficult sharing in both NA and AA. One condition of my initial employment, post treatment at Davidson County Drug Court (DC4), was to digest as much of the contemporary research / literature on my condition as I could. I gave weekly book reports to the owner of the agency, my supervisor and mentor. Research by Drake gave me my first insight into my condition. Somewhere in his works I recall reading that "addicts live to use and use to live; individuals with co-occurring disorders use on the 1st and 15th of the month."

Works by Scot Miller, Carlo Di-Clemente, William White, and Kim Muser soon followed. Might I add that my job happened to be the Resource Center Director, Foundation Associates, Nashville, TN. The agency received credits as one of the participating agencies in the drafting of TIP 42 SAMSHA's TIP 42 Substance Use Treatment for Persons With Co-Occurring Disorders.

Continuing on with my development as a subject matter expert was my next stop as Operations Officer of NAMI Tennessee. It was there that I learned about advocacy. It was not just knowing about advocating but, more importantly, it was knowing what to advocate for. It was there that I learned that advocacy is just so much hot air that benefits the one doing the advocating but few others.

At a recent forum featuring former Congressman Patrick Kennedy I learned that using our lived experience in the service of others is not a crime. I'm not ashamed of my humble beginnings from the wrong side of the tracks, nor my years in uniform as a commissioned officer in the U.S. Navy. On the contrary I benefited mightily from concepts like duty, honor, integrity, and ESPRIT DE CORPS. I did not grow up as a privileged individual but rather as a military brat, moving from one military installation to another not knowing the true meaning of childhood friends.

By the time I arrived at Beacon Behavioral Health (a Managed Care Organization formerly known as Value Options), I had already become familiar with true advocacy, knowledge, and understanding of contemporary thought leadership on behavioral health by virtue of my earlier years with Foundations Associates, which was my first job after first receiving care. And just as important as learning about true advocacy (beyond the hot air), was the strength derived from belonging to a group of organized individuals living with a common purpose and singular identity. Each one of us that identifies as a peer specialist has our own lived experience. When we're able to use that experience to benefit and serve others it becomes a force multiplier (which is when the whole is greater than the sum of the individual parts added together).

I believe that survivors of trauma, living a resilient life of recovery benefit from the collective strength of the entire team. Beyond treatment and therapeutics, the most important element of the team is the authentic lived experience of the peer specialist.

Discussion

Peer support services were recognized by Centers for Medicare and Medicaid Services (CMS) as an evidence-based practice in 2007 (Smith, 2007). The provision called upon states to develop their own peer specialist certification processes. Based on an Executive Order by President Obama, the Dept. of Veterans Affairs (VA) committed to more than 800 new peer support positions by the end of 2013 (White House, 2012; VA Press Release, 2013). This was a notable milestone not only for the numbers but for the early movement to provide a career later for peers. By April of 2018, 39 state Medicaid programs were covering peer support services for either individuals with mental illness or individuals with addiction disorders, or both groups (Open Minds, 2018). This was a rapid increase over the previous decade, in which only eight states funded peer services under Medicaid. Today most states reimburse for these services

How do individuals benefit from these services? Beacon enrollees have responded to surveys in which they indicated peer support helps in the following ways:

- Symptom remission is only the beginning:
- Safe, independent housing
- Gainful employment
- Meaningful social interaction

- Good nutrition
- Physical health and activity
- Emotional and spiritual wellbeing
- Self-monitoring and personal responsibility
- Hope, empowerment, healing, connection

On any given day, you can find peer support specialists serving in a variety of roles:

- Coach
- Mentor
- Guide
- Educator
- Health promoter
- Connector to resources
- Advocate
- Health system navigator
- First call for help
- Recovery planner
- Clinical team adjunct
- Role model for what's possible

Beacon provides services to benefit both individuals and families as whole units, just as we believe that recovery should be pursued from a whole person perspective. This perspective has enabled us to provide support services that:

- Provide one-on-one support and encouragement to young adults; assist with goal setting and identification of positive environments and resources; advocate for youth in team meetings
- Facilitate group meetings of young adult peers.
- Conduct outreach in the community; and provide education on youth engagement, youth peer support, and recruitment of young adults to access available supports and services.
- Provide safe, independent housing
- Offer gainful employment

Peer support for families is becoming an increasingly meaningful service and peer supporters are involved with making a difference at the local, state, and national levels.

Over the years Beacon has partnered with several different local and national consumer advocacy organizations. We've supported the National Alliance on Mental Illness (NAMI) by hosting the Welcome Center at the annual NAMI National Convention, which has provided meals for 3,400 conference attendees over the past 17 years.

Health Promoter is an integrated health training for peers that was developed in house at Beacon to help bridge the gap between behavioral and physical health. The training has been endorsed by the Mental Health Association (MHA) as a prerequisite for the National Peer Certification Program.

Beacon has also collaborated with like-minded organizations to address disparities in health care. We worked with the University of Tennessee Health Sciences on the BLUES Project. This initiative provided assistance to thousands of young adults to combat infant mortality rates.

Beacon was there in the formation of the Congregational Health Network of Memphis which has become a national model to support mental health care literacy and open the doors to behavioral health services in a unique faith-based model.

During the height of the COVID-19 pandemic Beacon peers provided a peer-run Virtual Peer Support Group to support plan members and effectively combat loneliness brought about by imposed COVID protocols.

Recovery is not easy for most, and it certainly wasn't for me either. Often it can be as messy if not more so than the periods when you feel seduced by the illness itself. I believe the thrust of the article on me in the National Council Magazine that celebrated the 50th Anniversary of the Community Mental Health Act (National Council Magazine, 2013) was the acknowledgement of the fact that many of us cannot do it alone. Once your perception of yourself changes and your basic social DNA is altered the journey forward can be extremely difficult because it's so easy to lose one's wellness compass. I liken it to episodes at sea where a ship loses its rudder. And just like episodes at sea when steerage is lost, even the smallest of tugs can provide an assist to the largest cruise liner.

Just as it doesn't make sense to send a tow truck to lend assistance to a rudderless ship, nor should we be deploying a skilled workforce that lacks lived experience in navigating the sea to aid those floundering in their recovery. At the core of Beacon commitment and passion for peer services are the National Practice Guidelines for Peer Specialists and Supervisors (N.A.P.S., 2019) alongside a set of Guiding Principles, Values, and Competencies developed by SAMHSA BRSS TACS (SAMHSA BRSS TACS, 2015). Beacon employs dozens of dedicated peer specialists and because we do, we believe that individuals affected by these behavioral health conditions do recover.

Our five core beliefs are:

- Everyone has the ability to learn and grow – Being diagnosed with a mental illness does not take away the ability to learn and grow; people can recover and move on with their lives
- Peoples' beliefs determine their behavior – What a person believes about himself, because he is diagnosed with a mental illness is the most important determinant of his success in creating a life he or she wants
- People think their way through life – Being diagnosed does not take away the ability to think strategically and creatively
- Whatever people focus on, they give power to – While symptoms and disability bring people in for services, the focus needs to shift to wellness and strengths as soon as possible
- Life's experiences are the best teacher – Your recovery experiences are your greatest gift to your peers

Our approach to peer staff development combines the N.A.P.S. nationally accepted values with the SAMHSA BRSS TACS peer competencies with an understanding of the impact of the illness coupled with the best scientific approach to individual change as promoted by the Appalachian Consulting Group Certified Peer Specialist Training, which was adopted by and offered through the Depression and Bipolar Support Alliance (ACG, DBSA, n.d.), see chart below:

Disabling Power of Personal Stigma	Stage of Change	Peer Intervention
Identity ~ Impact of Illness; shattering of world hopes & dreams	Pre-contemplation	Engagement ~ establishing rapport
Possibilities ~ Life is limited; giving up was a solution	Contemplation	Encouragement ~ believable hope
Risk ~ Change is possible; fragile flame of hope & courage	Planning	Empowerment ~ you've done it before and you can do it now
Support ~ Commitment to change; simple acts of courage	Action	Education ~ Identification of possible resources
Responsibility ~ Actions for Chang; we rebuild our lives	Relapse Prevention	Exit ~ development of meaningful support system

EVEN WITH ALL OUR BELIEFS, values, and competencies we still make a conscientious effort to eliminate the vestiges of stigma, abuse, and disparate treatment. Employ a comprehensive strategy to combat the undisputed, number one barrier to individual and organizational wellness, stigma.

Conclusion

Scholars and scientists have pointed to persistent stigma as a major barrier to the successful treatment of mental health and substance use disorders (National Academies of Science, Engineering, and Medicine, 2016). Stigma is real and needs to be addressed at multiple levels of society including the structural level of institutional practices, laws, and regulations; among both the public and groups, such as health care providers, employers, and landlords; as well as self-stigma, which reflects internalized negative stereotypes. The language that is used to discuss mental health and substance use disorders and to refer to people with these disorders, is often targeted for change as a strategy for reducing stigma. For example, many stakeholders prefer person-first language, which is language that describes a person as having a mental illness rather than as being mentally ill. The term "stigma" itself has been targeted for change by some stakeholder groups, and the Substance Abuse and Mental Health Services Administration (SAMHSA) is moving away from the use of this term.

In addition to a fragmented mental health care system, the community of stakeholders concerned about mental health and substance use disorders reflects a multiplicity of goals and at times different competing agendas. Peers play an essential role in combating stigma, in part because they model personal recovery. Their role is critical in helping individuals to overcome the debilitating forces of self-stigma. Peer support programs and services include social and emotional support, as well as practical support related to quality-of-life decisions, delivered by people with mental health and substance use disorders.

Peer support services have existed since the 1970's, but in 2001 several states began efforts to certify and train the peer specialist workforce. Today state peer certification for mental health, or addiction recovery peer support (or both) exists in all but one state, South Dakota. (Peer Recovery Center of Excellence, 2021). State programs vary in terms of stage of development and certification requirements, including the content and process of training, examination criteria and requirements for continuing education and recertification.

68

One would think given the mounting evidence attesting to the benefits of peer support services that there would be tens of thousands if not more certified peer specialists providing recovery support services wherever needed. Such is not the case, in most states the current number of certified peer specialists providing clinical support services are but a handful. Yet some experts in the field of psychosocial rehabilitation indicate that the most critical moment in the change process would be at that point the person begins to contemplate making such life changing decisions. I don't think it matters much if you receive care voluntarily or court ordered, most will have those moments when you think to yourself that you've had just about enough of the madness: doing the same thing over and over again expecting different results.

What happens when you enter care matters a lot; the reception you receive and by whom, how you are addressed and the tone that is established can be a make-or-break moment. First impressions; the cleanliness of the grounds, the state of repair of the facility, lighting, and sounds all contribute to your assessment of things to come. If what is being presented resembles what you're expected to leave behind, it's difficult to see, think, feel, and act any differently. Peer support can make a world of difference to anyone who is struggling with mental health and/or addiction challenges.

References

Appalachian Consulting Group (ACG) (n.d.) Certified Peer Specialist Training, as adopted by the Depression and Bipolar Support Alliance.

Jordan, C. (2019). Beacon's 'coach approach' earns accolades. MHA Endorsement. https://www.beaconlens.com/beacons-coach-approach-earns-accolades/.

Jordan, C. (2013). Recovery Story. The National Council for Behavioral Health Magazine 50 stories of recovery. Special issue to commemorate the 50th anniversary of the Community Mental Health Act signed into law on October 31, 1963 by President John F. Kennedy.

Kubek, P. & Weiland, M. (2008). "Stages of change" co-creator Carlo DiClemente discusses practical applications of his Transtheoretical Model for health, wellness and recovery. Center for Evidence-Based Practices, Case Western Reserve University. https://case.edu/socialwork/centerforebp/

stories/stages-change-co-creator-carlo-diclemente-discusses-practical-
applications-his-transtheoretical-model-health-wellness-and-recovery

National Academies of Science, Engineering, and Medicine (2016). Ending
Discrimination Against People With Mental And Substance Use Disorders:
The Evidence for Stigma Change Ending Discrimination Against People with
Mental and Substance Use Disorders: The Evidence for Stigma Change
(riprc.org)

National Association of Peer Supporters (2019). National Practice Guidelines
for Peer Specialists and Supervisors. Washington, DC: N.A.P.S. https://www.
peersupportworks.org/wp-content/uploads/2021/07/National-Practice-
Guidelines-for-Peer-Specialists-and-Supervisors-1.pdf

Open Minds (2018). https://openminds.com/press/39-states-cover-peer-
support-services-for-behavioral-health-open-minds-releases-reference-
guide-on-medicaid-reimbursement-for-peer-support-services/

Peer Recovery Center of Excellence. (2021). Comparative Analysis of State
Requirements for Peer Support Specialist Training and Certification in the
United States https://peerrecoverynow.org/documents/Comparative%
20Analysis_Jan.31.2022%20(003).pdf

SAMHSA BRSS TACS (2015). Core Competencies for Peer Support Workers.
Substance Abuse and Mental Health Services Administration. https://www.
samhsa.gov/brss-tacs/recovery-support-tools/peers/core-competencies-
peer-workers

Smith, D. (2007). Letter to the State Medicaid Directors. https://downloads.
cms.gov/cmsgov/archived-downloads/smdl/downloads/smd081507a.pdf

VA Office of Public and Interdepartmental Affairs (2012). https://www.va.
gov/opa/pressrel/pressrelease.cfm?id=2487

White House Archives. (2012). https://obamawhitehouse.archives.gov/the-
press-office/2012/08/31/fact-sheet-president-obama-signs-executive-order-
improve-access-mental-h

SECTION 3: MENTAL HEALTH PEER SUPPORT WORKFORCE DESIGNLINE

Jessica Wolf, Assistant Clinical Prof. of Psychiatry, Yale University
For the Central East MHTTC (Used with permission)

Central East (HHS Region 3)

MHTTC Mental Health Technology Transfer Center Network
Funded by Substance Abuse and Mental Health Services Administration

Mental Health Peer Support Workforce Designline

Jessica Wolf, PhD, Decision Solutions
Waymon Harrold, Graphic Designer
August 2020

Introduction

This "Designline" (Graphic Design Timeline) aims to increase awareness of the rich history, context and challenges of the mental health peer support workforce.

Peer support began in late 18th century France and in the mid-19th century in the U.S., with mutual support groups starting in the 1930s. The mid-20th century saw overcrowded "insane asylums," the introduction in the early 1950's of (now controversial) antipsychotic medications, and the community mental health centers movement in the 1960's. Deinstitutionalization efforts beginning in the 1970's were accompanied by active protests and advocacy, significantly contributing in the following decades to a shift from primarily medical-model treatment to a rehabilitation and recovery focus, including peer support and involving individuals with lived experience as key participants in service design and delivery. Emphasis on community support and psychiatric rehabilitation in the 1980's was followed by increasing attention to recovery and the participation of peers in the 1990's. In the 21st century, the peer workforce has grown considerably, with increasing attention to person-centered care and self-determination.

We consulted with current and past peer leaders and reviewed numerous books, articles and accounts in developing this Designline. While opinions may diverge about choice of events, our purpose is to increase awareness of peer support workforce history. A list of references offers additional depth to this important story.

We recommend the New York State Academy of Peer Services course on The Historical Roots of Peer Support for an extensive interactive history of the disability rights and consumer/survivor/ex-patients' movement that insisted on "nothing about us without us." Movement pioneers, together with other leaders who advocated for recovery from mental health conditions and a full community life, did the critical work that eventually resulted in current employment of thousands of certified peer specialists and other peer support workers in 43 U.S. states, the District of Columbia and the U.S. Department of Veterans Affairs. Thousands more are employed as recovery coaches in substance use prevention and treatment programs, as parent partners, youth peer support workers, forensic peer specialists, dual diagnosis peer specialists, peer supervisors, and peer support workers in primary and integrated care settings. In important ways, they support the recovery of individuals living with mental health and substance use conditions.

 1900-1950

Themes: Large public psychiatric hospitals are overcrowded and little more than warehouses for those locked up, many of whom are committed for indefinite periods. Many people die there and are buried in graves marked only by numbers.

1900

1920

1908:: *A Mind That Found Itself,* by Clifford W. Beers, published.

1909: Clifford Beers founds the National Committee for Mental Hygiene, now known as Mental Health America.

1930

1935: AA (Alcoholics Anonymous) founded by Bill Wilson and Dr. Robert Smith.

1937: Recovery, Inc. founded by Dr. Abraham Low.

1940

1948: Film "The Snake Pit" released, based on Mary Jane Ward's 1946 novel about her terrible experiences in a psychiatric institution.

1948: *The Shame of the States,* by Albert Deutsch published, about appalling conditions in state mental hospitals.

1950

1948: WANA ("We Are Not Alone"), former patients, found Fountain House.

 FOUNTAIN HOUSE

 Inspiring Communities for Mental Health

Themes: People with serious mental health conditions—then considered a "life sentence"—are hospitalized in large institutions. While the development of antipsychotic medications leads to discharges, continuity of care from hospital to the community is lacking. Some medications, such as Thorazine, have terrible side effects including tardive dyskinesia, an irreversible condition with disfiguring grimacing. The U.S. psychiatric institution population in 1955 is 558,000.

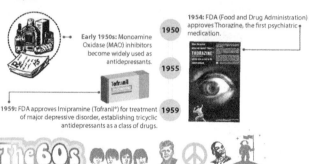

1950

Early 1950s: Monoamine Oxidase (MAO) inhibitors become widely used as antidepressants.

1954: FDA (Food and Drug Administration) approves Thorazine, the first psychiatric medication.

1955

1959

1959: FDA approves Imipramine (Tofranil®) for treatment of major depressive disorder, establishing tricyclic antidepressants as a class of drugs.

Themes: Large institutions are the worst places to care for people with serious mental health conditions; people do better with community-based services. Some federally funded community mental health centers tend to treat the "worried well," rather than people with serious mental health conditions. The first modern anti-psychiatry group is founded, sparking the social justice movement of people with psychiatric histories.

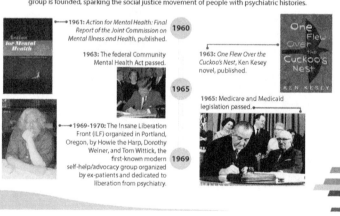

1961: *Action for Mental Health: Final Report of the Joint Commission on Mental Illness and Health,* published.

1960

1963: The federal Community Mental Health Act passed.

1963: *One Flew Over the Cuckoo's Nest,* Ken Kesey novel, published.

1965

1965: Medicare and Medicaid legislation passed.

1969-1970: The Insane Liberation Front (ILF) organized in Portland, Oregon, by Howie the Harp, Dorothy Weiner, and Tom Wittick, the first-known modern self-help/advocacy group organized by ex-patients and dedicated to liberation from psychiatry.

1969

Themes: Numerous "mental patients' liberation" groups are founded on the West and East Coasts; Madness Network News begins publication; advocacy/political action and self-help movement groups make successful demands for inclusion in federal program planning.

1971-1972: Mental Patients' Liberation Front founded in Boston; other groups are founded in New York City, San Francisco, and elsewhere.

1972: San Francisco-based *Madness Network News* begins publication.

1973: The first International Conference on Human Rights and Against Psychiatric Oppression.

1975: The U.S. Supreme Court, in O'Connor v. Donaldson, rules that people cannot be institutionalized in a psychiatric hospital against their will unless they are found to be a threat to themselves or others.

1975: IAPSRS (now PRA–Psychiatric Rehabilitation Association) founded.

1978: *On Our Own: Patient-Controlled Alternatives to the Mental Health System,* by Judy Chamberlin, published.

1978: National Institute of Mental Health (NIMH) Community Support Program (CSP) initiated.

1971: Emotions Anonymous founded.

1972: New York State consumer-operated programs underway.

1972: The Mental Health Law Project (now the Judge David L. Bazelon Center for Mental Health Law) founded.

1975: "One Flew Over the Cuckoo's Nest," released, based on 1962 Ken Kesey novel.

1978: : Adult Children of Alcoholics founded.

1979: NAMI (National Alliance for the Mentally Ill, now the National Alliance on Mental Illness, founded.

Mental health advocates, led by people with lived experience, call for the end of abusive treatment. The federally-funded Community Support Program begins to collaborate with individuals with psychiatric histories. Tension exists in the consumer/survivor/ex-patients' movement about the value of working outside versus inside "the system." NIMH Community Support Program funding continues through the 1980s as psychosocial rehabilitation is added to medical-model treatment of mental health conditions.

1980s: Dual Diagnosis self-help groups begin.

 1980

1980: The Civil Rights of Institutionalized Persons Act (CRIPA) gives the Department of Justice the power to sue state or local institutions that violate the rights of people held against their will, including those residing in institutions for the treatment of mental health conditions.

CRIPA

Civil Rights of Institutionalized Persons Act

 NARPA
NATIONAL ASSOCIATION FOR RIGHTS PROTECTION AND ADVOCACY

1980: National Association for Rights Protection and Advocacy (NARPA) founded.

 NARSAD
The Brain and Behavior Research Fund

1981: National Alliance for Research on Schizophrenia and Depression (NARSAD) founded.

 1981

1980s-1990s: Offices of Consumer Affairs are established in State Departments of Mental Health.

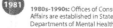

 NYAPRS
"Partners in Recovery"

1981: NYAPRS (New York Association of Psychiatric Rehabilitation Services) founded.

1982: Statement of Principles adopted at 10th International Conference on Human Rights and Against Psychiatric Oppression.

1982

1982: Survivors of Incest Anonymous founded.

1983

1983: The California Network of Mental Health Clients, first statewide peer-run organization, founded.

 On Our Own of Maryland, Inc.

1983: On Our Own, Inc. in Maryland first to receive state and federal funds to open a consumer-operated drop-in center.

 1984

 **NIMH**
NATIONAL INSTITUTE OF MENTAL HEALTH

1985: The National Mental Health Consumers' Association, the first national c/s/x organization, founded under Joseph Rogers' leadership.

1985

1985: The first annual Alternatives conference in Baltimore, MD, organized by and for individuals with psychiatric diagnoses, organized by On Our Own of Baltimore and funded by NIMH-CSP. Federally funded Alternatives conferences continue through 2017.

 Madness Network News

1985: The final International Conference on Human Rights and Against Psychiatric Oppression, in Vermont.

1985: *Madness Network News* ceases publication.

1985: Altered States of the Arts founded by Gayle Bluebird, Howie the Harp and others.

1986: The Rehabilitation Act of 1973, as amended, authorizes federal funding of employment services for people with "mental and physical disabilities."

1986: "Reaching Across: Mental Health Clients Helping Each other," by Sally Zinman, Howie the Harp, and Su Budd, published.

1986: The State Comprehensive Mental Health Plan Act (P.L. 99-660) mandates case management and other services as Medicaid benefits. Required stakeholder involvement in the State Block Grant program recognizes the importance of service user voices.

1986: The National Depressive and Manic Depressive Association founded; later renamed the Depression and Bipolar Support Alliance.

NDMDA

1987: "Vermont Longitudinal Study of Persons with Severe Mental Illness" published, demonstrating that people diagnosed with schizophrenia did not necessarily have to take drugs indefinitely; psychosocial services positively affected recovery.

NIMH
National Institute of Mental Health

1988-1991: NIMH CSP funds 14 consumer/survivor-run demonstration projects including drop-in centers, outreach, businesses, employment, housing, peer-run crisis respites.

1989: The National Association of State Mental Health Program Directors (NASMHPD) "Position Statement on Consumer Contributions to Mental Health Service Delivery System" approved.

1986

1986: The National Mental Health Consumers' Self-Help Clearinghouse, the first national technical assistance center serving the c/s/x movement, conceived and founded by Joseph Rogers in Philadelphia.

Clearinghouse

1986: The first peers including activist Pat Risser, trained to work as Consumer Case Manager Aides in Denver, Colorado, through the leadership of Paul Sherman, PhD Services were billable to Medicaid under the Colorado Medicaid Rehabilitation Option Waiver.

1986: The Protection and Advocacy for Mentally Ill Individuals (now the Protection and Advocacy for Individuals with Mental Illness) Act of 1986 passed.

1987: Selective Serotonin Reuptake Inhibitors (SSRIs) antidepressants introduced.

1987

1988

1989: FDA approves Clozapine as the first atypical antipsychotic drug. The danger of death required weekly blood tests.

1989

Themes: Advocacy against abusive treatment continues. The concept of recovery is promoted with a range of coordinated community rehabilitative services. "Nothing about us without us": c/s/x (consumer/survivor/ex-patient) voices gain more prominence, advocacy groups grow; and peer-designed and -operated programs are implemented in mental health systems. State hospitals continue downsizing; some close. In just over 40 years, U.S. occupied state hospital beds declined from 339 to 21 per 100,000 people. In 1998, 57,151 people were in state hospitals.

1990: The Americans with Disabilities Act becomes law.

1992: The National Empowerment Center (NEC) founded in Massachusetts by Dan Fisher and Laurie Ahern. The NEC and the Clearinghouse apply for and receive federal funding.

1990

1990: Bill Anthony, founder of the Boston University Center for Psychiatric Rehabilitation, labels the 1990s the "Decade of Recovery."

1992: The federal Substance Abuse and Mental Health Services Administration (SAMHSA) succeeds NIMH; the Center for Mental Health Services is created.

1991

1993: The Mental Health Law Project renamed the Judge David L. Bazelon Center for Mental Health Law.

1993: The first consumer Civil Service job title is created, in New York State.

1995: Paolo del Vecchio appointed SAMHSA Consumer Affairs Specialist.

1992

1992: National People of Color Consumer/Survivor Caucus launched at Alternatives Conference.

1994: Research by Drs. Phyllis Solomon and Jeffrey Draine demonstrates consumer case management is as effective as a non-consumer team in helping individuals with serious mental health conditions over a two-year period.

1993

1995: "Consumers as Peer Specialists on Intensive Case Management Teams: Impact on Client Outcomes" by Felton et al. is published, stating "Integration of peer specialists into intensive case management programs appears to lead to enhanced quality of life for clients and more effective case management."

1995: *Return to Community: Building Support Systems for People with Psychiatric Disabilities,* by Dr. Paul J. Carling, published.

1994

1995: SAMHSA issues first "National Consensus Statement on Mental Health Recovery," with updated versions in 2006 and 2010.

1995: The Howie The Harp Advocacy Center begins peer training program in NYC.

1995

1998-2004: Federally funded research by Jean Campbell, PhD, on Consumer-Operated Service Programs proves peer-run program effectiveness, leads to other research on c/s/x-run programs and establishes peer support as an evidence-based practice.

1999: *Mental Health: A Report of the Surgeon General,* published.

1999

1999: Georgia Mental Health Consumer Network with Larry Fricks' leadership makes Georgia the first state to receive Medicaid reimbursement for peer services.

1999: U.S. Supreme Court *Olmstead* decision affirms the right of people with disabilities to receive state-funded services in communities and be treated in the least restrictive setting.

1999: NAMI publishes *Families on the Brink: The Impact of Ignoring Children with Serious Mental Illness.*

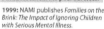

Themes: Recovery focus increasingly integral in federally funded and promoted concepts and programs, with people in recovery involved in planning and service delivery; PEER SUPPORT becomes a reimbursable workforce option; federally funded system transformation initiatives undertaken.

2000s: National People of Color Consumer/Survivor Network initiated.

2000 **2000:** Bill Anthony article published, "A recovery-oriented service system: Setting some system level standards."

2001: Institute of Medicine publishes *Crossing the Quality Chasm: A New Health System for the 21st Century.*

2002: *Mad in America*, by Robert Whitaker, published.

2001 **2001:** PRA (Psychiatric Rehabilitation Association) initiates CPRP (Certified Psychiatric Rehabilitation Practitioner) credential.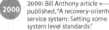

GEORGIA
CPS project

2001: *Mental Health: Culture, Race, and Ethnicity*, published as *A Supplement to Mental Health: A Report of the Surgeon General.*

2002 **2002:** National Council on Disability issues *National Disability Policy: A Progress Report.*

2002: NDMDA becomes Depression and Bipolar Support Alliance (DBSA).

Depression and Bipolar Support Alliance

2001: Georgia initiates peer certification.

2002: NTAC Report published, *Mental Health Recovery: What Helps and What Hinders?*

2003 **2004:** iNAPS (International Association of Peer Supporters) founded by Steve Harrington.

2003: President's New Freedom Commission on Mental Health Report, *Achieving the Promise: Transforming Mental Health Care in America*, calls for involvement of people in recovery and their families.

2004 **2005: Peer support training, certification and employment in 7 states**

2005: U.S. Veterans Health Administration begins funding peer support positions.

2005: Intentional Peer Support curriculum developed by Shery Mead.

2005 intentional peerSUPPORT

2005-2010: Federal mental health system transformation grants awarded and implemented.

2006 **2006:** National Coalition for Mental Health Recovery co-founded by Daniel Fisher, M.D., Ph.D., Joseph Rogers, Sally Zinman, Linda Corey, and Mike Finkle. National Coalition for Mental Health Recovery

2006: Institute of Medicine Report *Improving the Quality of Health Care for Mental and Substance-Use Conditions*, published.

PAT DEEGAN'S
COMMONGROUND

2007 **2007: Medicaid letter issued authorizing reimbursement for peer support services as an "evidence-based" practice.**

2007: Common Ground software launched by Pat Deegan Associates (long-time advocates); also developed Shared Decision-Making recovery-oriented, person-centered software.

2008 PILLARS OF PEER SUPPORT

2007: National Action Plan on Behavioral Health Workforce Development by Michael Hoge, John Morris, Alan Daniels et al. includes people in recovery and families as partners.

2009 **2009: First Pillars of Peer Support: Transforming Mental Health Systems of Care conference at the Carter Center, Atlanta, GA.**

Themes: Continued growth of peer support workforce; new forms of person-centered care underway; with change in federal administration, national focus shifts towards treatment and hospitals as peer workforce continues to expand. Digital peer support certification launched.

pcori

2010: Patient Centered Outcomes Research Institute (PCORI) created as a result of passage of the Patient Protection and Affordable Care Act (Obamacare).

2010: Hearing Voices Network USA founded (begun in Netherlands in 1986).

HEARING VOICES NETWORK USA

2010: Peer training, certification and employment in 26 states.

2010: *Anatomy of an Epidemic: Magic Bullets, Psychiatric Drugs, and the Astonishing Rise of Mental Illness in America,* by Robert Whitaker.

2011-2020: SAMHSA BRSS TACS (Bringing Recovery Supports to Scale Technical Assistance Center Strategy) initiated to promote recovery-oriented supports, services and systems.

BRSS TACS Bringing Recovery Supports to Scale

ROBERT WHITAKER

2010-2014: Pillars of Peer Support reports.

2012: The Foundation for Excellence in Mental Health Care (FEMHC) founded to undertake progressive research and fund innovative programs.

2012: Open Dialogue approach to schizophrenia initiated in U.S. (begun in Finland in 1980's).

2013: INAPS National Practice Guidelines for Peer Supporters circulated.

2014: Surviving Race: The Intersection of Injustice, Disability and Human Rights Facebook group founded by Celia Brown and others.

BRAIN & BEHAVIOR RESEARCH FOUNDATION
Awarding **NARSAD** Grants

2014: NARSAD becomes The Brain and Behavior Research Foundation.

2015: Peer support training, certification and employment available in 38 states.

2015: SAMHSA circulates Peer Support Core Competences.

2016: Over 25,000 peer specialists certified in 44 States, D.C., and the V.A.

2017: The federal Intergovernmental Serious Mental Illness Coordinating Committee (ISMICC) created.

2017: The V.A. employed 1,300 peer support workers with defined positions and career ladders.

2017: Mental Health America launches National Certified Peer Specialist certification.

MHA Mental Health America

2017: Final SAMHSA-funded Alternatives Conference.

2018: 2018: Federally-funded MHTTC (Mental Health Technology Transfer Network) created to accelerate adoption of mental health related evidence-based practices, improve workforce skills, foster alliances and assure availability of training and technical assistance across the nation.

Strategic Plan for FY 2019-2023
SAMHSA Substance Abuse and Mental Health Services Administration

SAMHSA Strategic Plan for FY 2019-2023 addresses peer delivered services (Priority 2 Objectives 2.3 & 2.5) and credentialed peer professionals (Priority 5, Objectives 5.2 & 5.3).

2018: Darby Penney article "Defining 'Peer Support'" addressing professionalization, peer support versus peer delivered services.

MHTTC Mental Health Technology Transfer Center Network

2018-2019: National Coalition for Mental Health Recovery presents independently-funded Alternatives Conference.

2018: International User/Survivor/Lived Experience Research Network founded at NCMHR-sponsored Alternatives Conference.

PEER SUPPORT

2019: 45 States, D.C. & V.A. train, credential and employ peer providers; the remaining 5 states appear to have non-state-sponsored peer support.

2019: National Association of Peer Supporters (formerly INAPS) releases National Practice Guidelines for Peer Specialists and Supervisors.

2010 · 2011 · 2012 · 2013 · 2014 · 2015 · 2016 · 2017 · 2018 · 2019

Current Themes: Defining paid peer roles; professionalization vs. cooptation; systems change from within vs. compromising core peer support principles; change from outside systems through advocacy; transforming traditional systems and promoting recovery-oriented practices; normalizing disclosure of lived experience, reducing stigma, increasing cultural humility and intersectionality; racial equity and social justice. Practice changes: early psychosis intervention; Hearing Voices Network, Open Dialogue; peer-run respites; certification, continuing education, career development and advancement; behavioral health and primary care integration; digital peer specialist certification; virtual and remote practice.

2020

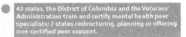
43 states, the District of Columbia and the Veterans' Administration train and certify mental health peer specialists; 7 states restructuring, planning or offering non-certified peer support.

Covid-19 pandemic spreads throughout the U.S. and the world.

Widespread racial justice demonstrations throughout the U.S. and globally.

NCMHR partners with Mental Health & Addiction Association of Oregon to include Alternatives presentations at July virtual Peerpocalypse conference.

SAMHSA BRSS TACS federal funding terminated as of September 30.

Peer workforce continues to increase; for example, as of July, 2,380 active Certified Peer Specialists in New York State with 941 pending applications; 747 Family Peer Advocates and 90 Youth Peer Advocates credentialed.

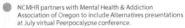
Digital Peer Support Certification launched by partnership at Geisel School of Medicine, Dartmouth College and peer specialists; 1,700 people from 30 states and 4 nations trained; 926 certified.

What will be the future of peer support?

Central East (HHS Region 3)

MHTTC Mental Health Technology Transfer Center Network
Funded by Substance Abuse and Mental Health Services Administration

Selected References

Academy of Peer Services, Virtual Learning Community (2019). *Gallery of History*. Gallery of History

Academy of Peer Services (2019). *The Historical Roots of Peer Support Services*, Historical Roots

Consumer Family Network of North Dakota (2010). Movement History of the Consumer/Client/Survivor/Ex-patient/Ex-Inmate/User Community (Timeline) Movement History Timeline

Gagne, C., Finch, W.L., Myrick, K.J, & Davis, L.M. (2018). Peer workers in the behavioral and integrated health workforce: Opportunities and future directions, *American Journal of Preventive Medicine, 54 (6S3),258-266*. Gagne et al. Peer Workers

Marill, M.C. (2019). Beyond twelve steps, Peer-supported mental health care. *Health Affairs 38*(6), 896-901. Marill Beyond 12 Steps

Kaufman, L., Kuhn, W., & Stevens Manser, S. 2016. Peer Specialist Training and Certification Programs: A National Overview. Texas Institute for Excellence in Mental Health, School of Social Work, University of Texas at Austin. PS Training & Certification Programs

Milestones of the Consumer/Survivor/Ex-patient (C/S/X) Movement for Social Justice (2012). Compiled by Risser, P., Rogers, S., & Spiro, L.

Penney, D. (2018). Defining "Peer Support:" Implications for Policy, Practice, and Research. Advocates for Human Potential, Inc. Retrieved from Penney Defining Peer Support

Psychiatric Services, Editor's Choice articles on Peer Support, March 2019, Peer Support Editor's Choice

Rogers, S. (2015). The Power of Peers: Peer support and the evolution of the peer provider workforce. Psychiatric Rehabilitation Association (PRA) Conference, Philadelphia, PA, June 2.

Wolf, J. (2018). National trends in peer specialist certification. *Psychiatric Services, 69(10), 1049*. Peer Certification Trends 2018

Zinman, S., Budd, S., & Bluebird, G. (2009). History of Mental Health Consumer Movement. U.S. Department of Health and Human Services, Substance Abuse and Mental Health Services Administration, Resource Center to Promote Acceptance, Dignity and Social Inclusion Associated with Mental Illness (Webinar; December 17). Consumer Survivor Movement History

Our sincere thanks to the many colleagues who contributed knowledge, information and perspective to the development of this unique Designline. We hope it will contribute to understanding our rich peer support history, will be widely circulated, and will guide future evolution of peer support practice. My personal thanks to Waymon Harrold, Graphic Designer, for his creative work and patience.

Jessica Wolf, Stratford, CT, August 2020

Decision
Solutions

SAMHSA
Substance Abuse and Mental Health
Services Administration

More Information

Bluebird, G. (2009). History of the Consumer/Survivor Movement. National Empowerment Center. https://power2u.org/wp-content/uploads/2017/01/History-of-the-Consumer-Survivor-Movement-by-Gayle-Bluebird.pdf

Budd, S. (2009). A History of the Mental Health Consumer/Survivor Movement. Presented at the SAMHSA ADS Center Training Teleconference on Dec. 17, 2009. https://virtualcommunityblog.files.wordpress.com/2021/04/su-budd-a-history-of-the-mental-health-consumer-survivor-movement.pdf

Brown, C. & Stastny, P. (2016). Peer workers in the mental health system: a transformative or collusive experiment? Chapter in J. Russo (Ed.) & A. Sweeney (Ed.) Searching for a Rose Garden: challenging psychiatry, fostering mad studies. PCCS Books, Ltd. https://www.pccs-books.co.uk/

Brown, C., (2012). Celia Brown speaking at Eugene's Opal Network, Oct. 15, 2012 [Video 3:53 min. excerpt from 19:55 min.] https://youtu.be/0-GJPBqgi4g

Campbell, J. & Leaver, J. (2003). Emerging New Practices in Organized Peer Support. U.S.: A Report from NTAC's National Experts Meeting on Emerging Practices in Organized Peer Support, Alexandria, VA. For the Dept. of Health and Human Services, Substance Abuse and Mental Health Services Administration (SAMHSA), Center for Mental Health Services, National Association of State Mental Health Program Directors (NASMHPD). https://virtualcommunityblog.files.wordpress.com/2019/08/2003-campbell-emerging-new-practices-in-organized-peer-support.pdf

Chamberlin, J. (1998). Confessions of a noncompliant patient. Psychosocial Nursing, 36(4), 49-52. Retrieved from https://cpr.bu.edu/app/uploads/2011/11/chamberlin1998b.pdf

Chamberlin, J. (1990). The Ex-Patients' Movement: Where We've Been and Where We're Going. National Empowerment Center. Retrieved from http://power2u.org/the-ex-patients-movement-where-weve-been-and-where-were-going/

Chamberlin, J. (1978). On our own. Patient controlled alternatives to the mental health system. New York: McGraw-Hill. (Book). For sale through the National Empowerment Center (NEC). https://power2u.org/store/on-our-own/

Copeland, ME (n.d.). WRAP is… Description of the Wellness Recovery Action Plan. https://www.wellnessrecoveryactionplan.com/what-is-wrap/

Davidson, L. (2015). The History of the Peer Support Movement. International Association of Peer Supporters. [Webinar]. https://youtu.be/U-nqTbz7ZmI

Deegan, P. (2013) The Historical Roots of Peer Support. Available through Pat Deegan's Recovery Library. https://recoverylibrary.com

Deegan, P. (2006). The Legacy of Peer Support. Blog dated July 24, 2006. https://www.commongroundprogram.com/blog/the-legacy-of-peer-support

Deegan, P. (2004). History and Self-Directed Recovery. Blog dated June 8,

2004. https://www.commongroundprogram.com/blog/history-and-self-directed-recovery

Deegan, P. (2002). The Politics of Memory. Five Part Documentary. Used with Permission. Available on YouTube: https://www.youtube.com/channel/UCcJj8EK37obMGjQhVmiEcuQ

Flannery, J. & MindFreedom International. (2019). Voices for Choices: 13 Part Video Series on the History of the Movement. https://mindfreedom.org/knowledgebase/voices-for-choices-video-series/

Harris, L. (2010). Judi Chamberlin: Her Life, Our Movement. National Coalition of Mental Health Consumer Survivor Organizations (NCMHCSO). [Video 5:18 min.] https://youtu.be/FGT4xJXgmoE

Hendry, P. Producer/Director (2017). From Asylums to Recovery. Mental Health America. [Video 23:38 min.; https://youtu.be/fFN-v_aT-y8

International Conference on Human Rights and Psychiatric Oppression (1982). Statement of Principles. Retrieved from https://www.madinamerica.com/forums/topic/statement-of-principles-from-10th-annual-conference-on-human-rights/

Jackson, V. (2001). In Our Own Voice: African American Stories of Oppression, Survival and Recovery in Mental Health Systems. Part 3 of the "It's About Time: Discovering, Recovering and Celebrating Psychiatric Consumer/Survivor History. https://power2u.org/wp-content/uploads/2017/01/InOurOwnVoiceVanessaJackson.pdf

Jackson, V. (2002). An Early History – African American Mental Health. Race, Health Care and the Law: Speaking Truth to Power! Part of the Reclamation Gallery. University of Dayton. https://academic.udayton.edu/health/01status/mental01.htm

Jackson, V. (2005). Separate and Unequal: The Legacy of Racially Segregated Psychiatric Hospitals – A Cultural Competence Training Tool. https://www.patdeegan.com/sites/default/files/files/separate_and_unequal.pdf http://www.healingcircles.org/uploads/2/1/4/8/2148953/sauweb.pdf

Harris, L. (2010). Judi Chamberlin: Her life, our movement. (Leah Harris, Narrator and Producer) National Coalition of Mental Health Consumer/Survivor Organizations (NCMHCSO). [Video 5:18 min.] Retrieved from https://youtu.be/FGT4xJXgmoE

Cohen, R. (2015). Leonard Roy Frank 1932-2015 "No Man Is An Island." An Unfinished Film by Richard Cohen. [Video 5:34 min.] Retrieved from https://youtu.be/4eKWcyOzsxI

Swarbrick, P., Schmidt, L. & Gill, K. (Eds.) (2010). *People in Recovery as Providers of Psychiatric Rehabilitation: Building on the Wisdom of Experience.*

United States Psychiatric Rehabilitation Association (USPRA). Linthicum, MD. USA. (Book available through the Psychiatric Rehabilitation Association)

Madness Network News (n.d.) Survivors Speak: Psychiatric Survivors Speak Out – United Against Forced Treatment. [Video 6:01 min.] https://www.youtube.com/watch?v=cKDuKFuDDq8

Mad People's History (2010) Presenting the consumer/survivor/ex-patient movement, Instructor, David Revelle. [Video 5:39 min.] Ryerson University, Canada Retrieved from https://youtu.be/9uTbEBPkAAk.

McKinney, J. (2012). Jacki McKinney speaking at the Eugene Oregon Opal Network, Oct. 15, 2012 [Video 4:13 min. excerpt from 27:34 min.] https://youtu.be/A6xthJYWBtE

Mead, S. (n.d.) Defining Peer Support. https://docs.google.com/document/d/1WG3ulnF6vthAwFZpJxE9rkx6lJzYSX7VX4HprV5EkfY/edit

Mead, S. & MacNeil, C. (n.d.) Peer Support: What Makes It Unique? https://docs.google.com/document/d/1cslJZuuh2r6h_R6U6IilRHrmszKg1wi9KtLBbhttuPs/edit

Mead, S. & Copeland, M.E. (n.d.) What Recovery Means to Us http://www.intentionalpeersupport.org/wp-content/uploads/2014/02/What-Recovery-Means-To-Us.pdf

Mental Health America (2017). From Asylums to Recovery. [Full length Video 23:38 min.] Retrieved from https://youtu.be/fFN-v_aT-y8

MindFreedom International Archive (n.d.) Celia Brown & Jacki McKinney Speak at MindFreedom Lane County Event. https://mindfreedom.org/affiliate-sponsors/as-archives/usa-as-archives/or/lane-county/celia-jacki/

MindFreedom International Archive (n.d.) Statement of Principles from the 10th Annual International Conference on Human Rights and Against Psychiatric Oppression.

National Empowerment Center. (No Date). Evidence That People Recover from Schizophrenia. National Empowerment Center Articles. Retrieved from https://power2u.org/evidence/

Penney, D. & Stastny, P. (2009). The Lives They Left Behind: Suitcase from a State Hospital Attic. http://www.suitcaseexhibit.org/index.php?section=about&subsection=suitcases

Penney, D. (2004). Documenting the History of Marginalized Groups: Organizations of People with Psychiatric Histories A Preliminary Guide to the Historical Records of Mental Health Consumer/Survivor/Ex-patient Organizations in New York State. The Community Consortium, Inc. Albany, New York.

Risser, P. (n.d.) Recovery and Real Systems Transformation. Timeline of the

Consumer/Client/Survivor/Ex-patient/Ex-inmate/User Community. Pat Risser's website: https://virtualcommunityblog.files.wordpress.com/2021/04/recovery-and-real-systems-transformation-landscape.pdf

Tenney, L. (n.d.) OurStory of Commitment: A Living Document. A collection of historical entries submitted by c/s/x members, compiled into a timeline by Lauren Tenney, Ph.D. http://www.laurentenney.us/ourstory-of-commitment.html

Unzicker, R. (2000). From Privileges to Rights: People Labeled with Psychiatric Disabilities Speak For Themselves. National Council on Disability. https://ncd.gov/publications/2000/Jan202000#exe

Unzicker, R. (2001). Mental Health Advocacy From Then to Now. National Association of Rights Advocacy and Protection (NARPA). https://narpa.org/reference/mental-health-advocacy-from-then-to-now

Unzicker, R. (1984) *To Be a Mental Patient* a poem by Rae Unzicker. Posted on the website of The Antipsychiatry Coalition. http://www.antipsychiatry.org/unzicker.htm

The National Association of Rights Protection and Advocacy. https://narpa.org/reference/mental-health-advocacy-from-then-to-now

Van Tosh, L. & del Vecchio, P. (2000). Consumer-Operated Self-Help Programs: A Technical Report. U.S. Center for Mental Health Services, Rockville, MD. https://virtualcommunityblog.files.wordpress.com/2021/04/consumeroperatedselfhelp-vantosh-delvecchio.pdf

Zinman, S. (2015). Mental Health Consumer Movement 101: The story of a social change movement. CAMHPRO. https://camphro.files.wordpress.com/2016/03/outreach-materials-mh-movement.pdf

Zinman, S. & Bluebird, G. (2015). History of the Consumer/Survivor Movement (2015) Recorded Webinar [Video 55:19 min.] International Association of Peer Supporters Webinar #22. Retrieved from https://youtu.be/H60_joPyO7c

References

Academy of Peer Services (2020). The Historical Roots of Peer Services. Online Course. https://www.academyofpeerservices.org/

Wolf, J. (2020). Mental Health Peer Workforce Designline. Central East, Mental Health Technology Transfer Center (MHTTC). Funded by Substance Abuse and Mental Health Services (SAMHSA). (no longer available online). Used with permission.

Wolf J (2019). The Logic of Scientific Revolutions: Peer Support Workforce and Mental Health System Transformation. [Webinar] Central East Mental Health Technology Transfer Center, July 18. https://mhttcnetwork.org/centers/central-east-mhttc/event/peer-workforce-and-mental-health-system-change-logic-scientific

PART 2: PEER SUPPORT VALUES AND STANDARDS

Chapter 4: The Underlying Values of Peer Support

- Chapter Introduction by the Editors
- Section 1: Building Utopia Through Peer Support
- Section 2: Welcome to the School of Hard Knocks: Using difficult situations to learn, grow, and produce recovery outcomes
- Section 3: Are Mental health Consumer/Survivors Forgetting their Rich Historical Heritage of Self-Help and Mutual Aid? Challenges that Peer Support Services Face and How to Tackle Them

Chapter 5: Peer Support Practice Standards

- Chapter Introduction by the Editors
- Section 1: The National Practice Guidelines for Peer Supporters: From Principles to Practice
- Section 2: First Year Findings of Certified Peer Specialist Career Outcomes Study
- Section 3: Supervision and the Development of Core Competencies with Peer Workers

Chapter 6: Values into Practice

- Chapter Introduction by the Editors
- Section 1: Equity, Ethics, and Peer Support
- Section 2: Advocacy 101. Making Your Voice Heard...And Matter
- Section 3: Strength in Numbers

Chapter 7: Efforts at Inclusion of Peer Support into Behavioral Health

- Chapter Introduction by the Editors
- Section 1: Resilience Road Map to Successful Organizational Integration of the Peer Role
- Section 2: Terms of "Enpeerment"
- Section 3: Managing Partnerships with Peer Supporters in the Workplace

CHAPTER 4
THE UNDERLYING VALUES OF PEER SUPPORT

CHAPTER INTRODUCTION BY THE EDITORS

AFTER PEER SUPPORT WAS DECLARED TO BE AN EVIDENCE-BASED PRACTICE, subject to Medicaid reimbursement, and as more and more states sought to certify peer support workers, discussions in the field, particularly among people who identified as psychiatric survivors, began taking place surrounding the question of whether the practice of peer support continued to embrace the values out of which organized peer support had evolved. Some viewed involvement by peers employed in traditional treatment settings as disregarding, or even being antithetical to, the values which had informed the notion of peer support arising from its roots in self-help and mutual aid practice. Table 1 lists the core values of peer support as found in the National Practice Guidelines for Peer Support.

Table 1. Core Value of Peer Support

Peer Supporters Are:	Peer Support Is:
1. Hopeful	7. Voluntary (supports choice)
2. Open minded	8. Mutual and reciprocal
3. Empathetic	9. Equally shared power
4. Respectful	10. Strengths focused
5. Agents of change	11. Transparent
6. Honest and direct	12. Person-driven

In the first reading, Yaffa views peer support through a social justice lens and makes the case that bringing peer support into alignment with mainstream culture deprecates peer values while amplifying traditional ideas of systems of care for individuals with mental health or substance use challenges. They advance the notion that for peer support to succeed, professional peer support would cease to exist, and close with a utopic vision of a world fully informed by peer support ethics and values. Next, Ashcraft and Blum look more closely at the foundational relationship between the peer supporter and the person being served, examining how peer support values can arise out of lived treatment experience when behaviors are not subject to treatment as usual. They offer a clear statement of values in terms of willingness to stay in relationship and adopt a self-regulating posture whereby the peer supporter can reflect upon mutual and empowering means of moving forward. Finally, Thomasina Borkman investigates whether the modern practice of peer support has lost touch with the principles which grounded the mid-20th century self-help/mutual aid and consumer/survivor movements. Borkman looks closely at the power differential inherent in government-funded and state-sanctioned peer support relationships, offering a historical overview of the roots of peer support along with actionable methods for coming into closer alignment with peer support values.

SECTION 1: BUILDING UTOPIA THROUGH PEER SUPPORT

Mx. Yaffa (Ahmad Abojaradeh) CPS, MA
Equity and Transformation Consultant, Meraj Consulting

"A map of the world that does not include Utopia is not worth even glancing at...
Progress is the realisation of Utopias."

— OSCAR WILDE (WILDE, 1891)

PEER SUPPORT IS INHERENTLY transformative and is a pathway to envision and
build a more just and equitable world. However, this vision of Peer Support
and the world it can build is less and less visible within Peer Support spaces as
Peer Support is absorbed into mainstream culture. Like with any movement
or philosophy, to gain mainstream standing core values that are in line with
the status quo are amplified and values that stand against the status quo that
necessitated the movements or philosophies creation are dampened.

Peer Support is meant to be self-explanatory, through shared recovery
language it is intended to be understood by everyone. This was definitely the
case for me. Being trained as a certified Peer Support specialist through RI
International seven years ago was the first time I heard the words Peer
Support, yet not a single thing was new. Peer Support gave words to experiences, values, and thoughts I had been having my entire life. These experiences were dampened over time, as I was told that something like Peer
Support could and should never exist, in fact, I was told it was Utopic and
impossible. Peer Support validated that not only was Utopia possible, it was
probable because it is what we yearn for most.

Discussion

In Cruising Utopia, Jose Esteban defines Utopia as a not yet fully realized
concept, a time and place that ought to be but is not here yet (Muñoz, 2009).
Similarly, the world that Peer Support aims to build, one grounded and
guided by the 12 National Practice Guidelines, ought to be but is futurity that
is not here yet.

Over the last twelve years, I have been doing justice and equity work
around the world. My purpose was to support building a better world, something I did not realize could be called Utopia when I started. Once I received
my certification, I realized that Peer Support was also intended to build a
Utopia. Through my work and academic research, I have defined Utopia in its
simplest form, a more justice filled world, a better world (Abojaradeh, 2021).

Peer Support, in its intent to build a better world and systems of care for individuals living with mental health and substance use challenges inherently leads to this.

The concept of Utopia is something that makes many individuals uncomfortable, as it had made me uncomfortable years ago prior to this work. For me, it was uncomfortable because it was easier to live in the despair of injustice than to be let down if Utopia never happened. I have learned through my work and Peer Support practice that for me, dreaming will sometimes lead to disappointment, but not dreaming is a constant state of disappointment. More often than not, I am able to use the disappointment stemming from an un-actualized vision as a stepping stone on the path to a greater vision. The opposite is not true.

The other reason that this vision is not readily accepted is that it threatens our survival, or what we believe is necessary for our survival. When I talk about how the vision of Peer Support is to no longer need professional Peer Support most hear that they will be out of a job, back on the job market, and back striving to survive. This is true - if we do not envision what the world would actually look like if Peer Support was truly not needed as a profession. The concepts of employment and healthcare that we know would need to be transformed, as will every relationship, and every space. Peer Support is a philosophy that must be all encompassing to build this ultimate vision of possibility, when it is not, or more so when we uphold a vision of it that is not then we ultimately uphold the status quo while participating in Settler-Colonial Capitalism and replicating the systems that made our societies unsafe for us as peers in the first place (Day, 2016).

I have presented in dozens of conferences, worked in over 30 countries, and hundreds of communities, and within mainstream Peer Support spaces, this idea is often met with resistance, partially due to the discomfort mentioned earlier and due to it being seen as an erasure of the labour of countless peers in building this movement into where we are today. Loving critically is necessary for growth, and if we cannot discuss the current and historic gaps and where we need to go then we have accepted the status quo and where we are as the end goal (hooks, 1999). We have achieved things that some may have believed impossible decades ago, and we have also lost in ways that some may have also believed impossible. And today, we can dream of the impossible and possible, so that others decades from now can benefit from this work and continue building beyond it, if they choose to.

The pathway to Utopia, to a world built on Peer Support values, is as simple as following the National Practice Guidelines, the values of voluntarism, hope, empathy, open-mindedness, respect, change, honesty and directness, mutuality and reciprocity, equally shared power, strengths-focused, transparent, and being self-driven in both our progression and our lives. As I have trained hundreds of individuals and worked with dozens of spaces I rarely hear of peer-run spaces or spaces that employ Peer Support specialists that honour all 12 values of Peer Support. I have always believed that pathways to move into a better world have been mapped out for us for hundreds and thousands of years. As an equity and transformation consultant, I see the enormous gap between the theory and practice of moving into Utopia within organizations and communities. This gap is rooted in a misunderstanding of both equity and transformation as foundational concepts, and in the realm of Peer Support a misunderstanding of ethics.

Conclusion

The road to Utopia is not without challenges. It is a road that challenges the status quo every step, and it is a road where you will deal with repercussions both from the non-peer and the peer communities. However, it is the road that leads us to a better world, to a world where the philosophy of Peer Support becomes universal. To me, that's a worthy journey any day.

References

Abojaradeh, A. (2021). Beyond Utopia: An autoethnographic account of living at the margins of marginalisation and searching for Home (dissertation).

Day, I. (2016). Alien capital - asian racialization and the logic of settler colonial capit.

hooks, bell. (1999). All about love.

Muñoz José Esteban. (2009). Cruising utopia.

National Association of Peer Supporters (2019). National Practice Guidelines for Peer Specialists and Supervisors. N.A.P.S. Washington, DC. https://www.peersupportworks.org/wp-content/uploads/2021/07/National-Practice-Guidelines-for-Peer-Specialists-and-Supervisors-1.pdf

SECTION 2: WELCOME TO THE SCHOOL OF HARD KNOCKS: USING DIFFICULT SITUATIONS TO LEARN, GROW, AND PRODUCE RECOVERY OUTCOMES

Patricia Blum Ph.D.
Vice President, Crestwood Behavioral Health
Lori Ashcraft Ph.D.,
Director, Resilience Inc. Crestwood

This narrative examines the value of leaning into difficult situations and learning new ways of being with people who are in pre-crisis mode. The unpredictability and heightened emotion of this pre-crisis occurrence is bursting with energy that can be channeled into a powerful *learning moment*. However, our fears often preclude the positive use of this energy, and instead of using it productively, we shrink and resort to controlling the situation with threats of reprimand and coercion. In extreme cases, the person may be secluded or restrained. There is a much better approach.

As peer support specialists we have the choice to work through the difficult situation or to try to avoid it. At Crestwood we can use this material to teach and reinforce courageous peer practices that lead to stronger relationships and recovery outcomes.

In this section, we describe skills and practices that peer support specialists can use to safely stay in uncomfortable moments, even though it's challenging, and create healing partnerships in which both the peer and the person served can learn new ways of being.

Peer support specialists, and other professionals for that matter, find it rewarding to work with people who are motivated to recover. The motivated person provides fertile ground for relationship building and for sharing ways to deepen the recovery experience, leading to resilience and fulfilling life experiences.

What happens when the person is not motivated? What happens when the person is angry and not interested in abiding by "house rules"? What happens when they are edgy and threatening to do harm to themselves or others? The first impulse is to control, to force the person into "compliance". The peer support specialist has often been the recipient of this reaction during their own treatment experience.

Do they repeat this behavior, or do they find a better way? When we repeat the behavior without thinking through the options, we miss the opportunity to use what's happened to us as motivation to find better ways of helping others. We pass up the opening to use this powerful moment for learning and growing, both for ourselves and for those we serve.

There is often a good reason for the person being served to be upset. When their "upset" is not taken seriously, when they are shut down, they easily recognize the lack of empathetic interest and resort to feeling disrespected and disregarded. This heightens emotions that can fuel a more explosive reaction. Perhaps they are trying to get our authentic attention in an attempt to connect with us even though it feels like they are trying to push us away.

Discussion

Gaining the courage to stay in relationship with a person who is in precrisis is key to having a successful outcome. As always, relationship is our most powerful healing agent and if ever there is a time to benefit from it, it's during a difficult and challenging moment. To do this requires us to step outside of the traditional consensual mindset (the person is wrong and needs to be controlled) and to move from having an outdated *point of view* and into having a *viewing point*. The *viewing point* allows us to observe the dynamics without locking into an opinion prematurely. It requires sitting with, rather than jumping in. It requires suspending our guiding and modeling so the person we are supporting can move through this challenging situation.

We are required to step into the willingness to be inspired by the person's courage to speak up. We are also required to expect a positive outcome, trusting the person and ourselves to be capable of reaching a positive resolution. We are further required to not be distracted by the behaviors demonstrated in the moment. As the situation cools down, we become willing to empower the person to find their next steps, shifting the power to them so they can find ways of using the experience as a learning moment (we discuss this further when we discuss reconciliation). In trusting the person to keep their agreements around moving forward, we learn to "let go" and not hold the person in the past by always seeing them through the lenses of their last pre-crisis event.

The list below describes the opportunities to view a situation differently, instead of being stuck in "the way we've always done this."

- Willing to step outside of the prevailing traditional mindset vs locked into "this is the way we've always done it"

- Willing to be known as an authentic person in a real relationship vs closing down and treating the person as "other"
- Willing to not be distracted by disruptive behaviors vs focusing entirely on the behaviors in the moment
- Willingness to participate in a collaborative process letting the person take the lead vs creating a hierarchical position and telling the person what to do, resulting in a power struggle
- Willing to be inspired vs being disappointed and judgmental about the person's presentation
- Willing to expect positive results vs expecting negative results with no learning or growth on the person's part
- Willing to stay close when things go backwards vs distancing and closing down
- Willing to empower and shift power vs holding tight and holding power, resulting in a power struggle
- Willing to let go at the right time vs expecting the person to need more structure and restriction

The prevailing traditional mindset often results in a power struggle where both parties attempt to win the struggle. When we find ourselves in the middle of a power struggle, we have already lost the opportunity for a learning, growing experience. There is a way out of this – it's not too late to turn the situation around. The first step has to do with self-regulation, or the ability to manage our own personal reactions in order to avoid escalating the situation. This is easier said than done, since in the moment we may be intent on convincing the person that we are right, and they need to listen to what we have to say. So, what is self-regulation and how do we learn to self-regulate our internal reactions?

Self-regulation is the discipline of using strengths in ways that bring about the best outcomes without being hijacked by our emotions and our ego's need to be right. It is a common process, often described in peer support trainings, of taking a step back, taking a breath, and noticing our state of mind. Self-regulation requires awareness and clarity. The challenge is to reset our mind, moving out of a state of fear and aggravation and coming into a place that reflects a loving approach. We ask, "What's coming up for me? What buttons are being pushed? What's my ego up to? How can I let go of the tendency to want to be right, to win?"

Viktor Frankl is often quoted as saying, "*Anything can be taken from a man but one thing: The last of the human freedoms to choose one's attitude in any given circumstance.*" Once we choose an attitude of hope and understanding, we can pull ourselves out of the power struggle and move into a collaborative process, with the person being encouraged to take the lead. When we avoid or mend the power struggle, we are better able to see the situation not so much as a problem, but as an opportunity.

Difficult situations are charged with energy that needs to be transformed. We can begin the transforming process by engaging in new ways that draw on the strengths of both ourselves and the person being served. This is when we get creative, thinking of new ways to be with people that will inspire them to come from their higher self.

Some may label the above process as *conflict resolution,* which means the conflict has been resolved. The most important step is holding the space for the conflict. We have learned that resolving the conflict leaves a lot of important unfinished business on the table. The conflict may have been diminished, but it doesn't address damage done to relationships. Reconciliation on the other hand focuses on the relationship instead of the problem. When the relationship has been mended; the problems are easier to resolve. This is why we put substantial attention on the process of reconciliation and the need for a reconciliation agreement.

Let's take a deeper dive into the meaning and practice of reconciliation. Most of us aren't born knowing how to reconcile relationships, and few of us ever get any training on how to do it. So now we have an opportunity to learn how to mend relationships and how to keep agreements and commitments as we move forward in the recovery process.

Timing is critical. Once the pre-crisis mode has been de-escalated, the peer support specialist and the person served need a little time to get centered and release the tension built up by the difficult situation. However, letting too much time pass before the reconciliation conversation takes place can drain off the energy needed to fuel the process. There is no formula for getting the timing perfect; it takes careful listening and an intuitive sense of knowing to determine when the time is right. The reconciliation conversation is not mandatory – we cannot force this, otherwise we are right back where we started – trying to control and manage the process. To initiate the conversation, the peer asks the person if they would be willing to talk about what happened and what can be learned from it.

The following script shows how this might play out:

Peer support specialist (PSS)
"Hey Jeff, I'd like to find a quiet place to debrief what happened today at the phone room. I just want to make sure we are both OK now and that we can move beyond any troubling feelings. OK with you?"

Jeff
Jeff rolls his eyes.
"I don't really feel like talking but I'll do it anyway. I want things to get back to where they were."
PSS
"Your case manager having you on hold for so long must have been really frustrating. I was upset by the event myself and could use some help in debriefing."

NOTICE how the PSS brings their own experience into the conversation in order to help normalize it and to show that we all need to learn how to sustain positive relationships.

Jeff
Jeff shuffles his feet restlessly and sighs.
"OK, I still feel upset too, so maybe it would be good to talk about it."
PSS
"OK, Let's meet in the blue room in a few minutes where we can have some privacy."
Jeff
Jeff stands up and ambles off.
"Yeah, OK, I'll see you there."
PSS
"Thank you for being willing to help us understand what happened at the phone room today and how to avoid this sort of upset in the future. We all need to help each other heal. We can't heal if we are feeling resentful and angry. I'd like us both to say what happened and how we feel about it so we can understand each other's perspective. I'll go first."

PSS GOES FIRST to role model the process. This is not a rule, just a suggestion.

"When I saw what was happening at the phone room, I felt a little anxious and worried that things would escalate. Then when I realized what you were dealing with, I felt helpless and wasn't sure how to support you. When Diane found a different phone for you to use, it relieved the tension, but we hadn't addressed the feelings or understood what was happening to each other. That's when I realized we needed to talk so we could move beyond the incident and have healing take place. What where you experiencing? By the way, this works best if we don't point fingers or blame each

other and don't interrupt each other. Just stick to what was happening to us and how we feel about it."

<u>*Jeff*</u>

"I was on hold for 10 minutes waiting for my case manager. When you came back, he had just gotten on the line. I didn't want to give up the phone because he is really hard to get ahold of. So that's what was happening to me."

<u>*PSS*</u>

"Now that we see things from each other's perspective we probably have a different feeling about it. I know I do. I see you trying hard to take responsibility for your issues and me trying to help. I have so much respect for you for taking responsibility to do your part in your healing, and especially for the maturity to work this through. Thanks so much for taking the time to work this through. How do you feel now compared to how you felt right after the incident?"

<u>*Jeff*</u>

"I feel much better. I'm glad we are back on good terms."

Here are some questions that can help us take this process a little further along:

- What can the PSS and Jeff suggest doing differently if this comes up again?
- What agreements can be made between the PSS and Jeff that will result in a positive outcome?
- What kind of training needs to take place to facilitate better relationships between person served and staff?

Conclusion

If Peer Support Specialists can comfortably work with people to de-escalate and move from a position of pre-crisis to reconciliation, both will have opportunities to learn and grow, using the energy generated by the pre-crisis event to fuel transformation.

References

Frankl, V. (1959). From Death-Camp to Existentialism: A Psychiatrist's Path to a New Therapy (First Edition of Man's Search for Meaning). Boston: Beacon Press

SECTION 3: ARE MENTAL HEALTH CONSUMER/SURVIVORS
FORGETTING THEIR RICH HISTORICAL HERITAGE OF SELF-HELP
AND MUTUAL AID? CHALLENGES THAT PEER SUPPORT SERVICES
FACE AND HOW TO TACKLE THEM

Thomasina Borkman, Ph.D.,
Professor of Sociology Emerita, George Mason University

Originally, peer support was intimately linked to and referred to the values
and principles of the self-help/mutual aid group movement of the 20th
Century. Unfortunately, developments of the last decades have ruptured those
connections. This essay describes the rich historical legacy, the contemporary
disconnects, the challenges stemming from it, and possible solutions.

Contemporary peer support is grounded historically in the self-help/mu-
tual aid group movement which occurred during and was inspired by the civil
rights movement, the feminist, disability and other movements of the 1960s
and 1970s. Then, mental health peer support was specifically linked to and
referred to the values, principles and practices of the self-help/mutual aid
movement.

I will briefly review the history as well as the values, principles, and practices of the ex-mental patient liberation movement that became the mental
health consumer/survivor movement and its successes. Accompanying the
successes were liabilities associated with government funding of mental
health consumer/survivor-run initiatives, especially the requirement of a
hierarchical nonprofit 501c3 form of organization that is antithetical to the
principle of egalitarian relationships among peers.

From the government's point of view, this form of organization allows
government oversight of expenditures and contracted outcomes (see Smith &
Lipsky, 1993). But from the self-help/mutual aid perspective, hierarchical
organization contradicts egalitarian peer relationships. Some of the resulting
challenges can be addressed by returning to the early research literature,
visiting relevant self-help support groups and supporting innovative
measures developed by peer supporters such as Intentional Peer Support
(Mead, 2009), and SHARE!'s Peer Toolkit (Borkman, 2020).

Discussion

I recently reviewed the history of research on self-help/mutual aid
groups/organizations and peer support from the mid-20th Century until the
present day in the US. By analyzing studies chronologically, I developed a

picture of how concepts and understanding of values, principles, and practices developed over time. This essay is based on that review and subsequent work (Borkman, 2020). Here, I will use self-help/mutual aid as a generic term and as a synonym for self-help groups. Self-help groups are also known by other names such as or self-help support groups, mutual help groups, self-help, mutual aid groups, etc.

My own research on self-help support groups dates back to 1970 when I began a participant observation study of a mutual help group of people who stutter. I then expanded my research to a patient group dependent on a medical device and Alcoholics Anonymous (Borkman, 1976). My professional training is supplemented with personal lived experience participating in 12-step/12 tradition anonymous groups for 44 years, a short-term grief group, a professionally-run support group, and a feminist consciousness-raising group. This combination of professional scientific research and lived experience of recovery in self- help/mutual aid groups gives me both an outsider and an insider perspective which has deepened and enlarged my understanding and appreciation of the phenomenon.

The mental health consumer/survivor movement began as the ex-mental patient's liberation movement (Bluebird, 2009; Campbell. 2005; Chamberlin, 1978, 1990). With deinstitutionalization, long term mental hospitals began to be emptied in the 1950s and 1960s in the US. Ex-mental patients were released to their communities without housing, treatment, jobs, or other support and they faced stigma, prejudice and indifference. In protest, angry ex-patients banned together forming local self-help groups similar to those of cancer survivors, recovering alcoholics and drug addicts, and people with disabilities. More moderate or conservative self-help groups also developed such as Recovery Incorporated (now Recovery International), founded in 1937, for ex-mental patients and nervous persons

The rich legacy created by the self-help and mutual aid group movement was based on a unique combination of values, principles, and practices (Riessman & Carroll, 1995). Self-help/mutual aid, although an awkward term, connotes two vital aspects which are reflected in the saying You alone can do it (self-help) but you can't do it alone (mutual aid). Self-help encapsulates self-determination or the individual's right to choose and self-direct their recovery and life decisions; their personal lived experiences are regarded as authoritative knowledge; they draw on inner strengths; and individuals take responsibility for their choices and their consequences.

Mutual aid connotes peers who identify as having significant commonalities with each other and participate in more trusting and egalitarian relationships with each other; utilize the 'helper-therapy' principle (Riessman &

Carroll, 1995) that helping others benefits the helper; practice reciprocal helping; and develop a culture and social network of peer support. A core practice of self-help groups is the "sharing circle" (Borkman, 1999), a face-to-face circle of peers who share their personal lived experience with each other in order to problem solve and to provide support to each other.

Practicing these values and principles over decades, the self-help group movement generated a rich legacy within society: people with a disease or disability became agents of their own recovery and destiny instead of being victims or perennial "patients." Individual's "lived experience" and the collectivized experience developed within self-help groups became newly acknowledged sources of knowledge (Borkman, 1976).

The essential social aspect of humanness—that people exist, recover, and thrive only in relationship to and with the support of others—is highlighted and made center stage (within the context of a highly individualized and psychologically oriented society and a medical system that emphasizes singleness, not connectedness). Further, new group and organizational tools had been created such as the 'helper-therapy' principle, the 'sharing circle,' and the major organizational models such as the 12-step/12-tradition anonymous group (of which there are almost 100).

The Alcoholics Anonymous 12-step/12 tradition model, founded in 1935 and probably the best recognized group, was imitated by drug addicts, compulsive gamblers, and compulsive overeaters, among others. While Alcoholics Anonymous, cancer survivor, disability and other self-help groups had many commonalities with the ex-mental patients' groups, the latter differed in emphasizing advocacy to change the mental health system.

The Insane Liberation Front was the first radical group formed in 1970 in Portland, Oregon followed by the Mental Patient's Liberation Project in 1971 in New York City, and the Network Against Psychiatric Assault in 1972 in San Francisco. National communication developed through newsletters & conferences (there was no internet then and telephone calls were expensive). The federal Community Support Program of the National Institute of Mental Health supported these groups funding yearly national conferences, among other support, which allowed them to develop advocacy activities (Campbell, 2005).

The radicals and moderates clashed for years. The radicals rejected psychiatric and medical definitions of mental illness and treatment and wanted to develop an alternative system. In contrast, the moderates were willing to work within the mainstream mental health system and believed they could change it from within. Judi Chamberlin's book *On Our Own: Patient Controlled Alternatives to the Mental Health System* (1978) became the bible of the movement and she became regarded as the mother of the movement (Bluebird, 2009). Self-help and advocacy became the twin goals of the movement. Self-definition and self-determination were among the major organizing principles. Chamberlin was adamant: exclude non-patients from ex-patient organizations and do not let outsiders dictate the organizations' goals.

The terminology changed from ex-mental patient movement to mental health consumer/survivors movement by the 1990s; the term survivors referring to those who had survived psychiatric treatment. The terminology of self-help and mutual aid or self-help groups gave way to peer support especially as more players and stakeholders got involved such as governments funding peer-run initiatives and professionals supporting or supervising them. Moreover, a newer generation of mental health peers never learned the connection with their historical heritage to self-help groups.

Movement successes developed as the advocacy bore fruit. As examples, 1986 federal legislation was passed that required mental health consumers and family members to be on advisory and planning committees; in 1989 the National Association of State Mental Health Program Directors endorsed the use of mental health consumers in their services. Research demonstrated that people with serious mental illness could recover to a fully functioning life in the community even with symptoms (e.g., see De Sisto et al., 1995), and mental health recovery became a movement to transform mainstream services (Ostrow & Adams, 2012). States developed peer support credentialing programs funded by Medicaid Insurance; credentialed peers worked within mainstream health care agencies (Myrick & del Vecchio, 2016). By 1993 46 state governments were funding 567 mental health peer-run initiatives (Segal, Silverman & Tempkin, 1995).

Government funding of mental health consumer/survivor-run organizations (CROs) came with conditions which challenged the movement (Borkman, et al., 2006). Government funders required an incorporated nonprofit form of organization, usually a 501c3 which by definition has a hierarchy as it assumes a board of directors, a director, and staff. In contrast, peer support requires an egalitarian non-hierarchical environment.

Perhaps most challenging was that mental health peer was defined by many governments as a person who had received/was receiving mental health services or self-identified as a mental health peer, or was in mental health recovery (McLean, 1995; Myrick & del Vecchio, 2016; Penny, 2018), but there were no requirements that a mental health peer know about or understand mutual help, self-help, self-help groups, or the original concept of peer support. Further, the definition of recovery was disputed and without standards. In addition, a further challenge was that some mental health peer leaders were negative toward self-help groups because they ignore advocacy; unfortunately, such leaders lacked appreciation of the value of robust recovery strategies practiced in self-help groups (Borkman et al., 2005; Hollman, 2009). Lack of space precludes discussion of other challenges, especially those involving peer supporters staffing professionally-based mental health services (see Myrick & del Vecchio, 2016; Penny, 2018).

What can be done about these challenges to the peer support movement? Three suggestions are made: (1) Learn the history of the ex-mental patient liberation movement and its close ties with other self-help groups and their values and principles during the mid-20th Century; (2) Visit and participate in mental health self-help groups such as Recovery, Inc., GROW, Hearing Voices Network, Depression & Bipolar Support Alliance, or Emotions Anonymous to learn about their robust programs of recovery and their dedicated practices that mirror the values and principles of self-help/mutual aid; and (3) Learn about and support innovations that overcome problematic features of mental health CROs or other peer support initiatives. There are many others that could be listed but I will amplify on one suggestion—to support innovations that deal with the challenges and shortcomings of mental health CROs and other peer support initiatives.

Two strategies, developed by dedicated peer supporters to overcome hierarchical environments in order to establish egalitarian peer relationships, among other advances, are particularly noteworthy and will be mentioned here: Intentional Peer Support (Mead, 2008) and SHARE! The Self-Help And Recovery Exchange Peer Toolkit. (SHARE! 2018) that is a radical interaction system of equal relations and inclusion for all.

Intentional Peer Support was developed in Maine to use in training of peer support specialists by Mead and associates (2008) for their credentialing program. The core principles are to change the peer support specialist role from that of helper to a role of equals learning together; shift roles from problem solver to peer support specialist as validator; instead of the usual perspective of an individual, taking a relationship lens; and substitute hope and possibility for fear.

SHARE! has developed an evolving interaction system known as the SHARE! Peer Toolkit (SHARE! 2018) with which it trains peer supporters; the State of California has funded SHARE! to conduct this peer support training and SHARE! is hopeful that the SHARE! Peer Toolkit will be the partial basis for the peer credentialing system that is being developed in California. The SHARE! Peer Toolkit consists of 12 Tools each of which refer to a principle of interaction; the Tools are couched in folksy language such as "Hit the Deck!" and are borrowed from various self-help groups and evolved over SHARE!'s 28-year history of working with people needing services or in recovery.

Some of the above-mentioned Intentional Peer Support is folded into the Tools. My analysis (Borkman, 2020) of the tools suggested that they served five major functions: a) develop respectful, personal peer relationships of unconditional regard; b) minimize the authority of staff in their paid position in order to have a more egalitarian relationship with peers; c) coach, guide or support a peer to encourage their self-directed and self-determined recovery; d) be a positive role model for constructive recovery; and e) prevent or neutralize conflict and disruptive situations in a manner that strengthens the relationship.

Conclusion

The current concept of "peer support" is interpreted quite differently by mental health peers and many professionals who work with them. The success of the mental health consumer/survivor movement in achieving government funding for many consumer/survivor-run initiatives needs to be tempered by accounting for the associated costs that leave peers in hierarchical non profit organizations that are contrary to the egalitarian relationships of peers. Some innovations developed by peers such as Intentional Peer Support and SHARE!'s Peer Toolkit are countering these challenges, but are they reaching a sufficiently wide audience of peer leaders?

More Information

SHARE! 2020 Conference on Supervision presentation, "Are mental health consumer/survivor services forgetting their rich historical heritage of self-help/mutual aid? Some challenges peer support services face and how to tackle them*–Thomasina Borkman, Professor of Sociology Emerita, George Mason University, Fairfax, VA & Affiliate Scientist, Alcohol Research Group, Emeryville, CA

References

Bluebird, G. (2009, December 17). History of the consumer/survivor movement. Center for Mental Health Services, Substance Abuse and Mental Health Services (SAMHSA), U. S. Dept. of Health & Human Services.

Borkman, T. (1976). "Experiential Knowledge: A New Concept for the Analysis of Self-Help Group," *Social Service Review*, 50 (September): 445-456.

Borkman, T. (2020). Self-Help/Mutual Aid Groups and Peer Support: A Literature Review. *Voluntaristics Review (journal), 5,2-3 and simultaneously published as book in 2021 by Brill Publishers.*

Borkman, T. (1999). *Understanding Self-Help/Mutual Aid: Experiential Learning in the Commons.* New Brunswick, NJ: Rutgers University Press.

Borkman, T., M. Karlsson, C. Munn-Giddings, and L. Smith. (2005). *Self-Help and Mental Health: Case Studies of Mental Health Self-Help Organizations in US, UK, and Sweden.* Stockholm, Sweden: Skondal Institute and University.

Borkman, T., Munn-Giddings, C., Smith, L. & Karlsson, M. (2006). "Social Philosophy and Funding in Self Help: A UK-US Comparison." *International Journal of Self Help & Self Care*, Vol. 4 (3): 201-220.

Campbell, J. (2005). The philosophical and historical development of peer-run support programs. Pp.17-64 in S. Clay, (Ed.). *On Our Own, Together: Peer Programs for People with Mental Illness.* Nashville: Vanderbilt University Press.

Chamberlin, J. (1978). *On Our Own: Patient -controlled Alternatives to the Mental Health System.* NY: McGraw-Hill.

Chamberlin, J. (1990). The ex-patient's movement: Where we've been & where we're going. The *Journal of Mind & Behavior,*11, ¾:323-336.

Clay, S. (Ed.) 2005. *On Our Own, Together: Peer Programs for People with Mental Illness.* Nashville: Vanderbilt University Press.

De Sisto, M., Harding, C., McCormick, R., Ashikaga, T., Strauss, J., & Brooks, G. (1995). The Maine and Vermont three-decade studies of serious mental illness. *British Journal of Psychiatry*, 167:331-41.

Hollman, R. (2009). Personal communication.

McLean, A. (1995). Empowerment and the psychiatric/survivor movement in the United States: Contradictions, crises, and change. *Social Science & Medicine*, 40 (8), 1053-1071.

Mead, S. (2008). *Intentional Peer Support: An Alternative Approach Workbook.* New Hampshire.

Myrick, K. & del Vecchio, P. (2016). Peer support services in the behavioral healthcare workforce: State of the field. Psychiatric Rehabilitation Journal, May 16.

Ostrow, L. & Adams, N. (2012). Recovery in the USA: From politics to peer support. Int. Rev. Psychiatry, 24 (1); 70-78.

Penney, D. (2018). Defining 'Peer Support': Implications for policy, practice, and research. Advocates for Human Potential, Inc.

Riessman, F, & Carroll, D. (1995). *Redefining Self-Help: Policy and Practice.* San Francisco: Jossey-Bass.

Segal, S. P, Silverman, C., & Temkin, T. (1995). Characteristics and service use of long-term members of self-help agencies for mental health clients. *Psychiatric Services*, 46,3, 269-274.

SHARE! (2018). Peer Toolkit Training Manual. Photocopied. Culver City, CA.

Smith. S. R., & M. Lipsky. (1993). *Nonprofits for Hire: The Welfare State in the Age of Contracting.* Cambridge, Mass.: Harvard University Press.

CHAPTER 5
PEER SUPPORT PRACTICE STANDARDS

CHAPTER INTRODUCTION BY THE EDITORS

DUE IN PART TO CRITERIA SET FOR MEDICAID REIMBURSEMENT, WHICH RESULTED in a plethora of patchwork state certifications, the need arose for a codification of practice standards to ensure that peer support work remained in alignment with peer support values. Making the case for putting forward standards of practice is the ever-present possibility of cooptation, or "peer drift," whereby peer support workers are expected to take on clinical or case management tasks, or even work entirely outside the peer support scope of practice, as with transportation or food service. The haphazard nature of certification, as managed separately by states to meet this federal mandate, can make it hard to know to what degree peer support ethics and values are part of any given certification training. The relationship of certification to career outcomes is also wildly variable.

Cronise, Bernstein, and Harrington introduce us to the historical basis of the development of peer support and explicate the differences between the traditional treatment model and that informed by consumer empowerment. They go on to describe the Task Force convened to review materials and identify common peer support values, and introduce the core values of peer support. They provide further information concerning the development of the National Practice Guidelines for Peer Specialists and Supervisors.

Pelot and Ostrow take a deep dive into career outcomes for certified peer specialists, pointing out the limitations on existing research. They offer an analysis of the certification process, including a discussion on eligibility requirements, which bear looking into as in many states peer support workers who excel in practice do not meet one or more state-mandated criteria, such as level of education or history of justice involvement. These, in combination with other exclusionary criteria having to do with, for example, driving requirements and writing skills, can disenfranchise potential peer support workers who would otherwise be well-qualified to provide services. While conclusions about job satisfaction and financial well-being are drawn, the need for more research on employment outcomes for certified peer specialists remains evident.

Closing the chapter, Gagne invites us to examine recovery-oriented supervision in the context of developing competencies for supervisors of peer support workers. She touches on SAMHSA's Core Competencies for Peer Support Workers in Behavioral Health Services, and enumerates the benefits of recovery-oriented supervision while explaining its core values. Gagne talks about the functions of supervision as she sees them, and argues in favor of two essential skills, giving feedback and problem solving.

SECTION 1: THE NATIONAL PRACTICE GUIDELINES FOR PEER SUPPORTERS: FROM PRINCIPLES TO PRACTICE

Rita Cronise, MS, ALWF,
Faculty, Rutgers University Academy of Peer Services

Andy Bernstein, Ph.D., CPRP,
Clinical Professor, University of Arizona College of Medicine, Department of Family and Community Medicine, Psychologist in Independent Practice

Steve Harrington, MA, JD, Founder,
International Association of Peer Supporters

PEER SUPPORT IS a natural human response to want to help others who are "like us". The "wounded healer" archetype describes how those who have been wounded are drawn to come to the aid of others who experience a similar wound. Mutual support arose as a more formalized phenomenon in the 1930's and again in the 1970's as groups of people who had experienced similar "wounds" found healing in coming together to share their "lived experiences".

"'You alone can do it, but you cannot do it alone,' is often used to describe the two aspects of self-help and mutual aid (Borkman, 2021)." Modern peer support evolved from three separate mutual support movements or traditions:

- Consumer/survivor/ex-patient (c/s/x) movement (1970's, Mental Patients' Liberation)
- Patient/family support groups (1930's, Recovery Inc., Fountain House)
- 12-Step and related programs (1930's, AA and 12-Step)

In 1978, Judi Chamberlin, a pioneer in the consumer/survivor movement wrote, *On Our Own: Patient Controlled Alternatives to the Mental Health System* that guided the movement to create peer-run programs as alternatives to the mental health system. People who attended these alternative programs found others "like them" and they gained hope, a sense of belonging, and the self-worth that comes with the ability to both give and receive. The helper principle states that peers who help each other benefit the most (Riessman, 1965).

In 1998-2007, Jean Campbell directed the Consumer Operated Services Program (COSP) Multi-site Research Initiative, a federally funded program that identified 46 common ingredients of consumer-operated programs and peer practices that promote psychological well-being. Based on the results of this study, peer-to-peer support in consumer-operated service programs was named an evidence-based practice. (Campbell, 2008 and 2009). In 2001, Georgia held its first Certified Peer Specialist (CPS) training. Georgia's training would go on to become a model program for training in many states. In 2004, Pennsylvania would launch its Certified Peer Specialist (CPS) training and be the first to access Medicaid funding for peer positions.

In 2007, following the determination through the COSP study that peer support was an evidence-based practice, the Centers for Medicare and Medicaid Services (CMS) issued a letter of guidance for States interested in developing peer support services under the Medicaid program. The guidance required a state authorized training program, care coordination, and supervision (Smith, 2007). The opportunity for traditional (non-peer) programs to receive Medicaid funding to provide peer support was a mixed blessing. On one hand, it provided organizations with the ability to fund new peer support positions. On the other, it did not require an organization to adopt recovery-oriented practices or to understand and preserve the "essence of peer support" that led to it being named an evidence-based practice.

Discussion

Since the 2007 introduction of Medicaid reimbursement for peer support services, there has been substantial growth in the peer support workforce, but it has also led to a sharp increase in role confusion and role drift (where peer support workers no longer understand or practice according to their core values). Role confusion and role drift are common in organizations that lack a recovery orientation. Role drift, in particular, is common when a supervisor is a licensed professional that lacks experience with mutual support or respect for the softer skills of peer support practice like building hope, trust, and choice based on sharing relevant lived experience toward empowerment through interpersonal relationships. This lack of experience or respect can be amplified when a supervisor's own professional training and code of ethics conflict with the sharing of relevant aspects of one's own personal recovery.

Figure 1 illustrates the differences between these orientations, which can lead to role confusion and the potential for role drift.

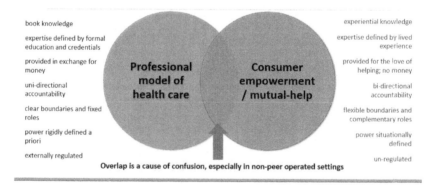

(Bernstein, et al., 2009)

THE PEER SUPPORT role was understood within consumer-operated services or peer-run programs where mutual support, strategic storytelling, and empowerment are core services. In traditional settings, however, where professional providers (as co-workers, supervisors, or other employees) lack exposure to mutual support or the power of the shared experience paradigm, it became easy to be dismissive of the value peer support offers to the organization and the recipients of services. Peer support workers in traditional settings often reported feeling invalidated, with a lack of respect for the importance their lived experience in comparison to academic training.

As more states developed peer support programs, friction and role confusion increased, and there was greater and greater demand for practice standards and guidelines that would help peer workers to better understand their own role and for supervisors and non-peer coworkers to receive additional guidance and training on the value of the wisdom of lived experience.

In 2010, as part of the grant it had received for the SAMHSA-funded Recovery to Practice (RTP) program, N.A.P.S. had conducted a situational analysis of the peer support workforce. The overall goal of the SAMHSA RTP program was to integrate recovery into professional practices, and recovery training was developed by and for six professional associations. The N.A.P.S. situational analysis described gaps between promising practices of peer support and actual implementation, highlighting areas where additional training was needed.

In 2012, N.A.P.S. convened a Task Force following its National Peer Supporter Conference in Philadelphia. The purpose was to identify common values for peer support practice that the workforce could agree upon. The Task Force reviewed codes of ethics, principles of practice, bills of rights, policies and procedures, community agreements, training manuals and handbooks used to guide peer support, peer advocacy, peer coaching and related practices. Workplace settings ranged from inpatient to housing to transitional programs to peer-run centers for wellness and recovery education.

After several meetings, the Task Force identified ten core values drawn mainly from peer-run mutual support programs, rights protection, and/or trauma-support guidance. The chosen core values captured the essence of peer support and seemed to fit all workplace settings where peers provided services. The Task Force avoided statements about what peer support workers "shall not do", and used simple, straight-forward, statements about what peer support workers "do" when practicing peer support. One Task Force member commented on some of the more patronizing and stigmatizing directives that the team had reviewed with, "you can't define a workforce by what it 'shall not do'."

The identified core values were discussed with the N.A.P.S. membership and at a series of listening sessions held in conjunction with N.A.P.S. Recovery to Practice training pilots in Cincinnati, Ohio; Grand Rapids,

Michigan; Oakland, California; Rochester and Syracuse, New York, and State College, PA. Over 200 people attended and provided feedback during these outreach efforts with members and in-person listening sessions.

Following these feedback sessions, the core values were refined and reviewed by a Peer Leadership Panel at SAMHSA. With additional feedback from the substance-use community at the SAMHSA meeting, 12 core values were sent via survey to the N.A.P.S. membership and related peer organizations. The values shown in Table 1, with the SAMHSA-approved definitions, were endorsed by the peer support workforce through a consensus process that led to a 98.5% approval rating from over 1,000 respondents from the mental health peer recovery, substance use peer recovery, and veteran peer support communities.

Table 1: Core Values of Peer Support

Peer Supporters are:	Peer Support is:
Hopeful	Voluntary (supports choice)
Open-minded (nonjudgmental)	Mutual and reciprocal
Empathetic	Equally shared power
Respectful	Strengths-focused
Agents of change (facilitate change)	Transparent
Honest and direct	Person-driven

In July of 2013, after compiling feedback from the focus groups and surveys into a companion section for each core value, "what this value looks like in practice," N.A.P.S. founder, Steve Harrington, issued the National Practice Guidelines for Peer Supporters (NPG) through the membership and affiliated channels. Since then, the guidelines have been recognized by the peer workforce in all 50 states. The World Health Organization (WHO) included the practice guidelines in its Quality Rights curriculum for training peer workers worldwide on how to respect and protect the rights of people with mental disabilities.

Conclusion

This section describes the historical context and origins of the N.A.P.S.

National Practice Guidelines for Peer Supporters. Familiarity with core values of mutual support is an essential element of good practice as a peer support worker but learning these guidelines is not a one-time event. Memorizing the bullet list of core values is akin to memorizing a motto, which can be a starting point, but putting those points into practice requires opportunities to try them out and reflect on how it went. Applying value-based guidelines such as these can be especially challenging because the practice is deeply rooted in establishing and maintaining good relationships. It is important to make a commitment to revisit and reflect upon the ways in which we (as individuals, groups, and communities) are living up to our values, the challenges we are having in putting the values into practice and exploring ways to overcome those challenges.

Some ideas for putting the guidelines into practice include setting aside a regular time for personal reflection such as focusing on one guideline per week; establishing time during supervision to discuss a particular guideline where you need feedback or are feeling stuck (this can be an opportunity to educate the supervisor if they are not familiar with these peer support values or practices); asking people you support to give you feedback on a particular guideline where you're not sure how you're doing and explain why their feedback on it is important to the way you provide peer support; scheduling a guideline per month to role play during group supervision or learning community meetings with other peer support workers and use the time to discuss and debrief challenges in applying the practice guidelines so that you can get feedback and fresh ideas from your colleagues. These suggestions can help to counteract the 'role drift' described earlier in this article by keeping the focus on mutual support values and practices strong individually, in supervision, with the people you support, and in your peer support worker learning communities.

In the years since the original NPG was issued, increasing attention has been placed on challenges related to supervision. In 2019, N.A.P.S. completed a nearly two-year process to include tips for supervisors in a revision to the NPG. The revision is known as the National Practice Guidelines for Peer Specialists and Supervisors (NPG-S) and the process of developing it is described in the article in the Reference section. Recommendations for applying the NPS-S guidelines would include all of the above with the addition of supervisors specifically making a similar commitment to individual, group, and community reflection and practice as was recommended to peer support workers themselves.

More Information

SHARE! 2020 Conference on Supervision presentation: National Practice
Guidelines for Peer Specialists and Supervisors—Rita Cronise, Instructional
Designer, Rutgers University & Jessica Wolf, Assistant Clinical Prof. of
Psychiatry, Yale University. Accessible though https://shareselfhelp.org/
conferences/2020peer-supervision-workforce-conference/
Access the SHARE! 2020 Conference on Supervision: https://shareselfhelp.
org/conferences/2022-peer-supervision-workforce-conference-video-
powerpoints/

References

Bernstein, A.D., Swarbrick, M, & Banes, J. (2009, June 20). Professional and
Mutual-Help Paradigm Tension in Serving People with Serious and Persistent
Mental Illnesses. SCRA 2009 Biennial Conference, Montclair, NJ.

Borkman, T. (2021). Self-Help/Mutual Aid Groups and Peer Support: A Literature Review. Voluntaristics Review. Brill, p.10.

Campbell, J. (2008). Key Ingredients of Peer Programs Identified. Missouri
Institute of Mental Health.

Campbell, J. (2009). Federal Multi-Site Study Finds Consumer-Operated
Service Programs are Evidence-Based Practices. Missouri Institute of Mental
Health.

Chamberlin, J. (1978) On Our Own: Patient-Controlled Alternatives to the
Mental Health System. National Empowerment Center, Lawrence, MA.

Foglesong, D., Knowles, K., Cronise, R., Wolf, J., & Edwards, J.P. (Jul 2021).
National Practice Guidelines for Peer Specialists and Supervisors. *Psychiatric
Services*. Published Online: https://ps.psychiatryonline.org/doi/10.1176/appi.
ps.202000901

National Association of Peer Supporters (N.A.P.S.) (2019). National Practice
Guidelines for Peer Specialists and Supervisors. https://www.peersupport
works.org/wp-content/uploads/2021/07/National-Practice-Guidelines-for-
Peer-Specialists-and-Supervisors-1.pdf

Riessman, F. (1965). The "Helper" Therapy Principle, *Social Work*, Volume 10,
Issue 2, April 1965, Pages 27–32, https://doi.org/10.1093/sw/10.2.27

Smith, D. (2007) Letter to Medicaid State Directors from the Director of the Center for Medicare and Medicaid Services (CMS). https://downloads.cms.gov/cmsgov/archived-downloads/smdl/downloads/smd081507a.pdf

Substance Abuse and Mental Health Services Administration. (2019). *Behavioral Health Workforce Report*. Retrieved from https://annapoliscoalition.org/wp-content/uploads/2021/03/behavioral-health-workforce-report-SAMHSA-2.pdf

Substance Abuse and Mental Health Services Administration (SAMHSA). (2011). Consumer-Operated Services: The Evidence. HHS Pub. No. SMA-11-4633, Rockville, MD: Center for Mental Health Services, Substance Abuse and Mental Health Services Administration, U.S. Department of Health and Human Services. https://store.samhsa.gov/sites/default/files/d7/priv/sma11-4633-theevidence-cosp.pdf

SECTION 2: FIRST YEAR FINDINGS OF CERTIFIED PEER SPECIALIST CAREER OUTCOMES STUDY

Morgan Pelot, BA, BS,
Live & Learn, Inc.

Laysha Ostrow, PhD,
Live & Learn, Inc.

Certified peer specialists (CPSs) use their lived experience of a behavioral health disorders plus skills learned in formal training to deliver support services (National Association of Peer Specialists, 2021).

The CPS workforce is positioned to address two persistent problems in mental health services: a severe shortage of behavioral healthcare providers and the need for services that integrate behavioral healthcare with primary care (Myrick & del Vecchio, 2016; University of Michigan Behavioral Health Workforce Research Center, 2019). Research is limited in this area, as only 17% of state CPS certifying entities collect outcome data (Wolf, 2018) and previous studies have failed to look at the outcomes for CPSs who are not working in peer support, which also excludes those who are unemployed (Lapidos et al., 2018).

Little has been done to compare these differences and limits our understanding of disparities and preferences in peer specialist employment. The CPS Career Outcomes Study is a three-year, national study of recently certified peer specialist in one of four participating states in four regions of the U.S. that gathers information on the work experiences, career perspectives, and financial well-being of CPSs (Ostrow, Cook, Salzer, Pelot, & Burke-Miller, in review).

Discussion

Currently, forty-five states and the District of Columbia offer peer specialist certification (Copeland Center for Wellness and Recovery, 2020) and there are over 25,000 CPSs nationwide (Wolf, 2018). The Substance Abuse and Mental Health Services Administration (SAMHSA) predicts that peer specialists will make up a quarter of the behavioral health workforce in the future (Substance Abuse and Mental Health Services Administration, 2019). Doors to Wellbeing, a national consumer technical assistance center and a project of the Copeland Center for Wellness and Recovery, maintains a Peer Specialist Database that describes certification requirements, process, supports, and entities in each state (Copeland Center for Wellness and Recovery, 2020). An important step in understanding certification outcomes is clarifying the process state to state.

Having lived experience of a behavioral health disorder is essential to being a CPS but states differ in how they define this requirement. Only 26% (n = 12) of states with certification differentiate between mental health and substance use disorder peer support; half have a separate certification for substance use. Most states (59%, n = 27) do not differentiate between the two and have a requirement to be "diagnosed with a mental health condition and/or substance use disorder." Some states have additional certification specializations that focus on specific populations, such as ones for parent or family mental health support (28%, n = 13), youth (17%, n = 8), forensic or justice involvement (8%, n = 4), veterans (7%, n = 3), and older adults (4%, n = 2). Other, less common, specializations focus on specific services include hospital Bridgers, supportive housing, crisis services, supported employment, and rights protection and advocacy.

Eligibility requirements typically include education level, age, meeting the state's definition of "lived experience," criminal background check, and work experience. Of the 41 states that specify an education requirement, 33 of them require at least a high school diploma or equivalent. The most common age requirement is being at least 18 years of age (25 out of 29 states with an age requirement) with a few states (n = 3) requiring applicants to be 21 years or older. Most states (89%, n = 41) require individuals to meet a definition of lived experience and some even go as far to require someone to be "well-grounded in recovery," which is usually defined as a specific amount of time without hospitalization or incarceration.

A little less than half (44%, n = 20) of states require a background check as part of the application for certification, with several clarifying that this may not disqualify someone from becoming certified. Of the states that do not require background checks, many remind applicants that background checks may still be required by an employer. More than half of states (57%, n = 26) have specific requirements that individuals have work experience in peer support or the state issues provisional certifications that require a specified number of hours in the field to gain full certification.

Other professional requirements include having a valid driver's license, leadership experience, and strong reading comprehension and written communication skills. These requirements are problematic because they may exclude the exact people who bring lived experiences of challenges that face the people the state is supposed to be serving, and the people who themselves may benefit from CPS employment opportunities the most.

Some aspects of the certification process are consistent across states. All states have specific training requirements (e.g., state created, state approved, training criteria requirements) and a majority of states (80%, n =37) use certification tests or testing as part of training. Certification expiry varies from one to a few years but most states (93%, n = 43) require CPS to attend between 2 to 20 hours of trainings or workshops per year to obtain continuing education units (CEUs) for recertification.

Training, CEUs, applications, and exams may be associated with fees depending on the state. Only 22% (n=10) of states cover all certification costs for individuals interested in becoming a CPS. Some states offer scholarships, but other funding supports can include an employer, employment supportive services, or other local organizations. If fees are not covered, this may exclude people with limited financial means from certification (common among the target population) and presents a challenge to having CPS with lived experience that "matches" the experiences of service users.

A final difference among states is certification for peer specialist supervisors. Only 9 states (20%) have additional training, certifications, or a defined amount of work experience as a CPS that allow peers to become a CPS supervisor. More states (28%, n = 13) define supervisors as "qualified practitioners" which are often described as another mental health professional (e.g., licensed psychologist, professional counselor, certified social worker) or a medical professional (e.g., registered nurse, psychiatrist, physician). This could be due to some states having Medicaid billable peer support services. The guidance provided by the Centers of Medicare and Medicaid Services on the implementation of peer specialists as a Medicaid reimbursable service is as follows: "Supervision must be provided by a competent mental health professional (as defined by the State)" (Smith, 2007). Most states define "competent mental health professional" as a non-peer provider, but this designation is not required for Medicaid reimbursement and is an indication of discriminatory attitudes towards people with lived experience in professional roles.

State qualifications, fees, and specifications for who can supervise CPSs represent barriers to certification, and therefore employment, of individuals with lived experience. The CPS Career Outcomes Study was designed to explore these barriers and how career opportunities and attitudes change after certification.

In 2020, the CPS Career Outcomes Study recruited recently certified peer specialist from North Carolina, Oregon, Pennsylvania, and Texas to take part in a three-year longitudinal study. The sample of 681 CPSs was 65% female (n = 440), 2% (n = 12) non-binary, 1% (n =4) genderqueer, 1% (n = 5) transgender. In terms of race and ethnicity, 67% were white (n = 450), 26% (n = 176) Black/African American, 5% (n = 32) American Indian, 1.3% (n = 9) Asian, and 9% Latinx (n = 63). CPS in this study were 47 years old on average, and 46% (n = 310) had an associate's degree or higher. A little over half (55%; n = 325) were working in peer support jobs; 123 (21%) were working in other types of jobs, and 143 (24%) not working for pay.

Using the first-year baseline data, we looked at relationships between participant characteristics and employment status and job type. First, we found that respondents who were receiving Social Security disability benefits, were veterans, had used outpatient counseling or therapy, and those that did not disclose their mental health status in the workplace were less likely to be employed.

Next, we explored what characteristics contributed to holding a peer support (PS) job versus a non-PS job. Not disclosing to colleagues and higher local unemployment rates contributed to a lower likelihood of working in PS jobs, whereas individuals reporting depressive disorders were more likely to have PS jobs than those with other diagnoses.

In addition to employment status and type of job, we looked at the quality of PS jobs compared to non-PS jobs. PS jobs had longer job tenure and more often provided employee benefits. Job satisfaction was significantly higher in PS than other jobs. Another aspect of job quality we examined was burnout – defined as a crisis in one's relationship with work characterized by exhaustion, cynicism, and low professional efficacy (Schaufeli & Buunk, 1996). We found relatively low levels of burnout in our sample of CPS. Importantly, respondents employed in PS jobs had fewer signs of burnout than similar respondents in other occupations.

There was no difference between wages and hours worked between PS and non-PS jobs. However, PS jobs paid relatively low wages when compared to national data from the Department of Labor for occupations in the Community/Social Services field, which are similar positions but do not require lived experience. The average hourly wage of PS jobs in our survey was $15.93, which is well below the average hourly wages for Community and Social Service ($25.09) and Community Health Work ($22.12) occupations, or even the lowest earning occupation in this category of Social and Human Service Assistants of $18.38 (U.S. Bureau of Labor Statistics, 2021). There was also a gender wage gap, with women earning less per hour than male counterparts. Veterans earned a higher hourly wage than the average CPS.

We also explored financial well-being (FWB) which is defined as a person being able to fully meet financial obligations, feeling secure in their financial future, and able to make choices that allow them to enjoy life (Consumer Financial Protection Bureau, 2017). Respondents who were employed full-time as a PS were more likely to have higher pay and greater FWB compared to other CPSs. At the same time, our sample had a lower average FWB score (52) than the median (54) among adults in the U.S. in 2017 (Consumer Financial Protection Bureau, 2017).

Our study also collected qualitative data through interviews with participants, which adds context to the survey data. Despite our finding from the survey data that certification may lead to high quality PS jobs, it is important to note that not everyone had a positive experience following certification. The quotes in Table 1 illustrate barriers faced by some respondents.

Barrier	Participant Quote
Getting Certified	"If you qualify for their [Office of Vocational Rehabilitation] services they pay for the two-week training at the state level. I didn't qualify, so I paid $1,100 out of pocket to take a two-week class so that I could take the certification tests."
Finding Work as a CPS	"I got a piece of paper that was required of me by the Agency and state, that's it. It has not gotten me a raise, bonus, stipend, respect, recognition or a pat on the head."
	"One major barrier has been entry into the field. One would assume that mental/behavioral health professionals would not only understand but expect a less-than perfect work history from a newly-certified PSS."
	"[Certification] hasn't helped me in a career, as I can't get anyone to hire me due to my charges and lengthy incarcerations...as well as lack of work history in 11 years."
	"I still can't get a job after that [training] because of my background, but yet that's what got me the certification is my background"
Negative Experiences in CPS Jobs	"I would've been in the car like five to six hours a shift....so I was like 'Okay, so are they hiring me to be a taxi driver instead of doing things that are actually beneficial to people?'"
	"The magic figure of $15.00 per hour being a living wage is only true if that's net income. And then it's a struggle. But there are rewards beyond income in this field."
	"I can't afford to get a job in the field. Pay is too low and organizations don't have enough funding to offer decent health insurance packages. I would inevitably relapse into crisis if I could not afford regular therapy. It's honestly very upsetting that a job specifically created for people in recovery from mental health conditions is unable to provide appropriate healthcare benefits."
	"She [boss] supervised people before, but I felt like she needed more training on how to supervise a peer and she-- we all lacked the ability to kind of communicate with each other."

Conclusion

While there are similarities among state requirements and certification processes, peer specialist certification is not transferable across states. Important areas where states differ include background checks, definition of lived experience, and supervision of CPS staff. Some of these requirements introduce barriers to becoming certified or in finding work following certification, which may also impact the quality of peer support relationships with service users. More research is needed to examine the career outcomes of individuals who become certified and explore if these jobs are more satisfactory and provide better opportunities for career advancement.

The first year of the CPS Career Outcomes Study found that while there are positive characteristics about PS jobs, including higher job satisfaction, tenure, benefits, and lower burnout, these positions were relatively low wage compared to other non-peer positions in the community health field. In terms of financial well-being, CPSs have at least a moderate likelihood of financial hardship. Employment in PS jobs did not result in greater financial well-being when compared to other types of work, suggesting that the financial commitment to this workforce is not strong enough to spur retention in these positions, which may lead CPS to seek better-paid employment.

Finally, while CPS appear not be at a particular greater risk of burnout, there is a strong relationship between burnout and likelihood of job turnover among PS. Aspects of the work life environment that can prevent burnout and increase retention include reasonable workload demands, fairness and respect from coworkers and supervisors, rewards that are consistent with expectations, and workplace community.

More Information

Certified Peer Specialist Career Outcomes Study website: https://www.peerspecialist.net/
Early Research Results Webinar (January 14, 2021): https://www.youtube.com/watch?v=4KHSY5bHbFQ
N.A.P.S. Webinar (May 27, 2021): https://www.youtube.com/watch?v=bpuObvH_hGI
Peer Specialist Database: https://copelandcenter.com/peer-specialists
Live & Learn, Inc.: https://livelearninc.net/
Team: https://livelearninc.net/team
Our other projects: https://livelearninc.net/projects-summary

References

Consumer Financial Protection Bureau. (2017). *Financial well-being in America*. Retrieved from https://files.consumerfinance.gov/f/documents/201709_cfp b_financial-well-being-in-America.pdf

Copeland Center for Wellness and Recovery, I. (2020). States with Certification. Retrieved from https://copelandcenter.com/peer-specialists. Peer Specialist Database Retrieved October 8, 2021 https://copelandcenter.com/peer-specialists

Lapidos, A., Jester, J., Ortquist, M., Werner, P., Ruffolo, M. C., & Smith, M. (2018). Survey of Peer Support Specialists: Professional Activities, Self-Rated Skills, Job Satisfaction, and Financial Well-being. *Psychiatric Services, 69*(12), 1264-1267. doi:10.1176/appi.ps.201800251

Myrick, K., & del Vecchio, P. (2016). Peer Support Services in the Behavioral Healthcare Workforce: State of the Field. *Psychiatric Rehabilitation Journal, 39*(3), 197-203. Retrieved from https://doi-org.ucsf.idm.oclc.org/10.1037/prj0000188

National Association of Peer Specialists. (2021). Leading Mental Health Organizations Strongly Support New Bipartisan Peer Support Legislation Introduced in the Senate. Retrieved from https://www.peersupportworks.org/leading-mental-health-organizations-strongly-support-new-bipartisan-peer-support-legislation-introduced-in-the-senate/

Ostrow, L., Cook, J., Salzer, M. S., Pelot, M., & Burke-Miller, J. (in press). Is there better job out there? Employment of peer specialists after certification. *Psychiatric Services.*

Schaufeli, W. B., & Buunk, B. P. (1996). Professional Burnout. In M. J. Schabracq, J. A. M. Winnubst, & C. L. Cooper (Eds.), *Handbook of Work and Health Psychology* (pp. 311-346): John Wiley & Sons.

Smith, D. G. (2007). *Dear State Medicaid Director, SMDL #07-011.* Retrieved from https://downloads.cms.gov/cmsgov/archived-downloads/smdl/downloads/smd081507a.pdf

Substance Abuse and Mental Health Services Administration. (2019). *Behavioral Health Workforce Report.* Retrieved from https://annapoliscoalition.org/wp-content/uploads/2021/03/behavioral-health-workforce-report-SAMHSA-2.pdf

U.S. Bureau of Labor Statistics. (2021). May 2020 National Occupational Employment and Wage Estimates. *Occupational Employment and Wage Statistics.* Retrieved from https://www.bls.gov/oes/2020/may/oes_nat.htm

University of Michigan Behavioral Health Workforce Research Center. (2019). *National Analysis of Peer Support Providers: Practice Settings, Requirements, Roles, and Reimbursement.* Retrieved from Ann Arbor, MI: https://behavioral healthworkforce.org/wp-content/uploads/2019/10/BHWRC-Peer-Work force-Full-Report.pdf

Wolf, J. (2018). National Trends in Peer Specialist Certification. *Psychiatric Services, 69*(10), 1049-1049. doi:10.1176/appi.ps.201800333

SECTION 3: SUPERVISION AND THE DEVELOPMENT OF CORE COMPETENCIES WITH PEER WORKERS

Cheryl Gagne, Sc.D.

C4 Innovations

Increasingly, peer support workers are being hired to provide peer support and other services in a wide range of behavioral health organizations. More peer workers are employed by behavioral health than by peer-run organizations. While peer support was a relatively new and widely misunderstood service, behavioral health organizations, perhaps motivated by workforce shortages, the modest cost of peer support workers, hired increasing numbers of peer support workers. Thus, peer support workers faced many challenges in the workplace with colleagues, including their supervisors, misinterpreting the role and code of peer support practice. Some peer workers found they had no job description and were asked to perform tasks that conflicted with the role of peer support. It became clear that peer support workers needed organizational changes and resources to overcome barriers to their success and satisfaction in delivering peer support in behavioral health programs.

With the expansion of the peer workforce has come the need for guidelines and training in the critical competencies needed by supervisors of peer support workers. This article presents the principles of recovery-oriented supervision and two critical competencies, *giving feedback* and *problem solving.*

Discussion

Supervision is a process and a relationship in which a worker is helped by a designated responsible staff person to make the best use of their knowledge, skills, and resources to perform the requirements of the position. Supervisors play a critical role in supporting work performance and the integration of peer workers into behavioral health organizations. Some peer support workers are employed by peer-run or family-run organizations that generally have a clear understanding of, and a commitment to, the unique and important role of peers in providing recovery support services. Most peer workers, however, are employed by behavioral health organizations that may not be grounded in the principles and practices of recovery and peer support.

With the expansion of the peer workforce has come the need for guidelines and training in the critical competencies of supervising peer workers. Peer support workers in behavioral health deserve high-quality supervision that provides support, advances reflective practice, promotes ongoing learning and education, and fosters understanding of administrative requirements.

In recent years, organizations have developed models for the supervision of peer support workers. Similarly, as peer workers have entered the workforce in various program models and environments, there have been attempts to configure supervision structures as they relate to peer practice in specific mental health and substance use recovery programs. At the same time, there is no single broadly accepted set of standards or even consensus regarding who is qualified to supervise peers. The following section outlines best practices in supervision and the main functions of supervisors.

All supervisors of peer support workers need have deep understanding of peer practice and knowledge of the organization and resources. They practice the skills of recovery-oriented supervision and act as a change agent within the organization.

Benefits of recovery-oriented supervision

- Support for all employees
- Learning of essential skills
- Improved communication
- Improved job satisfaction
- Reinforcement of valued roles of peers in the workplace
- Model of collaborative work relationships with peers
- Development of job performance
- Improved work culture
- Increased employee retention
- Positive outcomes for agency or program

Principles of Recovery-oriented Supervision

Recovery-oriented supervision is a process and relationship(s) that assist workers to grow professionally. For most workers, supervision is the only opportunity they have to concentrate on their own professional growth and satisfaction and, because so much of life is spent working, supervision is a worthy invest of time.

Recovery-oriented supervision as a practice is grounded in the core values of connection, collaboration, involvement, person-centered, strengths-based and growth oriented. These values can be universally applied to all supervisory practices in all behavioral health organizations.

- Connection: This value reflects the significance of workers' relationships to supervisors, colleagues, and mission of the service. The relationship between the worker and supervisor is the "gateway" connection to the rest of the organization and the supervisor has some responsibility in connecting workers to meaningful relationships in and with the organization.
- Involvement: Workers are active participants in their own supervision. Supervisors create conditions in the relationship and the supervision process that invites and encourages participation. Supervisors are sensitive that some workers may need more coaching and support to participate fully in supervision.
- Collaboration: In recovery-oriented supervision, the nature of the relationship between supervisor and worker is collaborative. While the supervisor has responsibility to ensure that the worker has what they need to deliver services in a manner that meets the organizational mission, they are transparent about their responsibility to the organization while engaged in a supportive and collaborative relationship with the peer support worker.
- Individualized: Supervision is tailored to the unique goals and needs of each worker. Each worker will have different strengths and areas that need improvement, and each has their own preferences and learning styles.
- Strengths-based: Supervisors recognize the unique strengths of each worker and engage workers to identify their own strengths. Supervisors and workers collaborate in developing work strategies that play to the worker's strengths. Feedback always begins with strengths. In a recovery-oriented workplace, the organization celebrates the unique contributions of their workers and creates a culture that affirms workers.

- Growth: Most workers want to improve some aspects of their work performance. Supervisors partner with workers to develop the competencies they need to improve their work performance or to prepare for their future career. Supervisors can assist either through modeling, training, or coaching. It's important to note that many issues in the workplace are not solved through the "growth" or professional development of the peer support workers, but rather meaning changes in organizational policies, practices, and culture.

Basic Functions of Supervision

Supervisors juggle multiple responsibilities to the worker and to the organization. These duties can be categorized as being administrative, formative, and supportive. Sometimes these basic functions are performed by one person and other times they are split between supervisors. For example, in one agency one supervisor, a peer support worker themselves, is responsible for all the formative supervision of peer support workers in the agency while other supervisors attend to administrative and support duties.

Administrative supervision focuses on the effective implementation of the agency's policies and procedures and the management of the peer worker's work performance. There is a focus on the quality of work, workload, conformance with program practices, and record keeping. Supervisors act as the liaison to operations like payroll and human resources.

Formative supervision focuses on the professional development of the worker though training, modeling, and structuring learning experiences. Formative supervision provides the venue and resources for supporting the peer worker's professional development. The majority of time in supervision should be spent providing the time and space for the worker to reflect on their peer practice. This reflection leads to discussions and exploration about what workers want to improve. Supervisors explore with workers, the possible competencies or resources that could assist a worker grow in an area they've chosen. Supervisors give feedback on the peer worker's work performance. Feedback is often perceived as supportive because it demonstrates a transparency that increases a person's sense of safety.

Supportive supervision focuses on the person's morale and job satisfaction. Supervisors will open discussions about the worker's personal reactions to the work. They will provide generous positive feedback and provide encouragement. Across the organization, supervisors will promote self-care practices through policies and practices that support all workers and advocate for peer support workers within the organization.

Two Essential Skills of Supervisors

Supervisors perform many roles and so need many different skills. Supervision skills may be developed through training and experience, but many supervisors haven't had the training or experiences needed to develop these skills. While other skills, like *listening, demonstrating understanding, praising, etc.* are critical, this section will focus on two essential skills, *giving feedback,* and *problem solving.* Although we describe these as skills for supervisors, recovery-oriented supervision enables the workers to learn these skills as well. Successful workers know how to give themselves feedback and how to solve problems.

Giving Feedback

Giving (and receiving) feedback may take practice and coaching. Many people have difficulty acknowledging strengths, while others may fail to see imperfections. Feedback can stir up uncomfortable feelings and could be a difficult trigger for people who've experienced abuse. It's important to be mindful of these facts and at the same time to talk about how getting feedback helps professional growth.

The Harvard Business Review article on building a feedback rich work culture made these suggestions, which align well with recovery-oriented practices.

1. Establish safety and trust in relationships. Supervisors and workers should get to know each other and talk about feelings about the job. Supervisors have to make it okay to say, "no" to the question, "Can I give you some feedback on that?"
2. Make certain that feedback is balanced. Colleagues should give each other praise related to job performance in private and in public. Positive feedback does not always have to be followed by an area to improve.
3. Make feedback a normal part of work. Supervisors can open conversations by asking how a certain task went. Supervisors can ask for feedback to be given about areas of their work performance. Workers can ask for feedback.
4. Leaders in feedback-rich workplaces are transparent and are open and act on feedback given to them.

Definition

Giving feedback means communicating your objective appraisal of the worker's performance of a specific work task or worker attribute

Benefits

> Helps workers discover areas they need to develop
> Contributes to a culture of growth and development
> Demonstrates supervisor's interest in helping the peer worker to grow in the role

Steps

1. Ask worker to give themselves feedback on a specific task or attribute
2. Share your objective appraisal of the worker's performance, starting with strengths and moving to areas that need improvement
3. Check in with the worker about their reactions to the feedback
4. Collaborate with the worker to develop activities for learning

Condition

Give feedback when the worker is ready to hear it and usually in private

---

Before giving feedback, the supervisor and worker must come to agreement on the job expectations. This is a task should be done regularly and whenever there are changes to a worker's job expectations.

One goal of giving feedback is to assist the worker to become more skilled at giving feedback to themselves. Supervisor and worker can come to consensus about the worker's strengths and problem areas at work. Nonjudgmental self-observation is the goal.

Supervisors are responsible to explore barriers or challenges that workers experience on the job and provide or identify needed learning opportunities, supports, and resources.

Problem Solving

Problem solving involves analyzing and resolving difficult situations. Problems or challenges are common in the workplace. Most often, problems or difficult situations are complex with several underlying causes. For example, a peer worker who frequently does not have required documentation completed. Exploring the causes with this worker may uncover potential solutions. Many adults have difficulty talking about or acknowledging problems and are hesitant to bring them to supervision so this skill, like giving feedback requires a safe and warm connection.

Definition
Problem solving is analyzing and resolving difficult situations

Benefits
➤ Supervisor and worker know how to identify contributing causes to the problem
➤ Supervisor and worker gain strategies for resolving working problems
➤ Supervisor and worker feel more confident in resolving problems at work

Steps
1. Define the problem
2. Determine underlying cause(s) of the problem
3. Brainstorm possible solutions
4. Decide on a solution after evaluating
5. Implement solution
6. Evaluate success of the solution

Condition
When a worker is confronted with difficulties that need resolution on the job

Defining the problem involves reflecting on the background, context, behaviors, and feelings related to the issue. There are many ways to define a problem from many different perspectives. In recovery-oriented supervision, the problem is seen through the worker's eyes. Supervisors contribute to the discussion about the issue and may offer other perspectives, but the final definition of the problem comes from the peer support worker.

Determining the underlying cause(s) of the problem is process of self-reflection and review of the context of the problems. One structure for listing possible causes is to think about barriers. Are there internal barriers (lack of knowledge, skill, experience, confidence)? What are the external barriers (people in the environment, place characteristics, resources, policies, practices, access etc.)? Once the barrier(s) is understood, it becomes easier to brainstorm possible solutions.

Brainstorming possible solutions, evaluating possible solutions, and selecting solutions is a collaborative process between supervisor and peer support worker. Possible solutions are based on how the problem is defined and underlying cause(s) identified. Solutions can be evaluated based on their expected effect, effort/cost, timeliness, and personal preferences. Solutions may involve training to improve a competency, changing an organizational procedure, providing organization-wide training, shifting work tasks or timelines, mentoring, and many other possibilities.

Once a solution is selected, it must be implemented. Some solutions may require more long-term planning while others can be implemented immediately. When effective solutions take months and the problem remains challenging, more immediate solutions are needed. Recycle the solutions list.

Supervisors and workers discuss how the solution is working. Sometimes solutions don't solve the problem while other times, the solution needs to be modified to make it more effective. Ongoing discussions about problems or difficult situations lead to problem solving and over time, the skill become very natural.

These are two essential skills for supervisors of peer workers. In addition to the many other skills that supervisors need, they need deep knowledge about peer support principles and practices and attitudes that align with the values of recovery. These required attitudes, knowledge, and skills combine to form the competencies needed by supervisors of peer support workers. (See resources for the link to Substance Use Disorder Peer Supervisor Competencies).

Core Competencies for Peer Support Workers in Behavioral Health Services

Competencies are the combination of observable and measurable knowledge, skills, and attitudes that contribute to enhanced performance. Competencies are also thought to improve workers' satisfaction in their work.

By 2010, many states and credentialing organizations were talking about the need for consensus about the competencies that peer workers need to be success in providing peer support in behavioral health programs. Core competencies, it was believed would increase recognition of peer-provided recovery-oriented services and supports. It was believed that describing competencies would better inform mental health and addiction programs on how to write their job descriptions for peer roles in their agencies and to establish and evaluate peer training programs. The BRSS TACS team hoped that describing competencies would prove helpful to peer support workers as a tool for self-evaluation of work performance and for communicating what peer support workers do. The team also felt strongly that it was unrealistic for peer support workers to develop all these skills during their training or experiences and the most workers gain their competencies on the job.

SAMHSA engaged the project *Bringing Recovery Supports to Scale Technical Assistance Center Strategy* (BRSS TACS) at C4 Innovations to assemble a team to draft, review, and develop the Core Competencies for Peer Support Workers in Behavioral Health Services. The BRSS TACS team contacted partners and other known experts in peer support and peer-provided services to help the BRSS TACS team identify multiple sources that would yield lists of potential competencies for inclusion in the draft core competency set. The sources gathered included published literature, grey literature, and existing sets of competencies for peer workers in a variety of roles.

The BRSS TACS team then organized and synthesized the lists of potential core competencies through a process of distilling the knowledge, skills, and attitudes, and eliminating redundancies. The team constructed competency language, categorized the competencies, and created an initial draft set of core competencies. The team and partners reviewed and revised the initial draft three times.

The draft core competencies then went through The Delphi process, a process of gathering feedback and input through a series of surveys. BRSS TACS recruited a panel of 26 experts with experience as peer support workers. After 3 rounds of surveys with changes made between each cycle, consensus was achieved. The Delphi process was chosen because it allows for anonymity and for minority opinions to be elevated to the whole panel.

Under SAMHSA's direction, BRSS TACS conducted a series of Regional Summits on May 19–20, 2015, in Atlanta, Georgia; on June 23–24, 2015, in Vancouver, Washington; and on July 29–30, 2015, in Baltimore, Maryland. In all, 209 people participated in the three summits. Participants gave feedback and made recommendations about the core competencies. The BRSS TACS team incorporated many of the recommendations—especially those that recommended using language more inclusive of family members—into the set of core competencies. SAMHSA also posted the set of core competencies on its website from March 2015–July 2015 for public comment. Again, many of the recommendations collected on the website related to adding inclusive language about the family. In response, the team incorporated or partially incorporated these recommendations into the set of core competencies.

Finally, BRSS TACS conducted the Core Competency Surveys and telephone interviews with a national sample of 100 peer support workers and peer recovery coaches currently working in these positions. They rated the relevance and importance of each competency in their jobs.

The work was complete in 2015. A best practice in competency development is to review the competencies every 5 years and making necessary changes.

Examples of Using Competencies in Recovery-oriented Supervision

Annette tells her supervisor that she wants to learn how to write advanced directives with people she supports. She and her supervisor discuss the goal with excitement and brainstorm possible learning experiences that would lead Annette to be competent at writing advanced directives.

Kevin, a peer recovery coach who provides harm reduction services in addition to peer support, sometimes reflected that he felt invisible in the organization. He believed himself to be a member of the SUD team, but he was never invited to meetings. Coming to the office felt weird since most of his work was in the community. The supervisor and he struggled to define the problem. They discussed the background, context, behaviors, and feelings related to the issue. Kevin moved from describing the problem as "I feel disrespected by my colleagues," to defining the problem, "The treatment team and the harm reduction team have high levels of mutual distrust." They brainstormed many possible solutions and landed on two solutions they felt would be effective and felt low-key enough for Kevin.

One solution was a monthly SUD team-wide meeting that would highlight different services offered by the team. This solution gave people some face-time together and they would learn about and from each other. The other solution came from the supervisor who had been tasked with incorporating harm reduction practices in the treatment services. She wanted to form a small committee comprised of treatment and harm reduction personnel to develop the protocols and lead the implementation. This activity would prove to be a partial solution to the problem of lack of connection between the treatment and the harm reduction teams.

Felicity has provided peer support to people visiting a peer recovery community and is beginning to work in the service that provides peer navigation/support to people transitioning from the hospital. Before she begins her work, she, with the help of the supervisor, assesses the competencies she will need for that specific peer navigation/support role. Felicity will participate in learning opportunities to gain the competencies she needs.

Conclusion

If the behavioral healthcare system continues to change and if peer support becomes part of every community's response to people in need of recovery support, core competencies and supervision strategies will continue to change. In the midst of change, supervisors and workers will retain the core principles and values that drive peer support services. What also is preserved is the passion of peer support workers who will continue to deliver powerful peer support services and make needed changes in behavioral healthcare systems.

References

Foglesong, D., Knowles, K., Cronise, R., Wolf, J., & Edwards, J.P. (Jul 2021). National Practice Guidelines for Peer Specialists and Supervisors. *Psychiatric*

Services. Published Online: https://ps.psychiatryonline.org/doi/10.1176/appi. ps.202000901

Foglesong, D., Spagnolo, A. B., Cronise, R., Forbes, J., Swarbrick, P., Edwards, J. P., & Pratt, C. (2022). Perceptions of Supervisors of Peer Support Workers (PSW) in Behavioral Health: Results from a National Survey. *Community mental health journal, 58*(3), 437–443. https://doi.org/10.1007/s10597-021-00837-2

Gagne, C., Olivet, J., & Davis, L. (2012) Equipping behavioral health systems and authorities to promote peer specialist/peer recovery coaching services. Expert panel meeting report. Retrieved from http://www:samhsa.gov/recov ery/docs/Expert_ Panel_02112013.pdf

Harvard Business Journal online, *Building a Feedback Rich Culture*. https://hbr. org/2013/12/building-a-feedback-rich-culture

Martin, E. & Jordan, A. (2017). Substance Use Disorder Peer Supervision Competencies. http://www.williamwhitepapers.com/pr/dlm_uploads/Peer-Supervision-Competencies-2017.pdf

Miller, R., Carr, E.R., Olezeski, C.L., Silva, M.A., & Ponce, A.N. (2020). Recovery-Oriented Supervision: A Missing Element in Systems Transformation. *American Journal of Psychiatric Rehabilitation 23*(1), 67-75. https://www.muse. jhu.edu/article/807526.

SAMHSA BRSS TACS (2015). Core Competencies for Peer Support Workers in Behavioral Health Organizations. https://www.samhsa.gov/brss-tacs/ recovery-support-tools/peers/core-competencies-peer-workers

Tucker, S. J., Tiegreen, W., Toole, J., Banathy, J., Mulloy, D., & Swarbrick, M. (2013). Supervisor Guide: Peer Support Whole Health and Wellness Coach. Decatur, GA: Georgia Mental Health Consumer Network. https://www.peer supportworks.org/wp-content/uploads/2021/05/Supervisor-Guide-to-Peer-Support-Whole-Health-and-Wellness-c-2013.pdf

CHAPTER 6
VALUES INTO PRACTICE

CHAPTER INTRODUCTION BY THE EDITORS

ONCE PEER VALUES ARE ESTABLISHED, IT IS HELPFUL TO HAVE GUIDANCE ON implementation in the many and quite varied spaces in which peer support work is practiced. It can be tedious, stressful, and even harmful to be expected to provide services in the face of conflicting mandates. Medical model institutions in particular, where an ever-increasing number of peer support providers are practicing, sometimes, even in the face of determined advocacy, are unable to nimbly accept modern peer support values such as mutuality and self-disclosure, simply because these are not practiced by other, more established disciplines. Another example might be the ethic of confidentiality, whereby in the case of an individual engaging in self-harm, peer values may hold that this is strictly between the individual and the peer support worker, but in a hospital where the peer support worker is part of a treatment team, such behavior is expected to be share among team members. Chapter 6 offers three views of how peer values may inform practice.

Mx. Yaffa (Ahmad Abojaradeh) leads off by deconstructing the meaning of peer ethics at the intersection of equity and marginalization. In Yaffa's view, despite what may be good intentions, peer support is subject to the same privileged viewpoint as what is termed the Medical Industrial Complex (Health Justice Commons, n.d.) unless rigorous attention is paid. Most disturbing is the view that people in the peer support community itself fails to practice equity and inclusion in more than a performative way.

Next, Foxworth takes us through different forms of the practice of advocacy, providing concrete on-the-ground examples. She continues by establishing a situation; the peer support worker shortage as promulgated by SAMHSA. Next, she leads us concisely through next steps of identifying and understanding barriers followed by strategy formation appropriate to both root cause and level of comfort on the part of the advocate. Foxworth speaks plainly and knowledgeably about legislative advocacy in particular and concludes with next steps for both budding and experienced advocates.

Ashcraft and Blum have created a protocol, which they call Strength in Numbers, designed to form capable teams utilizing an exchange of personal and professional strengths. They describe reasons that teams may not cohere, such as mistrust or competition, In order to extract vulnerability and honesty, the protocol is gamified so that individuals learn by having fun. A banking metaphor is used to teach the protocol. First, an assessment of social capital is made to establish a baseline of strengths and areas needing development. This is followed by an exchange of assessments among the team, and sharing ideas for relying on one another and working effectively as a group. Most important is the focus on recovery and resiliency, which can be addressed joyfully by enlightened teams.

SECTION 1: EQUITY, ETHICS, AND PEER SUPPORT

Mx. Yaffa (Ahmad Abojaradeh) CPS, MA
Equity and Transformation Consultant, Meraj Consulting

One of the major requirements for Peer Support to be effective and transformative is that it must be utilized in ethical ways that are created by Peers ourselves. Additionally, Peer Support without a lens of equity replicates the same Ableist systems within the Medical Industrial Complex (MIC) that created the necessity for Peer Support in the first place (Health Justice Commons, n.d.). In this narrative, we dive into defining equity rooted in Peer Support values and discuss why Peer Support without equity is not ethical. This session works on defining ethics, equity, and gaining an understanding of Ableism and the MIC.

Peer Support was always intended to be equitable. The concept of 'for us by us' is meant to challenge the status quo by ensuring the most marginalized are leading conversations about our needs and care. However, in most Peer

Support spaces 'for us by us' is limited to our mental health and substance use challenges and does not take any other form of marginalization into consideration. 'For us by us' inherently goes beyond any single identity and instead is rooted in intersectional marginalization. Instead, many spaces still utilize the outdated concept of equality in their Peer Support framing instead of equity, which would require us to ground Peer Support in the same framing that birthed it, one rooted in marginalization due to power imbalance.

Discussion

If Utopia is a not fully realized future, something that ought to be but is not here yet, then marginalization is the here and now. Marginalization is rooted in a time and place. It is the past and present, and idealistically not the future. Peer Support was a response to a specific type of marginalization, the marginalization of individuals living with mental health and substance use challenges. The marginalization of peers in the 60's and 70's, as the movement was being built, is not the same marginalization that exists today and the marginalization centered at the start of the Peer Support movement was not necessarily encompassing intersecting marginalizations of the time or the now. Every movement, rooted in a single identity of marginalization and not rooted at the intersection of marginalization, is bound to be inequitable, even if, like Peer Support, it is meant to be equitable.

The initial movement began around the same time as various other movements, the movement for Civil Rights, the Disability Rights Movement, the Feminist movement, and built off of the Recovery movement. These movements were all birthed due to specific types of injustice and marginalization that had been ongoing since the inception of the United States. They are all linked, however, as they all gained mainstream traction, they lost the intersectional framing that allowed them to all build in unison, supporting individuals who carry all the marginalized identities experiencing the injustice they aimed to transform.

Even prior to understanding Peer Support and becoming a certified Peer Support specialist, I was often told that as I conducted mental health awareness work that gender, race, religion, orientation, immigration status, or any other identities were not relevant to mental health. I was told they belonged in different spaces and I was doing harm by bringing up my other marginalized identities, identities that have and will always be intrinsically tied with my mental health and separating them will never be possible. Peer Support was refreshing after a few years of resisting mainstream ideas of how and what impacts our wellbeing. My training dug deep into conversations about spirituality and diversity, and covered ethics generously. We talked about system transformation and modeling our practice as a way to transform the mental health system.

I recommended Peer Support to every single person of color, various immigration statuses, and broadly within the queer and trans communities. Then I realized that a Peer Support specialist is just as likely to call the FBI on a Muslim peer as a councillor or social worker. I realized that white supremacy is still in the room with us, no matter how equipped we are to leave our baggage outside. I realized that a Peer Support specialist was just as likely to misgender me in every session and apologize because I am abnormal and they just need more time to get used to it, something acceptable at times for a loved one but never for a professional. I realized that Peer Support specialists are still conditioned into a white supremacist heteronormative capitalist society that still values identities that the majority of people experiencing the worst the system has to offer do not carry.

I learned there were two visions of Peer Support out there, one that includes me and other marginalized individuals within the realm of mental health and substances and for various other identities, and a more mainstream one that doesn't. I have been talking about this for seven years now, at keynotes and conference presentations, and although many rally behind the call for a more transformative Peer Support, many in power within the Peer Support universe do not. In such spaces I will still experience every microaggression that I experience outside the Peer Support community. As an example, outside of a trans Peer Support space, I have been misgendered during every single meeting and space. In my experience, Islamophobic, anti-black, ageist, and anti-immigrant comments are routine in most Peer Support spaces.

Despite all this, I still believe in Peer Support, and I believe that there is only one Peer Support. I believe and know this to be the case because everything I mentioned above is in direct opposition to the twelve National Practice Guidelines and any Peer Support ethics I have ever seen. Peer Support is about honoring people as experts in their lives and acknowledges that many systems of care were never built for our wellbeing. They were built to remove us from view or rehabilitate us only to be able to be used as additional bodies in service of capitalism. We cannot honor people if we do not comprehend everything that people can be. We do not need to know or understand, we need to ground ourselves beyond systems of oppression, allowing us to live in a realm of limitless possibility for individuals, their identities, experiences, and everything else that they are or can be.

Honoring people includes a vision of equity that seems to be missing from many spaces. This is not only my experience, I have yet to find a person with other marginalized identities who has not experienced unethical behavior from our fellow Peer Support specialists.

Equity is about acknowledging and addressing the systemic challenges and barriers that prevent us from living our lives wholeheartedly and providing care and attention to individuals differently to compensate for these challenges and barriers. Although the systems themselves are the same, the impact of inequity varies drastically between communities and individuals from the same community. If this is not what the core of Peer Support is supposed to be, then I do not know what is.

Equity is ethics and ethics is equity within Peer Support. If as a cis- Peer Support specialist you treat a trans peer as if they are an anomaly and a burden for 'making' you learn about pronouns then you are not acting ethically. If as a white-Peer Support specialist you have not done work to move outside of white supremacy then you are showing up in white supremacist ways and are not acting ethically. If as a non-black or a non-indigenous POC Peer Support specialist you do not equip yourself with knowledge about this land and its history and how immense injustice is still enacted to black and indigenous communities then we are not acting ethically. The list goes on and on because our identities are endless.

When I train individuals and organizations on Peer Support ethics and the necessity of honoring individuals, I am often asked about the difficulty of trying to learn everything about every marginalized group to show up in better ways. My response is simple, in Peer Support we do not need to share the same challenge to be able to step back and honor peers as is our job. We continuously work on bettering ourselves, and when we show up, we show up as supports, walking side by side with our peers, allowing our peers to lead and guide the journey. It is the same for equity. No one will ever know every single culture or identity, and we do not need to. With that said, if we have not done *any* work, even as these identities are sitting across from us and in our spaces then we are purposefully acting in unethical ways. You should not wait to work with a trans person to learn about pronouns, or any other example from identities listed above. I have known some in the Peer Support Movement for years now and they have not taken the initiative to grow. This is privilege and must be addressed if we are ever going to truly honor peoples' power instead of hoarding it.

Conclusion

Peer Support, rooted in a value of lived experience, understands marginalization and ought to be equitable. However, like many other movements, it understands single identity marginalization and is thus not equitable.

References

Terms defined- Medical Industrial Complex. Health Justice Commons. (n.d.). Retrieved February 9, 2022, from https://www.healthjusticecommons.org/terms-defined

SECTION 2: ADVOCACY 101. MAKING YOUR VOICE HEARD...AND MATTER

Phyllis Foxworth, Vice President Peer and Policy Advancement, Depression and Bipolar Support Alliance

Advocacy means different things to different people. It can also encompass several major categories, including self-advocacy, corporate policy reform, or legislative and public policy reform. An example of self-advocacy is following all appropriate steps to reverse a mental health care insurance claim that has been denied. Mobilizing a boycott of a television show and its advertisers that promote mental health stigma is an example of corporate policy reform. Legislative or public policy reform focuses on changing laws and regulations that create barriers to quality mental health care.

The one thing these different types of advocacies have in common is a desired outcome of increasing positive perceptions and attitudes around mental health. The most successful advocacy efforts create strategies to influence those holding power to acknowledge equity for people living with mental health conditions. The discussion in this chapter will focus on legislative or public policy reform.

Discussion

Advocates have many tools at their disposal to bring about legislative and policy reforms depending on their level of comfort. First and foremost is becoming knowledgeable about the issue. Take for example the issue around developing the peer specialist workforce.

According to SAMHSA, workforce shortages are a key driver of the unmet need for behavioral health services—55 percent of counties in the United States do not have any practicing behavioral health workers. As a result, SAMHSA officials and other experts have called for using peer support specialists to help address shortages in the behavioral health workforce. To fill this need, the agency's Behavioral Health Workforce Report states the country needs 777,326 mental health peer support specialists. Yet that same report states there are only 23,507 peer support specialists available. (SAMHSA, 2021).

The next step is to understand barriers that contribute to the workforce shortage of state-certified peer specialists. Is it a state funding issue for education and training? Do you live in a state that has not chosen to bill the Center of Medicare and Medicaid Services for peer support services through its state Medicaid program?

Once you have identified a root cause, you can create a strategy to influence those who can bring about change. For example, could a solution be legislation that authorizes and provides funding to the state mental health department for increased training, or allows the state Medicaid program to bill for peer support services? Perhaps the solution resides with the executive branch that can directly influence the agency to make those changes.

Depending on your comfort level there are several options you can take to move your advocacy issue forward. The easiest one is to reach out to local, state, and national mental health organizations that include advocacy as part of their mission, such as the Depression and Bipolar Support Alliance (DBSA), or Mental Health America (MHA). Go to their website and read about the work they are doing around the issues that concern you. Register to receive advocacy communications from them. This will enable you to stay abreast of the issue and respond to action alerts. These alerts will provide you with step-by-step instructions on how you can lend your name in support of or opposition to a law or policy. The alert typically provides information about the issue and includes an easy-to-fill-out form that sends an email to the appropriate legislator or government official.

If you are comfortable being more public, you can write a letter to the editor of the news outlets in your area. In your letter identify the issue and why you think it is important that your elected officials take action in favor or against the issue.

As your confidence grows, you can schedule a meeting with your state representative or senator. Generally, you won't need to travel to your state capital to have that meeting. Most state representatives and senators have local offices. When you call the office, you might first speak to one of their aides. Tell them you would like to schedule a meeting with your legislator and why. If appropriate, tell them you represent the organization you are affiliated with, such as DBSA, MHA or NAMI. Before the meeting gather the facts around the issue and rehearse your conversation. You'll want to share with them why you are in favor of the policy or why you oppose it. While personal stories are valuable, it is important to not make the visit about you. Your lived experience provides context but should not be the focal point of your conversation. You'll want to be sure they understand you feel strongly about this issue because it benefits everyone in the mental health community, not just you. Finally, you'll want to conclude the meeting with a direct ask, such as, "Representative Smith, I am asking you to support funding for peers to enroll in peer specialist course work." Don't leave the meeting without an answer to your ask. "Mr. Smith, can we count on your support for this issue?" The answer might be "No." But better to know where your representative or senator stands on the issue.

Conclude your meeting with a "thank you" if the answer was "Yes." If the answer was "No," be sure to leave as friends. Graciously accept their position by stating, "While I don't agree with your position, I thank you for your time, and hope to have the opportunity to change your mind in the future."

Conclusion

Anyone can become involved in legislative and policy advocacy. If advocacy is new to you, start out small by learning about the issues that are important to you. Get involved with local mental health advocacy organizations and seek out mentors. You'll soon find that advocacy can be a fun, social way to build a community for yourself. As your confidence builds, you'll look back years later and recognize that you not only brought about change but made friends along the way and mentored others as they began their advocacy journey.

More Information

Depression and Bipolar Support Alliance: https://www.dbsalliance.org/
Mental Health America: https://mhanational.org/
National Alliance on Mental Illness: https://nami.org

References

SAMHSA Behavioral Health Workforce Report: https://annapoliscoalition. org/wp-content/uploads/2021/03/behavioral-health-workforce-report-SAMHSA-2.pdf

Terms defined- Medical Industrial Complex. Health Justice Commons. (n.d.). Retrieved February 9, 2022, from https://www.healthjusticecommons.org/terms-defined

SECTION 3: STRENGTH IN NUMBERS

Lori Ashcraft PhD
Director, Resilience Inc.

Patricia Blum Ph.D.
Vice President, Crestwood Behavioral Health

The *Strength in Numbers* protocol provides a creative and fun way of building team capacity by developing and exchanging personal and professional strengths. This deliberate engagement of strengths, both individual and collective strengths, can build strong, effective work teams of peers, or a blend of peers and other professionals.

Most of us who work in the behavioral health field have had the experience of working on teams that don't function very well, whether they are composed exclusively of peers, or peers blended with other professionals. There are several reasons for this common dilemma:

- Often there is not enough trust among team members to create a platform for honest communication and vulnerability.
- Sometimes there is competition among team members that precludes supporting each other's growth and successful delivery of a meaningful contribution.
- There are also times when team relationships are weak and unable to support the bonding that needs to take place for teams to function effectively.

These conditions keep teams from being creative and finding new ways to solve old problems.

The *Strength in Numbers* protocol is an effective approach to moving past the things that interfere with creative teamwork. The protocol was first developed as a process for helping participants who are ready for community living build social capital in order to have meaningful contributions to make, solidifying their value in their neighborhood. It was later used to help families create respectful and productive relationships in the interest of becoming a strong well-functioning family unit. Once we saw the effectiveness of the process, we adapted it for working teams to maximize the engagement of skills and contributions of each team member resulting in the development of meaningful and productive team relationships.

Discussion

The *Strength in Numbers* protocol provides a creative and fun way of building team capacity by developing and exchanging personal and professional strengths. This deliberate engagement of strengths, both individual and collective strengths, can build strong, effective work teams of peers, or a blend of peers and other professionals.

The process for embedding the *Strength in Numbers* protocol is presented in the form of a game, making it fun and less threatening for people to be vulnerable and truthful. The process focuses on building reciprocity and developing relationships that can sustain the rigors of daily problem solving and find new creative ways of addressing intractable problems that keep us from having optimal outcomes.

Peer team capacity is expanded and strengthened by recognizing and exchanging strengths in each other. Supervisors and coaches can easily capitalize on the process by pointing out strengths and providing accountability for staying on track, thus reinforcing team growth and development.

What is the outcome of using the *Strength in Numbers* game? Regardless of the players, the purpose is to learn and practice a smooth give-and-take process of reciprocity among team members. Team members learn to develop and embody their own strengths and to also rely on, and draw on, the strengths of others. This results in an interdependent network of ongoing natural supports that creates synergy—the whole being much more effective than the sum of the parts.

What are the consequences of using the *Strength in Numbers* protocol? Here's a brief summary to help you grasp the concept:

- Regardless of the players, the purpose is to learn a smooth give-and-take process, learning reciprocity in relationships

- Players learn to develop and own their strengths
- Players learn to rely on the strengths of others
- Interdependent network for ongoing natural supports is created

Table 1 below outlines the skills teams can learn, and even more important, can role-model for people in recovery, helping them learn, by example, how to create meaningful relationships that growth and healing can be transported upon. This type of reciprocity is key to building supportive mutual relationships.

1	Learn how to give in ways that make self and others stronger
2	Learn how to take in ways that appreciate the giver without creating dependency
3	Learn to ask for help without being clingy
4	Offer support to others while supporting their independence

Relationship is the first principle of peer support. it is the bridge that links our higher selves, in a healing partnership, with other team members and with the people in recovery. A relationship built on strengths, while not overlooking the painful aspects of life, creates the type of rapport necessary for learning and growing.

The *Strength in Numbers* approach is based on mutuality and the assurance that we both have something to give and receive. It teaches team members how to build strong connections and yet not become swamped with team problems —the team acknowledges the problems but they don't embody them. They stay connected without losing their own sense of self.

	Here are the first steps we take in order to get the game off to a good start.
1)	We begin by assessing our individual net worth much like we would if we went into a bank to ask for a loan. The banker will ask us for a list of our assets and also a list of our liabilities. Here we are not talking about financial issues but issues of social capital--what we have to offer our team in terms of skill, ability, and personality traits. Our liabilities are our areas that need further development--things we want to get better at doing.
	It takes a mature attitude to honestly and transparently complete our lists. We start by trying to be as honest as we can about our strengths and our areas needing development. We are willing to be vulnerable with each other which is a key principle of teamwork. Part of what we are building is a safe place to take risks and teachability.
2)	Next, we share our lists and ask for feedback from our team members. Have we left out strengths that others see in us? If so, we add them to our list. Have we listed areas of development that seem right to others? Are there strengths that others would like us to develop further? Make any changes we think will give a more accurate picture of our areas for development. Finally, we look to see if there are things we do that get in the way of being a great team player.
3)	Once each team member has their own list, we will build a joint account by putting our list together. We start by listing all the strengths of all team members and we ask if anything's missing. We move on to listing areas for team development. Are there new skills and abilities that need to be added to the team?

Now that we have an understanding of the team status, we are ready to put our "joint account" into action. We begin by asking the following questions and collectively agree on responses:

- How can we help each other develop our real and potential strengths more quickly?
- What agreements will we have for exchanging strengths?
- How can we use our strengths most effectively?

The final step includes creating ways to evaluate the team's progress. One of the ways to do this is to set team goals for recovery and resilient outcomes. The goals can include how well the team is functioning as well as outcomes the team hopes to achieve with those they serve. If the team is reaching their goals, we can assume they are working well together. If there are glitches and fallout, we know the team needs to go back and examine the way the team is working together.

Conclusion

Good teamwork focused on recovery and resilient oriented goals can make the difference between ordinary outcomes and amazing outcomes. The time and effort spent to get a team on track and keep it there is well spent, given the increase in positive outcomes.

CHAPTER 7
EFFORTS AT INCLUSION OF PEER SUPPORT INTO BEHAVIORAL HEALTH

CHAPTER INTRODUCTION BY THE EDITORS

INCLUSION OF PEER SUPPORT INTO BEHAVIORAL HEALTH SYSTEMS OF CARE HAS been an ongoing challenge. Originally peer services were offered informally through either community- based self-help support groups or through the efforts of peer run agencies. As the impact of peer support became more widely known, organizations moved to harness the benefits of peer support. After 2007 when peer support services became Medicaid reimbursable, the challenges of including peer support workers into systems of care were even more apparent. The literature is replete with the barriers and challenges to these efforts. In part these challenges arise from the difference in perspectives between non-peer professional staff and peer support workers. Earlier chapters have discussed the underlying values of peer support. The table below distills some of the challenges:

External or Organizational Challenges	Individual/PSW Practice Guideline Challenges
Lack of recovery orientation in work setting, medical model primary orientation	Recovery orientation: practice of shared power, reciprocity and mutuality
Emphasis on academic training	Lived experience
Lack of job description or clarity	Role confusion or ambiguity
Provider concerns about confidentiality, dual relationships, and role conflict	Role blurring; suppression of peer identity; concerns about cooptation
Absence of peer training or leadership	Role minimalization; disempowerment
Low wages and lack of career ladder	Perceived tokenism; job attrition
Negative staff attitudes	Perceived stigmatization
(Bennetts et al., 2013; Goodwin & Happell, 2013; Kemp & Henderson, 2012; Lawn, Smith & Hunter, 2008; Repper & Carter, 2011; Smith et al., 2016; Vandewalle et al., 2016).	

The readings included in this chapter suggest approaches that have been successful in promoting inclusion of peer support workers into existing behavioral health systems. In the first reading, Palluck suggests a process that prepares an organization for the role of the peer support worker. It has long been suggested that inclusion of peer support work is successful when there is total management and organizational understanding and support. This reading offers a creative step by step process to accomplish that goal. Next, Martin's reading highlights the importance of the peer support worker's responsibility for endearing themselves to the non-peer professionals with whom they work. Of course, it is a shared responsibility but each and every peer support worker can do their share. The instructional materials for this workshop which include, an interactive workbook and PowerPoint are available at the chapter's end. Finally, the reading by Ashcraft and Bernstein emphasizes the importance of a top- down, bottom-up process to include peer support workers in systems of care. The differences between the two helping paradigms (peer and professional) are explored, and then they focus on how service recipients as well as the whole behavioral health system benefit from the incorporation of peer support principles and practitioners into it. Assisting non-peer staff to recognize the value of role modeling recovery is often an important tipping point. These readings in their aggregate can help both peer support workers and the organizations which seek to include them to identify and address the barriers and challenges to inclusion.

SECTION 1: RESILIENCE ROAD MAP TO SUCCESSFUL
ORGANIZATIONAL INTEGRATION OF THE PEER ROLE

Scott Palluck, MA - Director of Operations Process Analysis
Crestwood Behavioral Health, Inc.

Successful integration of peers into the workforce can be challenging, but the rewards can be huge for an organization and for the people being served. Creating a "resilience road map" to support this integration process can result in reducing or eliminating the potential bumps in the road during this journey. Using the Resilience Action Planning process as part of your "road map" is one effective way an organization can successfully support the integration of peers into the workforce.

When you travel by car on a vacation....do you just jump into the car and start driving? If you do, it will likely result in numerous challenges within the first several hours. If you decide to drive from San Diego, California to Myrtle Beach, South Carolina – it is in your best interest to do some planning before you embark on such an adventure. You need to pack essential items that you will need for your road trip like, food, water, and extra clothing. In addition, it is also helpful to plot out the directions for navigating your journey and much more!! The same is true for integrating peers into the workforce. With the proper preparation, planning and information, this road map can lead your organization to accomplishing the goal of integrating peers into the workforce.

Discussion

If your organization is at the beginning of the peer role integration process, you may be asking the question – where do we start? It is a good idea to identify the framework that you will use to start creating a "map" for your journey. One such framework is called DCAS. That stands for Discover, Create, Activate and Sustain.

Discover

This is a team-based exploration of your organization's vision for the future related to integration of the peer role and the values that will support this vision. Remember, this is a team-based exploration – not a solo journey.

Ensure that you have representation from the various departments within your organization as you begin the exploration process. If you are having trouble identifying who should be a part of this process – consider developing an ART. An ART is an acronym for - Activate Resilience Team. The ART is comprised of a group of individuals that: 1) are in alignment with the integration of peers into your organization – as well as your mission and vision; 2) supports the use of recovery and resilience principles and philosophies; 3) will actively participate in meetings; 4) will act as a role model of integrity and accountability; 5) will promote quality in the execution of the plan; and 6) effectively communicates with the rest of the team. If you have an effective ART to support the integration of peers into your organization out of the gate – you are headed for success!!

Create

This is the Resilience Action Planning stage. A detailed plan – the Resilience Action Plan - will be developed to support the integration of the peer role into your organization and will have a compelling impact to move your organization toward their vision. The Resilience Action Plan is a "living-breathing" document that will continue to be updated and enhanced during the integration process. It is helpful to have your ART actively engaged in this process. You can certainly have others from your organization involved as well. Create a schedule that reflects that dates and times the Resilience Action Plan will be developed. This will support the development of a first draft of the Resilience Action Plan. Once you have created a working Resilience Action Plan, it is time to move to the next step.

Activate

This is the execution of the plan. Everyone will be empowered to participate in the plan's implementation and celebrate the success. Although your ART may be driving the plan, it is wise to get as many individuals involved in this process as possible. For example, if your Resilience Action Plan includes staff training – make sure ALL staff participate.

Sustain

The vision and values of integrating the peer role will become embedded into your organization's culture and practice. Your organization will learn during the *activate* phase and the new opportunities will support a level of accountability with the resilience to thrive.

During this journey, many organizations encounter some "bumps in the road" – which can often be avoided by using the DCAS framework. Some of the most common "bumps in the road" include:

- Not having a common definition of a peer within your organization. In my experience, an organization can easily say that everyone is on the same page regarding their understanding of the definition of a peer. After some exploration, often this is not the case at all. Try this. Take a quick survey by asking a variety of staff within your organization what they understand to be the definition of a peer. If you find that staff are not on the same page, here are a few things to consider: Create a clear definition of a peer for your organization; Create a Scope of Practice for the peer; Create job descriptions for programs supported by peers. The definition and scope of practice can remain the same ensuring that job tasks/requirements are specific to each program.
- Lack of awareness, knowledge or understanding of the peer role within your organization. In working with numerous counties and community-based mental health organizations, it often becomes evident that staff within an organization do not have an awareness of the peer role within an organization, and sometimes are not even aware that there is a plan in place to develop a peer workforce. If this is the case, here are a few recommendations:

1. Develop an organizational communication plan. Including a process to ensure that updates on peer initiatives or peers being hired is provided to staff – in a newsletter or emails to staff from the organization's CEO or other creative communication strategies.
2. Provide training to all existing staff. This is an important way to ensure that everyone within an organization – regardless of role – has an awareness and understanding of the peer role within your organization.
3. Provide information on the peer role during new hire orientation for ALL new staff. If you have successfully provided training to your existing staff, consistently providing this information regarding the peer role during new hire orientations will ensure that all staff are well-versed in the peer role at your organization.

- Lack of opportunities for peers in an organization. If you are on your journey of integrating peers into your organization, it is important to provide opportunities for growth and development. Remember, the DCAS framework…SUSTAIN. If you are not able to keep your peers on staff, consider conducting a Classification and Compensation Study. It is important that peer positions can meet an individual's financial needs. You can also create a peer classification series with the ability for advancement. And ensure that job descriptions reflect new peer positions.

Resilience Action Planning – what is it and how to use it.

As noted earlier, part of a solid framework is the "create" phase. During this time is when the actual planning takes place. The Resilience Action Plan is a detailed, "living-breathing" plan that you can use to guide your organization to successful integration of the peer role. Using the metaphor of a garden, the Resilience Action Planning process includes:

Here and Now Garden – Pause. During this phase of planning, you want to pause….to identify some strengths and what benefits your organization will gain from integrating the peer role. Strengths are definitely what you want to keep in your "garden."

Here and Now Garden – Letting Go. During this phase, you will identify what things you let go of that could get in the way of integrating the peer role into your organization? Try not to overlook this step!! It is extremely important to be able to focus on those aspects of the integration plan that will lead to your success. If there are things that you can let go of to increase your focus – do it!!

The Greenhouse. Now that you have let go of things that could get in the way of integrating the peer role into your organization, you should experience some freedom and healing. You are now in the perfect position to begin to identify the concrete goals that you would like to achieve.

The Resilience Garden. This is a critical part of the Resilience Action Planning process. This is where the very specific details of your plan are developed.

- For each goal, identify the actions steps that are necessary to achieve them.
- Identify your "gardeners"-the individuals who are responsible for completing each action step.

- When will your "garden" flourish? Meaning – what timeframe/dates do you expect to accomplish each action step?
- Identify what "weeds" may pop up and how will you eliminate them? This is an opportunity to explore what barriers may develop and create a "Plan B" so that your Resilience Action Plan is not derailed.
- How will you celebrate your beautiful garden…meaning, how will you celebrate your accomplishments? This is a very important step that should not be missed. When an organization is successful in integrating the peer role – it is worth a celebration!! Make sure you develop a plan that leads to celebrating your achievements!!

Although this process may sound very easy, to be successful using the Resilience Action Planning process – it requires a great deal of dedication from an organization to reach your goals.

New Findings: At Crestwood Behavioral Health, Inc., we used the DCAS framework and the Resilience Action Planning process to successfully implement an innovative pilot project called, the Peer Employment Learning Center (PELC). The PELC pilot project is designed to increase opportunities for residents in our Adult Residential Programs and Mental Health Rehabilitation Centers (MHRC) to participate in a rigorous 80-hour Peer Support Specialist training program and a 106-hour paid internship leading to employment opportunities in peer roles. This means that individuals receiving services in one Crestwood program, were trained, and then participated in an internship within another Crestwood program.

On January 20, 2022, the first PELC graduation took place at our San Diego campus. There were 18 graduates and many of these graduates are now transitioning from people being served to individuals providing peer support services at our campuses!! Click on the link to see a short video of the graduation ceremony. http://recoveryresiliencesolutions.com

This same pilot will now be rolled-out to four additional Crestwood Behavioral Health, Inc. campuses. This pilot project is a unique way of increasing the peer workforce at Crestwood. And, using the DCAS framework and the Resilience Action Planning process were primary tools that led to our success.

Conclusion

We know the positive impact that a peer workforce can have within an organization. Having some helpful tools to get you started will support your organization's success. By using a solid framework as a guide (DCAS) and the Resilience Action Planning process, you will not only put your plan in motion, but also steer your organization to the pathway of sustainability. Through the use of these tools on the road to integrate peers into the workforce, you will likely find that these tools can also be used to support other projects or initiatives within your organization. Enjoy your journey!!

More Information

Palluck, S. (2019). A resilience road map to successful organizational integration of the peer role. Presentation on October 23, 2019, at the N.A.P.S. Conference – San Diego, California

If you would like to download the instructional materials for this workshop which include, an interactive workbook and PowerPoint, visit our website at http://recoveryresiliencesolutions.com

References

Martin, C., Ashcraft, L. (2015) Peer support learning for the 21st century. Crestwood Behavioral Health, Inc. 4th edition.
Johnson/Ashcraft, Resilience Inc., 2015, Resilience Action Plan

SECTION 2: TERMS OF "ENPEERMENT"

Chris W. Martin, MA in Ed. & Ed. Counseling
Director of Learning and Performance I for Crestwood Behavioral Health, Inc.

Under what terms do our professional colleagues desire, embrace, and promote the inclusion of Peer Support Specialists on the team? What can we do to make our peer support services irresistible to our behavioral health team? If you want the answers to these questions and other related ones, then you'll really want to participate in the "Terms of Enpeerment" workshop.

This 90-minute fun, engaging, and value-added learning experience will prepare participants to develop a personal or team action plan for peer support inclusion in your program and organization.

The lively and interactive workshop starts with what the experts (that's every peer support specialist) already know and provides for collaborative sharing on lessons learned. The course identifies six myths held by some professional colleagues as a rationale for not including peer support specialists on the team. Participants will review ten bedazzling ways to enhance endearment of "enpeerment." And they'll learn in concrete terms how they, as peers, can take the leadership role toward transforming the program and organization with peer support inclusion. Finally, participants will draft an action plan to move forward the *terms of enpeerment* within their work environment.

Discussion

So Why Hasn't the System Engaged More Peer Support Specialists? - We can easily understand the value of an organization hiring people on the team who have the experience of "having been there" and who can share their recovery experience with others. Many of us have witnessed first-hand how peer support inspires recovery and increases the recovery outcomes for an organization. Some of us have even found our own path to recovery as a result of having connected with a Peer Support Specialist. Because of the effectiveness of peer support, thousands of Peer Support Specialists now work in peer run organizations and as members on integrated behavioral health teams across the U.S. and in other parts of the world. We've come a long way in the last 50 plus years. Yet, we haven't come far enough! Too many behavioral health agencies, crisis services, and psychiatric hospitals have too few Peer Support Specialists or none at all. Peer Support Specialists are rarely used on first responder teams, and very few of them are staff at general hospitals serving those with chronic health conditions such as cancer, cardiac issues, and diabetes complications, to name a few.

The French Connection - Sometimes when we look back into the past, we can uncover solutions we've forgotten. In the late 1700's, peer support was thriving as a treatment approach in at least one French asylum. In fact, the late 18th Century ushered in several progressive steps toward recovery in Europe that ultimately spread to the U.S. This brief era of mental health enlightenment was called "Moral Treatment." It started in France by Dr. Philippe Pinel who was hired for the position of chief physician at the Bicêtre Hospital in Paris. Pinel was to soon become inspired by the amazing work of a former patient, Jean Baptiste Pussin, who had become the governor (superintendent) of the Bicêtre Hospital in Paris. Pussin through his own "having been there" experience had a kind and compassionate approach with patients. As a result of his *peer approach*, he successfully eliminated all the chains and shackles of patients who had been previously seen as violent and dangerous. (Martin & Ashcraft, 2015).

In a 1793 letter to his director, Dr. Pinel had asked Pussin to provide background on how the hospital was running prior to his arrival. Pussin wrote him a letter detailing his recruitment and hiring strategy for the hospital. "As much as possible, all servants are chosen from the category of mental patients. They are at any rate better suited to this demanding work because they are usually more gentle, honest, and humane" (Davidson, et al, 2012). This was the first documented example of people with a lived recovery experience being hired to support the recovery of people with mental illness, i.e., the very first…" *Peer Support Specialists* (Davidson, et al, 2010).

"In addition to being "gentle, honest, and humane", Pinel found these former patients recruited by Pussin to be "averse from active cruelty" (which was a common management strategy in the asylums of the day) and "disposed to kindness" toward the patients in their care. It was then to a significant degree through the hiring and deployment of such staff that Pinel and Pussin were able to do away with shackles and abuse…."3 Now, these were some wonderful recovery outcomes!

Endearment Can Lead to "Enpeerment"- When it comes to hiring Peer Support Specialists in adequate numbers, what we need today is a little *French twist* ourselves. Can you imagine what it could mean for recovery outcomes if we could staff a critical mass of Peer Support Specialists in our behavioral health organizations, crisis services, and hospitals? It would mean that we would not only see recovery outcomes increase, but we would experience the organizations and system becoming more recovery oriented. In order to make this transformation happen, we still need to engage in system and organizational advocacy to promote and hire more Peer Support Specialists. But we as Peer Support Specialists can also make headway by raising the endearment level that our colleagues have for us. When we do that, we'll know we've shifted the environment to *Terms of "Enpeerment."*

More Information

If you would like to download the instructional materials for this workshop which include, an interactive workbook and PowerPoint, visit our website at http://recoveryresiliencesolutions.com

Resources

12 Principles of Servant Leadership: Larry Spears, CEO of the Greenleaf

Center for Servant Leadership; retrieved from http://library.nsuok.edu/admin/minutes/servantleadership.pdf

Shlain, T. & Let It Ripple Studio. (2015, Oct. 8) *The Adaptable Mind*. (Video) YouTube. https://www.youtube.com/watch?v=937iCwJd3fI&t=5s

Shlain, T. & Let It Ripple Studio. (2012, Sept. 19) Engage: A New Cloud Film from the Let It Ripple Studios. (Video) YouTube. https://www.youtube.com/watch?v=jLjcuDDTUTo&t=7s

References

Davidson L., Bellamy, C., Guy, K., Miller, R. (2012) Peer support among persons with severe mental illnesses: a review of evidence and experience; World Psychiatry. (11)2, 123-128.
Davidson L., Raakfeldt J., Strauss JS. (2010). The roots of the recovery movement in psychiatry: lessons learned. Chichester, West Sussex, UK: John Wiley and Sons Ltd.
Martin, C., Ashcraft, L. (2015) Peer support learning for the 21st century. Crestwood Behavioral Health, Inc. 4th edition.
Weiner, D.B. (1979). "The Apprenticeship of Philippe Pinel: A New Document, 'Observations of Citizen Pussin on the Insane,'" 136 (1979): 1128-1134

SECTION 3: MANAGING PARTNERSHIPS WITH PEER SUPPORTERS IN THE WORKPLACE

Lori Ashcraft, PhD,
Director, Resilience, Inc.

Andy Bernstein, PhD, CPRP, Clinical Professor,
University of Arizona College of Medicine, Department of Family and Community Medicine, Psychologist in Independent Practice

This narrative is a summary of material which was prepared for and also generated interactively during a morning session at the 10th Annual iNAPS Conference in Philadelphia, on August 28, 2016. The original presenters were the two co-authors (Ashcraft and Bernstein) and two guest speakers, Chris Cline, MD, and Ken Minkoff, MD, who were presenting with us as the princi-

162

pals of Zia Partners Consulting, Inc. Our plan was to review how peers have been moving into the workplace as helping professionals in their own right, and then to identify some of the challenges which have arisen with this workforce change.

Since the core values and key practices of peer supporters differ from those of more traditionally- and clinically-trained professional helpers, we chose to highlight some of the differences between these two helping paradigms, and then focus on how service recipients as well as the whole behavioral health system benefit from the incorporation of peer support principles and practitioners into it. Finally, we wanted to offer our own suggestions and tap participants' knowledge and wisdom around creating and maintaining synergistic partnerships which integrate peer support into organizations which are attempting to blend the two models.

While peer support is arguably older by several millennia than any professional helping model, it is only in recent years that behavioral health settings have begun to utilize peers specifically to bring their own lived experience and recovery narratives to help clients/patients/service recipients move forward in their own journeys of recovery and healing.

The recovery movement—both in addiction and in mental health—has contributed to this phenomenon, and we see several forms of this throughout the public behavioral health systems during the 1970's and 1980's. In some instances, people with lived experience of receiving psychiatric services (i.e., consumers/survivors/ex-patients) developed and staffed their own "consumer-operated service" agencies, eschewing the more traditional helping professions. At the same time, some traditionally-staffed agencies simply caught on to the benefits of hiring peer support specialists, though formal job titles were--and still are--quite varied, including such names as recovery coaches, health navigators, peer counselors, etc.

The results of these efforts depended on numerous factors which we'll address shortly, but a third model was exemplified by organizations which effectively integrated peer support concepts and actual leadership, simultaneously employing some traditionally-trained staff to perform functions which fell outside the purview of peer support but also hewing true in their policies and procedures to the ethical principles and practices of peer support.

As a theoretical framework, let's look at two very distinct models of helping—the pure mutual help paradigm and the professional help paradigm (see Table 1, below). The former is exemplified in its most pure form by self-help groups such as A.A. or N.A., and the latter shows up in almost all of the formal mental health agencies and professions, such as psychology, social work, counseling, and psychiatry.

Table 1. Mutual Help and Professional Help Paradigms

Professional Help	Mutual Help (in pure form)
Book knowledge	Experiential knowledge
Expertise defined by formal education and credentials	Expertise defined by lived experience
Provided in exchange for money	Provided for the love of helping
Uni-directional accountability	Bi-directional accountability
Clear boundaries and fixed roles	Flexible boundaries and roles
Power rigidly defined *a priori*	Power loosely defined situationally
Externally regulated	Un-regulated

(Bernstein, et al., 2009)

Clearly, when peer supporters are hired as employees by an agency and paid a salary to do their work, a number of the mutual help elements either disappear or are significantly diluted, and the result is a kind of hybrid model which incorporates elements of both paradigms. While the benefits of offering peer support to people working through their own recovery are generally acknowledged by now--as evidenced by peer support being recognized as an emerging best practice--integrating peer supporters into formal agency work presents challenges for everyone involved. The rest of this chapter will address the benefits both to individuals and to the system of employing peer supporters, some of the ways in which the resulting challenges can be overcome, and strategies for developing and maintaining effective partnerships between peer support staff and non-peer colleagues.

Discussion

Let's start with a quick look at what are the core ethical and practice guidelines of the peer support profession as developed via a national survey in 2013 by the *International Association of Peer Supporters*, now the *National Association of Peer Supporters* (See Table 2, below). There was an extraordinary degree of agreement among the over 1000 survey respondents, and these National Guidelines have been adopted as the basis for peer support training throughout the United States.

Table 2: Ethical and Practice Guidelines for the Peer Support Profession

Peer Support Is:	And therefore, in practice, peer supporters:
1. Voluntary	Support choice
2. Hopeful	Share hope
3. Open minded	Withhold judgment about others
4. Empathic	Listen with emotional sensitivity
5. Respectful	Be curious and embrace diversity
6. Facilitative of change	Educate and advocate
7. Honest and direct	Address difficult issues with caring and compassion
8. Mutual and reciprocal	Encourage peers to give and receive
9. Equally shared power	Embody equality
10. Strengths focused	See what's strong not what's wrong
11. Transparent	Set clear expectations and use plain language
12. Person driven	Focus on the person, not the problems
* Adapted from National Practice Guidelines for Peer Supporters (NAPS, 2019).	

Next, we'll look at the rationale for adding peers to the staffs of behavioral health programs, and some ways to ensure that this transition is successful.

The practice of adding peers to the workforce can be a win/win/win proposition if care is taken to prepare both the peers and the workplace which they are entering. The first win is related to peers' own recovery process. Having a meaningful job strengthens and expands the peer's own recovery.

The second win is gained is by the person receiving services from the peer. Peers sharing their own personal experience of recovery gives hope for, *"If you can do it, maybe I can too."* The mutual stance and the recovery-oriented approach often succeeds where other approaches have failed.

The third win is the organization employing peers and the whole behavioral system: having peers on the team promotes new hope and high expectations, as staff work alongside people in recovery and learn from them. Also, having peers present as colleagues minimizes systemic and professional stigma. Partnering with peers moves the organization from having a "mental patient" orientation to becoming a community of colleagues, thus expanding the organizational vision for recovery and resilience.

Table 3. Benefits to Agencies and to the System of Adding Peers to the Workforce

- Peer support workers can create an immediate connection with the people they serve
- Peer support workers that are well trained know how to use their story and lived experience to inspire hope in the people they serve
- Peer support workers can help build a bridge to assist in engagement with the other providers on the treatment team
- Peer support workers can bring a different perspective to other team members during team meetings
- Peer support workers can role-model healthy relationships that people can replicate in the community by being trustworthy and supportive in an intentional relationship
- Peer support workers on the team help everyone remember that people recover: They are the evidence
- Peer support workers demonstrate to family members and other supporters that their loved one can recover
- Peer support workers help support the use of recovery language, and minimize the use of labels and diagnoses that can unfortunately become a person's overriding status
- Peer support workers, through the depth and breadth of their own experiences, have given all of us a better understanding of what it really takes to support others in the recovery process

How then do we add peers to the workforce in ways that bring about successful outcomes and lead to healthy, productive partnerships? The first and most important step is to invest in solid peer training. Sometimes there is a temptation to rush past this step, offering minimal training to save time and money. However, it quickly becomes apparent that inadequate or absent peer training leads to failure on the part of the organization trying to add peers to the workforce and often a demoralization of the peers themselves. A well designed 80-hour training plus a meaningful internship will get peers off to a good start, and will minimize problems when peers join the workforce with other professionals.

A second critical step is to have clear job descriptions for peers and ongoing support and guidance on how to function as part of a team. In the early days of peer employment, peers were sometimes left to try and figure out what to do, and often felt lost. With little or no direction on how to be part of a team or how to work in tandem with other professionals, missteps were often made, and this eroded the peer's sense of personal competence and efficacy as well as the receiving team's view of what peers could bring to the workplace. We learned that having clear job descriptions and expectations on teamwork is vital to creating a peer friendly workplace.

And a key to this which results in that win/win/win result is in the hands of the peer supervisor. There are many ways to stack the deck so that the supervisory relationship works well, and one way is what we call the *Resilience Coaching Method**. This coaching method begins with the peer creating their own professional development plan with the support of the peer supervisor, and consists of four elements: vision, action, sustaining, and celebrating.

Table 4, below, lists the points that can be included in what we call the Professional Resilient Employee Plan (PREP):

VISION	What are my hopes and dreams for my present job?
	What specific areas of my performance will help me reach my hopes and dreams?
ACTION	What plan of action will it take?
	What new skills will I need to develop?
	What are the things I can do on a regular basis to help me consistently practice my new skills?
	How can I use my past successful experiences to develop new skills?
	What supports do I want my coach to provide so I can develop new patterns and approaches?
SUSTAINING	How will I know if I'm starting to slip?
	What new things will I need to keep from slipping back into old patterns when under pressure?
	What will I do to use my resilience and get back on track?
CELEBRATING	How will I know when I have reached my goals?
	What are some ways I can celebrate my success?

Once the plan is agreed upon, the supervisor supports the peer in completing their work in ways that fulfill the goals of the plan. This is a bottom-up process, planned by the peer, and supported by the supervisor. Adjustments are made if some points need different supports or learning experiences to be carried out successfully. Supervisors who coach peers need training in what peers are capable of; they need to learn how to motivate and coach them to make their best contribution. Supervisor training needs to include ways to reach agreement on problem solving methods so there is alignment on enhancing strengths and also on making corrections in practices. The supervisor and the peer work together to be accountable for professional growth on both their parts.

In the early days of peer employment, we had many opportunities to learn from our mistakes. Now we know there are a few fail-safe steps we can take to create a successful peer workforce. One of these, for example, is to offer peers the option of having part-time jobs for their initial employment experience. This creates an easy startup, lowering the stress of moving from unemployment to full-time work. Once the peer is comfortable with part-time employment, they can amp up the number of hours they work to full-time if they so desire.

Another step which should be taken is to provide continuing education, similarly to how CE is provided to and required of other professionals. This allows peers to stay current with new recovery practices and to grow both in their personal and their professional roles. Peers also need opportunities for advancement, and this calls for the development of career ladders that give peers the hope and incentive of moving to more advanced levels of work when they are ready for it. It's also helpful to encourage peers to join professional associations (e.g., N.A.P.S. and PRA) so they have opportunities to learn what other peers are doing and to experience themselves as part of a larger community of practice, much more extensive than just at their own place of employment or even in their own geographic region.

Once peers are adequately trained and supervised, the rest of the organization needs to step up and be ready to collaborate in meaningful and effective ways with peer employees. This is a critical step in the development of a blended workforce, and can be thought of as *"workplace development."* When other professionals are not prepared to accept and integrate the gifts that peers bring, or worse, when they persist in having stigmatizing attitudes towards people in recovery, the result can be peers leaving their jobs, sadly and cruelly confirming some of the negative beliefs held about them by unenlightened non-peers.

In addition to front-line co-workers and supervisors, staff in departments of human resources and agency administrators need to be educated in ways which peers add value to their organizations, and this sometimes means unlearning the stereotypes and stigmatizing beliefs which ironically and all too often are held by people in the mental health field. Experiential workshops and retreats can accomplish this, but they require careful planning and execution in order to comport with a particular agency's culture and staff composition.

In general, however, it's critical for non-peer staff to see their peer colleagues as successful in their own recovery, and to have knowledge about the peer role, what peers are trained to do, and what is not appropriate for them to be asked to do, such as serve as drivers or medication compliance monitors. And perhaps most important, they need to see how the role-modeling effect that peers have on service recipients can increase their motivation and sense of hope regarding their own recovery, thus supporting the efforts of non-peer providers when they do their own work competently and compassionately.

Conclusion

It should be clear by now, especially since this chapter is being written in 2022, how much benefit accrues to everyone involved in behavioral health services when peers are effectively brought on board and successfully integrated into treatment teams. Research which has been done on the impact of peer support—both in traditional clinical settings and in peer-operated service environments--confirms these benefits, especially to service recipients. But the evolution of peer support as a discipline in its own right has had other consequences, not only to these systems which care for people working through mental health challenges, but also to those of us who cannot call ourselves peers, because whatever challenges we faced in our lives--or treatment which we sought--did not stigmatize, marginalize, or derail us, did not interrupt our journeys to self-actualization. Getting to know and work side by side with people who were successfully meeting those challenges allowed us to see them in much more human terms, and conversely to see and accept ourselves as humans on the same continua, with the same vulnerabilities, faults, strengths and potentials that they have.

For me (Bernstein), that meant becoming more comfortable in my own humanness, and becoming more willing to share that with the people I was seeing in my professional role as a psychotherapist. I took a more personally disclosive stance when I thought it might increase the level of trust that my own clients/service recipients would have in me and in our interactions, identifying peerness in realms other than just whether we both had been consumers of mental health services. These could include social and familial roles, ways of looking at the world and universe and even physical and mental health itself.

With the concept of peerness thus expanded in my work, I found a kind of recalibration taking place in the power dynamics of my helping relationships, and I believe that many of the people with whom I worked became empowered in the process. I know of other "non-peers" in the behavioral health field who have had similar experiences; this is an area which I believe warrants further investigation. In the meantime, let us agree that bringing people who have received mental health services into roles where they can provide those services to others has started an important change process in how people help each other, and all of us are better for it.

For More Information

Palluck, S. (2019). A resilience road map to successful organizational integration of the peer role. Presentation on October 23, 2019, at the N.A.P.S. Conference – San Diego, California
If you would like to download the instructional materials for this workshop which include, an interactive workbook and PowerPoint, visit our website at http://recoveryresiliencesolutions.com

References

Bernstein, A.D., Swarbrick, M, & Banes, J. (2009, June 20). Professional and Mutual-Help Paradigm Tension in Serving People with Serious and Persistent Mental Illnesses. SCRA 2009 Biennial Conference, Montclair, NJ.

Davidson L., Bellamy, C., Guy, K., Miller, R. (2012) Peer support among persons with severe mental illnesses: a review of evidence and experience; World Psychiatry. (11)2, 123-128.

Davidson L., Raakfeldt J., Strauss JS. (2010). The roots of the recovery movement in psychiatry: lessons learned. Chichester, West Sussex, UK: John Wiley and Sons.
Johnson/Ashcraft, Resilience Inc., 2015, Resilience Action Plan

Martin, C., Ashcraft, L. (2015) Peer support learning for the 21st century. Crestwood Behavioral Health, Inc. 4th edition.
National Association of Peer Supporters (2019). National Practice Guidelines for Peer Specialists and Supervisors. Washington, DC: N.A.P.S. https://www.peersupportworks.org/wp-content/uploads/2021/07/National-Practice-Guidelines-for-Peer-Specialists-and-Supervisors-1.pdf

Weiner, D.B. (1979). "The Apprenticeship of Philippe Pinel: A New Document, 'Observations of Citizen Pussin on the Insane,'" 136 (1979): 1128-1134

Part 3: The Practice of Peer Support

Chapter 8: Advice from Communities of Practice

- Chapter Introduction by the Editors
- Section 1: Overcoming Our Fears as Peer Supporters
- Section 2: Peer Specialists as Human Rights Officers
- Section 3: Conflict Resolution Skills for Peer Specialists
- Section 4: Vocational Peer Support
- Section 5: Human Resources Practices for Growing and Sustaining the Peer Workforce
- Section 6: Toward an Effective Peer Support Workforce: Integrating Research and Practice

Chapter 9: What Helps What Hinders

- Chapter Introduction by the Editors
- Section 1: Career Chat: Sharing Tips and Strategies for Pursuing Professional Development and Personal Goals through Education and Life Experience
- Section 2: At the Margins of Marginalization and Peer Support
- Section 3: Addressing Spiritual Concerns in Peer Support Settings
- Section 4: Building Bounce-Back Families

CHAPTER 8
ADVICE FROM COMMUNITIES OF PRACTICE

CHAPTER INTRODUCTION BY THE EDITORS

THE VALUES OF PEER SUPPORT CALL FOR, AMONG OTHER THINGS, TRANSPARENCY, mutuality, and a constant belief in collaboration. This book reflects our attempt to join with our fellow peer supporters to bring to the reader the experiences, strength and knowledge derived from the vast community of peer support workers and supervisors. Learning collaboratives, communities of practice, and educational networking are ways to continue to inform and expand the practice of peer support. Continuing to learn and grow personally and professionally is often accomplished with the assistance and support of others. This chapter offers you previously presented knowledge and wisdom about various aspects of peer support that has been presented at various conferences

In the first reading, Sunderland and Peek tackle a common experience for peer supporters entering the workforce: fear. We question ourselves, our journey, our abilities. This reading discusses these fears and offers some useful tips and strategies.

In the second reading, Woodhouse, et al., tackle an oft underappreciated role of many peer supporters. As advocates with a particular point of view, the rights of those we are supporting often take front and center in our concerns. This reading discusses the formal role of Human Rights Officers as they address violations that are directly Page 2 of 68 observed and reported. It suggests all our responsibility as advocates to protect the rights of our peers.

The third reading addresses another topic that often does not get the attention it deserves. Peer supporters are as diverse as any other profession. In that diversity can come misunderstandings and conflict. Berstein offers suggestions on how to deal with conflict.

The fourth reading by Legere speaks to what is required to offer vocational peer support. It can be a specialty certification. For the majority of peers, work of some kind is an important part of recovery. This reading presents helpful information for those who want to bring focused employment, career, and educational supports to people within or beyond behavioral health services.

Finally, Wolf addresses the topic of human resources. The two readings consider evidence-based Human Resources approaches to recruiting, training, and retaining peer support workers with lived experience. They also identify essential organizational leadership and culture, together with knowledgeable human resources departments, competent supervision, and clear peer support worker job descriptions that together successfully support and retain peer supporters in the workforce.

Section 1: Overcoming Our Fears as Peer Supporters

Kim Sunderland, Peer Support Consultant

Hayley Peek, Mental Health Consultant

It is common for peer supporters to experience their own fears and insecurities in relation to being able to offer quality peer support. These fears exist for those of us who are new to the role as well as for those who have been doing the work for years. Fear can challenge our ability to connect empathetically and to inspire hope in an open-minded and authentic manner. Therefore, fears warrant of our attention. Even when we know we are capable of something, our fears can get the best of us and prevent us from achieving our full capabilities.

Acknowledging our fears and knowing that we are not alone in experiencing them is a valuable first step. This paper will offer simple practices to help us begin to notice when we may be experiencing uncomfortable emotions. Practical exercises to help manage the impact of fears will also be provided, in an effort to strengthen our ability to offer peer support in a healthy and sustainable manner.

As peer supporters, we have experienced our own recovery journeys; in fact, these journeys of self-awareness and day-to-day learning continue through life. Throughout our unique journeys of recovery, we have developed a greater sense of awareness with our emotions, including our emotional reactions. Emotions are human and often occur deep down in our subconscious. This can make it difficult for us to process them and self-regulate since we can be impacted by an emotion even before we are aware that we are reacting. Even though some emotions can be more uncomfortable to experience than others, it's important to remember that there are no 'bad' emotions. As humans we can expect to experience the full breadth of emotions as we move through life. The goal is to recognize and work with the uncomfortable emotions as they occur so we can minimize the amount of time we spend with them as well as the impact they might have on us and our actions. This takes practice but is a worthwhile goal to strive towards.

This discussion is focused on the emotion of *fear* (and its various iterations including feelings of worry, insecurity, insignificance, and overwhelm) in relation to our roles as peer supporters.

Discussion

The identified fears, shared by peer supporters over several years of workshops, include ones such as:

- "I might say or do the wrong thing / not be helpful or make it worse"
- "I might become impatient or judgmental / I might lose hope for another's recovery"
- "The person I am supporting may attempt suicide"
- "I might be triggered or retraumatized / become too busy or overwhelmed"
- "If others knew of my fears, they might lose faith in my peer support abilities"

TAKING the time to acknowledge that you may share some of these fears is of value (and a practice of self-awareness). Consider taking a moment to reflect on what you might add to the list based on your experience.

When we do this exercise, we notice that fears exist for both new and experienced peer supporters. Noticing that fears like these are shared among

176

all members of our community reminds us that we are not alone in experiencing them. Fears and concerns can change over time which is why it is important to continue to reflect on them. By reflecting with an open mind, we may choose to adjust our approach to working with the fears that we experience.

Developing strength and resilience to manage your fears can support you throughout your workday; this is something to be recognized and celebrated. However, it is also important for your mental wellness and your professional development to take the time to reflect on what may be happening under the surface.

If we were together in this discussion, each of you would be asked to share helpful insights on how to notice when a fear-based thought may be impacting our confidence and behavior. One approach that we would offer as an option is to carry a small slip of paper with you as you go through your day, marking every time you notice your inner critic talking to you in a judgmental, critical, or fearful manner. The more times you notice, the more credit you can give yourself for having a strong self-awareness practice. Becoming more aware of those times that we are saying to ourselves, *"I'm afraid I'm going to make this worse"* or *"I don't think I can do this the way others are expecting me to do it"* can be enlightening as it shows us that fear is present. When fear (rather than calm or confidence) is influencing our thoughts and emotions, we are more likely to become self-centered and in turn have less empathy or hope, making it more challenging to be present in our peer support interactions.

Another suggested approach for working with fear is to identify what is in our control and what is out of our control. We suggest the teachings and wisdom brought forward by Dr. Nicole LePera as a resource in reflecting on what we can have impact on compared to what we cannot. For example, we can work towards managing or adjusting our own emotional state, verbal responses, and meanings that we attach to a situation. Those are all things within our control; we cannot however control another person's emotional state, verbal or behavior responses, or their interpretation of a situation. We can strive to communicate clearly and objectively so that others feel safe in our presence; we cannot control another person's communication style or choices.

An example specific to peer support might be if we feel like we have said or done something that is not helpful, possibly due to our own impatience or loss of hope. We can control the way we move forward by acknowledging our misstep, apologizing if they found it upsetting or insensitive, and asking what they may find more helpful.

Another example might be if we are triggered (having a strong emotional reaction) to something another person shared with us. Although we cannot always control our natural reactions, we can control how we handle it after the fact. This can be done by calmly discussing our reaction with the person and acknowledging that sometimes things can impact us in ways we didn't expect. It is also in our control to decide if it is wise for our own health to continue supporting this person or if we are both better served with suggesting another peer supporter who is better suited to step in to provide support.

I CAN HAVE IMPACT ON (WORK ON):	I CANNOT CONTROL:
My emotional state and verbal or behavioral responses	Another person's emotional state and verbal or behavioral responses
The meaning I attach to a situation	Another person's interpretation of a situation
Communicating clearly and objectively so the other person feels safe and able to express fully	Another person's communication choices
Setting and maintaining clear personal boundaries	Another person's reaction or response to my boundaries
	Source: Adapted from LaPera, Nicole, 2021.

Compassion for both ourselves and others should accompany this practice. Criticizing ourselves if we didn't manage to 'control' an emotional outburst or if we slipped and crossed a personal boundary is not helpful to our growth and development. Treating ourselves with understanding, kindness, and compassion when we notice slip-ups, helps us to feel more empowered to try again. It allows us to embrace mistakes as a critical part of the growing process; it is possible to be accountable to yourself while remaining in compassion.

An additional strategy for managing fear and other uncomfortable emotions is to be proactive by learning new information and/or skills. Ongoing learning is critical for both newcomers to peer support and for those with experience in the field to reinforce our skills. There is value in continued learning around topics such as applying trauma-informed practices or suicide intervention strategies, just to name a few. This can support us in feeling more prepared and empowered for handling difficult situations. *In what area do you feel that additional training may help you to feel more confident and capable?*

Peer support is not only something we can offer to others; we often require it ourselves. Take time to reflect on who you can reach out to when you feel the need for support, whether that's to debrief, reflect, or brainstorm – or just to have fun. Our needs are constantly changing as we progress through life. Our supports (including therapy or other clinical needs) also adjust as we learn, grow, and experience diversity in our peer support connections. It is wise for us to reflect on this to ensure that we have others in our community who 'get it' when we need to talk about our fears, concerns and challenges. *Do you feel that it would be helpful to have other resources (possibly different types of resources) available to you for when you require support?*

As we work with our fears, we may notice that with some fears it is wise that we honor their impact by creating a personal boundary for the sake of our own wellness. If there is something that is harmful for us to work with at this point in our recovery (or ever), then it may require attention. Confide in a trusted friend or supporter to consider if it is wise for you to set a boundary and find compassionate, yet firm ways, to maintain that boundary. Setting and maintaining a personal boundary can be done in a compassionate manner; this is an example of strong role-modeling. *Are there any situations in your peer support relationships or in your personal life that might be causing you excessive overwhelm or to be emotionally unwell? Would it be appropriate to discuss this with a trusted friend to determine if a boundary would be helpful so you can continue to work in this role in a healthy and sustainable manner?*

Conclusion

Working in peer support can be both rewarding and challenging. As individuals with lived experience, it is critical for us to maintain our mental wellness as our top priority to ensure we remain in a strong place of recovery and to continue providing quality peer support in a sustainable manner. When fears such as insecurity, overwhelm or inadequacy are present in our subconscious, it can impact our ability to remain empathetic, authentic, and hopeful in our peer support connections.

There will always be room for growth and learning in our work, especially with our self-awareness. Being able to notice, name and explore our fears can help us long term with both personal growth and professional development. It's natural to have fears, no matter how long we have been working in peer support; we are human.

This paper proposes practical exercises to help you to overcome the negative impact that your fears may be having on you. As you consider implementing some of these practices, we encourage you to do so from a place of understanding, kindness and self-compassion.

Clarifying what is within our realm of control versus what is not, can be helpful for balancing where we spend our energy. Letting go of our desire to control the thoughts or reactions of others allows us more room to focus on how we want to show up in our relationships as our most authentic selves.

Remaining open to ongoing learning supports us in becoming well rounded peer supporters and sharpens our skill sets. It helps us feel more capable to face diverse situations, reduces fear, and strengthens our individual resilience.

Caring for our own wellness is of primary importance in becoming and remaining a strong peer supporter. It's critical to pay attention to the supports we have in place for ourselves, including ensuring that we have relationships with trusted individuals who we can debrief, confide, and strategize with.

Finally, as we consider how to support our own wellness, setting and maintaining compassionate boundaries where necessary plays an important role. Much like fears, boundaries can shift and change over time. Identifying where a boundary is helpful will support us in continuing our work in a healthy and sustainable manner.

Fears are a natural part of our human experience and at times can be challenging to work through. However, taking the time to identify what is impacting us can help us reflect on how to work through our fears and minimize the impact they can have.

More Information

www.KimSunderland.ca
www.HayleyPeek.com
www.SupportingThroughStruggle.com

References

LaPera, N (2021). How To Do The Work: Recognise Your Patterns, Heal From Your Past, and Create Your Self. Orion Spring, London.

Sunderland, Kim, Mishkin, Wendy, Peer Leadership Group, Mental Health Commission of Canada. (2013). Guidelines for the Practice and Training of Peer Support. Calgary, AB: Mental Health Commission of Canada. Retrieved from: http://www.mentalhealthcommission.ca

Section 2: Peer Specialists as Human Rights Officers

Robyn Woodhouse, Human Rights Coordinator

Michelle Love CPS

Nicole MacAskill-Kaylie

Ashley Sproul CPS

The Human Rights apparatus for Advocates Behavioral Health Residential Services (BH Res) has evolved over time and is currently structured to have Peer Specialists assume the role of Human Rights Officers (HROs). The dual relationship of having a direct service staff functioning as an HRO for a program in which they work poses a potential barrier to identifying and reporting human rights concerns or violations. The benefits of having a Peer Specialist with lived experience as the HRO for the programs we operate are increased mutuality, a significant reduction in the power differential, and minimal risk of a conflict of interest that would compromise the process. This opens the door to honest conversations about the human rights concerns of those we support as well as greater likelihood that Human Rights violations are directly observed and reported.

Prior to 2008, there was no full-time, designated person who worked as the Human Rights Coordinator of BH Res Services at Advocates. During that period, volunteers from the Senior Management team would take on the tasks related to the oversight of our Human Rights Officers and the operation of Human Rights Committee. In 2008, the first full-time, dedicated Human Rights Coordinator was hired, and direct service program staff continued to function as program HROs. Assigning staff who work in the programs to hold the responsibility for monitoring human rights, assisting people we support to file complaints (often on their colleague or supervisor) and educating the staff and the people served in the program about human rights was not effective or even ethical. It was not consistent with our commitment to support the autonomy of the people we serve, nor our commitment to provide assistance with each person's recovery.

The monthly Human Rights Committee meetings did not meet the Department of Mental Health (DMH) requirements for membership that requires an attorney, community members, and people receiving services to be voting members of the Committee. We began to have conversations regarding how to make changes, as it was essential that program and clinical staff understand that self-determination and recovery are not possible without a strong focus on human rights. In 2013, the Vice President of Peer Support and Self-Advocacy, the Human Rights Coordinator, and the Client Advisory Board all agreed that Peer Specialists should take on the role of HROs.

Discussion

Between 2013 and 2017, the human rights process at Advocates was improved to better identify violations while increasing opportunities for staff and people using services to be provided with more education about human rights. A Human Rights 101 training was developed and put online to create easier access for staff and persons supported. A 72-hour orientation training was also created for newly hired direct service staff and residents within 72 hours of moving into a program.

In 2017, BH Res Services began to implement a new process where clinical program staff are required to write and present Restrictive Plans and Staff Action Plans (SAPs) to the Human Rights Committee before they can be put into action. A Restrictive Plan is written by clinical staff when supporting a person who is engaging in behaviors that pose imminent risk to their health and safety, when all other less restrictive interventions have been exhausted.

The most common example is when staff are working to support someone who habitually smokes inside the program and does so unsafely. Smoking indoors is prohibited in both the Service Agreement residents sign before moving in, and their occupancy agreement, as there is a serious risk of fire. When staff are creating any sort of restrictive plan, they are expected to involve the person about whom the plan is being developed and solicit consultation form the Human Rights Coordinator and the Peer Specialist HRO.

It is a firm expectation that the steps the person would have to take to eventually eliminate the need for the restriction are spelled out clearly in the plan; all other interventions that have been tried are documented, and there is an identified review period that is as short as possible. Once a plan is completed, the clinician must attend the next Human Rights Committee meeting and present the plan for review. The Human Rights Committee will have the opportunity to ask questions, provide feedback, make recommendations and even request amendments. The Committee then votes to either pass the plan as is, with recommended amendments, or not pass the plan. Staff are also instructed to ask the subject of the plan if they would also like to attend the Human Rights Committee meeting to share their perspective, adhering to the "Nothing About Us Without Us" Peer Support principle. Staff Action Plans are similar in that they are designed to target specific behaviors that a person may be struggling with, but the SAP is designed for staff to have a plan for addressing the behaviors that cause concern. SAPs are only enacted when collaboration with the person supported is not possible, and they must also be presented and reviewed by the Committee.

There are many benefits to requiring a more thoughtful process around identifying potential human rights violations. Checks and balances promote accountability, increase knowledge about how and why violations occur, and foster a culture of responsibility through the education of staff and people supported in the programs. It is acknowledged that staff are not typically violating someone's rights intentionally, but unless they are provided with education explaining why something is a violation, these transgressions will continue to occur. Peer Specialist HROs are in a natural position to be objective, third-party observers when supporting programs and the people they serve and can provide consultation to staff while advocating for those in services.

Peer Specialist HROs are responsible for conducting Quarterly Human Rights Forums in the programs they support. These forums are informal conversations with staff and residents about varying topics regarding human rights that are designed to raise awareness about human rights and facilitate dialogue. Some of the topics covered include voting rights, the Six Fundamental Human Rights, Health Care Proxies, Advanced Directives, Representative Payees, Guardianships and more. Peer Specialist HROs also distribute small, foldable pamphlets called Human Rights Pocket Guides. These guides are easily carried in a wallet or pocket and offer information about the Six Fundamental rights, as well as the name and contact details of the current HRO, the numbers for the Disabled Persons Protection Commission (DPPC) and Elder Abuse Hotline, and the contact information for the Human Rights Coordinator.

Peer Specialist HROs are responsible for conducting biannual Human Rights Inventories for each program they support. These inventories assist with identifying potential human rights violations occurring in programs, program structures, program rules, and policies and highlight what areas need to be addressed and improved. If restrictions or violations are found in a program, the inventories can help explore the reasoning for the restriction and assist staff with finding other solutions that minimize or eliminate restrictions.

There are several examples of potential restrictions an HRO may be looking for, including: kitchen knives being locked up in the staff office, residents not having keys to their bedrooms and front door of the building, or locked covers on house thermostats. Peer Specialist HROs are also looking for guardianships, representative payees, and conservators that we might help staff and the people we support work to have those constraints removed. Taking inventories twice a year can help us stay aware of which programs need extra support with human rights and what specifics the programs should be focusing on. The data from the inventories helps the Peer Specialist HRO determine how they can best support the residents and staff within the program.

In addition to the Human Rights 101 training, HRO's also receive ongoing trainings internally through the Human Rights Coordinator & Human Rights Assistant. These trainings include but are not limited to, introduction to becoming a Human Rights Officer, an annual team wide human rights training, monthly group supervision where a portion of the time is dedicated to teachings on a particular topic, and a general Human Rights training that is offered across BH Res Services. HRO's are also encouraged to attend external human rights trainings that are offered.

The role of Peer Specialists as HROs is an organic relationship founded in self-determination, advocacy, and mutuality. A person in services may feel more comfortable going to an HRO who has lived experience in the mental health system as there may be less of a power differential than if the HRO was a direct care staff who works in the program. If a person supported wishes to file a human rights complaint, they may feel less inclined to exercise their rights if the complaint is against a staff or manager who regularly works at the program. Now that the HRO is a Peer Specialist who does not work at the program, (and isn't supervised by the Program Manager) the power differential is diminished. People supported hopefully feel more secure in voicing their concerns without fear of real or perceived retaliation. When this change first happened, some program staff felt as though the HRO was just there to scrutinize their work or "catch" them in wrongdoing. This is not the point; a lot of care is taken in providing HROs with tools on how to best collaborate with the programs they support. Through relationship building and education between HROs and staff around the different roles, the process now feels more official, collaborative, powerful, and validating for the person filing the complaint.

Peer Specialist HROs can be an objective person to provide clarification and information, as well as real-time consultation when staff have concerns that may lead to restrictions. Someone who is not directly involved (or as emotionally invested) in the situation can provide an outside perspective and suggest alternatives to control to avoid creating unnecessary restrictions. The natural tension that can develop between Peer Specialist HROs and the programs they support is important, healthy, and necessary. Occasional conflict eventually leads to dialogue, greater understanding, and growth.

Ideally, a strong relationship is built between staff, persons supported, and the HRO so that each can see the other as mutually invested in safeguarding human rights. Having Peer Specialists as HROs will hopefully help both residents and staff feel empowered to reach out for support and consultation.

Additionally, the Human Rights Committee hosts an annual Human Rights Award Celebration, where staff in clinical roles as well as people we support, are nominated, largely by the Human Rights Officers, for their exemplary commitment to honoring, protecting, and advocating for Human Rights. This event recognizes and celebrates the great work that is being done across Behavioral Health Residential Services.

Conclusion

Peer Specialist HROs operate under the universal principle that people in the mental health system are autonomous adults who are entitled to the same human rights as any other person. Recovery is not possible without an acute awareness of and respect for human rights, and fierce advocacy is needed to ensure that the voices of those who have habitually been oppressed by the mental health system are heard and honored. The role of peer specialists as HROs is an organic relationship founded in self-determination, advocacy, and mutuality. Checks and balances in the human rights process is essential for identifying potential human rights concerns as well as improving services. Peer Specialist HROs can be more objective when recognizing potential violations, and people supported will hopefully feel more empowered to voice their concerns to an impartial advocate.

More Information

Human Rights Inventory Data 2013-2020

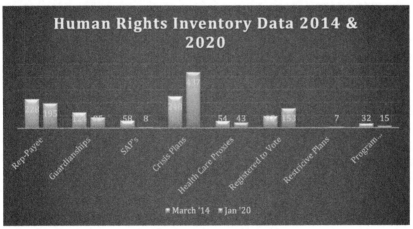

Human Rights Inventory Data 2014 & 2020

SECTION 3: CONFLICT RESOLUTION SKILLS FOR PEER SPECIALISTS

Dan Berstein, MHS, Founder MH Mediate

Peers have conflicts with co-workers, clients, and others. How do we stop them from escalating? Mediators have tactics for addressing conflicts, and MH Mediate adapted them to mental health settings. This narrative will allow readers to learn to validate different beliefs, appreciate diverse perspectives, act impartially, and demonstrate neutrality. It also includes resources for addressing conflicts.

Conflicts are a normal part of life. Conflict resolution skills can help us prevent them, de-escalate them, and resolve them. Whether the conflicts you experience are related to role confusion, professional boundaries, different treatment, clashing mental health philosophies, interpersonal difficulties, workplace transitions, communication styles, or something else entirely there are skills that can help.

Discussion

Appreciate and Validate Someone's Perspective

People may make different mental health choices based on their role (peer, supporter, provider), cultural background, experiences with different mental health clinicians and services, membership in various mental health communities with diverse philosophies, language they use to label problems, beliefs about causes and treatment, and lived experiences including side effects and trauma. Or they may have other reasons for making different choices.

When you validate someone's perspective, you are not agreeing with their beliefs - you are agreeing they have a right to form their own beliefs. By listening to them, you help them feel heard, you remind yourself to be open-minded to different views, and you learn what this person's views are to help set the stage for better conflict resolution. You can use a Reflective Listening Tip sheet to practice ways to listen to someone else by repeating back what they say and avoiding sharing your own perspective. Access a tip sheet at http://bit.ly/31HIXXS

Discuss Needs Instead of Arguing About Positions

When people are in conflict, they often argue about their positions rather than discussing their underlying needs. A position is something someone wants. For instance, if a person is in a conflict with their roommate regarding when they should have quiet hours, their position might be that all noise needs to stop after 10PM. We can imagine that the roommates will be in an intense argument about whether or not 10PM should be the quiet time, especially if the other roommate's position is that they would rather be free to make noise late at night.

It might be very difficult to resolve this conflict if we stay stuck in these positions. But what if we figured out why these people had those positions? The answer is their needs. Their needs are the reasons that they want whatever it is they want. Why did the first person want quiet hours after 10PM? Perhaps those are the rules of the community, and this person is a stickler for the rules. Or maybe they have deep fears about having interrupted sleep as part of a self-care need. They might also simply not want to hear something specific that the other roommate is doing late at night and this is the reason. There are infinite possibilities as to why this person wants quiet, just as there are all sorts of reasons their roommate might feel it is important to be able to make noise later at night. To resolve conflicts, we need to ask people why they want the things that they want. Then the conversation can shift to brain-storming ways to balance and meet each person's needs, instead of simply fighting about positions.

You can access a Positions and Needs Worksheet at http://bit.ly/2LGb862 and you can access some additional resources for getting past positions by downloading the Talking Mental Health Toolkit at www.mhmediate.com/toolkit

Reach Effective Agreements

Whenever we resolve a conflict, even if we do so informally, the result is an agreement. But sometimes these agreements end up being dysfunctional, and they can even become a source of an entirely new conflict if people start arguing about whether the other party did not live up to its terms. In order to prevent these problems, it is important to reality-check an agreement. Ask questions to be sure it is specific, realistic, sustainable, balanced, and updatable.

Take the example of two people who have been having very escalated verbal fights involving yelling and name-calling and now they agree to be "nice" to each other. We ask if this is specific. The answer is no, because nice can mean different things to different people. So, then the parties get more specific and say they will refrain from name-calling and yelling going forward. Now we ask if this is realistic - can they really do this? After all, they have a pattern of past conflicts. Perhaps they do say they believe they realisti-cally can control themselves, so we also ask if this is a sustainable plan. Will they be able to do this forever? Most likely, they will decide it is not realistic or sustainable for them to suddenly stop this behavior. Perhaps then they will agree that, going forward, they will apologize to one another as soon as they calm down. This may be a more realistic agreement than simply planning to be nice.

The other things we check are if the agreement is balanced - meaning both parties have something to gain and both give something, rather than having a lopsided or one-sided agreement. Finally, we make a plan to ensure it is updatable. That means we create an outline of what to do if there are any problems with the agreement and it needs to be updated. This may simply mean saying something like "either of us can let the other know if the agreement is not working and we can talk about adjusting it." This is an important step, so people do not end up fighting about the agreement later on when there are new problems that arise.

You can access a checklist for reality-checking an agreement at http://bit.ly/2mZ8Wrl

Demonstrate You Are Trying to Be Fair

A mediator is an impartial third party who does not know anyone in a conflict, and they have credibility from being an outsider. Normally, at work, we do know the people who we are in conflict with or who we are helping. In either case, that means it is not possible for us to function as a neutral because we have our own biases. Perhaps we like one person and not another, or we are more familiar with one person, or we just generally want to steer the situation to less escalated outcomes because we are invested in our work environment. All of these biases mean we cannot be completely fair. That said, we can still tell people we are trying to be as fair as we can be knowing that we have these limitations. Often, demonstrating a commitment to fairness can help build good will in a conflict. This can be done by saying that your goal is to try to be fair, and inviting people to share feedback if they think things are not fair. It can also be incorporated as a value that is written into policies.

Conclusion

Conflict resolution skills can help us have better communication in our day-to-day lives. This section has provided an overview of four key skills - appreciating peoples' perspectives, getting past their positions, reaching effective agreements, and demonstrating fairness. Though they may sound simple, these skills take practice. Consider using the resources provided to start developing conflict resolution skills and perhaps you will be able to more comfortably and confidently navigate the challenging situations you encounter.

More Information

Dan Berstein, MHS is the founder of MH Mediate, the Co-Founder at the CUNY Dispute Resolution Center's Dispute Resolution in Mental Health Initiative, and the Co-Chair of the Diversity Committee at the American Bar Association Section of Dispute Resolution. He is the author of the book,

Mental Health and Conflicts: A Handbook for Empowerment (available at https://www.americanbar.org/products/inv/book/420367133/) and his TEDx Talk "How to Talk About Mental Health Without Offending Everyone" can be viewed at https://youtu.be/nstRHTVv0Aw

Visit the Dispute Resolution in Mental Health Initiative to access more resources, by visiting www.mhmediate.com/drmh

THE MATERIAL from this section is derived from Dan Berstein's work in the areas of conflict resolution and mental health. Read his book Mental Health and Conflicts: A Handbook for Empowerment (American Bar Association, 2022) or visit the Dispute Resolution in Mental Health Initiative website (www.mhmediate.com/drmh) to access more in-depth coverage of these topics.

SECTION 4: VOCATIONAL PEER SUPPORT

Lyn Legere, MS, CPSS (Massachusetts and North Carolina)
Sr. Training Associate, Boston University, Boston, MA.

Debbie Nicolellis, MS, CRC, CPRP,
University of Massachusetts Chan Medical School, Implementation Science and Practice Advances Research Center (iSPARC), Transitions to Adulthood Center for Research, Shrewsbury, MA.

Vocational Peer Support (VPS) is an advanced specialization for trained/certified peer support specialists who want to bring focused employment, career, and educational supports to people within or beyond behavioral health services. VPS offers peer supporters a new set of skills that build on peer support foundations by adding a keen focus on vocational recovery. VPS adapts key elements of psychiatric rehabilitation (Anthony & Farkas, 2009) and fundamental components of peer practice (Legere et al., 2020) such as sharing one's own "recovery story" to inspire hope. VPS prepares peer support workers to scaffold existing employment supports while also inspiring hope for a meaningful vocational or avocational journey.

Vocational Peer Support (VPS) developed from a longstanding desire of the authors to integrate two training courses that were impacting practitioners supporting people with lived experience of a mental health condition: the Massachusetts Peer Support Training/Certification and the Certificate Program in Psychiatric Vocational Rehabilitation (PVR; Nemec et al., 2003; Nicolellis, 2001). The former prepared people with lived experience to become Certified Peer Specialists while the latter introduced recovery-oriented vocational practice to vocational rehabilitation (VR) and mental health counselors. The authors understood that it was as important to bring peer support values and learnings to VR practitioners as it was to bring the vocational process of PVR to peer support workers who were being asked to support the vocational aspirations of the people using those supports. It was hoped that the integration of the two, the comprehensive and supportive vocational processes of PVR, and the powerful hope-inspiring practices of Peer Support, would be beneficial to people considering work and to those in the process of actively seeking employment. Our vision was to enhance foundational peer support practice with the information, skills and tools that can help to inspire hope for and support vocational recovery, thus maintaining the essence of peer support rather than creating employment specialists with lived experience.

The Boston University Center for Psychiatric Rehabilitation was awarded a 5-year, federally funded grant from the National Institute on Disability Independent Living and Rehabilitation Research (NIDILRR) to create, pilot, and test VPS. VPS was tested in a randomized clinical trial under the direction of Sally Rogers and was developed in consultation with vocational rehabilitation and peer support training experts from around the country with the consultation and support of Marianne Farkas. The following will detail how VPS teaches peer support providers to encourage vocational recovery, and initial outcomes from related studies.

Discussion

VPS Training: VPS is a 6-day comprehensive training that increases the competency of peer support providers in 10 skill areas:

Vocational Recovery and Vocational Peer Support	Partnering to Support Vocational Recovery
Motivational Foundations of Vocational Change	Supporting Choice in Work and Career
Scaffolding Getting into Jobs and School	Keeping Work and School
Coordinating with Vocational and Employment Providers	Researching Information
Supporting the Use of the Social Security Work Incentives	Utilization Planning (VPS Skills in Practice)

Vocational Recovery: VPS teaches peer support specialists who are trained/certified in peer support to engage people in the activities that inspire and support vocational recovery. Vocational Recovery is described as an individualized journey of claiming or reclaiming one's right and capacity to pursue, attain and achieve meaningful vocational paths. In other words, it's more than getting a job; it is considering, pursuing, and sustaining—for as long as the person wants or needs—the vocational experiences that give meaning, purpose, and activity to their life.

The Importance of Sharing One's Vocational Recovery Story: Peer supporters in VPS learn how to share their "vocational recovery story." They learn to share relevant pieces of their own journey: considering work and overcoming internal and external barriers and how they have come to eventually enjoy a life of meaning and purpose through work, school, and other vocational experiences. By honing in on the vocational portion of the recovery journey, peer supporters are able to identify those specific experiences that led them to reframe their own work and/or school possibilities. Like recovery stories, vocational recovery stories are shared to foster connection, inspire hope, and provide resources and tools.

Supporting Employment: VPS skills are designed to help "scaffold" available employment supports to ensure that people are not falling through the cracks of systems and services. Common employment systems, such as the federal Vocational Rehabilitation system (VR) and evidence-based supported employment (e.g., Individualized Placement and Support), are reviewed to enable VPS-trained peer specialists to support people as they navigate through these systems.

The Choose-Get-Keep Approach (Psychiatric Rehabilitation) (Rogers, Anthony & Farkas, 2006): Choose-Get-Keep (C-G-K) was created as a way to integrate recovery-oriented practices for providers supporting people in attaining valued roles in the community, such as worker or student. C-G-K outlines the person-driven philosophy as well as the skills and tools needed to assist people *as they*

consider, choose, enroll, keep, and leave these preferred roles. "Tools" consist of activities, worksheets or conversations that can facilitate exploration or information gathering along the process. For example, "Identifying Preferences" is an activity related to "choosing" that may help someone as they're thinking about what they would like to do for work or school.

Since the underlying philosophy of person-driven practice in C-G-K is consistent with peer support practice, only the tools that were originally created for providers needed to be adapted to ensure that mutual peer support remains the foundation throughout. *Motivational Foundations of Change* focuses on factors that help people *feel* prepared to consider a vocational change and vocational dreams and aspirations. *Supporting Choice in Work and School* helps peer supporters learn how to support people to apply what's important to them to potential work or educational choices and make an informed choice about the kind of employment or educational setting they want to be in, based on preferences and vocational research. *Scaffolding Getting into Jobs and School* is an exploration of ways to support application to valued, preferred vocational settings. *Keeping Work and School* brings a focus on sustaining participation in vocational activities for as long as needed and wanted, through development of any needed skills, supports, and accommodations.

Partnering. Finally, the VPS training teaches the skill and art of "partnering." Steeped in the seminal work of Carkuff's Empathy Model (e.g., Carkuff & Benoit, 2019). Trainees learn and practice the skills of listening to learn, paraphrasing, asking open-ended questions, and related skills that facilitate person-driven mutual peer support.

How VPS differs from traditional employment support

It is worth stating again that peer specialists trained in Vocational Peer Support maintain their "peerness" as they support people in their vocational process. That is, the relationship is voluntary, nonjudgmental, empathic, respectful, requiring honest and direct communication, mutual responsibility, power-sharing and reciprocity (Myrick & DelVecchio, 2016). A key differentiating factor in the VPS role from other employment support positions is that peer specialists with VPS training operate out of their lived experience of *vocational recovery* and related experiential knowledge (Penney, et al. 2020, SAMHSA, 2015). The experiential expertise of the VPS trained peer supporter covers the gamut from reframing self-limiting beliefs to navigating the Social Security system and brings a unique component to employment support not replicated elsewhere.

Structure of the Training: Six days of in-person training were developed to be offered over several sessions to provide information, and skill practice to increase confidence in using the tools. VPS Training is highly interactive in order to enhance learning. Community-based practical assignments are completed in between class meetings to inform real-world practice. Ongoing support is offered post classroom through recurring technical assistance sessions to help trainees incorporate learnings and fine-tune their practice.

VPS Tools. Several comprehensive toolkits were developed to equip systems, programs, and peer specialists themselves incorporate VPS to support vocational recovery.

VPS Tools include:

- Vocational Peer Support Training Program: Trainee Handbook and Toolkit (Nicolellis & Legere, 2015): Divided into 10 modules, the Toolkit provides overviews of each content area, Learning Discussion Questions, Skill Information, Process Examples, Practice Exercises, Discussion Prompts for use in peer-to-peer conversations, and essential Tools/Worksheets.
- Vocational Peer Support Training Program: Trainer's Guide (Nicolellis & Legere, 2015): The Trainer's Guide provides an overview of the principles and key concepts addressed in the VPS training, trainer tips, training preparation and a lesson plan for each module. Lesson Plans are presented to increase accessibility to the training and ease the burden on new trainers, providing suggested schedules, instructions and scripts that offer specific

orientations, questions, definitions and points to make, discussion prompts, demonstration prompts, and instructions for activities.

- Vocational Peer Support Training Program: Implementation Guide (Nicolellis, Farkas & Legere, 2015): The Implementation Guide is an essential resource for program administrators who are considering how to build capacity to support vocational recovery and success in vocational environments. The Implementation Guide introduces pertinent considerations, offers key conceptual information, and guides the development of programming that includes VPS supports. Guiding programmatic needs assessment, recruitment of VPS-trained peer supporters, and the development of organizational readiness, the Implementation Guide offers organizations what they need to successfully implement VPS. Supervisors are offered what they need to support the practice of VPS-trained peer supporters in general and by skill set. Peer Supporters can also use the Practice Checklists to assess their own fidelity to the approach.

THE EVIDENCE. A randomized clinical trial was conducted to test this new VPS approach to providing vocational supports (Maru, et.al., 2021). 166 people were recruited into a study in which 83 received VPS-trained peer support, with the other 83 receiving peer support as usual. Results included positive outcomes across several areas of "work readiness," including reported greater mental wellbeing, greater awareness of the world of work, and feeling greater support to pursue vocational goals.

Operationalizing VPS Supervision

To support the Peer Support specialist in the most concrete way, observe a peer support interaction and be available to facilitate feedback. *Facilitating* feedback is different from *providing* feedback, in that the supervisee is very much involved in the supervision.

We suggest using the following as an effective framework for providing supervision which facilitates feedback: "Get-Give-Merge"

Get: Ask supervisee for successes, struggles, strategies	**Give**: your perspective, and your support to the person	**Merge:** perspectives and find possible solutions

Use VPS concepts, tools and skills

People also reported that there was a stronger working alliance with the VPS-trained peer specialist, especially in the areas of goal support and bond of relationship, which appeared to have a positive effect on quality of life, and increased hope for work. There were modest differences in the vocational activity between the two groups within the one-year follow-up period, perhaps because employment wasn't the exclusive support offered by the VPS-trained peer supporters.

You don't feel like you're a client or the consumer or whatever they want to call people. You just feel like who you are. And it feels good to feel like who you are.

— FROM BALOGUN-MWANGI, ET.AL., 2018

In our experience, peer specialists in the study acted as generalists, and employment-related support may have taken a back seat to more pressing crises. This study found that having peer supporters equipped with the knowledge and skills needed to provide vocational peer support resulted in greater hope for employment. It also demonstrated that people getting VPS peer support felt a greater readiness to go after vocational goals with a sense of hope about their own vocational future.

"Unlike [my] family and friends who just expected me to go back to work without any preparation, she [vocational peer support specialist] was willing to acknowledge that there were challenges along the way and that she overcame."

— FROM BALOGUN-MWANGI, ET.AL., 2018

196

A second, qualitative study (Balogun-Mwangi, et.al., 2018) explored whether having employment support from a peer specialist, as opposed to a vocational provider, had any impact. The most fundamental component identified by program participants was that of mutual support and sharing of lived experience.

This study found that peer specialists trained in VPS provided a model of vocational possibility for those in the study as they themselves were successfully employed as peer specialists. The study identified that several factors made an impact: a sense of *Equality*, or "an absence of hierarchy and formality," and not treatment in orientation; *an Absence of Judgment*; a sense of *Empathy*, or the ability to relate to their experiences; *Role Modeling; Prioritizing the Person*, including what the person wanted to focus on; *Creativity* and *Hope*. This study confirmed that the lived experience of vocational peer support specialists appears to be a unique and effective element in building strong interpersonal connections, which can be leveraged for improving vocational outcomes among individuals with psychiatric disabilities.

Conclusion

Peer support specialists have been trained to be members of employment programs in a number of settings. However, many peer specialists in this situation become "employment specialists with lived experience," where the core elements and values of peer support practice may be minimized. Vocational Peer Support intentionally builds upon Peer Support core values and principles with the belief that the ingredients of mutuality, shared lived experience and empathy of a fellow traveler are critical. VPS has been found to have positive effects on hope for a meaningful vocational life, as well as immediate impact on peoples' overall quality of life and a greater sense of readiness for work.

Learn More

Let us know how we can help with your efforts to support vocational aspirations through mutual peer support!
Boston University Center for Psychiatric Rehabilitation website: https://cpr.bu.edu/
Vocational Peer Support Tools: https://cpr.bu.edu/store/vocational-peer-support/

References

Anthony, W. A., & Farkas, M. D. (2009). *Primer on the psychiatric rehabilitation process*. Boston: Boston University Center for Psychiatric Rehabilitation.

Balogun-Mwangi, O., Rogers, E.S., Maru, M. & Magee, C. (2018). *Vocational Peer Support: Results of a Qualitative Study*. Journal of Behavioral Health Services & Research, 2017. 1–14.

Carkuff, R.R. & Benoit, D.M. (2019). *The Art of Helping*, 10th Ed. HRD Press, Amherst, MA.

Cohen, M., Danley, K., & Nemec, P. (1985, 2007). *Psychiatric rehabilitation training technology: Direct skills teaching*. Boston, MA: Boston University Center for Psychiatric Rehabilitation.

Nemec, P., Nicolellis, D., Wolpow, S., MacDonald-Wilson, K., Restrepo-Toro, M. (Eds.) (2003). *Psychiatric Vocational Rehabilitation: A training curriculum*. Unpublished manuscript. Boston, MA: Boston University Center for Psychiatric Rehabilitation.

Legere, L. & Peer Voice North Carolina (PVNC). (2020) *Best Practices in Peer Support: It All Starts Here*, White paper created for the NC Division of Mental Health, Developmental Disabilities and Substance Use Disorders.

Maru, M., Rogers, E.S., Nicolellis, D.N., Legere, L., Placencio-Castro, M., Magee, C., and Harbaugh, A.G. (2021). Vocational Peer Support for Adults with Psychiatric Disabilities: Results of a Randomized Trial, *Psychiatric Rehabilitation Journal* 44(4): 327-336

Myrick, K., & del Vecchio, P. (2016). Peer support services in the behavioral healthcare workforce: State of the field. *Psychiatric Rehabilitation Journal, 39*(3), 197–203.

Nicolellis, D. & Legere, L. (2015). *Vocational Peer Support Training Program: Trainee Handbook and Toolkit*. Trustees of Boston University, Center for Psychiatric Rehabilitation: Boston, MA.

Nicolellis, D. & Legere, L. (2015). *Vocational Peer Support Training Program: Trainer's Guide*. Trustees of Boston University, Center for Psychiatric Rehabilitation: Boston, MA.

Nicolellis, D., Farkas, M., & Legere, L. (2015). *Vocational Peer Support Training Program: Implementation Guide*. Center for Psychiatric Rehabilitation, Boston University, Boston, MA.

Nicolellis, D. (2015). Vocational Peer Support: Bringing Psych Rehab, Employment, and Peer Support Together. *PsyR Connections. Issue 1.*

Nicolellis, D. & Farkas, M. (2014). Vocational Peer Support: A New Specialization for Peers Supporting Employment. *Recovery & Rehabilitation Newsletter; Special Interview Issue.* Spring Issue, Vol. 14 (1). Boston, MA: BU Center for Psychiatric Rehabilitation.

Penney, D., Ostrow, L., & Burke-Miller, J. (2021). Development and properties of a measure designed to assess core competencies in intentional peer support. *Psychiatric Rehabilitation Journal* , 44(2), 118–123.

Rogers, E. S., Anthony, W. A., & Farkas, M. (2006). The choose-get-keep model of psychiatric rehabilitation: A synopsis of recent studies. *Rehabilitation Psychology, 51*(3), 247–256.

Substance Abuse and Mental Health Services Administration (SAMHSA), U.S. Department of Health and Human Services, *Core Competencies for Peer Workers in Behavioral Health Services*, Rockville, MD. 2015

SECTION 5: HUMAN RESOURCES PRACTICES FOR GROWING AND SUSTAINING THE PEER WORKFORCE

Jessica Wolf, PhD
Decision Solutions Consulting and Yale Department of Psychiatry

The 2020 webinar addressed evidence-based Human Resources approaches to recruiting, training, and retaining peer support workers with lived experience. It explored job qualifications, peer employment, supervision, and career advancement together with agency leadership and commitment to recovery values and practices.

Peer support workers are increasingly employed in public health and mental health systems. Peer specialists offer emotional, informational, instrumental, and affiliation support (SAMHSA, 2017). Peer specialists may work in mental health, substance use, and forensic settings, as parent partners, youth peers, with veterans, in primary care, and specific health settings. Peer support is non-clinical, builds on lived experience, and helps individuals identify and attain individual life goals.

"Peer support workers are people who have been successful in the recovery process who help others experiencing similar situations. Through shared understanding, respect, and mutual empowerment, peer support workers help people become and stay engaged in the recovery process and reduce the likelihood of relapse." (BRSS TACS, n.d.).

"Peer support is valuable not only for the person receiving services, but also for behavioral health professionals and the systems in which they work." "Peer workers educate their colleagues and advance the field by sharing their understanding of how practices and policies may be improved to promote wellness and recovery." "Peer workers play vital roles in moving behavioral health professionals and systems towards recovery orientation." (SAMHSA, 2017).

However, service agencies struggle with high turnover, burnout, and uncertainties about boundaries between peer workers and other staff. Peer workers are challenged by role confusion, "peer drift," and scarcity of knowledgeable supervisors.

Committed agency leaders and human resources practitioners are essential to the success of peer workers and the practice of peer support. This presentation addressed human resources practices for growing and sustaining the peer workforce.

Discussion

Challenges for Human Resources (HR) staff include: addressing disclosure; knowledge of the Americans with Disabilities Act (ADA), clarification of peer roles; developing clear peer support worker job descriptions; pairing HR and peer support consultants/staff and team leaders to design and structure peer roles; serving as a resource for staff role clarification, conflict resolution, and career development.

HR tasks include recruitment, interview practices and regulations, job postings and descriptions. benefits management, creating equitable compensation and career development opportunities.

Challenges for peer workers include being the "new staff;" joining and connecting with pre-existing teams; sometimes being the only peer or one of a few dispersed peer workers; dealing constructively with benefits and challenges of lived experience disclosure; avoiding "peer drift" (sliding into non-peer roles and work); isolation and lack of community; lack of organizational support; stigma, including micro-aggressions and micro-affirmations.

Table 1 presents recruitment and hiring best practices and problematic practices.

Table 1. Recruitment and Hiring

Recruitment and Hiring Best Practices	Recruitment and Hiring Problematic Practices
Hiring peer workers (PW) with at least a year of self-help support group attendance	Viewing all lived experience as equal (a person who has never received services or training is likely to have difficulty providing them)
Hiring trained peer workers with demonstrated competence in evidence-based peer services	Assuming anyone with lived experience can offer peer support without training and mentoring
Clear agency vision of peer role; active support of peer practice	Lack of knowledge of differences between peer services and supportive employment; hiring peers without role clarity, job descriptions not grounded in evidence-based peer services; undefined career paths
Hiring peer workers in recovery with histories of serious mental health conditions and difficult life experiences	Giving hiring priority to peers with least difficulty in recovery
Assuring supervisors and staff are knowledgeable about peer support	Assuming peer services are not as effective as clinical services and thus do not need to be delivered by trained peer workers
Actively including peer workers in addressing agency and staff stigma, microaggressions and working environment	Hiring peers to do policing jobs; peers working in isolation
Encouraging peer workers to support each other at work	Assuming all peer jobs should be at agency sites and not in the community, hiring co-dependent workers without good self-care plans in place

Table 2 presents best and problematic employment practices.

Table 2. Employment Practices

Best Employment Practices	Problematic Employment Practices
Clear scope of work	Using peers inappropriately such as policing, case management or clinical roles; unclear scope of work
Agency-wide trust building: all-staff meetings, good communication, high recovery orientation, training on stigma, allyship, bias reduction	Not demonstrating agency commitment to inclusion of peers as partners
Peer workers and all staff included in brainstorming and decision making about clients and agency goals	Peers excluded from agency decision making and brainstorming.
Defining and implementing continuing education plans for peers and all workers	Viewing licensed positions as the sole career path for peer providers and encouraging peer drift; low expectations of peer workers
Acknowledging and reducing staff members' lack of understanding of peer services and fears that peers will take their jobs	Overprotective interactions with peer workers; discounting peer workers' expertise
Eliminating "othering" language and negative agency practices such as using derogatory language about people being served or requiring separate restrooms	Viewing mistakes or missteps as caused by peer workers' mental health issues rather than as correctible mistakes or missteps
Assuring peer workers and all staff have and use self-care plans and support networks	Establishing or maintaining therapeutic relationships with peer workers

Table 3 describes best and problematic supervision practices.

Table 3. Supervision Practices

Best Supervision Practices	Problematic Supervision Practices
Recognition of impact of staff traumatic histories	Failing to recognize staff traumatic histories
Supporting and providing collaborative supervision	Exclusively authoritative supervision
Using a continuous improvement approach	Making supervision a therapeutic relationship; undermining peer workers by repeatedly asking if they are OK, overwhelmed, need time off, taking meds, etc.
Equally valuing supervisors of peer workers	Devaluing role of supervisor of peer workers
Educating all staff on peer services and benefits	Lack of education about recovery, recovery values, and peer services
Rewarding all staff including peer workers for success; viewing failure as a path to learning	Using mistakes and failures to reduce peer worker responsibilities or autonomy
Developing career ladders for all staff, including peers; not leaving peers stuck in dead-end jobs	Lack of career ladders or arrangements for increased peer worker compensation
Incorporating peer services into all treatment plans, programs, and agency activities	Limiting peer work to mundane tasks
Encouraging staff including peer workers to participate in support groups	Expecting staff including peers to work in isolation; segregating peers from other staff

Table 4 shows Best Practices in Promoting Career Development

Table 4. Promoting Career Development

Supervisors discuss career advancement with supervisees
Promotion, merit increases, added job responsibilities and increased compensation opportunities included in regular performance review
Release time and funding available for staff continuing education and academic studies
Peers employed in senior management roles
HR and Supervisors advocate for peer advancement
Leadership and HR create and implement agency career and compensation ladders
Leadership assures peer voice throughout the agency/system

Table 5 contains suggested training topics for all staff.

Table 5. Training Topics for All Staff

Recovery values: people with mental health conditions can and do recover
Definition of peer support, what peer support workers do, and evidence for peer support
Learning about and using recovery-oriented and person-first language
Understanding and avoiding peer drift
Building communications skills such as dialogue rather than debate
Practicing cultural humility, recognizing, and reducing micro and macro-aggressions, "othering" and stigmatizing behaviors
Challenging negative attitudes about employment of people with lived experience

Table 6 offers Tips for HR Staff: "Do's"

Table 6: Tips for HR Staff to Do

Hire people with lived experience who have at least one year of attendance in 12-Step, Recovery International or other self-help groups.
Hire people with lived experience who have had to overcome many obstacles to recovery rather than a few.
Hire people with lived experience who have training in evidence-based peer services from a reputable training program,
Develop and use ethical guidelines specific to the peer role.
Address boundary issues so that peer workers are not working at an agency where they receive or recently received services or on a team where a clinician had previously provided services.
Make sure to have clear job descriptions that assign peer supporters to evidence-based peer services rather than assisting clinicians in clinical tasks.
Train all staff on peer roles and effective anti-stigma and discrimination approaches.
Arrange for new peer workers to have mentors who are not their supervisor to help them understand the organization and its culture.
Wherever possible, have peers trained and supervised by peers.
Assure that supervisors are using collaborative supervision and data-informed plans of action.
Create opportunities for career advancement in peer services.
Implement policies and procedures that articulate inclusiveness, the value of peer workers and promotion of a non-stigmatizing environment.
Make sure peer workers receive continuing peer services education

Table 7 includes two important Tips for HR Staff: "Don'ts":

Table 7: Tips for HR Staff to Avoid

Do not exclude people with lived experience who have a criminal justice record.
Do not exclude peers because of résumé gaps.

Conclusion

Human resources team members are key in peer worker recruitment, employment, supervision, career development and retention. HR and related staff, as well as all agency staff, must be familiar with peer support values and practice. Whole-of-organization commitment to peer support values and practice is essential for successful peer employment and partnering of peer support and non-peer staff. Effective engagement and training of all staff are essential in reducing stigma, assuring diversity and successful working relationships. Agency leaders must proactively support all staff in fulfilling these goals.

Employment and full inclusion of peer support workers in mental health and substance use agencies requires leaders' conscious and proactive approach to involvement of lived experience workers as partners with clinical providers. Successful inclusion requires a reorientation of organizational culture, practices, and partnerships at all agency levels.

More Information

SHARE! 2020 Conference on Supervision presentation: Growing & Sustaining the Peer Workforce: HR Best practices—Jessica Wolf, Assistant Clinical Professor of Psychiatry, Yale University, New Haven Connecticut

Acknowledgments

Ruth Hollman, Chief Executive Officer, Libby Hartigan, Director of Training, and Quality Assurance, and Jason Robison, Chief Program Officer at SHARE! the Self-Help And Recovery Exchange, all contributed significantly to the content of the March 25, 2020 SHARE! Supervision Conference presentation, "Human Resources Practices for Growing and Sustaining the Peer Workforce." Their substantive assistance is acknowledged with appreciation.

References

Byrne. L., Roennfeldt, H., O'Shea, P., & Macdonald, F. (2018). Taking a gamble for high rewards? Management perspectives on the value of mental health peer workers. *International Journal of Environmental Research and Public Health, 15, 746.*

Byrne, L., Roennfeldt, H., Wing, Y., & O'Shea, P. (2019). 'You don't know what you don't know': The essential role of management exposure, understanding and commitment in peer workforce development. *International Journal of Mental Health Nursing 28, 572-581.*

Byrne L, Roennfeldt H, Wolf J, Linfoot A, Foglesong D, Davidson L, & Bellamy C (2021).
Effective Peer Employment Within Multidisciplinary Organizations: Model for Best Practice. *Administration and Policy in Mental Health and Mental Health Services Research* Sep 3. doi: 10.1007/s10488-021-01162-2. Epub ahead of print. PMID: 34478040.

City of Philadelphia Department of Behavioral Health and Intellectual Disability Services and Achara Consulting, Inc. (2017). Peer Support Toolkit https://dbhids.org/wp-content/uploads/1970/01/PCCI_Peer-Support-Toolkit.pdf

Gagne, C.A., Finch, W.L., Myrick, K.J., & Davis, L.M. (2018). Peer workers in the behavioral and integrated health workforce: Opportunities and future directions. Special Article. *American Journal of Preventive Medicine, 54 (6S3), S258-S266. https://www.ajpmonline.org/article/S0749-3797(18)31637-4/fulltext*

Moran GS, Russinova Z, Gidugu V, et al. (2013). Challenges experienced by paid peer providers in mental health recovery: a qualitative study. *Community Mental Health Journal, 49*(3):281– 91. Epub 2012 Nov 2. https:// doi .org/ 10.1007/ s10597-012-9541-y PMed:23117937

National Association of Peer Supporters (NAPS) Supervision resources and Supervision Guidelines: www.inaops.org/supervision

New York City (NYC) Peer and Community Health Workforce Consortium (2019). Workforce Integration of Peer and Community Health Worker Roles: A needs-based toolkit to advance organizational readiness. https://www1.nyc.gov/assets/doh/downloads/pdf/peer/needs-based-toolkit.pdf

New York City (NYC) Peer and Community Health Workforce Consortium (2020). Workforce Integration of Peer and Community Health Worker Roles, Action Planning and Implementation Guide. https://www1.nyc.gov/assets/doh/downloads/pdf/peer/action-planning-and-implementation

U.S. Department of Health and Human Services, Substance Abuse and Mental Health Services Administration (SAMHSA), (2017). Peers Supporting Recovery from Mental Health Conditions https://www.samhsa.gov/sites/default/files/programs_campaigns/brss_tacs/peers-supporting-recovery-mental-health-conditions-2017.pdf

U.S. Department of Health and Human Services, Substance Abuse and Mental Health Services Administration (SAMHSA), Bringing Recovery Supports to Scale Technical Assistance Center Strategy (BRSS TACS) (n.d.) Peers https://www.samhsa.gov/brss-tacs/recovery-support-tools/peers#; and Supervision of Peer Workers https://www.samhsa.gov/sites/default/files/brss-tacs-peer-worker-supervision.pdf

Wolf J (2020). Human Resources Practices for Growing and Sustaining the Peer Workforce. [Presentation]. SHARE! Conference on Supervision of the Peer Workforce, March 25. https://shareselfhelp.org/programs-share-the-self-help-and-recovery-exchange/supervising-peers-conference/

Wolf J (2019). Chop Wood, Carry Water: Key Elements in Progressive Peer Workforce Practice. [Webinar] Central East Mental Health Technology Transfer Center, July 30.

Wolf J (2019). The Logic of Scientific Revolutions: Peer Support Workforce and Mental Health System Transformation. [Webinar] Central East Mental Health Technology Transfer Center, July 18. https://mhttcnetwork.org/centers/central-east-mhttc/event/peer-workforce-and-mental-health-system-change-logic-scientific

SECTION 6: TOWARD AN EFFECTIVE PEER SUPPORT WORKFORCE: INTEGRATING RESEARCH AND PRACTICE

Jessica Wolf, PhD
Decision Solutions Consulting and Yale University Department of Psychiatry

SHARE! the Self-Help And Recovery Exchange Supervision of Peer Workforce Project (2018-2020) sought to help transform the Los Angeles County mental health system as peer support worker employment increased. Project components included four training sessions built on evidence-based research findings and project evaluation research. The INAPS 2019 workshop (Wolf and Robison, 2019) described the research and training process, and anticipated outcomes. Discussion addressed challenges and rewards of integrating research and practice.

During the past twenty years, peer support workers have become increasingly important in the public and private mental health workforce. As the peer support workforce grows, organizational leadership and culture, together with knowledgeable human resources departments, competent supervision, and clear peer support worker job descriptions are essential. These are necessary to support and encourage viable partnerships and collaborations among clinically-trained workers and peer specialists; peer specialists' emphasis on lived experience and promotion of self-determination bring new hope and opportunities both to service users and team members.

The SHARE! Supervision of Peer Workforce Project was funded by the California Office of State Health Planning and Development to assist in transforming the Los Angeles County mental health system as it trains and employs more peer support workers and seeks to create new partnerships between peers and traditionally trained clinical and management staff.

To help people in Los Angeles pursue personal growth and change, SHARE! empowers individuals to change their own lives and provides a loving, safe, non-judgmental place where they can find community, information, and support. SHARE! officially opened its doors at an abandoned warehouse with a leaky roof in Venice, CA in 1993.

Since 1993, SHARE! the Self-Help And Recovery Exchange has served people through self-help support groups and communities that provide recovery and social support. Participants develop skills to cope with substance use, trauma, mental health disorders, and dysfunctional relationships. They learn to better their own lives, become employed, reconnect with family and friends, and reintegrate into the community.

SHARE! programs are designed to support self-sufficiency through social support and community integration. This innovative, peer-run approach was honored with the Los Angeles County Mental Health Commission Outstanding Program Award in 2013.

Supervision of Peer Workforce project leaders intentionally included available research knowledge and findings in each project component. The project evaluation was designed and undertaken via the creation of a control and an intervention group. A total of 169 peer workers and 86 supervisors from 68 sites completed baseline and 10-month follow-up surveys assessing peer worker, peer supervisor, and site outcomes. The measures and scales used are described in a forthcoming article by Brown et al (see Brown, 2020 and References).

The intervention was the provision of four trainings, each based on existing research knowledge, using didactic and interactive components: 1) Strategies for an Effective Peer Workforce; 2) Cultural Competence: Becoming an Ally; 3) Trauma-informed Developmental Peer Supervision; and 4) Stigma…in Our Work and in Our Lives.

Discussion

Research was relevant to this project both in selection of the control and intervention groups, as well as in the selection and presentation of training topics.

Identifying the control and intervention groups presented complex methodological and procedural challenges. Los Angeles County has a population estimated in 2019 at 10,000,000 with the Los Angeles County Department of Mental Health directly operating many sites and contracting with many others. Sites employing peer workers and supervisors were invited to participate in the study, with a few non-affiliated sites also allowed to enroll. Site recruitment was undertaken from June-October 2018 through email, telephone, follow-up email, contact with supervisors and directors. Sites were then randomly assigned to the control or intervention group.

Study participants were peer workers or supervisors of peer workers at a participating site. They were all invited to complete a baseline survey between October 2018 and March 2019. The response rate was 72% of 251 peer workers and 80% or 115 supervisors. The ten-month follow-up survey was completed by 169 peer workers and 86 supervisors, with response rates of 80% and 86% respectively (Brown, 2020; Brown et al, in draft).

The content of each training included evidence-based practices developed from research on the topics. For example, "Strategies for an Effective Peer Workforce" built on SAMHSA Infographics providing extensive references on the evidence for effectiveness of peer support for people with mental health conditions (SAMHSA, 2017, Hollman 2020). "Cultural Competence: Becoming an Ally," drew on research and findings about allyship, behaviors supporting dialogue, and steps in speaking up against bigotry (Almeida, 2013; California Survey on Othering and Belonging, 2018; Powell, 2017; Sabat, Martinez & Wessel, 2013; Schneider, Wesselmann & DeSouza, 2017; Southern Poverty Law Center 2015; Yankelovich, 2001); "Trauma-informed Developmental Supervision" was based on the work of Stoltenberg and McNeill (2011), as well as trauma-informed supervision (Berger & Quioros, 2014; Blanch, Filson, & Penny, with Cave 2012; Institute for Health and Recovery, 2014), and others. "Stigma…in Our Work and in Our Lives," was presented by On Our Own of Maryland, based on research by Michaels, Corrigan et al (2014). Each training curriculum was submitted to the Los Angeles Department of Mental Health Program Support Bureau Training Division for approval of Continuing Education Units (CEUs) and was required to include a list of relevant references.

Conclusion

Integrating research and practice yields challenges and reaps rewards. In the SHARE! Effective Supervision of Peer Workforce Project, challenges included SHARE! project and research team members working with various sections of the Los Angeles Department of Mental Health in order to identify, define and randomize the control and intervention groups; selecting the peer and supervisor participants; and, with the collaboration of LACDMH offices, assuring that as many as possible completed the baseline and follow-up surveys, and attended all four of the training sessions; obtaining and meeting the criteria for Continuing Education Units by submitting descriptions of each training session, including relevant references; arranging for multiple in-person training sites at numerous locations convenient in different geographic L.A. County locations likely to attract as many participants as possible; reminding participants of the training and encouraging attendance; developing training presentations and PowerPoints and collaborating with knowledgeable trainers; and providing and assuring submission of completed evaluations of training events.

The benefits of meeting the challenges of combining research with practice included the resulting evidence that the trainings made a difference to organizational culture in Los Angeles agencies, particularly around knowledge of and support for peer workers (Brown et al, in press).

In conclusion, "one size does not fit all," in combining research with practice. It's important to recognize the complexities and challenges involved, while also maintaining a high bar for the possible rewards: well-constructed research can lead to important practice gains.

Acknowledgment

Jason Robison, Chief Program Officer at SHARE! the Self-Help And Recovery Exchange, co-led the 2019 INAPS Workshop presentation and discussion. His ideas and contributions are acknowledged with appreciation.

References

Almeida R. (2013). Cultural Equity and the Displacement of Othering. DOI10.1093/acrefore/9780199975839.013.889

Berger R. & Quioros L (2014). Supervision for trauma informed practice. *Traumatology 20*(4), 296-301.

Blanch A, Filson B, & Penny D with contributions from Cave C (2012).

Engaging women in trauma-informed peer support: A guidebook. National Center for Trauma-Informed Care. https://www.nasmhpd.org/sites/default/files/PeerEngagementGuide_Color_REVISED_10_21012.pdf

Brown, L.D. (2020). An intervention to improve peer supervision: Evaluation of the supervision of peer workforce project. [*Presentation*] SHARE! The Self-help And Recovery Exchange Peer Supervision Conference, March 25. https://shareselfhelp.org/programs-share-the-self-help-and-recovery-exchange/supervising-peers-conference/

Brown LD, Vasquez D, Wolf J, Robison J, Hartigan L, & Hollman R. (2022). Supporting peer workers and their supervisors: Cluster randomized trial evaluating a systems-level intervention. (In draft)
California Survey on Othering and Belonging: Views on Identity, Race and Politics. https://haasinstitute.berkeley.edu/survey-majority-californians-oppose-bordr-wall-suppport-racial-inclusion. Haas Institute for a Fair and Inclusive Society Press Release, April 18, 2018.

Hollman, R. (2020). Evidence-based Peer Practices for Supervisors. [*Presentation*] SHARE! The Self-help And Recovery Exchange Peer Supervision Conference, March 25. https://shareselfhelp.org/programs-share-the-self-help-and-recovery-exchange/supervising-peers-conference/

Institute for Health and Recovery (2014). Trauma-Informed Supervision, in Trauma-Informed Organizations: A Tool Kit, Cambridge, MA.

Jones, N., Kosyluk, K., Gius, B., Wolf, J., & Rosen, C. (*2020*). Investigating the mobility of the peer specialist workforce in the United States: Findings from a national survey. *Psychiatric Rehabilitation Journal, 43(3), 179-188.* doi.org/10.1037/prj000039

Jones, N., Teague, G.B., Wolf, J, & Rosen, C. (2020) Organizational climate and support among peer specialists working in peer-run, hybrid and conventional mental health settings. *Administration and Policy in Mental Health and Mental Health Services Research, 47(1),* 150-167. doi.org/10.1007/s10488-019-00980-9

Michaels, P. J., Corrigan, P. W., Buchholz, B., Brown, J., Arthur, T., Netter, C., & MacDonald-Wilson, K. L. (2014). Changing stigma through a consumer-based stigma reduction program. *Community Mental Health Journal, 50(4),* 395–401. https://doi.org/10.1007/s10597-013-9628-0

212

powell, ja (2017). Us vs Them: The Sinister Techniques of Othering and How to Avoid Them. *The Guardian (November)* https://www.theguardian.com/inequality/2017/nov/08/us-vs-them-the-sinister-techniques-of-othering-and-how-to-aoid-them

Reddy SB, Wolf, J, Brown, LD (2020). Capacity-building in the peer workforce: A systems-level approach. *Psychiatric Services 71(3):*307 DOI: 10.1176/appi.ps.71301.

Sabat IE, Martinez LR, & Wessel, JL (2013). Neo-Activism: Engaging allies in modern workplace discrimination reduction. *Industrial and Organizational Psychology 6*(4), 480-485. https://doi.org/10.1111/iops.12089. First published 19 November 2013.

Schneider, KT, Wesselmann, ED, & DeSouza, ER (2017). Confronting subtle workplace mistreatment: The importance of leaders as allies. *Frontiers in Psychology 8*, 1051. doi: 10:3389/fpssyg.2017.01051.

Southern Poverty Law Center (2015). Responding to Everyday Bigotry. https://www.splcenter.org/20150125/speak-responding-everyday-bigotry

Stoltenberg, CD, & McNeill BW (2011). *IDM Supervision: An Integrative Developmental Model for Supervising Counselors and Therapists.* Routledge, Third edition.

Wolf, J. (2018). National trends in peer specialist certification. *Psychiatric Services 69* (10, October), 1049. doi: 10.1176/appi.ps.201800333

Wolf J, & Robison J (2019). Toward an Effective Peer Support Workforce: Integrating Research and Practice [Presentation] INAPS (International Association of Peer Supporters) Conference, San Diego, CA.

U. S. Department of Health and Human Services, Substance Abuse and Mental Health Services Administration (SAMHSA), (2017). Peers Supporting Recovery from Mental Health Conditions. https://www.samhsa.gov/sites/default/files/programs_campaigns/brss_tacs/peers-supporting-recovery-mental-health-conditions-2017.pdf

Yankelovich D (2001). *The Magic of Dialogue; Transforming Conflict into Cooperation.* Touchstone.

CHAPTER 9
WHAT HELPS WHAT HINDERS

CHAPTER INTRODUCTION BY THE EDITORS

LONG BEFORE PEER SUPPORT SERVICES WERE DEEMED MEDICAID REIMBURSABLE, peer supporters and self- help groups had identified those practices, values and attitudes that were helpful and those that were not. In 2002, a team of researchers set out to discover from a consumer's perspective what helps and what hinders recovery. This research identified ten domains and consumers detailed what was either helpful in their recovery or hindered their recovery in that domain. Peer Support was identified as one of the ten domains that could either help or hinder recovery. Peer support was helpful if there was adequate funding, if it was widely available, if there were diverse models, available role models and mentors, exposure to self-help philosophy, support resources run by consumers, and if support was found within traditional resources (Onken, S., et al, 2002). Peer supporters continue to lead the way in identifying those environments, practices, attitudes and values that are helpful and those that are not. This chapter seeks to add to that body of knowledge.

The first reading by Edwards and Enders brings into focus the importance of choice and personal and professional goals. This reading speaks directly to processes that help peer support workers think about their career goals and choices. The next reading by Mx. Yaffa (Ahmad Abojaradeh) takes on the continuing challenge of stigma and marginalization of peer support workers and peer support as a tool of recovery. He adds to this discussion a focus on diverse populations that remain unrepresented. What hinders recovery is being marginalized and dismissed. In the next reading, Welle discusses incorporating spirituality into wellness plans. Spirituality in all its forms has been heralded as a practice that helps recovery. Finally, Martin discusses how to create successful relationships with the people most important to you. What helps recovery is a support network either of people related by blood or through strong bonds, i.e., "family.". This reading describes a workshop providing participants with concrete tools and a process to build and strengthen resilient "family" relationships

SECTION 1: CAREER CHAT: SHARING TIPS AND STRATEGIES FOR PURSUING PROFESSIONAL DEVELOPMENT AND PERSONAL GOALS THROUGH EDUCATION AND LIFE EXPERIENCE

Jonathan P. Edwards, Ph.D., LCSW, ACSW, NYCPS
Workforce Development Consultant, Facilitator and Researcher
Former Board Member, National Association of Peer Supporters (N.A.P.S.)

Gita Enders, LMSW, MA, NYCPS
Workforce Training and Development Consultant

Career Chat is a facilitated 90-minute dialogue which seeks to look at one's own life through a lens of healing and recovery while exploring the terrain of educational, vocational or other meaningful goals, and incorporating National Practice Guidelines for Peer Supporters (NPG). Participants are encouraged to share liberally about goals, and other personal and professional development aspirations. To operationalize change as both a concept and choice, we introduce Twelve Actionable Ideas© to foster self-determination and autonomy.

During a conference several years ago, we were asked to facilitate a dialogue about peer specialists seeking career advancement in other fields such as social work or addiction counseling. We thought that one way of continuing this discussion was to briefly share our experience as peer supporters balancing work, going back to school, and maintaining personal recovery. The goals of the dialogue were to promote hope and identification, share our stories, ignite each other's courage and determination, build community through ongoing mutuality, and finally, to provide context for our experiences by referencing specific National Practice Guidelines for Peer Supporters (NPG) personally and professionally.

Discussion

Career Chat is a facilitated dialogue in which workshop facilitators offer their experience and perspective on pursuing higher education and meaningful activities in the face of challenges, setbacks, stigmatizing beliefs, and other structural barriers that often stand between individuals and attainment of their goals. Consistent with the values of hope, identification, and mutuality, one person's account of overcoming feelings of fear can ignite another person's courage and determination. We have found that many of our colleagues experience the ageing process as another barrier to pursuing personal goals, higher education and career advancement.

Common themes that have emerged from previous Career Chat workshops include: 1. It's never too late to go back (to school or work); 2. All you need is one drop of hope; 3. Going back to school gave me options, but I am happiest when I am doing peer work; 4. I want to get certified and stay in peer services, but how can I also obtain the skills to be a supervisor; 5. I want to learn how to talk about the gaps in my resume; 6. I want to enhance my personal growth through learning.

Career Chat draws upon and advances three National Practice Guidelines for Peer Support Specialists, namely:

TO SHARE HOPE

By telling strategic stories of their personal recovery and helping others reframe life challenges as personal opportunities for growth, Career Chat encourages dialogue about how life experiences impacted goals and opportunities and how lessons gleaned from those situations can become cornerstones of present and future success. Facilitators and participants can discover in a supportive environment how resilience and self-determination needed to navigate previous challenges can inform strategies for addressing current concerns.

SEE WHAT'S STRONG NOT WHAT'S WRONG

CAREER CHAT PROVIDES A STRENGTH-BASED, supportive and respectful setting where participants are asked to be present for each other and honor each other's experiences through active, non-judgmental listening and by showing compassion when elicited. Simply hearing that one is not alone in contemplating change (or working around fear of change) can be a major element in facilitating change. Choosing not to change is also an option and not indicative of being wrong, but indicative of personal autonomy, choice, and self-determination. Career Chat is not a forum in which to assess, diagnose, prescribe or give advice. Rather, it is an opportunity to share about where one might be in their career development or process, where they might like to be, and what steps might be necessary or recommended to achieve a goal. It is important to stipulate that the concept of education is applied broadly across the scope of this discussion; it is not necessarily about achieving academic degrees but more about the value of learning and how learning enhances our range of choices.

FOCUS ON THE PERSON, NOT THE PROBLEMS

Dignity, respect and positive regard are essential in peer support relationships, whether dyadic or in group settings. Career Chat, as stated earlier, is strengths-based and provides opportunities to affirm each other for merely exploring career change/growth. Past decisions, experiences and consequences are not viewed here as problems but as resources in one's toolkit. People are valued for being present and their experiences, albeit informative, educational and identifiable, are secondary to the living person in the room.

To build the rapport within the cohort, we ask participants:

- How many people are attending this conference for the first time?
- How many people are working as a peer specialist?
- How many people are working as a supervisor?
- How many people think about going back to school or pursuing another meaningful goal?

There followed a discussion of interest in and/or motivation for going back to school or pursuing other meaningful goals, and areas of specific interest. Participants shared their thoughts on how going back to school or pursuing other meaningful goals would support personal growth or professional development.

EACH FACILITATOR SHARED their experience for 5-7 minutes incorporating some of the following themes:

- What education and other meaningful goals meant to us personally (e.g. "It's cool to learn stuff about things")

- It wasn't necessarily about professional development (at the time) but about personal fulfillment / interests, opportunities (e.g., poverty scholarship, talk to the astronauts)
- Needed structure but was not confident enough to return to work yet; needed to get out of bed and into the world. (prodded by an interested and supportive supervisor.)
- Working and going to school under heavy medication was not the easiest thing

Questions were then invited from participants about what the facilitators had shared, or anything else they wanted to ask.

Participants were instructed to find a partner or form a small group to discuss where they were currently at and where they might want to be. If a participant was considering a career change, they were then asked to name something that might support them getting from one point to the next. To facilitate this interactive segment, we used a non-hierarchical illustration, "Where I Stand", to illustrate the following states or "life locations" for participants to assess where they're currently at and where they might want to be short, moderate, or long-term:

- Happy where I'm at
- Curious about making change
- Ready to make a move
- On my way!
- I'm here and figuring it out

This was followed by sharing about the activity; what people had learned from each other, and about themselves. Finally, to summarize the activities and dialogue, participants were acknowledged for bringing themselves into the space and contributing to the activity. One participant was asked to read the quote by Socrates, "The secret of change is to focus all of your energy not on fighting the old, but on building the new," and another was asked to share about what the quote meant to them.

At the end of the activity, the group discussed Career Chat Principles: Twelve Actionable Ideas©

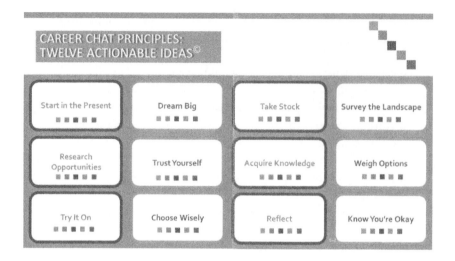

As we parted, participants were gifted with a tasseled bookmark explicating the Twelve Actionable Ideas© in greater detail.

Conclusion

Many participants seemed relieved that they were not alone; we certainly felt validated by the honesty and sense of hope from our peer support community. No matter where you stand in your feelings about [peer] work or additional education; there is dignity in all choices, and input, questions, and comments in this forum add value to an ongoing dialogue.

References

National Association of Peer Supporters (2019). National Practice Guidelines for Peer Specialists and Supervisors. Washington, DC: N.A.P.S. https://www. peersupportworks.org/wp-content/uploads/2021/07/National-Practice-Guidelines-for-Peer-Specialists-and-Supervisors-1.pdf

SECTION 2: AT THE MARGINS OF MARGINALIZATION AND PEER SUPPORT

Mx. Yaffa (Ahmad Abojaradeh) CPS, MA
Equity and Transformation Consultant, Meraj Consulting

At its onset, Peer Support was created as a transformative practice for and by individuals who are marginalized by the Medical Industrial Complex (Health Justice Commons, n.d.). This movement, rooted in a concept of "for us, by us" has been instrumental in moving the mental health system to better support individuals receiving services worldwide. However, in the process, Peer Support stopped being about marginalization and instead watered down to only individuals with mental health and substance use challenges from privileged communities, while de-centering any other areas of marginalization.

For most individuals who are not Cis-Straight-White-Global North Citizens Peer Support does not offer a sanctuary and spaces of belonging, and although more effective than non- Peer Support spaces, does not reach its transformative capacity. In response, many non-white-cis-straight-global north spaces have built their own frameworks and movements to better support our communities. Arenas of Disability Justice, Trans Peer Support, and Mutual Aid are three such examples. Collaboration within and outside mainstream Peer Support is necessary for us to build pathways for accountability and create a movement and profession that is comprehensive and accessible to the most marginalized of the most marginalized.

Peer Support exists as a movement, a profession, and more importantly a way of life that has always existed. The concept of individuals with shared identities supporting one another is not something that was developed in the last 50 years, or even the last thousand years. For humans to survive we learned to build communities, at the onset, being alone was the most dangerous thing. We survived by coming together. Today, we live in a world where the most dangerous thing to us is another human being, depending on your identity, it is usually someone more privileged. I mention that last part because in the last few hundred years the concept of Peer Support, particularly in Colonizer and Settler Colonizer nations is seen as radical and unheard of (Learning for Justice, 2019). Peer Support in those countries is seen as a different way of being, a step away from our nature. Doing this work in over 30 countries, and learning about the various cultural practices to be able to do my work effectively, has led me to see that Peer Support, named differently everywhere, has always been the way. This is validated by my own family and Palestinian culture. Years ago, when I first got into Peer Support, talking to my grandfather about Peer Support felt surreal because I realized that to him Peer Support never needed a name, it was the way our community was and has always been.

Often, I find that we ground our Peer Support work in the Peer Support movement, and not necessarily in the intrinsic humanity of it. For most of our history Peer Support was more the reality than what we see in our daily lives today. For this section I will centre some alternative models that I believe go hand in hand with Peer Support that are created by and for the most marginalized communities.

Discussion

In 2018, at a then INAPS conference, the Youth and Young Adult Peer Supporters committee hosted a full day of events. One of the sessions was centered around the transformation of Peer Support to be inclusive of the realities and desires of youth and young adults. Justice and Equity came up first, then a desire to entirely transform the mental health and substance use support systems. Fifteen minutes into it, with a fairly comprehensive list, I felt that we arrived at Disability Justice.

Disability justice is "a framework that examines disability and ableism as it relates to other forms of oppression and identity (race, class, gender, sexuality, citizenship, incarceration, size, etc)" (Piepzna-Samarasinha, 2018). To some Peer Support Specialists this definition may feel very similar to the work we are doing or aim to do, for others it might be seen as unnecessary and completely different. Disability Justice was formed during the 90's and early 2000's at the start of the tech revolution which made it possible for Disabled individuals to organize. To me, Disability Justice is the Intersectional and Transformative vision of Peer Support as a pathway for systemic transformation.

Over the last 20 years, Disability Justice has grown around the world, but has not reached mainstream consciousness to the same level as Peer Support. Many of the gaps I have spoken about within Peer Support spaces are resolved within most Disability Justice spaces. Within Disability Justice spaces individuals are honored for everything that they are. Accessibility is paramount, alternative pathways for participation and leadership exist and are at the forefront of the work, the land and the bodies that exist on the land are honored. Disability Justice is intersectional, honoring that disability is always connected to everything else that we are, and rights in one area of our lives are not enough if we are still being murdered and marginalized for other areas. These frameworks are not new, but having them brought together into a structure that works for and by the most marginalized disabled individuals is powerful and offers alternatives to individuals who do not feel at home within the disability rights and Peer Support movements.

Another example that comes to mind is the Trans Peer Support community. Translifeine (TLL) is one of the biggest examples of Trans-led Peer Support, as the only organization operating an entirely trans operating helpline for trans individuals and their families (Translifeline Principles, n.d.). TLL was built outside of the Peer Support movement and community, and to this day there is little intersection between TLL and the broader Peer Support community. Outside of TLL, there are various other vibrant Trans communities and organizations practicing Peer Support in their daily practice. At the time of writing this I am currently in a Trans and Queer Muslim support space that leverages Peer Support to support us in navigating a society that despises us (*Queer Crescent*, n.d.). Many pride centers across the country will also utilize some Peer Support practices within their spaces and programming.

The final area of work I would like to highlight is the Mutual Aid space. Mutual Aid, like Peer Support, has existed as long as humans have and the two concepts can be identical in certain ways. Mutual Aid, like Peer Support, is a concept that everyone needs support and everyone is capable of providing support, building relationships beyond the dichotomy of those who support and those who are supported. Although Mutual Aid has been around as long as we have, in the United States it reached mainstream consciousness at the start of the COVID-19 pandemic in 2020. At the time, the peer-run organization I was running, Life in My Days, Inc stepped into creating a central statewide mutual aid hub in CT (*CT Mutual Aid,* n.d.). Built on a foundation of Peer Support values and grounded by indigenous Palestinian mutual aid practice we supported the launch of 13 local mutual aid groups or organizations supporting the most marginalized within our communities. Within our mutual aid hub, we also offered free virtual Peer Support in three languages for anyone in the state. Peer Support was also offered in every interaction within the network that collectively was supporting over 20,000 a week.

Conclusion

Both within and outside the Peer Support community there is incredible work happening. Unfortunately, a lot of it is siloed and separate, rarely visible from the outside and grows separately. There is no perfect movement or space, and all groups and movements benefit from cross collaboration and walking towards accountability with one another. Doing so would build a much more efficient and transformative Peer Support.

References

CT Mutual Aid. (n.d.). Retrieved January 9, 2022, from https://ctmutualaid.com/

Piepzna-Samarasinha, L. L. (2018). *Care work: dreaming disability justice.* Arsenal Pulp Press. "A framework that examines disability and ableism as it relates to other forms of oppression and identity (race, class, gender, sexuality, citizenship, incarceration, size, etc)"

Principles. Trans Lifeline. (n.d.). Retrieved February 6, 2022, from https:// translifeline.org/about/#princples
Queer Crescent. (n.d.). Retrieved February 1, 2022, from https://www. queercrescent.org/

Terms defined- Medical Industrial Complex. Health Justice Commons. (n.d.). Retrieved February 9, 2022, from https://www.healthjusticecommons.org/ terms-defined

What is settler colonialism? Learning for Justice. (2019, January 22). Retrieved February 5, 2022, from https://www.learningforjustice.org/magazine/what- is-settlercolonialism

SECTION 3: ADDRESSING SPIRITUAL CONCERNS IN PEER SUPPORT SETTINGS

Victoria (Vic) Welle,
MTS (Master of Theological Studies)
CPS (Certified Peer Specialist)

Spirituality can be a significant topic when a person is seeking support related to mental health and related challenges (such as trauma or substance use). Spirituality is frequently associated with religious belief, but it is much broader than religion. It can be a way of thinking about one's life purpose, personal values, cultural rituals, and how a person makes meaning of their experiences. Peer supporters need to be skilled at approaching the topic of spirituality in a way that is trauma-aware, culturally sensitive, and aware of any personal bias they might bring to a peer support interaction. Many peer support trainings do not cover this topic in-depth, and some peer support workplaces discourage discussions of religion or spirituality. It's important for peer supporters to have strategies for exploring spiritual concerns in a way that is validating and respectful.

The peer support field can learn from other support systems, such as hospice and palliative care, to explore ways to effectively incorporate spiritual considerations into peer support interactions. These, combined with peer support best practices (such as approaching with curiosity, honoring multiple perspectives, centering self-determination, etc.) can make it possible to engage in meaningful conversations about spirituality.

Discussion

This topic began as an area of interest for me because of my own experiences navigating the intersections of spirituality and mental health during times of crisis and significant upheaval in my life. In my experience, both the psychiatric system and formal religious institutions did not provide adequate supports to help me heal and make sense of what happened to me. Instead, it was the support of my peers, along with my own exploration and adaptation of spiritual practices that provided the meaningful spiritual support I needed. Bringing together my own experiences, formal theological studies, peer support work, and over fifteen years of conversations and reflection with others, I developed workshops for those wanting to explore spirituality as part of their healing and recovery. The title of my original workshop on this topic was "Incorporating Spiritual Practices into a Wellness Plan." Over the course of five years, I shifted into a broader framework and now present workshops on "Addressing Spiritual Concerns in Peer Support Settings." This approach acknowledges that not everyone finds wellness planning useful or helpful, and also gives space for individuals who may instead be seeking conversation, exploration, and a safer space to talk about what they consider sacred. My findings are not the final word, and I hope they can serve as a starting point for those unsure of how to approach spiritual matters when they arise in peer support settings.

For many people seeking healing and recovery related to a mental health challenge, spirituality can be an essential part of the process. "Spiritual wellness" is recognized as one of components of a holistic health framework known as the Eight Dimensions of Wellness (SAMHSA 2016). Spirituality can be understood in many different ways; here it will be defined as "the aspect of humanity that refers to the way individuals seek and express meaning and purpose, and the way they experience their connectedness to the moment, to self, to others, to nature and to the significant or sacred (Puchalski, et al, 2009)." This may or may not involve formal religious beliefs, or beliefs in a divine higher power. Each person will have a different way of understanding how they define what is meaningful and sacred. As peer supporters, it is important to always create space for spiritual exploration, rather than telling another what should or should not be considered sacred or significant.

It's important for peer supporters to know how to navigate conversations about spirituality because it may be one of the few settings where a peer feels comfortable sharing deeply about the role of spirituality in their lives. Barriers exist in both clinical mental health settings and formal religious settings that can prevent meaningful exploration of spiritual matters. Some of the barriers are related to histories of harm experienced in either or both settings.

In clinical settings, a person receiving services related to a mental health challenge might be reluctant to bring up spiritual matters with a mental health clinician due to fear of how they will be judged. For example, if a person is experiencing unusual or extreme experiences (seeing visions, hearing voices) that they interpret as spiritual, a person might be afraid of those experiences being pathologized as symptoms. If pathologized and given a psychiatric label, it is often the case that, rather than explore whether these experiences hold meaning and significance, the experiences are labeled as problematic symptoms to be medicated away. Clinical providers might also lack expertise about spirituality beyond their own belief system, or may be reluctant to speak about spiritual topics, fearing it's beyond their scope of practice. Even if a provider is open to exploring spiritual matters with a person, the provider might also be limited by systemic barriers such as billing, health insurance, and time constraints that make it difficult to talk about spirituality or what it might look like to integrate spiritual considerations into a person's recovery plan.

It is not uncommon for clinical providers (and also peer supporters) to encourage a person to seek out spiritual support from a local faith community, religious leader, or similar faith-based "natural support" to discuss spirituality. While often well-intentioned, this may also be a challenging thing to do. This is especially true if a person has experienced exclusion, discrimination, or abuse in faith communities in the past. This can include members of the LGBTQIA+ community, survivors of clergy abuse, or individuals who were rejected due to their mental health status. Further harm can happen if trying to re-engage with a faith community without sufficient support. Clergy and other religious leaders also may not have training or sensitivity in mental health matters. Similar to a clinician who imposes a psychiatric diagnosis to explain a person's experience, a religious leader might instead impose a spiritual explanation, without taking the time to ask the person how they have come to interpret their experiences with emotional distress. (In my own experience, this happened to me on more than one occasion when well-intentioned clergy told me what my experiences meant, rather than offering guidance on what possibilities existed for discerning my own spiritual understanding of what happened.)

In contrast to formal psychiatric and religious systems, peer support settings are uniquely positioned to offer the time, flexibility, and open-mindedness to support an individual wanting to explore spirituality as part of their healing and recovery. Because a peer supporter is not in a position of diagnosing a peer or assessing what their experience means, a supporter instead has the freedom to provide a nonjudgmental space to explore with a curious, open mind about what a person's experiences might mean, and what if anything, the peer might want to do in response to their experiences as part of their healing process. The question then becomes: how can peer supporters effectively bring up the topic of spirituality, especially when some have been specifically instructed to avoid potentially "controversial" topics like religion?

When I first began doing peer support work, I felt comfortable talking about spirituality because of my prior work in ministry and faith-based settings, which is not an experience all peer supporters have. I was also aware of how to integrate spiritual concerns with holistic health plans in non-religious settings, such as end-of-life hospice and palliative care. In thinking about peer support, I saw a lot of parallels. In peer support, we're often meeting people in the midst of significant turmoil and life changing experiences. They may be asking themselves what it all means or trying to figure out how to make big changes in their life. If care professionals are able to talk about the role of spirituality at the end of a person's life, it's also possible for peer supporters to talk about it when a person is in the midst of re-envisioning what their life is going to look like after a significant mental health crisis or similar life-altering event. I decided to draw on some of the wisdom, resources, and techniques already in use and adapt them for peer support.

One of the frameworks I drew from was the FICA Spiritual History Tool developed by Dr. Christina Puchalski and colleagues at the GW Institute for Spirituality and Health (Puchalski, 1996). Although created for medical providers to assist in talking to patients, the format of the FICA tool can be adapted by peer supporters. Rather than doing a "spiritual assessment," it can instead be a guide for conversation, or offered to the peer to do their own self-guided reflection. The tool offers a semi-structured way for person to reflect on what kind of role they would like spirituality to play in their vision of wellness. Here is the FICA format for self-reflection, with minor adaptations for a peer support setting.

Faith: Do I have spiritual beliefs that help me cope with my life? With my mental health? What gives my life meaning? What do I value? (Note: these beliefs do not have to involve belief in a higher power.)

Importance: How important are these beliefs to me? Do they influence how I think about my emotional well-being? Do they influence my healthcare decisions (such as the role of medication, advocating for alternative therapies, etc.)?

Community: Do I belong to a spiritual community? Am I happy there? Do I need to search for another community? If I don't have a community, how might it help if I found one?

Address/Action: What should be my action plan? What changes do I need to make? Are there spiritual practices I want to develop?

Based on how a person answers the above questions, a peer supporter can offer support in a number of ways. It might be the case that spirituality is not a high priority for the person, in which case other areas of wellness can be explored. If the person decides that part of the action to be taken is exploring spirituality further, there are ways that a peer supporter can encourage spiritual activities that do not endorse a specific belief system. The following are some possibilities that a peer supporter could explore with a peer.

Music can be a simple yet meaningful starting point for spiritual exploration. Songs do not need to be religious songs in order to have significance for a person. Singing, playing, and listening to songs that hold significance is often a powerful way to connect. Books can be another opportunity for reflection and discussion. Reading a memoir or biography of a mystic, saint, or other significant person (such as a sports hero or performing artist) can assist with helping identify values, aspirations, and hopes for what a meaningful life might look like for a person. Another possibility is reading verses or a few pages daily from a sacred text, poetry collection, or self-help book that the peer chooses. Finally, service to others is a value found in many spiritual traditions. Volunteering can help cultivate a sense of meaning and purpose, and has additional benefits such as meeting new people, or building new work experience. All of these are activities are examples of activities that a peer supporter could do with a peer that would likely not be seen as promoting or endorsing a particular religious belief system.

When considering activities that could be seen as explicitly religious, such as prayer, rituals, or some forms of meditation, it may be more appropriate for a peer supporter to not take the lead in initiating these practices, especially if it gives the appearance of a peer supporter attempting to convert someone to the peer supporter's belief system. Instead, the peer supporter can facilitate conversation that equips a peer to initiate their own spiritual practices. One possibility is for the peer supporter to assist in creating a "spiritual wellness plan," in which the peer can decide how and when they will practice their spirituality. This can be a stand-alone plan or combined with a wellness and recovery plan that addresses the many dimensions of a person's healing process. Here are some questions a peer supporter can use to assist a person wanting to make such a plan for themselves.

What? Do you already have spiritual practices you know how to do? What are you interested in learning more about? This could include prayers, rituals, meditation practices, or non-religious activities that have meaning, such as taking a walk in nature on a regular basis.

How often? Do you want to incorporate daily practices into your plan? Weekly? Once in a while, during times of distress, or to mark significant events?

When? Are there daily routines you already do where you can add a prayer or ritual? This could include a blessing before a meal, or a prayer before taking medication.

Who? Do you want to practice with another person? Alone? In a small group, or larger faith community? Is there a religious mentor, guide, or elder you want to seek out for more information?

Where? Do you want to set aside a space where you live for spiritual practices, or have a less formal routine? Will there be a need to adapt practices for your living situation (such as electric candles if your building doesn't allow burning actual candles)?

I often encourage people to start small, incorporating one or two spiritual practices into their routine at first. Then, after the person has had time to practice, I offer space for them to reflect in follow up meetings. What did they notice? What did they find useful or meaningful? Encourage the person to continue adapting their plan, in the same way that a peer support would encourage the development of other self-directed wellness plans.

Cultural considerations and trauma awareness are also significant aspects of exploring spirituality as a peer supporter. It's important to be aware that exploring spirituality can be an emotional journey, particularly if a person is from a marginalized community, or has experienced harm related to faith. Some examples of this are survivors of clergy abuse, survivors of historical or generational trauma (such as First Nations communities whose religious practices were banned or suppressed in the United States and Canada), or rejection from faith communities due to gender identity or sexual orientation. Exploring spirituality can be a healing experience, but it can also reignite memories of hurt and trauma. Peer supporters can provide validation of the impact of these past harms and encourage exploration of spirituality at a pace that feels right for the person receiving support.

As peer supporters, we may not always agree with the choices a person makes in their expression of spirituality. I have encountered situations where a person wanted to attend a church that held discriminatory beliefs, or a person wanted to adopt ritual practices that were not meant to be used outside of a particular religious and cultural tradition. It can be challenging as a peer supporter to withhold judgement and honor these choices, yet also maintain one's own personal values when faced with these kinds of situations. I have found it helpful to first ask the person I'm supporting if they're open to hearing feedback about a point of disagreement. If they are, I try to share my own thoughts in a respectful way and listen with an open mind to their response. Peer supporters are skilled at having complex, nuanced conversation about difficult topics including trauma and suicide, and this also extends to hard conversations about spirituality and deeply held beliefs. As with conversations around other potentially controversial topics, it is possible for peer supporters to model curiosity, open-mindedness, and respect.

Conclusion

Peer support offers a unique opportunity to explore meaning, purpose, and what connects us to a sense of what is sacred in our lives. When peer supporters are prepared to navigate conversations that include spiritual beliefs and practices, a more holistic vision of wellness can be imagined and put into practice for a person healing from mental health, substance use, or other life-altering challenges. Peer supporters are not meant to be spiritual guides. Rather, peer supporters can be prepared to offer the people they support the tools to create their own maps of meaning for a spiritual path.

Learn More

victoriawelle.com

References

Eight Dimensions of Wellness: Creating a Healthier Life: A Step-By-Step Guide to Wellness April 2016, Substance Abuse and Mental Health Services Administration (SAMHSA) https://store.samhsa.gov/sites/default/files/d7/priv/sma16-4958.pdf (accessed January 30, 2022)

Spirituality definition from Christina Puchalski, et al., "Improving the quality of spiritual care as a dimension of palliative care: the report of the Consensus Conference," Journal of Palliative Medicine, 2009; 12:885-904.

The FICA Spiritual History Tool: A Guide for Spiritual Assessment in Clinical Settings 1996, 2020, Christina Puchalski, MD https://smhs.gwu.edu/spiritual ity-health/sites/spirituality-health/files/FICA-Tool-PDF-ADA.pdf (accessed January 30, 2022)

SECTION 4: BUILDING BOUNCE-BACK FAMILIES

Chris W. Martin, MA in ED Counseling, ITE
Director of Learning and Performance I for Crestwood Behavioral Health, Inc.

Building Bounce-Back Families is a 90-minute fun, engaging, and highly interactive workshop providing participants with concrete tools and a process to build and strengthen resilient family relationships.

Peer Support Specialists can share these tools individually in a one-to-one setting or deliver them to a group of participants in a classroom. In fact, the workshop can even be delivered to a whole family or groups of families in a classroom setting. The learning package contains inspiring music, videos, and opportunities for small team sharing. The materials and family building tools can also be used by the participants for enhancing their own family relationships.

Discussion

It's All Relative - What is a family? There are many answers and examples for that question. One universal answer might be: *it's all relative*. We're not only talking here about a relative by blood, adoption, and/or marriage. A family might include some or all of those characteristics or perhaps none of those at all. We believe a family is *relative* to the persons who are its members. A family is a social unit consisting of two or more people who are connected by a bond of love and a commitment that "no matter what, we are there for each other." We might also think of a family as "bio-logical." A family is "bio" in the sense that it's comprised of living beings; we can also include pets as family members. And a family is logical in the sense that our rational mind helps us consider who to include and exclude as supportive family members.

Families can be comprised of people who are not related by blood at all but are bonded like kindred spirits.

Will the Circle Be Unbroken? - As a consequence of mental illness, addiction, and/or trauma, fractures and divisions can happen within families. In fact, these types of struggles often take a toll on each family member. This is why it's often said that recovery is for the whole family. Some recovering people may lose their family connections altogether. For them it may be about putting together a new family that will be more supportive in their recovery. Regardless of its makeup, any family can experience good times, bad times, growth, healing (reconciliation), and resilience. And as Hemmingway wrote, "[families] can become strong in the broken places."

Stronger in the Broken Places - Whatever family we choose or that chooses us, we can take some steps to strengthen those family bonds. Building a bounce-back family or ... *Family Resilience Planning* is a dynamic relationship building process that can help a family become more hopeful and optimistic; increase their courage to face challenges and fears; develop a stronger sense of belonging to each other, enhance their family and community wellness; and develop a durable family spirit. This meaningful family self-help experience involves four separate and progressive activities which build upon each other. These intentional activities are: 1) creating a family meeting agreement; 2) developing a family mission statement and values; 3) completing a Resilient Family Survey; and 4) completing a Resilient Family Action Plan.

If We Build It, Resilience Will Come - Building resilience for achieving a bounce-back and spring-forward family takes unified and intentional work. And the payoff is totally worth the effort. A close, resilient family provides a harbor where members can find shelter in times of storms; it serves as a power station where they can recharge what might be in short supply; it can be a source of unconditional love that nourishes their spirit; and it projects a glowing light to help them see what's best and strong in themselves.

An old story recounts the tale of two brothers living on adjoined farms who had been very close, but they gradually drifted apart due to some small, long-forgotten offense that one committed against the other. Over the years, many offenses and defenses flew back and forth between them.

One day, the older brother dug a deep gully to reroute a fast-running river to separate their two properties. The younger brother retaliated by hiring an engineer to build a massive wall along the property line so he would never again see his brother or the river. The wise engineer, who knew a lot about family structure, instead built a beautiful sturdy bridge (Figure 1) over the raging river.

When each brother saw the bridge and his brother standing on the other

Figure 1. Sturdy Bridge

side, they walked forward to meet each other in the middle. A long, tearful, and happy hug commemorated the opening of the bridge that day.

The moral to this story is... when we take down the "fences" (those offenses and defenses) that can separate a family and do the intentional work of bridge-building, we can strengthen ourselves to become a resilient family, staying connected and resilient over smooth and rough waters.

In the 50's & 60's, TV shows like "Father Knows Best," "Leave It to Beaver," and others presented a perfect picture of a wholesome family. Chris Martin came from a family that was more like the Adams Family, but perhaps not so funny. His biological father spent most of his life in prison while his mom was frequently absent due to long hospitalizations in the state mental hospital. And his stepfather had a strong addiction to alcohol with a tendency toward emotional and physical abuse. As a result of Chris's own recovery and resilience, he learned a lot about how to create a resilient family.

More Information

If you would like to download the instructional materials for this workshop which includes an interactive workbook and PowerPoint, then visit our website at http://recoveryresiliencesolutions.com

PART 4: SUCCESSFUL SUPERVISION OF PEER SUPPORT

Chapter 10: Peer Voices in Supervision

- Chapter Introduction by the Editors
- Section 1: Supervision Strategies: A Dialogue on Best Practices for Supervising Peer Supporters
- Section 2: Supervision as Collaboration: An Emerging Dialogue for Peer-Informed Practice
- Section 3: SUD Peer Supervision Competencies
- Section 4:: Recovery First, Family Second, Work Third: Supervising & Supporting Peers
- Section 5 Supervision and Co-Supervision for Family (Peer) Support Specialists

Chapter 11: Supervision Research and Resources

- Chapter Introduction by the Editors
- Section 1: What We Have Learned from Peer Support Workers Supervised by Non-Peer Supervisors
- Section 2: Five Components of Peer Support Services with Keys to Supervision
- Section 3: Supervision and Successful Employment: Overview of the National Peer Worker Supervision Survey

CHAPTER 10
PEER VOICES IN SUPERVISION

INTRODUCTION BY THE EDITORS

IN THE HELPING PROFESSIONS, SUPERVISION IS INTEGRAL TO PROFESSIONAL development, and supervisors help staff members fulfill (and hopefully thrive in) their organizational roles by offering clarity and guidance on the vision and mission of the organization, and how the employee's workplace contributions directly and ultimately support these pillars. Soundness and integrity of supervisory practice is correlated with job satisfaction, retention, productivity, and impactful outcomes with respect to individuals and communities who engage with services, or benefit from goods, provided by an organization. Research indicates that the quality of supervision is a contributing factor in staff decisions to stay at or leave a job (Kuhn et al., 2015).

Chapter 10, Peer Voices in Supervision, is the first of three chapters on supervision covered in this volume. Given the default and familiar configuration of top-down supervision, which is characteristic of many clinical and other occupational environments, we are excited to offer important perspectives on supervision envisioned and developed by people with lived experience. These contributions subvert what has historically constituted familiar supervision paradigms that are often unidirectional, reactive, and punitive rather than trauma-informed, developmental, and strengths-based.

Departing somewhat from didactic and theoretical models cited from the extant literature on supervision, we are pleased to offer an account given by one of the editors of and contributors to this first volume of Narratives by

Peer Support Specialists. We feel this account epitomizes a real-world example of crafting on-the-ground supervisory practice— an amalgam of lived experience, academic training, professional development, and a huge dose of introspection.

Affirmed and encouraged by my supervisor in 2009 to take stock of the myriad functions and tasks embedded in my role as a program director and supervisor of nearly 30 peer specialists, I began to think more critically about how my workplace roles and my own personal lived experience both inform and potentially limit my judgment when conducting supervision. Two key things came to mind: 1) I needed to flesh out the layers and tasks of supervision in an organized matrix; and 2) I needed to be deeply reflective about fairness and accountability when engaging supervisees and responding to their workplace concerns, including personal situations and circumstances that would inevitably impact how they show up in their job. Since my major concern was that I would be too stringent or too lenient when responding to supervisees' concerns and requests, I initially conceptualized a multi-function supervision model as an accountability tool to help guide me through the maze of workplace situations and decisions I would be faced with as a supervisor. This was a vital process since I embodied both lived experience and academic training; in fact, I identified as a peer supporter even though I had a management position; I was also a licensed master social worker and a doctoral candidate, a researcher, a coach, a change agent, and oftentimes just another a person navigating my own recovery process. (The Five Critical Functions of Supervision, Conference Presentation, SHARE!, 2022).

Renowned for addressing the breadth and depth of supervisory practice, The Peer Support Toolkit developed by the Philadelphia Department of Behavioral Health and Intellectual Disability Services (DBHIDS, 2017), delineates 11 promising practices for investing in, supporting, and supervising peer support staff. These are shown below in Table 10.1. Forthcoming is a brief overview of Chapter 10 readings which incorporate and draw upon many of these promising practices. Our vision in this initial chapter on supervision is to enhance the roadmap that guides both supervisors and peer support staff in establishing enriching, mutually respectful, and fruitful workplace partnerships. Ultimately, the goal is to learn from each other and advance peer support practice and supervision through collective wisdom and collaboration.

Table 10.1 Philadelphia Toolkit Promising Practices for Supervision

Promising practices for investing in, supporting, and supervising peer support staff
P1. Provide Diverse Types of Supervision
P2. Provide the Right Supervisory Structure
P3. Ensure that Supervision Is Consistent, Accessible, and Helpful
P4. Ensure that Supervisors Are Skilled in Building Trust and Maintaining Boundaries
P5. Collaboratively Assess Strengths and Areas for Growth
P6. Familiarize Supervisors with Common Concerns of Peer Staff
P7. Help Peer Staff Develop Time-Management and Documentation Skills
P8. Hold Peers Accountable to Recovery Values
P9. Support Continuing Education and Career Mobility
P10. Watch For and Redirect "Peer Drift"
P11. Promote Self-Care

The five readings in this chapter provide a cross-section of peer-informed perspectives, as well as various tools with which to design, conduct, and evaluate supervision processes and performance. First, we learn about three approaches to supervision that embed peer support principles and provide hands-on guidance for documenting supervision sessions using a template. We also learn about the relationship between core competencies and effective supervision pertaining to Family Support Specialists (FSS), an emerging specialization of peer support practice. To foster and support the inclusion of peer support practice among FSS, there is also an outline of the purpose and best practices related to co-supervision with peer and clinical supervisors. This important alliance cannot be overestimated, as many settings in which peer support staff practice are integrated settings where mutual understanding of respective philosophical and practical approaches to engagement is paramount.

Supervision Strategies: A Dialogue on Best Practices for Supervising Peer Supporters summarizes a didactic and interactive workshop given at the 2016 International Association of Peer Supporters (iNAPS) Conference in Philadelphia. The scenario-based workshop activities illustrate opportunities for participants to navigate the "murky terrain" of supervision in a supportive space where responses to challenging situations that could arise in supervision are collectively brainstormed and analyzed.

Wacker et al. speak specifically to what is needed to maintain recovery from SUD. However, the title and content are also instructive for all peer supporters as the reading offers a way to prioritize the myriad demands of life, recovery and work, with handy tips for supervision. Supervision as

Collaboration: A Continuing Dialogue for Peer-Informed Practice presents a five-function model of supervision that provides a framework for organizing, applying, and evaluating (including self-assessment) supervisory practice. Although the five-function model of supervision is designed primarily preliminarily for supervisors, it embeds transparency as a key principle in promoting equity among supervisors and those whom they supervise. For example, the five-function model can be adapted for a self-assessment template that can be used by the supervisor in reviewing their own performance with those whom they supervise, promoting within the supervisor-supervisee dyad principles based on core values such as mutuality, accountability, complementarity, and teamwork.

A timely inclusion to this chapter, SUD Peer Supervision Competencies, helps bridge the gap that reflects an historical bifurcation of what is termed behavioral health. Not only are there ongoing misconceptions, policy barriers, and resistance among practitioners to intentionally address the high incidence of co-occurring mental health and substance use disorders, understanding this in the context of peer support services raises even greater concern. Competency-based performance evaluation standards for staff who provide supervision to peer supporters working in SUD settings have, until recently, been almost nonexistent. This contribution advances our knowledge in a rapidly growing arena.

Finally, Recovery First, Family Second, Work Third: Supervising & Supporting Peers and Supervision and Co-Supervision for Family (Peer) Support Specialists speak to the importance of family support and the supervision necessary for it to thrive.

Reference

Philadelphia Dept. of Behavioral Health and Intellectual Disabilities Services and Achara Consulting Inc. (2017). Peer Support Toolkit. Philadelphia, PA: DBHIDS https://dbhids.org/wp-content/uploads/1970/01/PCCI_Peer-Support-Toolkit.pdf

Kuhn, W., J. Bellinger, S. Stevens-Manser, & L. Kaufman. (2015). Integration of Peer Specialists Working in Mental Health Service Settings. Community Mental Health Journal, 51(4), 453–458. doi:10.1007/s10597-015-9841-0

SECTION 1: SUPERVISION STRATEGIES: A DIALOGUE ON BEST
PRACTICES FOR SUPERVISING PEER SUPPORTERS

Jonathan P. Edwards, Ph.D., LCSW, ACSW, NYCPS
Workforce Development Consultant, Facilitator and Researcher
Former Board Member, National Association of Peer Supporters (N.A.P.S.)

Yumiko L. Ikuta, MBA
Director of Rehabilitation Programs, Office of Rehabilitation Programs
Bureau of Mental Health
NYC Department of Health and Mental Hygiene

In 2007, The Centers for Medicare and Medicaid Services (CMS) recognized
peer support services as both an evidence-based mental health model of care
in which a qualified peer support provider assists individuals with their
recovery from mental illness and substance use disorders, and an important
component in a state's delivery of effective mental health and substance use
treatment (NACBHDD, 2016).

In 2009, the Substance Abuse and Mental Health Services Administration
(SAMHSA) recognized peer supporters as important service providers in
mental health service delivery and designated what was then the International
Association of Peer Specialists (iNAPS) to be among the five mental health
professional organizations charged with developing recovery-oriented educational materials and training thousands of staff providing mental health
services.

On October 1, 2015, New York became the 33rd State to implement a
certification process for peer specialists. In accordance with the 1915i
Medicaid waiver, which includes Home and Community Based Services
(HCBS), mental health peer specialists who met the requirements, could
provide specific peer support services within organizations that had been
designated to offer these services. Accordingly, the formalization of peer
support services necessitated clarity of peer support specialists' roles and
tasks and ensuring ample infrastructure within organizations to provide
ongoing supervision and support to peer support staff. Without these
supports, role drift, inordinate stigma and exploitation compromised effective inclusion of peer support as full-fledged employees with accountability
and compensation commensurate with their co-workers (Davidson et al.,
2012; Gates & Akabas, 2007).

Despite the increasing visibility of peer support specialists, their recognition by CMS and SAMHSA as important service providers in mental health treatment, and funding streams created by Medicaid to cover specific peer support services, many organizations that either employed peer supporters, or indicated interest in expanding their workforce to include peer supporters continued to overlook important factors that negatively impacted optimal inclusion of this emerging workforce. These included but were not limited to 1) misperceptions regarding readiness and stability of potential peer supporters to adapt and function effectively on the job; 2) lack of career advancement opportunities for peer support specialists; and 3) lack of experienced supervisors especially those who understood important considerations and concerns working with peer support staff. Supervision in particular continues to be one of the grand challenges in terms of optimally addressing successful identification, onboarding, training, and retention of peer support specialists.

Discussion

Supervision Strategies: A Dialogue on Best Practices for Supervising Peer Supporters is both didactic and interactive. Following introductions and overview to the workshop, learning objectives were shared: Participants who attended this workshop 1) learned about some of the unique considerations involved in supervising peer support specialists; 2) described the critical functions of supervising peer supporters; and 3) articulated best practices for supervising peer supporters.

We first proposed our working definition of supervision as a structured relationship with the goal to help the worker gain attitudes, skills and knowledge needed to be a responsible and effective worker; concerned with guiding the worker in supporting the needs of participants and customers; and as encompassing administrative, support, educative, advocacy, and evaluative functions (NYCHHC, 2012). This multi-faceted model of supervision had first been introduced several years earlier as a four-function model of supervision; during a last-minute planning discussion for this workshop, we realized that, given the nuances of supervisors advocating for both the worker and the approach to care employed by peer support specialists, we should add advocacy as fifth function to capture supervisory tasks not necessarily addressed within the other domains.

We also spoke to the paradox faced by many peer support specialists—that they are neither in the "patient" nor the clinician role; therefore, a critical function of the supervisor will be to provide guidance and support that helps peer employees grow a meaningful identity, set appropriate boundaries with other staff, and minimize role ambiguity.

Additional material which addresses a number of issues for which supervisors of peer support staff express concern includes "Myths & Facts" (See Table 1) and "Supervision Situations & Solutions" (See Table 2). This material is excerpted from two widely known resources: An article by Davidson and colleagues (2012) and the Peer Specialist Toolkit developed by Philadelphia Department of Behavioral Health and Intellectual Disability Services (DBHIDS, 2017).

MYTH / CONCERN	FACT
Aren't peer staff too "fragile" to handle the stress of the job?	Focus should be on whether the peer staff is able to perform the essential functions of the job
Don't peer staff relapse?	All employees, including peer staff, take off time because of illness, including mental health issues
Can peer staff handle the administrative demands of the job?	Supervision and specific job-skills training can support peer staff in managing these tasks
Won't peer staff cause harm to clients by breaking confidentiality or by saying the "wrong" things?	Given their own experiences, peer staff may in fact be more sensitive around issues of participant confidentiality
Won't peer staff make my job harder rather than easier?	The perspective of a peer specialist provides an important and useful complement to traditional mental health services; they can enrich participants' lives while other staff focus on their own roles

SITUATION / CHALLENGE	SOLUTION / RECOMMENDED PRACTICES
Lacking formal supervision structure	Establish formal supervision guidelines Establish a clear agenda Clarify tasks and expectations
Distinguishing supportive supervision from therapy	Establish clear and professional boundaries Redirect or identify appropriate support
Understanding and respecting peer supporter role	Discuss the value of peer support Clarify expectations and tasks
Resolving interpersonal conflicts	Listen to all "sides" of the story Facilitate mutual respect and resolution
Evaluating performance	Document regularly, keep a journal Provide feedback, guidance, and support Implement progressive discipline when necessary

Source: Peer Support Toolkit. Philadelphia, PA: DBHIDS., 2017

GIVEN the complex nature of supervision as it pertains to myriad roles and mindsets of manager, coach, mediator, and in some cases, a person who draws on their own lived experience, we proposed a model designed specifically to address some of the nuances of supervising individuals in the peer specialist role. The Five Critical Functions of Supervision (Edwards, 2018) guides a supervisor to reflect critically on their role including range and depth of responsibilities. This model suggests that supervision can be conducted with compassion without being infantilizing or setting a double standard. Further, this model fosters accountability for supervisors and promotes collaboration between supervisors and people whom they supervise (Foglesong et al., 2021).

The Five Critical Functions of Supervision are operationalized as examples of three tasks beneath each of the five functions (See Table 3). Although not exhaustive, these tasks cover a broad array of a supervisor's responsibilities beginning with recruitment and hiring to promoting professional development.

Table 1: Five Critical Functions in Practice

ADMINISTRATE	SUPPORT	EDUCATE	ADVOCATE	EVALUATE
Hire staff who meet job qualifications	Build rapport by providing constructive feedback	Explain the big picture; provide context for value and role and value in supporting the mission	Foster good morale and a respectful work environment	Clarify expectations with respect to job performance
Orient staff to organizational structure	Inspire excellence and promote wellness and self-care	Coach staff on methods for engaging and educating participants	Strengthen the practice of peer support by promoting its value	Conduct performance evaluations
Help staff understand practices, policies, and procedures	Utilize a strengths based and trauma-informed approach to help staff problem-solve	Offer relevant training and conference attendance opportunities	Negotiate reasonable work accommodations when appropriate	Address areas needing improvement; progressive discipline

Source: Edwards, J.P. (2018). The Critical Functions of Supervising Peer Supporters. (Presentation Slide)

Activity (operationalization of presentation concepts)

To encourage participation and interaction, we invited five volunteers to read scenarios that were used to prompt discussion in small group discussions based on Supervision Situations and Solutions. Instructions for setting up the activity are listed in Table 4.

GUIDELINES FOR ACTIVITY

Instructions
- Join the group based on your assigned number
- Review and discuss in ten minutes your group's scenario
- Prepare and share in three minutes your group's response to the
  question that follows the scenario

Topics for Scenarios
- Lacking formal supervision structure
- Distinguishing formal supervision from therapy
- Understanding and respecting the peer specialist's role
- Resolving interpersonal conflicts
- Evaluating performance

TABLES 5 through 9 are the scenarios used by small groups to complete the activity.

SCENARIO #1
LACKING FORMAL SUPERVISION STRUCTURE

A peer specialist complains that he is not receiving the necessary support
from his supervisor on a regular basis. In fact, he can't even remember
the last time he sat down with his supervisor to discuss specific work
issues. The supervisor states that she has an open-door policy and that he
can knock on her door to discuss any issues at any time the peer specialist
wants.

Activity Prompt: Using at least one the Five Critical of Functions of Supervision in
Practice, what steps could you take to address this situation?

244

SCENARIO #2
DISTINGUISHING SUPPORTIVE SUPERVISION
FROM THERAPY

A peer specialist begins to talk about personal problems she is having with her partner and goes into great length in detail about the challenges. The supervisor is struggling with not knowing how much and what kind of support to give his peer specialist supervisee. He wants to do as much as he can to help the peer specialist because she is a consumer but doesn't know where to draw the line. He understands that the peer specialist is not a client on his caseload, but a peer specialist staff.

Activity Prompt: Using at least one the Five Critical of Functions of Supervision in Practice, what steps could you take to address this situation?

SCENARIO #3
UNDERSTANDING AND RESPECTING THE
PEER SPECIALIST'S ROLE

Many supervisors are new to supervising peer specialists and don't understand their role or value. Some non-peer staff feel as though peer specialists rest on the laurels of their lived experience. Peer specialists sometimes believe that simply by the fact that they have shared experience enables them to provide quality services.

Activity Prompt: Using at least one the Five Critical of Functions of Supervision in Practice, what steps could you take to address this situation?

SCENARIO #4
RESOLVING INTERPERSONAL CONFLICTS

Jane is a social worker who feels threatened by Tom who is a peer specialist. Tom provides many of the same case management services and does a good job engaging program participants. Jane hears that there may be budget cuts within the organization and feels threatened by Tom because he can provide the same services for less pay. As a result, Jane feel anxious about job stability and begins to behave disrespectfully to Tom. Tom complains to the supervisor who manages both Jane and him.

Activity Prompt: Using at least one the Five Critical of Functions of Supervision in Practice, what steps could you take to address this situation?

SCENARIO #5
EVALUATING JOB PERFORMANCE

Cheryl is a peer specialist who seems to do an excellent job of engaging consumers who are disconnected from mental health services. However, her attendance is poor, and she is often late. On occasion she has even been absent without notifying her supervisor. Although she has been given a verbal warning, her attendance has not improved. Cheryl believes that because she does a good job at consumer engagement her attendance should not be an issue.

Activity Prompt: Using at least one the Five Critical of Functions of Supervision in Practice, what steps could you take to address this situation?

Conclusion

What matters most at the end of this workshop is that participants not only articulate comprehension of the learning objectives, but that they also glean a sense of accomplishment in their own practice wisdom as new, intermediate, or seasoned supervisors. In other words, what we consistently observe is that participants bring a great deal more into the room than they tend to give themselves credit for. Perhaps this is part of the inherent downside of being a supervisor; holding a great deal of responsibility often without commensurate formal power. Discussing approaches to and solutions for addressing issues that arise in supervision can be a tremendously empowering experience, especially in small group dialogue with other supervisors. Similarly, supervisors can gain additional perspectives on the nuances of situations that peer specialists navigate in their myriad role of advocate, change agent, companion, champion, and role model for both their colleagues and those whom they support.

References

Centers for Medicare and Medicaid Services (CMS) (2007). SMDL #07-011. Retrieved from: https://downloads.cms.gov/cmsgov/archived-downloads/SMDL/downloads/smd081507a.pdf

Davidson, L., Bellamy, C. B., Guy, K., & Miller, R. (2012). Peer support among persons with severe mental illnesses: A review of evidence and experience. World Psychiatry, 11(2), 123–128. doi: 10.1016/j.wpsyc.2012.05.009

Edwards, J. (2018). Five critical functions of supervising peer supporters, supervision track: An introduction to supervising peer specialists, key concepts. Academy of Peer Services.

Foglesong, D., Spagnolo, A. B., Cronise, R., Forbes, J., Swarbrick, P., Edwards, J. P., & Pratt, C. (2021). Perceptions of Supervisors of Peer Support Workers (PSW) in Behavioral Health: Results from a National Survey. *Community mental health journal*, 1–7. Advance online publication. https://doi.org/10.1007/s10597-021-00837-2

Gates, L. & Akabas, S. (2007). Developing Strategies to Integrate Peer Providers into Mental Health Agencies. Administrative Policy in Mental Health & Mental Health Services Resources 34:293–306. doi 10.1007/s10488-006-0109-4

National Association of County Behavioral Health and Developmental Disability Directors [NACBHDD]. (2016). Under the Microscope: Perspectives on peer support.

National Association of State Mental Health Program Directors (NASMHPD) (2014)
Enhancing the Peer Provider Workforce: Recruitment, Supervision and Retention

New York City Health and Hospitals Corp. (2012). Guide for Supervisors of Peer Counselors at HHC.

Philadelphia Dept. of Behavioral Health and Intellectual Disabilities Services and Achara Consulting Inc. (2017). Peer Support Toolkit. Philadelphia, PA: DBHIDS.

SECTION 2: SUPERVISION AS COLLABORATION: AN EMERGING DIALOGUE FOR PEER-INFORMED PRACTICE

Jonathan P. Edwards, Ph.D., LCSW, ACSW, NYCPS
Workforce Development Consultant, Facilitator and Researcher
Former Board Member, National Association of Peer Supporters (N.A.P.S.)

Gita Enders, LMSW, MA, NYCPS
Workforce Training and Development Consultant

Over the past 15 years, peer support within behavioral health settings has grown exponentially. SAMHSA predicts an additional one million peer support workers are needed to meet demand and there are multiple pending legislative bills that would expand peer support services in Medicare, the Veteran's Administration, and through telehealth peer support. Peer support is shown to improve quality-of-life and has financial implications for emerging service delivery models, yet many organizations struggle to mean-ingfully utilize peer support workers and recognize the value-add of peer-delivered services. As these services expand, opportunities and barriers have become better understood. However, if organizations do not receive guidance and support in systematically integrating a lived experience perspective into the workforce, challenges will persist despite documented effectiveness of peer support services. Several decades of experience supervising peer special-ists in multiple practice settings, as well as developing, implementing, and managing peer support services and programs in the government, private, and nonprofit sectors, the presenters of this workshop integrate best prac-tices based on national studies and workgroups they led and participated in.

Supervisors should minimally be familiar with principles and values informing the work of those whom they supervise. Supervision should there-fore integrate the National Practice Guidelines for Peer Support staff in their entirety. In this workshop we focus on the principle, "Peer support is mutual and reciprocal." Both peer support staff and effective supervisors (1) are receptive to constructive feedback; (2) use their own experiences in mutual exchanges to encourage and inspire those they support; (3) inspire others to explore dreams and goals meaningful to those they support; and (4) communicate equitably, acknowledging strengths, informed choice, and shared decision making as a foundation of recovery/growth. Lastly, although both peer support staff and effective supervisors may use role-modeling, they do not fix or do for others what those individuals can do for themselves.

Discussion

Supervision as Consultation: A Continuing Dialogue for Peer-Informed Practice is both didactic and interactive. Following a robust and warm introduction, presenters poll participants to get a sense of who is in the room (e.g., peer support staff, supervisors, program directors) and to get feedback on what participants consider their favorite attribute in a past or present supervisor. Rationale for offering a workshop on supervision responds to: (1) an emerging peer support workforce in the U.S. with recent estimates of more than 25,000 certified peer specialists in the U.S. alone (NACBHDD, (2016); (2) uptake in organizational interest and buy-in of peer support staff, in programs serving mental health, substance use disorder (SUD), family, youth, and justice-impacted populations; and (3) historic underutilization of established models guiding supervisory practice in human services.

Learning objectives state that by the end of the workshop, participants will be able to: (1) define the "Five Critical Functions of Supervision"; (2) operationalize at least three supervisory functions; and (3) identify one specific approach to address a supervisory situation. Learning objectives are also reviewed at the end of the workshop session; participants are asked to verbalize how each objective was demonstrated.

Introducing the element of comic relief, we look at a few examples of what supervision is not: (1) The number of clients seen during the day; (2) The number of forms completed; or (3) The number of cases filed. In contrast, we define supervision as, "An alliance between staff in differing roles working towards common goals." Supervision is further described as an opportunity to develop knowledge, skills and abilities to become an effective worker; that teamwork, communication, mutual respect and professional development are essential; and that supervision inherently encompasses administrative, supportive, educative, advocacy and evaluative functions. See figure 1: Five Critical Functions of Supervision (Edwards, 2018).

Figure 1: Five Critical Functions of Supervision

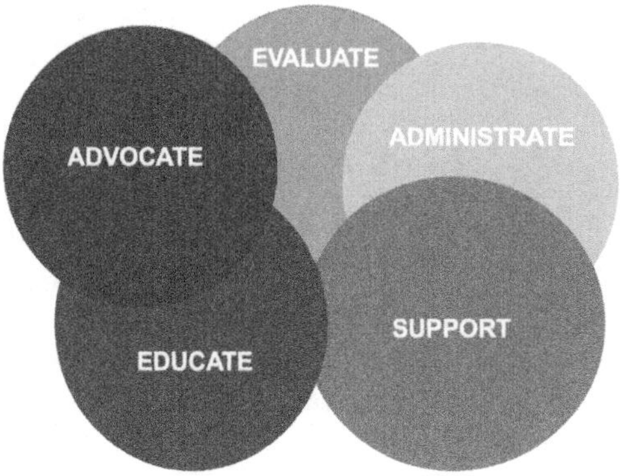

Given the complex nature of supervision as it pertains to myriad roles and mindsets of manager, coach, mediator, and in some cases, a person who draws on their own lived experience, we propose a model designed specifically to address some of the nuances of supervising individuals in the peer specialist role. The Five Critical Functions of Supervision (Edwards, 2018) guides a supervisor to reflect critically on their role including range and depth of responsibilities. This model suggests that supervision can be conducted with compassion without being infantilizing or setting a double standard. Further, this model fosters accountability for supervisors and promotes collaboration between supervisors and people whom they supervise (Foglesong et al., 2021).

The Five Critical Functions of Supervision are operationalized as examples of three tasks beneath each of the five functions (See Table 1). Although not exhaustive, these tasks cover a broad array of a supervisor's responsibilities beginning with recruitment and hiring to promoting professional development.

Table 1: Five Critical Functions in Practice

ADMINISTRATE	SUPPORT	EDUCATE	ADVOCATE	EVALUATE
Hire staff who meet job qualifications	Build rapport by providing constructive feedback	Explain the big picture; provide context for value and role and value in supporting the mission	Foster good morale and a respectful work environment	Clarify expectations with respect to job performance
Orient staff to organizational structure	Inspire excellence and promote wellness and self-care	Coach staff on methods for engaging and educating participants	Strengthen the practice of peer support by promoting its value	Conduct performance evaluations
Help staff understand practices, policies, and procedures	Utilize a strengths based and trauma-informed approach to help staff problem-solve	Offer relevant training and conference attendance opportunities	Negotiate reasonable work accommodations when appropriate	Address areas needing improvement; progressive discipline

Source: Edwards, J.P. (2018). The Critical Functions of Supervising Peer Supporters. (Presentation Slide)

Additional material which addresses issues for which supervisors of peer support staff express concern includes "Myths & Facts" (See Table 2) and "Supervision Situations & Solutions" (See Table 3). This material is excerpted from two widely known resources, an article by Davidson and colleagues (2012) and the Peer Specialist Toolkit developed by Philadelphia Department of Behavioral Health and Intellectual Disability Services (DBHIDS, 2017).

Table 2: Myths & Facts

MYTH / CONCERN	FACT
Aren't peer staff too "fragile" to handle the stress of the job?	Focus should be on whether the peer staff is able to perform the essential functions of the job
Don't peer staff relapse?	All employees, including peer staff, take off time because of illness, including mental health issues
Can peer staff handle the administrative demands of the job?	Supervision and specific job-skills training can support peer staff in managing these tasks
Won't peer staff cause harm to clients by breaking confidentiality or by saying the "wrong" things?	Given their own experiences, peer staff may in fact be more sensitive around issues of participant confidentiality
Won't peer staff make my job harder rather than easier?	The perspective of a peer specialist provides an important and useful complement to traditional mental health services; they can enrich participants' lives while other staff focus on their own roles

Source: Davidson, Bellamy, Guy, & Miller, 2012

(Davidson & Harrington, 2012)

SITUATION / CHALLENGE	SOLUTION / RECOMMENDED PRACTICES
Lacking formal supervision structure	Establish formal supervision guidelines Establish a clear agenda Clarify tasks and expectations
Distinguishing supportive supervision from therapy	Establish clear and professional boundaries Redirect or identify appropriate support
Understanding and respecting peer supporter role	Discuss the value of peer support Clarify expectations and tasks
Resolving interpersonal conflicts	Listen to all "sides" of the story Facilitate mutual respect and resolution
Evaluating performance	Document regularly, keep a journal Provide feedback, guidance, and support Implement progressive discipline when necessary

Source: Peer Support Toolkit. Philadelphia, PA: DBHIDS., 2017

Time for a typical workshop is 90 minutes. We endeavor to move from introduction, polling and didactic to interactive 35-40 minutes into the workshop. Over time, we have learned that the "heart of the learning" emerges from dialogue between participants with workshop presenters serving as facilitators.

Activity (operationalization of presentation concepts)

To encourage participation and interaction, we often invite participants to volunteer to read segments of workshop content. Below are steps to setting up the main activity:

Introduce Supervision Situations (aka scenarios). These are based on practice knowledge, current trends, and potential concerns supervisors may face when helping staff work through a range of issues.

Refer to The Five Critical Functions of Supervision in Practice Reference Tool, which provides examples of tasks within each of the functions; these can be used in formulating responses to various situations that come up in supervision.

Divide participants into small groups ranging from 3-6 people depending on size of workshop.

Provide groups with 20 minutes to (1) read and discuss their specific scenario; (2) use the Five Critical Functions of Supervision in Practice to formulate their response to the prompt at the end of the scenario; and (3) prepare a brief summary to report out to the other groups.

We have found that simply reporting out on groups' processes generates rich dialogue; this is where the workshop becomes more organic as new themes and approaches emerge.

Conclusion

What matters most at the end of this workshop is that participants not only articulate comprehension of the learning objectives, but that they also glean a sense of accomplishment in their own practice wisdom as new, intermediate, or seasoned supervisors. In other words, what we consistently observe is that participants bring a great deal more into the room than they tend to give themselves credit for. Perhaps this is part of the inherent downside of being a supervisor; holding a great deal of responsibility often without commensurate formal power.

Discussing approaches to and solutions for addressing issues that arise in supervision can be a tremendously empowering experience, especially in small group dialogue with other supervisors. Similarly, supervisors can gain additional perspectives on the nuances of situations that peer specialists navigate in their myriad role of advocate, change agent, companion, champion, and role model for both their colleagues and those whom they support.

References

Centers for Medicare and Medicaid Services (CMS) (2007). SMDL #07-011. Retrieved from: https://downloads.cms.gov/cmsgov/archived-downloads/SMDL/downloads/smd081507a.pdf

Davidson, L., Bellamy, C. B., Guy, K., & Miller, R. (2012). Peer support among persons with severe mental illnesses: A review of evidence and experience. World Psychiatry, 11(2), 123–128. doi: 10.1016/j.wpsyc.2012.05.009

Davidson, L. & Harrington, S. (2012). Common Practitioner Concerns: Myths About Peer Support. Part 2 of a 3 Part Series. SAMHSA Recovery to Practice Weekly Highlight. Volume 2, Issue 10 (March 18, 2011).

Edwards, J. (2018). Five critical functions of supervising peer supporters, supervision track: An introduction to supervising peer specialists, key concepts. Academy of Peer Services.

Foglesong, D., Spagnolo, A. B., Cronise, R., Forbes, J., Swarbrick, P., Edwards, J. P., & Pratt, C. (2021). Perceptions of Supervisors of Peer Support Workers (PSW) in Behavioral Health: Results from a National Survey. *Community mental health journal*, 1–7. Advance online publication. https://doi.org/10.1007/s10597-021-00837-2

National Association of County Behavioral Health and Developmental Disability Directors [NACBHDD]. (2016). Under the Microscope: Perspectives on peer support.

Philadelphia Dept. of Behavioral Health and Intellectual Disabilities Services and Achara Consulting Inc. (2017). Peer Support Toolkit. Philadelphia, PA: DBHIDS.

SECTION 3: SUD PEER SUPERVISION COMPETENCIES

Linda May Wacker, M Ed., CADC I
Program Director of Morrison Child & Family Services' Parent Mentor Program

Discussion

THIS TOOL REMEDIES a significant gap in the field of SUD peer services and represents a crucial body of specialized knowledge developed by practicing peer supervisors to date. The DACUM Workgroup has created a highly accessible and relevant teaching tool now used widely by peer programs in the state of Oregon and throughout the United States.

While the tool has been peer reviewed and developed utilizing an academic literature review, the resulting tool is a practical framework that provides any easy-to-use structure for any person supervising SUD peers.

The SUD Peer Supervision Competencies offer a 35-page training and assessment tool for supervisors of peers designed for in-class training which can be accessed online here: Peer-Supervision-Competencies-2017.pdf (williamwhitepapers.com)

The competencies are divided into these 4 sections:

1. Recovery-Oriented Philosophy
2. Providing Education & Training
3. Facilitating Quality Supervision
4. Performing Administrative Duties

It is important to note that this competency tool is specifically designed for teaching purposes. Competencies with specific KSA's (Knowledge, Skills, and Attitudes) are described in checkboxes for classroom participant self-assessment. The brief and straightforward instructions appear below.

Classroom Directions

1. Review and discuss a competency.
2. Ask each participant to complete the associated self-assessment. The self-assessment check box can also be used as an "agency self-assessment" check box.
3. In groups, have participants discuss their strengths and areas needing improvement based on their self-assessment.
4. Facilitate a class discussion around the insights gained by individuals through self-assessment and group discussions.
5. Move on to the next competency and repeat the process.

As an example, an excerpt of one of the competencies appears below:

* COMPETENCY SIX: *Ongoing Training - Supervisor acknowledges that requisite entry level education is modest and that their role includes ongoing training & education, including coaching/mentoring peers regarding: competencies, skills development, documentation, data collection systems, ethical standards, professional boundaries, community resources, applicable laws, and client rights.*

SELF-ASSESSMENT CHECKLIST: *Ongoing Training*

☐ *Supervisor has the capacity to provide education and ongoing coaching on a variety of topics and understands basic principles of adult learning strategies.*

☐ *Supervisor designs and implements ongoing education in staff meeting formats, agency in-services, and individual instruction/coaching as indicated.*

☐ *Supervisor provides ongoing education/training/coaching regarding documentation standards and data entry systems, motivational enhancement techniques/micro-skills, outreach, engagement, rapport- building, peer competencies (SAMHSA, IC&RC, etc.), regulations, legal compliance, ethics, professional boundaries, cultural awareness, self-care, and community resources.*

☐ *Supervisor supports peer staff in obtaining ongoing training to advance their personal efficacy and competencies in delivering peer support services through participation in classes, conferences, webinars, and other forms of education and training.*

. . .

DURING TRAINING, the supervisor completing the assessment is able to reflect on their practice, and identify, for example, that they frequently provide "ongoing education in staff meeting formats" but may need to research and better understand "adult learning strategies." They can then use this information to inform their annual performance evaluation, professional development or other goal-setting plan. A thorough self-assessment that includes reflection and enriching discussion with fellow supervisors takes several hours. (An in-depth training offered locally by the authors for a group of approximately 30 local peer supervisors lasted 6 hours.) This training process could be offered at a retreat or other extended team meeting setting.

Conclusion

The final three pages of the curriculum are a condensed Peer Employee Evaluation Form that is ready-to-use for anyone supervising SUD peers. While many organizations employing peers have their own annual evaluation forms, it is rare that these documents developed by HR professionals are relevant to peer work or include the specialized competencies required to perform high quality peer support work.

A meaningful way to evaluate peer performance is especially important for peers working in a medical or broader behavioral health context, where role clarity and distinction from clinical or administrative roles can be an ongoing challenge for those supervising peers. Utilizing this tool provides a meaningful supplement to more generic agency HR forms and empowers peer supervisors to evaluate their staff in the proper context.

More Information

SUD Peer Supervision Competencies curriculum —Linda May Wacker, Program Director, Morrison Child & Family Services, Portland, Oregon SUD Peer Core Competencies

Acknowledgements

DACUM Facilitators/Authors: Eric Martin, MAC, CADC III, PRC, CPS & Anthony Jordan, MPA, CADC II, CRM

DACUM Workgroup: Michael Razavi, MPH, CADC I, PRC, CPS Van Burnham IV, B. Accy., CRM Ally Linfoot, PSS Monta Knudson, CADC II, CRM Erin DeVet, B.S., CADC II Linda Hudson, MSW, CSWA, CADC III LaKeesha Dumas, CRM, PSS, CHW Edited by J. Thomas Shrewsbury, MSW,

LCSW, BCD, MAC Jeff Marotta, PhD, CADC III, CGAC II Ruth Bichsel, Ph.D., HS-BCP, MAC, FACFEI, FABPS Kitty Martz, MBA, CGRM
Qualitative Review by William White

About the Authors

Linda May Wacker, M Ed., CADC I is Program Director of Morrison Child & Family Services' Parent Mentor Program and has been a peer mentor trainer and supervisor for 9 years. She contributed as an editor to <u>Substance Use Disorder Peer Delivered Services Child Welfare Best Practices Curriculum</u>. Smith, K. Debban, C. Sanden, S. Martin, E. Wurscher, J. Wacker, L M. Klapperich, M. Paul, J. (2017). Linda May learned everything she knows about addiction, recovery, and peer supervision from people in recovery.

References

Boyd, J. PhD CPRP, O'Brien-Mazza, D., M.S. VA Psychology Leadership Conference, conference presentation, Frontiers in Peer Support Supervision (2014).

BRSS-TACS, Meeting Transcript, Supervision Strategies for Peer Recovery Support Providers, November 21, 2014, 12:00-1:00pm ET (2014).

Camp, D. ALWF, CPS, CCAR-T, course syllabus, Supervising Peer Recovery Specialist.

Chinman, M., PHD, conference presentation, Peer Specialist: Implementation, Evidence and Effective Supervision

Community Care, Performance Standards Peer Recovery Support Services - Certified Peer Specialist Services (2014).

Daniels, A. S., Tunner, T. P., Powell, I., Fricks, L., Ashenden, P., Pillars of Peer Support – VI: Peer Specialist Supervision (2015).

Delaware Certification Board, Certified Peer Support Specialist Supervisor Endorsement, (2016).

Denverdrugstrategy, Colorado, Implementing Peer Recovery Services Handbook adapted from: Implementing Peer Support Services in VHA

Hendry, P., Hill, T., Rosenthal, H. Peer Services Toolkit: A Guide to Advancing and Implementing Peer-run Behavioral Health Services. ACMHA: The College for Behavioral Health Leadership and Optum (2014).

Idaho Certification Board, Peer Supervisor Requirements
Lesesne, B., CCETT, Roberts, K. M. MPH, conference presentation, Code of Professional Conduct: Clarifying and Establishing Boundaries in SCDMH Peer delivered services.
Magellan Health, Peer Support e-course 4: Effective Supervision of Peer Specialists

Martin, E. & Jordan, A. (2017). Substance Use Disorder Peer Supervision Competencies & The Systematic Review of the Literature. The Regional Facilitation Center. http://www.williamwhitepapers.com/pr/dlm_uploads/Peer-Supervision-Competencies-2017.pdf

Martin, E., Razavi, M., Gage, J., Marotta, J. (2016). MetroPlus Substance Use Disorder Peer delivered services Survey

Martin, E. Oregon Peer delivered services Business Best Practices Manual (2016).

Massachusetts Department of Mental Health, Supervision Meeting the Needs of CPS's in a System in Flux

Mental Health Coordinating Council, New South Wales, Workforce Development Pathway 8 – Supervision, Mentoring & Coaching

National Association of State Mental Health Program Directors, Enhancing the Peer Provider Workforce: Recruitment, Supervision and Retention (2014)

NJPRA November Conference Living the values of recovery in policies, programs, and practice, conference presentation, Practices in Peer Specialist Supervision and Employment (2010).

Schwenk, E.B., Brusilovskiy, E., & Salzer, M.S. Results from a National Survey of Certified Peer Specialist Job Titles and Job Descriptions: Evidence of a Versatile Behavioral Health Workforce. The University of Pennsylvania Collaborative on Community Integration: Philadelphia, PA (2009).

Sheff-Eisenberg, A. Psy.D., MFT, Walston, G., MA, MFT, San Fernando Valley Community Mental Health Center, Recovery Oriented Supervision in PSR Programs, A Summary of the Presentation at the Israel Psychiatric Rehabilitation Association (ISPRA) Conference (2011).

State of Tennessee, Certified Peer Recovery Specialist Supervision Requirements

Substance Abuse and Mental Health Services Administration, Center for Substance Abuse Treatment. Perspectives on the Evolution and Future of Peer Recovery Support Services. Rockville, MD (2012).

Substance Abuse and Mental Health Services Administration, Center for Substance Abuse Treatment, TIP 52, Clinical Supervision and Professional Development of The Substance Abuse Counselor Swarbrick, M., Peer Wellness Coaching Supervisor Manual. Freehold, NJ: Collaborative Support Programs of New Jersey, Institute for Wellness and Recovery Initiatives (2010).

Swarbrick, M., Peer Wellness Coaching Supervisor Manual. Freehold, NJ: Collaborative Support Programs of New Jersey, Institute for Wellness and Recovery Initiatives (2010).

Tucker, S. J., Tiegreen, W., Toole, J., Banathy, J., Mulloy, D., & Swarbrick, M. Supervisor Guide: Peer Support Whole Health and Wellness Coach, Georgia Mental Health Consumer Network (2013)

Veterans Administration, A Report on Peer Support Supervision in VA Mental Health Services Depression and Bipolar Support Alliance (DBSA)

White, W., Illinois Department of Human Services Office of Alcoholism and Substance Abuse, The Delivery and Supervision of Outreach Services

White, W. Peer-based addiction recovery support: History, theory, practice, and scientific evaluation. Chicago, IL: Great Lakes Addiction Technology Transfer Center and Philadelphia Department of Behavioral Health and Mental Retardation Services (2009).

White, W., Schwartz, J. & the Philadelphia Clinical Supervision Workgroup. The Role of Clinical Supervision in Recovery-oriented Systems of Behavioral

Healthcare. Philadelphia: Department of Behavioral Health and Mental Retardation Services (2007).

SECTION 4: RECOVERY FIRST, FAMILY SECOND, WORK THIRD: SUPERVISING & SUPPORTING PEERS

Linda May Wacker, M Ed., CADC

Anna Rockhill, MPP

Brittany Kintigh, MA

In this asubmission we describe our approach to supporting and supervising peer parent mentors. We introduce a framework that includes a recovery-oriented workplace, team connectedness, effective supervisory relationships, role clarity and meaningful performance evaluation. We describe the rationale behind these components as well as practical tips that support their implementation. While our experience is based on working with peers within a child welfare context, we believe it has broad applicability beyond that arena.

Background

For 18 years, the Parent Mentor Program at Morrison Child & Family Services in Portland, Oregon has operated a highly successful parent partner program serving parents involved in Child Welfare. The program hires parents with prior child welfare involvement to mentor parents who currently have an open child welfare case. All Parent Mentors are in recovery from substance use disorder, have at least 2 years of sobriety and work an active program of recovery. The program has taken an intentional approach to supporting a team of staff who use their lived experience of trauma, addiction & recovery in their work every day. Each of the essential components of our approach is rooted in the belief that healing, growth and change are possible for each person, at all levels, in communities, organizations and systems.

Discussion

Fostering a Recovery OrientedOrientated Workplace

The Parent Mentor Program motto, "Recovery First, Family Second, Work Third" has specific meaning, and places value on recovery and family. First, all program staff understand that actively living a life in recovery is what allows peers to provide unique support to others with shared experiences. Recovery activities and perspectives keep them healthy, sober, and practicing ethical boundaries.

Many peers express that they believe losing their recovery practices would jeopardize their relationships, their housing, their job, their income, their transportation and everything else of value, including their families. Second, we also understand that when people are experiencing grief, loss or a crisis in their families, it can be nearly impossible for them to focus on performing their job. Only by maintaining their recovery can peers effectively navigate the inevitable challenges of family life that can include birth, illness, death, and constant change and stress. When both recovery and family are stable, we know peers can perform their best work.

Programs may operationalize these values by removing some of the traditionally held dominant culture values around productivity and overwork. In organizations where value is placed on getting work done for the organization over individual employee health & wellness, for example, it is common for employees to feel guilty for taking a sick day and may push themselves to show up to work despite illness. Recurrence of use (relapse) often occurs during times of stress or change, whether positive or negative, and peers may demonstrate or express needing time off to seek counsel from a sponsor, support network or go to a recovery meeting during times of change. When an aging parent or young child is ill, employees may fear asking for time to care for their family member.

In a "Family Second" work environment, it becomes normal to ask for time off for these family caretaking responsibilities, and supervisors are flexible and supportive (not shaming) when staff ask for this time off. For this reason, it is important for peers to have full time, benefitted positions with paid time off available to them. When the explicitly stated value of the program is recovery and health maintenance, and family stability over "showing up no matter what," peers are able to bring their authentic selves to work *and* minimize potential harm that can be caused to teammates and clients if a peer comes to work when their recovery practices are lacking, or they are otherwise unfit to be professional helpers due to family or life stress, grief or loss.

Other important ways supervisors promote a recovery-oriented work environment are:

- Modeling a strength-based approach & language (not gossiping or encouraging negativity)
- Normalizing asking for help
- Modeling resolving conflicts; not holding resentments
- Expressing belief that change is possible – holding hope for each employee and client

Building Team Connectedness & Trust through Regular Team Meetings

An old parenting quote tells us, "Children spell *love*, T-I-M-E." This quote has been attributed to numerous people, but a parallel for the workplace might go something like, "Employees spell trust, T-I-M-E." If we place value on promoting health and preventing burnout, creating a sense of trust and connection within our teams is an incredibly potent way to disperse stress and communicate that none of us is alone in the difficult work of being helping professionals. At the Parent Mentor Program, staff begin each week with a 90–120-minute team meeting that includes sharing professional and personal successes and challenges, and completing program business.

An important value of an effective team meeting in the peer services setting is consistently holding space for staff to share their personal and professional experiences. Beginning each meeting intentionally with a way for staff to share how they are feeling, what happened over the weekend, and what they are bringing with them to work that day is key. And, using a tool that creates a container and prevents emotions from taking over the meeting is equally important. The Parent Mentor Program uses a tool from the Sanctuary Model called the Community Meeting. Each team member asks another team member in turn, "How are you feeling?" "What is your goal for today?" and "Who can support you if you need it?"

This method of checking in accomplishes several important goals:

1. It encourages presence, everyone makes eye contact and listens actively each of their teammates for a few moments.
2. It normalizes that we are all human beings with emotions and lives outside work
3. It helps each person experience feeling seen, heard and valued, briefly, to begin their work week

4. It signals to supervisors and teammates if a team member is struggling and may need additional support that day
5. It creates opportunities for staff to ask for the support they need, from specific people
6. It is a structured "container" for sharing personal information within a timeframe that allows for a person-first approach and leaves plenty of time for discussing business needs.

When team members check in as feeling "anxious," or "worried," "sad," or any upset or negative emotion, the person asking the questions asks, "Would you like to check in about that?" giving them the opportunity to share more and receive encouragement or support, or to pass. If the check-in begins to take up a lot of time, the person asking the questions can prompt with the final question, "Who can support you today," or the more nuanced, "What does support look like for you today?" to help the team member articulate what they need from the group. And at that point the supervisor, the supervisor knows to check in with their supervisee later that day.

Expressing and listening to the shared ups and downs of life together, over time, creates the glue that can help hold a team together. In the team setting, this process can also model and mirror the process of peer support. While other techniques than the Community Meeting may be used to accomplish this goal, a regular and intentional plan to hold space for a check-in is vital.

While business must also be conducted in team meetings, there are important checks in place to create safety and predictability for the team. Consistently providing a written agenda helps to minimize surprises and provides a structured routine for gathering together. Including brief announcements to share community events or program deadlines peers need to know is helpful, so long as the meeting does not become an "information dump." Business updates should be minimal to make the team meeting function as a trust-building gathering that provides meaningful connection and skill-building. Regular communication from leadership with built-in opportunities for staff to ask questions about any organizational changes will help build trust between peers and management. Team meetings are also a venue to gather feedback from peers to inform program decision-making. Through regular updates and opportunities to provide input, teams learn to trust that leadership will not "drop bombs" in the team setting and will seek the input of peers during times of change.

Other specific practices during team meetings include:

- Shared facilitation of the meeting; everyone takes turns sharing in the challenge of keeping the meeting focused, holding space for feelings, and getting through the agenda, developing understanding of and appreciation for facilitation skill
- Intentional case staffing – modeling strength-based language about clients and community partners
- Making regular times to share successes
- Gratitude and self-care practices in team setting
- Supervisors encourage peers to consult with and support one another
- Regular team-building activities – make time for fun! Productive teams spend fun social time together

Building Trusting Supervisory Relationships

IN PEER SUPPORT, as in any helping relationship, building a trusting relationship is primary. In order to support individuals through the difficult business of change, peers must first earn the client's trust. This is typically accomplished by the peer consistently showing that they will show up when they say they will show up, that they can make time for the client, that they will follow through on any agreed-upon tasks, and that they generally demonstrate honesty and integrity in their words and actions. This process can be helped with some limited self-disclosure in which the peer communicates their shared lived experiences with the client.

All of this is also modeled by supervisors in building trust with peers they supervise. Supervisors of peers should hold regular (weekly is preferable) supervision & prioritize availability for peers. Supervision is a time to check in personally, staff each client the peer is supporting, and to coach around professional development.

Peers may come into their role with limited professional experience; supervisors should expect to spend time in workforce development activities that help peers develop professional office, writing and communication skills. Supervisors ensure resources and support for ongoing training for each mentor to support their skill development and advance their careers.

An important way supervisors build trust with mentors is by role modeling honesty & integrity in way that aligns with principles of recovery. During inevitable times of stress or conflict, supervisors can help to minimize surprises and communicate openly, encouraging peers to communicate directly and honestly when a coworker or community partner does or says something that upsets them. Supervisors can offer to coach staff in resolving interpersonal conflicts and can role model the concept of "making amends" by acknowledging harm and initiating repair work with team members. This is a process that has repeatedly played out in the Parent Mentor Program – when a team member (whether a mentor or supervisor) says something that impacts another team member during a meeting, they follow up in the same meeting setting to acknowledge their mistake and its impact and apologize.

Supervisors also have ongoing discussions about personal and professional boundaries with peers, and help staff establish and adhere to professional boundaries. Since the role of peers is not widely understood in many settings, the role of the supervisor in helping the peer know when they can say no is crucial. On the one hand, peers will have vulnerable clients who regularly test boundaries, often due to their personal desire for connection, reassurance and concrete assistance; on the other hand, peers may have community partners who ask them to break confidentiality due to their professional desire to have more information about a client. Supervisors provide guardrails for peers in both areas.

Other important supervisory practices include:

- Praise regularly; honestly validate effort
- Know their story/trauma history & ask about how recovery works for them
- Learn about their cultural identity and how it impacts recovery, family, and work
- Take a holistic approach: provide personal and professional support
- Encourage and be flexible about self-care, share resources with peers who may benefit from outside professional support
- Allow staff to come up with their own solutions
- Defer to staff experience whenever possible
- Have staff participate in hiring
- Model what you want peers to do with clients

Role Clarity and Meaningful Performance Evaluation for Peers

Whether operating and maintaining a peer services program or considering start-up of a new program there is a series of helpful questions supervisors and program leadership can ask to assess how they will effectively support people with lived experience in their peer roles:

1. Providing role clarity for peers is a crucial supervisory activity; do I – or do our supervisors – have a thorough understanding of the peer role?
2. If not, how will we commit to developing this understanding?

- Starting points include: Use of SUD Peer Supervision Competencies Peer-Supervision-Competencies-2017.pdf (williamwhitepapers.com)
- Use of Peer Employee Competency Evaluation Form

1. What is our understanding of what it means to support principles of recovery at work?
2. How can we engage staff in recovery to help us build this understanding?
3. Peers will regularly be in touch with their own lived experiences of trauma in their work; What is our understanding of what it means to support a trauma-informed workplace?
4. Is our organization a learning organization?
5. How much tolerance does our organization have for mistakes as staff learn?
6. How committed is our organization to continued professional development for staff providing direct services?
7. What opportunities exist for peers to advance in their peer roles or beyond?
8. How do we provide accountability to staff for their job responsibilities? (i.e., we value learning enough to expect that people will learn from their mistakes; there is a limit to how many times someone is allowed to make the same mistake)

Using a tool that is designed to evaluate peer performance helps provide role clarity for peers and supervisors and provides meaningful prompts for discussions about professional goal setting.

A central function of peer supervision is to reinforce that the peer is not alone in their work, and that the client is not alone in their change. Supervisors should reinforce that a crucial role of the peer is *to help clients build support networks that do not include them*. It is important to note that the supervisory activities described here all occur in context: the supervisor should not be the "only one" who can support the peer, just as the peer should not be the "only one" who can support the client. *Quality peer supervision that prevents burnout and promotes growth occurs in a supportive context where peers build trusting connections on their team aside from their supervisor, in addition to the support networks that they have developed outside of work as a part of their recovery practice.* Supervisors and program leadership can support an effective peer services program by attending to the interconnected values of social connection and professional boundaries. In their unique roles, peers feel valued and supported when their specific context is understood, and they see their skills and expertise reflected back to them in performance evaluation.

Conclusion

Effectively supporting and supervising peers is multifaceted and may require intentional culture change work in organizations. Creating recovery-oriented workplace, team connectedness, effective supervisory relationships, role clarity and meaningful professional development and performance evaluation for all staff contributes not only to effective peer services, but also supports retention and an environment where all employees love their jobs.

More Information

Recording of original conference presentation: "Linda May Wacker & Stacy Rivera: Recovery First Peer Supervision" - YouTube: https://youtu.be/g4OSSq6EjQQ
PowerPoint from SHARE! 2020 Conference: Slide 1 (sccgov.org)
https://bhdp.sccgov.org/sites/g/files/exjcpb716/files/Wacker_Supervising-Supporting-Peers-ppt-February-2020.pdf
SUD Peer Supervision Competencies curriculum —Linda May Wacker, Program Director, Morrison Child & Family Services, Portland, Oregon SUD Peer Core Competencies

References

Martin, Jordan, Razavi, Burnham, Linfoot, Knudson, DeVet, Hudson, & Dumas (2017). Substance Use Disorder Peer Supervision Competencies, The Regional Facilitation Center, Portland, Oregon.

Sanctuary Model – Sanctuary Institute (thesanctuaryinstitute.org)

SECTION 5: SUPERVISION AND CO-SUPERVISION FOR FAMILY (PEER)
SUPPORT SPECIALISTS

Tammi S. Paul, Family Support Specialist
Deputy Director, Oregon Family Support Network

The three core elements of supervision include 1) observing behavior in the way an employee shows up, what they know, how they demonstrate what they know and how they are growing and adapting new skills 2) giving and receiving feedback as demonstrated by the ability to receive information about performance, knowing one's strengths and challenges and knowing what can be done to address their challenges and 3) motivating employees to learn new skills and tasks, develop strong relationships and the ability to invite employees to contribute thoughts and ideas in supervision.

Supervision of FSS is a regular, predicable, planned time to reflect, in a safe place, that is respectful of and honors what each participant brings with meaningful preparation. It is not *just* listening, as needed, therapy, for only those with less experience or easily done!

FSS supervision includes three distinct types of conversations and can be done in any order and often flows from one type to another in any single discussion item. **Reflective Supervision** is relationship based, operates in a parallel process, uses reflective questions as a function of the conversation, includes mindfulness practice, includes the courage to face conflict, attends to feelings and offers grace to self and others. **Administrative Supervision** includes contractual or employment logistics, scheduling and policy discussions, information sharing and operational knowledge. **Practice Supervision** is specific to the peer practice and principles. It often includes strategies for gaining mutuality, creating and sustaining boundaries and ethics specific to the peer practice, strategic sharing, resiliency strategies, self-care and modeling peer principles.

When Family Support Specialists work in clinical settings or their services are billed to Medicaid, there is an additional requirement for **Clinical Supervision** or consultation. This type of supervision or consultation includes diagnostic impressions, intervention strategies, clinical guidance/advice and other discussion related to the clinical treatment plan. The best supervisory practice is to provide a regular hour in which the clinical and peer supervisor meets with each FSS and this is often referred to as co-supervision.

Using core competencies in the work of supervising Family Support Specialists supports effective supervision by setting fidelity measurements for the workforce, identifying and measuring strengths in self and others, and identifying areas for growth and skill building.

Discussion

As the field of peer support has matured, it is incumbent upon us to guide the consistency of practice across environments and organizations by setting up measurable fidelity standards that incorporate lessons we have learned and to reflect the evolution of the field. In addition, we must develop a keen understanding of how peer work is grounded in a set of principles, competencies, ethics and values that is unlike other clinical work.

In 2014, Oregon Family Support Network was contracted to convene national think tank conversations on the practice of supervision specific to family support specialists (defined as a family member or primary caregiver raising a child experiencing mental health, behavioral health or other complex health needs). The development, vetting and implementation of 43 family support specialist competencies serve as the core of competence in the work. The 43 competencies are divided into six subject areas that include legal, wellness and recovery, research data and documentation, planning, family support specialist skill sets, and system supports. The following are the competencies associated with each core area:

LEGAL

- Confidentiality
- Mandatory
- Reporting
- Federal/State Laws
- Protocols and Mandates
- Informed Consent
- IEP/504
- Rights/Responsibilities
- Ethics/Standards

WELLNESS AND RECOVERY

- Recovery Principles

- Promotion
- Holistic Approach
- Trauma Impact
- Trauma Healing
- Wellness and Self Care

RESEARCH, Data and Documentation

- Diagnosis and Screening
- Psychoeducation
- Systems of Care
- Family Support vs Clinical Support
- System Plans
- Information Gathering
- Family Support Profession

PLANNING

- Family Driven
- Young Adult Transitioning
- Crisis and Safety

FAMILY SUPPORT SPECIALIST Skill Sets

- Person 1st Language
- Strategic Sharing
- Cultural Humility
- Holistic Approach
- Boundaries
- Strengths, Needs, Outcomes
- Collaborative Problem Solving
- Relationships
- Listening Skills
- Myths and Stigma

- System Navigation

- Co Occurring/Morbid
- Adult Systems
- Adult Mental Health
- Youth Mental Health
- Addiction
- Family and Youth

USING core competencies in supervision expands shared language, supports assessment of work expectations, connects everyday challenges to competencies of the practice, elevates the peer practice to fidelity benchmarks, and guides consistency of practice.

Best practice supervision includes documentation of the conversation essence, reflections and discussion points. The use of a Supervision Note serves as a record of the supervision conversation between supervisor and employee (see attached). The supervision note includes all three types of peer supervision (Administrative, Practice, Reflective) along with a stress level and workload discussion. These elements mirror the principles of peer support by ensuring that the supervisor models the skills sets expected of Family Support Specialists. These include mutuality, strategic sharing, self-care, person first language, cultural humility, and others. The supervision note is always shared with the FSS and available to add, correct, or clarify discussion items.

Co-supervision between a clinical supervisor or consultant and a family support peer supervisor is often used as a best practice and recommended when peer positions are out-stationed or hired by a community agency/mental health organization other than a family organization. For Family Support Specialists working in a Medicaid billing environment, clinical supervision is required. The benefits of a co-supervision model include the opportunity for clinical partners to learn the benefits and challenges of peer delivered services, sharing of knowledge, expertise and experience, and sustaining high fidelity family peer support services work in the clinical environment. When both clinical supervision and peer supervision occurs simultaneously, it creates an environment in which diagnostic impressions, intervention strategies, and treatment plans are discussed in relevance to peer delivered services, peer practice standards and needs that maintain the unique peer role.

Conclusion

The development of competencies that serve to guide the work of Family Support Specialists elevates the fidelity, consistency and delivery of peer delivered services using a distinct role of lived experience to build mutuality with others. Using competencies in the process of supervision guides the professional and personal development of the workforce by providing supervisors and Family Support Specialists a road map to work at the highest level of competence. The FSS Competency Assessment Tool can be used by the supervisor to evaluate strengths and areas of growth for each Family Support Specialist while also acknowledging that there is a baseline skill or ability expectation for each competency. The importance of using a co-supervision model for peer delivered services is to maintain the autonomy and purity of the family support peer practice within a clinical model of service delivery. This model reduces the inconsistency of peer services across systems and environments, increases effectiveness by centering lived experience at the core of service delivery and, finally, models mutuality in the clinical and peer relationship.

More Information

SHARE! 2020 Conference on Supervision presentation: Supervision and Co-Supervision for Family Peer Support*–Tammi S. Paul, Deputy Director, Oregon Family Support Network (OFSN) POWERPOINT

The following worksheets are provided

- Family Support Specialist (FSS) Competency Assessment Tool.pdf
- Family Support Specialist (FSS) Competency Definitions.pdf
- Family Support Specialist (FSS) Overview Visual.pdf
- FSS Supervision Note.pdf

Oregon
Family Support
Network

Family Support Specialist Competencies Tool

(adapted from the Parent Support Partner (PSP) Certification Commission, National Federation of Families on Children's Mental Health)

Knowledge/Skill levels are adapted from the National Certified Parent Support Provider (CPSP) minimal standards.

Aware of *means that the prospective trainee has been introduced to the information and can discuss it as a concept but will likely need to again locate the information for detailed use & process*
* Recovery Principles * Screening Tools * Chronic conditions commonly co-morbid with MH/A&D conditions

Knowledgeable about *means that the prospective trainee has been introduced to the information or the skill and can discuss it or utilize it at a beginning level and may need to look it up.*
* Resiliency * Holistic approach to wellness * Impacts of trauma, compassion fatigue & burnout * Adult Service Systems * Common Adult MH treatment options * Common addictions treatment options

Understands *means that the prospective trainee has utilized this information or skill and can discuss it or utilize it at an intermediate level without referencing.*
* Person 1st language * Family-Driven Holistic Planning Processes * Collaborative Approaches to Problem Solving * Trauma Healing Strategies * Common Children/Young Adult treatment options * Value of Diversity and strives for cultural and linguistic responsiveness * Child and Family serving systems

Proficient *means that the prospective trainee has utilized this information and skill, can discuss or utilize it in a manner that would be considered advanced or able to teach others.*
* System of Care Principles * Peer Support principles * Self-Care prioritization & strategies

Expert *means that the prospective trainee can discuss, utilize and teach others how to implement the competency. Generally, this applies to those who have a certification in the competency.*

FSS Competencies

Name: Date:

#	Skill/Knowledge Area	Not aware	Aware		Knowledgeable		Understands		Proficient		Expert
		1	2	3	4	5	6	7	8	9	10
1	Recovery Principles		X								
2	Promoting Resiliency				X						
3	Holistic Approach to Wellness				X						
4	Impact of Trauma, Compassion Fatigue, Burnout and Grief				X						
5	Trauma Healing Strategies						X				
6	Family Support of Wellness/Self Care Strategies								X		
7	Diagnosis and Screening Tools		X								
8	Psychoeducational Information				X						
9	System of Care Principles								X		
10	Peer Support vs Clinical Support Principles								X		
11	System Support Plans: Wraparound, Spec Educ, Case Plans				X						
12	Information Gathering Techniques						X				
13	Family Support Profession and Movement				X						
14	Holistic Driven Planning Process								X		
15	Young Adult Transition Challenges				X						
16	Young Adult Transition Resources				X						
17	Crisis Intervention and Crisis Planning				X						
18	Confidentiality		X								
19	Mandatory Reporting		X								
20	Additional Federal and State Laws/Regulations		X								
21	Interagency Protocols and Mandates		X								
22	IDEA (IEP) and Section 504 Laws/Regulations		X								
23	Informed Consent						X				
24	Rights and Responsibilities in System Supports						X				
25	Professional Ethics and Standards						X				
26	Co-Occurring/Co-Morbid Conditions		X								
27	Adult Service Systems				X						
28	Adult Mental Health Supports and Services				X						

	Skill/Knowledge Area	Not aware	Aware		Knowledgeable		Understands		Proficient		Expert
		1	2	3	4	5	6	7	8	9	10
29	Youth Mental Health Supports and Services						X				
30	Addiction Supports and Services				X						
31	Family and Youth Supports and Services								X		
32	Person First Language						X				
33	Strategic and Appropriate Sharing								X		
34	Cultural Humility/Responsiveness								X		
35	Holistic Approach Model								X		
36	Peer Support Role Limits and Boundaries						X				
37	Identifying Family Strengths, Needs, Outcomes								X		
38	Collaborative Problem Solving						X				
39	System Partner Relationship Building						X				
40	Family Relationship Building								X		
41	Active Listening and Perspective Taking						X				
42	Addressing Myths, Stigma, and Discrimination						X				
43	Local Community and System Navigation				X						

Oregon
Family Support
Network

Family Support Specialist (FSS)
Competency Descriptions

(adapted from Parent Support Partner (PSP) Certification Commission, National Federation of Families on Children's Mental Health)

Competency Category: Wellness and Recovery

	Competency	Description
1	Recovery Principles	Knows and can discuss recovery as an aspect of addictions and mental heath recovery programs. Can access more in-depth information on current approaches.
2	Promoting Resiliency	Can discuss the principles of resiliency including the use of protective factors to foster the building and strengthening of individual as well as family resiliency. Models behaviors promoting resiliency.
3	Holistic Approach to Wellness	Understands and can discuss the incorporation of a holistic approach to wellness when addressing mental and physical health challenges. Includes, but not limited to, family dynamics, family environment, siblings, housing, food, finances, pets, family culture, etc.
4	Impact of Trauma, Compassion Fatigue, Burnout and Grief	Understands and can discuss the physical, emotional, and mental impacts of trauma across the life-span. Is self-aware regarding signs of compassion fatigue or burnout. Can discuss the Adverse Childhood Experiences study (ACEs). Models healthy boundaries. Readily can access current trauma information and supports.
5	Trauma Healing Strategies	Understands, can discuss, and models multiple individualized self-care

4275 Commercial St. SE, Suite 180
Salem, OR 97302

276

Oregon
Family Support
Network

		strategies as it relates to trauma and toxic stress impact. Includes, but not limited to, patterned sensory interventions, scent interventions, brain activation interventions, and disassociation.
6	Family Support of Wellness and Self-Care Strategies	Can identify family strengths and use these to create or build upon current personal, individualized support networks and practices that promote the healing of toxic stress impact and increased wellness.

Competency Category: Research, Data, and Documentation

	Competency	Description
7	Diagnosis and Screening Tools	Familiar with a broad scope of typical signs and symptoms of various diagnosable disorders, such as anxiety, mood and thought disorders, and autism spectrum. Knows and understands a variety of assessment and screening tools for mental health and addiction challenges. Can readily research these tools as requested by the family.
8	Psychoeducational Information	Familiar with various tools for families to access information on mental heath and addiction challenges. Includes, but not limited to, websites, research papers, library, training sessions, support groups, and books.
9	System of Care Principles	Knows and understands the three principles of the Systems of Care philosophy model. Understands where families as well as family support fits

Oregon
Family Support
Network

		within this model, and strategies to support a Systems of Care community.
10	Peer Support vs Clinical Support Principles	Understands and can explain the key similarities and differences of Peer support vs Clinical support strategies. Can readily explain the principles and practices of each.
11	System Support Plans: Wraparound plan of care, special education, case plans, etc.	Understands and assists in connecting the FPSS work to the development of system plans for families, the data collection process, as well as the design of outcomes, goals, and strategies.
12	Information gathering techniques	Understands various strategies and can utilize methods for gathering information based on peer support principles. Includes, but not limited to, technology, organic conversations, active listening, getting "curious", observation, motivational interviewing, and more.
13	Family Support Profession and Movement	Understands and can demonstrate knowledge on current family support movement strategies, principles, research, best practice, supports, and skill sets that promote the profession. Can describe the differences and similarities among peer support, family support, and youth support in the context of the Traditional Health Worker.

278

Oregon
Family Support
Network

Competency Category: Planning

	Competency	Description
14	Holistic Family Driven Planning Process	Understands and can coach to the model of family driven/person centered practice. Can assist in using this model with a variety of audiences in wellness and recovery services and supports.
15	Young Adult Transition Challenges	Knowledgeable in adolescent and young adult development and emerging challenges and can facilitate exploring developmentally appropriate strategies with families to address identified needs holistically.
16	Young Adult Transition Resources	Knowledgeable in young adult transition resources and supports and can discuss with families the local resources for transitioning youth such as Youth ERA, EASA, Youth Empowerment Programs, Housing resources, etc. that are available.
17	Crisis Intervention and Crisis Planning	Understands the difference between Crisis Intervention and Crisis Planning with families. Aware of proactive vs reactive strategies. Can assist families, when desired, in intervention or crisis planning. Plans are created with the family in a holistic manor based on all 12 life domains and the family's strengths.

Competency Category: Legal

	Competency	Description
18	Confidentiality	Knows, understands, and follows all agency, state and federal confidentiality

Oregon
Family Support
Network

		laws/policies. Can communicate these policies and laws to families.
19	Mandatory Reporting	Knows, understands, and complies with all agency, state and federal mandatory reporting laws. Can comfortably explain mandatory reporting responsibility with families and partnering providers.
20	Additional Federal and State Laws/Regulations	Consistently maintains safe and lawful behavior on and off duty. Models such behavior. Can readily access laws, policies, and procedures.
21	Interagency Protocols and Mandates	Knowledgeable in typical mental health and addiction services and supports, and interagency protocols, legal mandates, and barriers that may be present within them. Understands and can help a family navigate these as they intersect.
22	IDEA (IEP) and Section 504 Laws/Regulations	Knowledgeable about protections for children and parents under IEDA (IEP's) and Section 504 of the Rehabilitation Act. Can assist families in understanding these laws, as well as navigate the educational system as advocates for the child.
23	Informed Consent	Understands informed consent definition, and practice. Models informed consent with families and provider partners in a variety of situations such as plan of care, case planning, treatment options, educational options, medication management, release of information, etc.
24	Rights and Responsibilities in System Supports	Can access and assist families in increasing knowledge about current

Oregon
Family Support
Network

		rights and responsibilities for various systems the family may be navigating.
25	Professional Ethics and Standards	Understands and can model commitment to family support provider professional ethics and standards, as identified in the Peer Support Provider Code of Ethics created via the National Federation of Families on Children's Mental Health.

Competency Category: System Navigation

	Competency	Description
26	Co-Occurring / Co-Morbid Conditions	Understands common co-occurring and co-morbid conditions that affect a persons mental, emotional, and physical health. Can assist a family in gathering information on co-occurring and co-morbid conditions from providers.
27	Adult Service Systems	Knowledgeable of commonly used adult services and supports. Can share appropriate resources with the family. Includes, but not limited to, employment, housing, nutrition, financial, as well as physical health.
28	Adult Mental Health Supports and Services	Knowledgeable of, and can refer to, local providers and supports who specialize in adult mental health wellness and recovery.
29	Youth Mental Health Supports and Services	Knowledgeable of, and can refer to, local providers and supports who specialize in youth mental health wellness and recovery.

Oregon
Family Support
Network

30	Addiction Supports and Services	Knowledgeable of, and can refer to, local providers and supports who specialize in addiction wellness and recovery.
31	Family and Youth Supports and Services	Knowledgeable of, and can refer to, local family providers and service supports. Can assist in the navigation of these supports with a family based on their identified need.

Competency Category: Peer Support Provider Skill Sets

	Competency	Description
32	Person First Language	Understands the philosophy and use of person first language. Can model use of person first language in communication (verbal and written) with a variety of audiences in multiple settings.
33	Strategic and Appropriate Sharing	Models the sharing of appropriate and relevant content from lived experience that is dependent on the audience and purpose. Can coach a family member on this strategic sharing strategy for advocacy purposes.
34	Cultural Humility/Responsiveness	Can affectively set aside personal culture and beliefs to support, understand and honor the individual culture/values/beliefs of the family. Can readily navigate and advocate for culturally and linguistically appropriate services, supports, and plans of care for the family as a holistic entity.
35	Holistic Approach Model	Understands and utilizes the 12 life domains in promoting and working toward a holistic approach to addressing

282

Oregon
Family Support
Network

		a family's needs, health, wellness, goals, and recovery.
36	Peer Support Role Limits and Boundaries	Understands and adheres to the limits and boundaries set forth within the family support provider role, as well as agency protocols. Can identify, and model, abstaining from taking on the roles of family members, partnering providers, clinical supports, etc.
37	Identifying Family Strengths, Needs, Outcomes	Understands and can utilize best practice strategies for identifying a family's strengths, needs, and desired outcomes. Adept at navigating this process with families in an organic and supportive manor.
38	Collaborative Problem Solving	Has knowledge of the Collaborative Problem-Solving approach to understanding challenging behavior by identifying the "problem to be solved" and the lagging skill. Can use this approach to assist in resolving conflicts.
39	System Partner Relationship Building	Can build cooperative partnering relationships with provider agencies/organizations via various communication and problem-solving strategy skill sets. Can model for, and coach families on, how this can enhance the family's level of active participation and satisfaction with system providers and supports.
40	Family Relationship Building	Can build positive, trusting, transparent relationships with families based on mutuality of lived experiences. Relationships emphasize the family strengths, needs, desires, culture and contributions.

Oregon
Family Support
Network

41	Active Listening & Perspective Taking	Models and can coach to the active listening practice. Can use active listening as a tool to enhance the ability to identify and validate a perspective that may differ from our own.
42	Addressing Myths, Stigma, and Discrimination	Can identify common social and cultural myths and misunderstandings around mental health and addiction challenges. Utilizes, and can coach families in using, best practice advocacy skills to address stigma and discrimination when identified in family, community, and system settings.
43	Local Community and System Navigation	Is aware of, and validates, various local community and system dynamics. Understands how the systems cultural norms and dynamics can be used in individual and family support and planning.

4275 Commercial St. SE, Suite 180
Salem, OR 97302

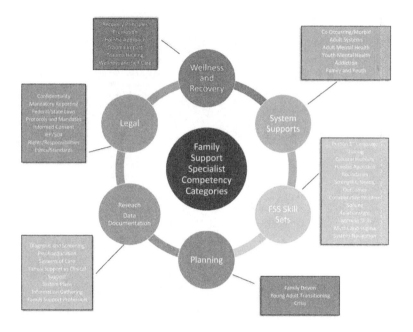

Oregon
Family Support
Network

Supervision Notes

Date:_____   Length: _____

Participants: Strengths/Successes:

New SOP/Policies since last meeting:

Workload Check In:

Take Care Check In

☐   ☐   ☐   ☐   ☐

No stress   Extremely Stressed

Where are you now? Why? What would help?

Supervisor Agenda Items	Staff Agenda Items
Supervision agendas should include an item from each of the following categories: Administrative (contractual obligations, vacation, staffing, etc.), Peer Supervision (peer practice, boundaries and ethics, mutuality, etc.), and Reflective Supervision (emotional intelligence, courage, mindfulness, self reflection, etc.)	

Statewide Office / 4275 Commercial St SE, Ste 180, Salem, OR 97302 / 503-363-8068(p) / 503-390-3161(f)/ www.ofsn.org

OFSN 2019

Carryover Agenda Items or Tasks:

Agenda Item:	Discussion/Action to be Taken:	Timeline:

OFSN 2019

Upcoming Training or Staff Development Plans:

Statewide Office / 4275 Commercial St SE, Ste 180, Salem, OR 97302 / 503-363-8068(p) / 503-390-3161(f)/ www.ofsn.org

OFSN 2019

CHAPTER 11
SUPERVISION RESEARCH AND RESOURCES

CHAPTER INTRODUCTION BY THE EDITORS

THE TOPIC OF SUPERVISION ALONE CAN CONJURE UP VARIOUS IDEAS RANGING from potentially punitive feedback sessions with higher ups to collaborative and encouraging brainstorming sessions with a mentor. The former example might describe how a worker experiences the process of *attending* supervision, whereas the latter example may describe the process of preparing for, and *participating* in supervision. In addition to what may appear to be a binary within supervisory practice are countless scenarios that illustrate a plethora of concerns about supervision of peer support workers (often denoted somewhat awkwardly as *peer supervision*, which actually connotes a number of possibilities).

Among contributors to this chapter, Supervision: Research and Resources, are several fundamental acknowledgements about supervision; that it 1) derives from casework models of guiding and overseeing the work of human service professionals; 2) provides and reinforces policies, procedures, and structures within which to produce the work; and 3) employs a hierarchical approach rather than a collaborative approach. While these acknowledgements do not constitute an exhaustive list of characteristics of supervision, they are often commonly agreed upon and understood as standard practices

Given ongoing debate (and sometimes controversy) regarding the supervision of peer support workers [in mental health and substance use service areas], this chapter explores perspectives of both peer support workers and supervisors. Two disparate perspectives posit 1) supervision of peer support workers should only be Page 1 of 45 provided by a supervisor who is also a peer; and 2) States' interpretation of Medicaid policy written in 2007 has resulted in a disproportionate number of supervisors being non-peer. Essentially, although they too may have personal lived experience, they are not disclosing that experience in their supervisory roles. Among the many complexities and nuances of these perspectives, this chapter provides results from research and resources on supervision of peer support workers. During this time of change and opportunity, the peer support workforce can leverage skills, education, vision, and personal lived experience to advocate for peer and trauma informed supervision policies and practices along with other models that support the integrity of peer support values. We maintain that collaboration is not simply a good approach to [conducting] supervision; it can also optimize supervision models that recognize peer support workers' unparalleled contributions and eliminate infantilizing them.

This chapter begins by sharing results from a groundbreaking study on the experiences of peer support workers supervised by non-peer supervisors. In addition to learning about supervisor attitudes, the importance of role integration, various supervisory techniques, and mutual learning, we get a glimpse into lesser-known workplace phenomena such as cooptation, moral injury, emotional labor, the apprenticeship model of supervision, and "the unanimous desire for a supervisor who was a more experienced peer support worker."

Five Components of Peer Support with Keys to Supervision points to, and draws upon, underlying psychosocial processes that provide the theoretical underpinnings of peer support. For example, Riessman's Helper Therapy Principle parallels with the notion that one of the benefits of peer support is that the person offering the support can sustain their own recovery in the process of helping another person. Implications for applying Helper Therapy Principle and four other components of peer support to the practice of supervision, as well as a rubric for assessing performance, are offered.

In contrast to the earlier contribution that presented results from a study on the experiences of peer support workers supervised by non-peer supervisors, results from a 2017 national survey of supervisors of peer support workers focuses on the quantitative information provided by supervisors to the survey with a brief summary of responses to open-ended questions that were published in a subsequent paper, Perceptions of Supervisors of Peer Support Workers (PSW) in Behavioral Health: Results from a National Survey.

Lastly, "You do what, how well? Integrating the peer's voice in supervision" introduces the Partners for Change Outcome Management System (PCOMS). This routine outcome monitoring process informs service effectiveness using and privileging the service recipient's voice, adds value to existing services, and increases efficiencies and improves retention rates and outcomes in public and other behavioral health systems. This article 1) illustrates how to integrate PCOMS' data into performance support that ultimately leads to a mastery level of peer service provider (PSP) competence and confidence; and 2) addresses a missing vital element – including and privileging the service recipient's voice.

SECTION 1: WHAT WE HAVE LEARNED FROM PEER SUPPORT WORKERS SUPERVISED BY NON-PEER SUPERVISORS

Joanne Forbes, PhD

A qualitative study examining the experiences of peer support specialists (PSS) supervised by non-peer supervisors (NPS) in adult community mental health settings across the United States revealed the following major themes: supervisor attitudes; importance of role integration; trauma informed supervisory techniques, promoting a facilitative/supportive environment which includes perspective taking and mutual learning; opportunities for peer networking; and the unanimous desire for a supervisor who was a more experienced peer support worker.

Peer support has become part of the mental health landscape as health systems move towards a system of care that includes the patient as an active participant (Anderson & Funnell, 2004; Cronise, Teixeira, Rogers, & Harrington, 2016; Salzer, Schwenk, & Brusilovsky, 2010; Wallerstein & Bernstein, 1994). Peer support is understood as a factor in promoting wellness and autonomy with a focus on mutuality, strengths and recovery (Mead, 2003). And peer support has been shown to impact service use, satisfaction with care, quality of life and increase in hopefulness (Davidson et al., 2006 ; Mead et al., 2001; Mead & McNeil, 2006; Simpson et al., 2014). Given the transformative nature of peer support in integrated settings, it is critical that PSS receive the support and supervision aligned with peer values.

Discussion

Guidance from Medicaid suggests that PSS be supervised by a competent mental health professional which has been interpreted in practice to mean a licensed practitioner. However, clinical supervision of PSS by non-peer supervisors is poorly understood. PSS, using their lives as a primary experience-based intervention, function in ways that are distinct from mental health professionals. These experience-based interventions may differ from professional interventions as they may involve dual relationships, personal self-disclosure; a focus on empowerment, and role modeling hope and recovery (Davidson et al., 2012; Lammers & Happell, 2003; Mead, 2003). Since there is little known about the experiences of PSS supervised by non-peer supervisors, this study contributed to an understanding not only of the basic experience itself but also about the elements perceived as important in supervision between a peer and a non-peer supervisor. The experiences of PSS reflect the challenges inherent in role innovation. NPS supervisors are the necessary guides who assist the PSS in navigating a system not yet aligned with peer values.

The major findings of this study suggest that supervision between a PSS and NPS is a potential mismatch that can result in communication difficulties. The most important but not surprising finding is that PSS want to be supervised by an experienced PSS (i.e., someone who has actually done the job) has not been previously documented. Inherent in clinical supervision is the goal of role-modeling practice behaviors for the less experienced supervisee and thus assisting the supervisee to increase their expertise (Goodyear & Bernard, 1998). The non-peer supervisor in all likelihood has not had the experience of accomplishing peer goals or interacting as a peer, making it difficult to role model for a peer.

The second finding is that PSS continue to experience poor role integration. Frequently there is no job description or if there is one it is at odds with peer values and standards of practice. Working in partnership to create a viable job description frequently addresses this problem. Also, including the PSS in team meetings and discussion allows non peer members to begin to understand what the PSS does.

The third finding is that the NPS attitude toward the PSS is a critical factor. A positive NPS attitude includes respect for the peer role, positive nonjudgmental communication and support for autonomous functioning. Respect for the peer role is foundational. It is true that any supervisee wants to be treated with respect. The importance of this attitude for PSS is in part a consequence of the lack of fit between NPS and PSS views and expectations. The PSS is often a role innovator: A role innovator integrating into a treatment system that may have disparaging elements. PSS are accustomed to stigmatizing attitudes from others, even non-peer professional staff. The attitude of respect role modeled by the NPS can set the tone for acceptance and support within the work setting.

The fourth finding supports the necessity of employing trauma informed supervisory techniques. The Pillars (Daniels et al., 2015) recommended that the supervisor should promote both the professional and personal growth of the PSS. One of the elements of personal growth is recognition and support provided by trauma informed supervisory techniques. Trauma informed supervisory techniques with an emphasis on self-care, acceptance of early compassion fatigue, and/or moral injury and prevention of re-traumatization are necessary for PSS to do their job. A possible explanation for the early onset of compassion fatigue is that the PSS use of self is different from the non-peer professional use of self. In the context of PSS self-disclosure, empathy can take on a different, even more personal meaning. Reliving difficult experiences could trigger shame and reinforce internalized stigma. A NPS can offer frequent debriefings to address this eventuality and provide adequate ongoing sensitivity to situations that could be retraumatizing.

Finally, the need for NPS to create a facilitative/supportive work environment was identified as important to PSS. Whether or not PSS intend to be role innovators, the role they occupy is relatively new so that PSS frequently feel isolated and at odds with the existing culture. Differences in values and approach require an environment that is open to such changes and an NPS that is supportive. Perspective taking is a skill that supports mutual learning. Both the PSS and NPS benefit from an open-minded curiosity about what the other has to offer. An environment that is less about the power differential and more about the shared goal of assisting someone into recovery facilitates collaboration and respect for other. Opportunities for peer networking both inside the organization and outside in the form of conferences and continued education provides PSS with a chance to learn from other PSS.

Conclusion

Peer Support Specialists are integrating into a mental health service system transitioning from a medical model to a recovery-oriented model of care. NPS are the necessary guides who assist the PSS in navigating a system not yet aligned with peer values. If the mental health system is going to successfully become recovery oriented, NPS need a unique skill set to support those with lived experience whose recovery can help point the way.

More Information

SHARE! 2020 Conference on Supervision presentation, Supervision of Peer Support Workers: Is Supervision by Non-peer Supervisors a Mismatch? —Joanne Forbes, Department of Psychiatric Rehabilitation, Rutgers University, New Jersey.

References

Anderson, R., &. Funnell, M. (2004). Patient empowerment: reflections on the challenge of fostering the adoption of a new paradigm. *Patient Education and Counseling 57*, 153–157.

Cronise, R., Teixeira, C., Rogers, E. S., & Harrington, S. (2016). The peer support workforce: Results of a national survey. *Psychiatric Rehabilitation Journal 39*(3), 211-221. doi:10.1037/prj0000222

Daniels, A.S., Tunner, T.P., Powell, I. Fricks. & Ashenden, P. (2015). Pillars of peer support-VI: Peer Specialist Supervision. Www.pillarsofpeersupport.org. March, 2015.

Davidson L, Bellamy C, Guy K, & Miller R. (2012). Peer support among persons with severe mental illnesses: A review of evidence and experience. *World Psychiatry, 11(2)*: 123-128.

Davidson, L., Chinman, M., Sells, D. & Rowe, M. (2006). Peer support among individuals with mental illness: A report from the field. Schizophrenia Bulletin, 32(3) 443-450.

Goodyear, R. & Bernard, J. (1998). Clinical supervision: Lessons from the literature. *Counselor Education and Supervision, 38*(1), 1998.

Lammers, J. & Happell, B. (2003) Consumer participation in mental health services: looking from a consumer perspective. *Journal of Psychiatric and Mental Health Nursing,*10, 385-392.

Mead, S., Hilton, D., & Curtis, L. (2001). Peer support: A theoretical perspective. *Psychiatric Rehabilitation Journal, 25*(2), 134-141.

Mead, S. (2003). Defining Peer Support. Unpublished paper.
Mead, S. & McNeil, C. (2006). Peer support: what makes it unique? *The International Journal of Psychosocial Rehabilitation,*10 (2),29-37.

Salzer, M., Schwenk, E. & Brusilovsky, E. (2010). Certified Peer Specialists Roles and Activities: results from a National Survey. *Psychiatric Services 61,* (5), 520-523. https://doi.org.10.1176/ps.2010.61.5.520.

Simpson, A., Flood, C., Rowe, J., Quigley, J., Henry, S., Hall, C. Evans, R. Sherman, P. & Bowers, L. (2014). Results of a pilot randomized controlled trial to measure the clinical and cost effectiveness of peer support in increasing hope and quality of life in mental health patients discharged from hospital in the UK. *BioMed Central Psychiatry, 14*(30),1-14. http://www.biomedcentral.com/1471-244X/14/30.

Wallerstein, N. & Bernstein, E. (1994). Introduction to community empowerment, participatory education, and health. *Health Education Quarterly, 21*(2), 141-148

SECTION 2: FIVE COMPONENTS OF PEER SUPPORT SERVICES WITH KEYS TO SUPERVISION

Ruth Hollman, PhD candidate, UCLA
Founder/CEO of SHARE! the Self-Help And Recovery Exchange

This narrative presents five components: 1) the Helper Therapy Principle; 2) Peer Listening and Disclosing; 3) Recovery Planning; 4) Self-help Support Groups; and 5) Peer Bridging. Each of the components of peer services is followed by Key Questions for supervisors to ask and also signs of a highly skilled peer worker or performance that needs to be improved.

The Helper Therapy Principle

The Helper Therapy Principle (Riessman, 1965) states that the person who helps gets more out of the interaction than the person being helped. Riessman was studying self-help support groups—another evidence-based peer service —and noticed that everyone in the groups was both giving and receiving help, but the giving of help had greater benefits than receiving help.

Since then, scores of studies have shown that helping others has positive health and mental health benefits—and heals the Helper more than the person being helped. For example, when teens tutor younger children, the younger children's grades improve with tutoring, but the teen tutors' grades improve even more (Rogeness & Badner, 1973). A majority of Community Health Workers felt helper benefits including positive feelings about self, a sense of belonging, and valuable work experience when helping others (Roman, L.A. et al., 2002). Recovery rates for alcoholics doubled if they were helping other alcoholics (Pagano, 2010). Helpers report a distinct physical sensation associated with helping, sometimes referred to as the "Helper's High".

In one study about half of helpers' report that they experienced a "high" feeling, 43 percent felt stronger and more energetic, 28 percent felt warm, 22 percent felt calmer and less depressed, 21 percent experienced greater feelings of self-worth, and 13 percent experienced fewer aches and pains after helping. (Luks, 1988). When people help others, or even *perceive* they are helping others, they feel good about themselves in ways that improve their mental health, health and functioning.

Peer workers give the people they serve opportunities to help others, so the people they are serving get the benefits of helping. They create opportunities for people to help which improves the health, mental health and self-esteem of those they serve.

Key questions for Supervisors to keep in mind in the supervision of peer workers using the Helper-Therapy Principle:

- Are you letting the person you are serving help you?
- Are you encouraging the people you are serving to help others?

The chart shows how to recognize a highly skilled implementation of the Helper Therapy Principle versus one that requires improvement.

Table 1. Helper Therapy Principle – Effective and Ineffective Practices

Highly Skilled	Needs Improvement
Peer worker is adept at creating opportunities for people to be the person helping. For example, finding a skill that someone has and having them teach that skill to others; teaching the person to use Word today and having them train someone else in Word tomorrow; volunteering in the community; going to self-help support groups.	Peer worker lacks structure and approach to create leadership opportunities. Peer worker does projects and accomplishes things themselves, rather than giving others the satisfaction of being leaders and making a difference.
Peer worker listens for and implements participants' suggestions such as having a Kwanzaa celebration, writing their legislative representative about something they want changed, starting their own business, putting on a program, inviting people to a recovery panel, etc. The Peer worker lets the person help them.	The only opportunities to help are those created by staff and/or directed by staff. The Peer worker sees their role as helping the person and rarely lets the person help them.

Peer Listening and Disclosing

Peer listening and disclosing is using active-listening techniques and sharing one's own lived experience of the situation the person being served is going through. Peer workers do not give suggestions or advice unless the person being served specifically asks for advice. Peer listening and disclosing is different from and complementary to clinical expertise because it represents a relationship of equals in which each is benefiting from the relationship with the other. Peer workers help others with similar challenges by sharing their own experience using "I" statements. They listen fully the whole time someone is talking without thinking about the response they want to give. Only after the person stops talking does the peer worker respond. It is okay to have a few seconds of silence to gather thoughts. Peer workers disclose only those parts of their stories that speak directly to what the person has shared.

Peer listening and disclosing has been shown to increase self-esteem and confidence, feelings of control and ability to make life changes, sense of hope and inspiration, empathy and acceptance, engagement in self-care and wellness, social support, social functioning, empowerment scores, and the sense that treatment is responsive and inclusive of needs (SAMHSA, 2017).

Key questions for supervisors to keep in mind in the supervision of peer workers using peer listening and disclosing:

298

- Is your listening free from judgement or suggestion?
- Are you regularly sharing your own similar experiences in such a way that the person you are supporting feels connection and hope, and is empowered to experience growth and change?

The next chart shows how to recognize a highly skilled implementation of peer listening and disclosing versus one that requires improvement.

Table 2. Peer Listening and Disclosing – Effective and Ineffective Practices

Highly Skilled	Needs Improvement
Peer worker listens the entire time to the person with eye contact and other positive body language and only thinks of their response after the person stops talking.	Peer worker multitasks while listening and thinks of how they are going to respond to the "gist" of what they heard.
Peer worker discloses their own experience with similar issues, including how they felt, what they thought at the time and what worked and did not work, without being asked. They use "I" statements in disclosing.	Peer worker discloses only when asked and does not include their feelings or thoughts at the time. They express their experience in the form of advice or say things such as "You should do what I did."
Peer worker discloses both their successes and challenges, including current challenges that they are encountering in their recovery that relate to what the person is going through. Peer worker is open about their lived experience, treats the person being served as an equal, and uses boundaries appropriate for peers. The Peer worker concentrates on connecting the person to non-paid social supports in the community.	Peer worker only discloses their successes and appears to be perfectly recovered without any problems, hiding their own setbacks from the people they are serving. Peer worker provides support using a clinical approach and/or clinical boundaries. The person receiving support has a social network limited to professional relationships and other people at the clinic.
	(SAMHSA 2017)

Recovery Planning

Recovery Planning is a way for a person to take charge of and control their recovery process by developing a written plan to help in their recovery. Two main Recovery Planning tools:

- Wellness Recovery Action Plan or WRAP®
- SHARE! Plan for Success

Wellness Recovery Action Plan (WRAP®)

WRAP "...is a self-designed prevention and wellness process that anyone can use to get well, stay well and make their life the way they want it to be (Copeland, 2002)." WRAP® has been linked to significant improvements in self-reported symptoms, recovery, hopefulness, self-advocacy and physical health (Cook, et al, 2009; Copeland et al, 2012).

SHARE! Plan for Success

SHARE!'s Plan for Success creates a pathway from today to success in 5 years using Backwards Design. Backwards Design is an evidence-based best practice that is effective in helping people achieve their goals faster (Wiggins & McTighe, 1998). The effective principle in Backwards Design is to start where you want to be in the future and work backwards to today, rather than vice versa.

To begin the SHARE! Plan for Success, each person comes up with their notion of what success in five years will look like for them. Working with an individual or group, the peer worker says: "Exhale fully, close your eyes and inhale. Take five more deep breaths. Now imagine five years from now when you are successful... What are you doing...? What makes you feel proud...? What is worth celebrating...? What makes you feel good about yourself...? What makes you feel accomplished...? Dreaming, what would satisfy you in terms of being successful...? Now write down what your success will look like in five years. Then working backwards from five years write down where you will be in four years if you achieve success in five years." Then three years, two years, one year, 9 months, six months, 3 months, 2 months, 1 month, two weeks, one week, tomorrow, today. The next chart provides an example of a SHARE! Plan for Success.

Table 3. Sample SHARE! Plan for Success

5 years—Living in Hawaii in a beach house that I own working as a Real Estate Agent.	9 months—Take the California Real Estate Exam
4 years—Sell houses in Hawaii, saving all my commissions, sell my condo and buy a beach house	6 months—get a supervising Real Estate Broker to sponsor me for my Real Estate License
3 years— Move to Hawaii with all my savings. Buy a cheap condo to live in. Get Hawaiian Real Estate license and start selling houses.	3 months—Finish Real Estate school
	2 months—Research Real Estate Brokers to find ones likely to sponsor me
2 years—Sell 20 houses in Los Angeles. Save as much as I can.	1 month— Continue at Real Estate school
1 year-- Get a job at a real estate agency and begin selling houses, saving every penny I can.	2 weeks-- Start Real Estate school
	1 week—Fill out and submit Real Estate school application
	Tomorrow—Get all the documentation needed for Real Estate school application
	Today—Research Real Estate Schools in Los Angeles and pick one to apply to.

Once the plan is developed, daily, weekly or monthly commitments are made to a friend, a support group and/or the peer worker. People who share a commitment are more likely to meet it. There are no consequences for not keeping a commitment, but the peer worker should give lots of praise for any progress toward the commitment. They should also reframe attempts that did not work as learning opportunities rather than as failures. Most people achieve their 5-year success in two to three years.

Key questions for Supervisors to keep in mind in the supervision of peer workers using Recovery Planning.

- Does the person have a WRAP Plan?
- Does the person have a SHARE! Plan for Success?

This chart shows how to recognize a highly skilled implementation of Recovery Planning versus one that requires improvement.

Table 4. Recovery Planning – Effective and Ineffective Practices

Highly skilled	Needs improvement
Peer worker shows their own WRAP and SHARE! Plan for Success, with their goals and commitments and talks about how it has helped them. They also talk about things that did not work out as planned and how they coped.	Peer worker gives someone the forms to use in recovery planning. Peer does not disclose their own recovery planning process or difficulties they had to overcome or are still working to overcome.
Peer worker encourages the person to be ambitious and accepts the goals that the person wants to work on, even if they appear to be unrealistic.	Peer worker tries to make sure that the person's goals are easily achievable and realistic to where they are now.
Peer worker supports the person in starting anywhere to reach their goals.	Peer worker suggests what the next step toward the person's goals should be.

Self-help Support Groups

The American Psychological Association defines a self-help support group as: "A voluntary, self-determining, and non-profit gathering of people who share a condition or status; members share mutual support and experiential knowledge to improve persons' experiences of the common situation." https://www.scra27.org/what-we-do/policy/rapid-response-actions/resolution-self-help-support-groups/

Key components of self-help support groups include: (1) everyone in the group being an equal (2) sharing and/or interaction between members (3) no paid leader (4) decisions affecting the group are made by the group members, not the leader or the agency where they meet (5) leadership is shared or rotated and any member of the group could be part of the leadership (6) groups often use a written document called a "format" to explain the rules of the meeting at each session, rather than having one person explain the rules, and (7) safety, anonymity and confidentiality are protected. Table 5 shows some of the demonstrated benefits of Self-Help Support Groups.

Table 5. Benefits of Self-Help Support Groups

Research as described in the Reference section listed on our website on self-help support groups show that they: Cut the rehospitalization of mental health consumers by 50 percent Reduce the number of days spent in the hospital by one third Reduce significantly the amount of medication needed to treat mental health issues Move large numbers of people out of the system into productive lives Result in participants collaborating with clinical staff regarding taking medications Realize effects in weeks that are sustained for years Reduce drug and alcohol abuse Reduce demands on clinicians' time Increase empowerment	Provide community support—the suspected reason that people in developing countries recover from schizophrenia at nearly twice the rate that they do in developed countries Provide mentoring opportunities that improve the outcomes of both the mentor and the person being mentored Reduce criminal behavior Increase family resources and reduce family stress Increase consumer satisfaction Are underutilized by clinicians because of incorrect preconceived ideas about self-help and the lack of professional training on self-help Note: For references go to https://shareselfhelp.org/about-share-the-self-help-and-recovery-exchange/research-shows-self-help-works

Key questions for supervisors regarding self-help support groups:

- Are you or your peer worker attending self-help support groups and using the lived experience with them to give the benefits of them to others?
- Does the peer worker put people in touch with someone attending a particular self-help group as part of the referral process?
- Does the peer worker match the worldview of the person served with the self-help groups they refer the person to?

Self-help groups can be found almost everywhere. SHARE! operates the self-help referral service for Los Angeles County and tracks more than 12,000 groups in Los Angeles County with 750 different focuses alone. Studies show that matching a person's worldview with a group with a similar worldview brings the best outcomes. For example, in groups for substance abuse recovery, 12-Step programs work best for people with belief in a single god, SOS, or Secular Organizations for Sobriety, works best for agnostics & atheists, SMART Recovery works for people who do not want to share their personal business in public, and Recovery Dharma works better for Buddhists.

Self-help meetings mostly do not require an appointment or a reservation to attend. In most groups, people just show up at the day and time of the meeting. Better self-help support groups have tools that help members change and grow that the members have developed over time. It is easy to find or start a self-help group in any language, as long as you have potential members who speak the language in question. Most groups ask for a small donation ($1 to $5), but no one is turned away for lack of funds. A rule of thumb is for a newcomer to try a group six times before you decide if it is working, as the way self-help support groups help people is different than a class or therapy. To find out more about self-help support groups and how to access them, start them, etc. contact SHARE! www.shareselfhelp.org.

The next chart shows how to recognize a highly effective self-help support group versus one that will have less robust outcomes.

Table 6. Self-Help Support Groups - Effective and Ineffective Practices

Highly Effective	Less Effective
Peers with the same level of power—none of whom are paid—attend a support group addressing a common concern. Leadership and decision-making are provided by the members.	Paid peer specialist leads the support group and discussions, addresses disruptive behavior and makes decisions for the group.
The group makes referrals and information about community-based self-help support groups is available to all participants.	Groups are held only at a mental health facility and/or are canceled when the room is needed for other uses.
Crosstalk, where others interrupt or comment on someone's sharing, is not allowed and is enforced by any member of the group with gentle reminders.	The leader has the right to ask anyone to leave without hearing their side of the issue or giving them opportunities to improve. People who are not peer members of the group enter the group without the group's permission.
Anonymity and confidentiality is expected and protected.	Staff create clinical notes about what happens in the group identifying individuals. Members sign in.
Each person has a right to due process in the group and is given opportunities to change disruptive behavior before the group takes action to exclude the member. If someone is asked to leave, it is for only one or two meetings, not forever.	Disruptive people are banned from attending the group without being given a chance to change their behavior.

Peer Bridging

Peer Bridging is "supporting a person in moving from one situation to another by a peer worker with similar experience." (Hartigan 2019). Peer bridging can happen when inpatients move to outpatients, when homeless people become housed, when an incarcerated individual is released to the community, or other transitions.

Ideally a peer worker doing peer bridging should get to know the person they are bridging before they are in their new situation. The peer worker normalizes people's fears, concerns and feelings by disclosing their similar lived experiences. They should be connected to self-help support groups and use Recovery Planning to empower the person to move forward. Part of peer bridging is using the Helper Therapy Principle by finding situations where the person being served is the one providing the help. The peer worker serves as both support and a role model.

Peer workers doing peer bridging reduce rehospitalization and days in the hospital. (Sledge 2011) The New York Association of Psychiatric Rehabilitation Services (NYAPRS) evaluated its Peer Bridger program designed to help people leaving psychiatric hospitals to re-integrate into the community and avoid/reduce further hospitalization. They reported that 71% of the people who got Peer Bridging stayed out of the hospital in 2009. They also reduce the use of psychiatric emergency rooms in favor of outpatient services. (NYAPRS 2009) SHARE! Peer Bridgers regularly succeed in getting at least 60 percent of people going to self-help support groups which reduce costs of treatment, increase employment, reduce drug & alcohol abuse, etc. https:// shareselfhelp.org/about-share-the-self-help-and-recovery-exchange/ research-shows-self-help-works/

Key questions for Supervisors to keep in mind in the supervision of peer workers using peer bridging:

- Is the peer worker empowering the person served and walking together as the person makes their own decisions in moving from one situation to another?
- Is the peer worker using the Helper Therapy Principle, Peer Listening and Disclosing, Recovery Planning and Self-Help Support Groups?

The next chart shows how to recognize a highly skilled implementation of Peer Bridging versus one that requires improvement.

Table 7. Effective and Ineffective Peer Bridging

Highly Skilled	Needs Improvement
Peer worker integrates the practical parts of the change with their own experience with a similar change including their feelings, hopes, fears, challenges, etc. They respect the feelings, fears, etc. of the person being served.	Peer worker sees that the practical parts of the change are taken care of. Peer worker does not connect with the person regarding their feelings, hopes, fears, and apprehensions. They reassure with little or no disclosing.
Peer worker recognizes the individuality of the person they are working with and supports them where they are, even when they have different assessments of the situation and/or different perspectives or worldviews. They recognize that everyone has a different recovery journey. One size does not fit all.	Peer worker expects that the person they are working with has the same worldview as they do, and thus will handle the situation in a prescribed way. They may assume that people need the same recovery tools that the peer worker has used. They judge the person served as "wrong" rather than as a human being able to make the best decisions for themselves.
Peer worker sees their primary role as helping someone discover their own path to recovery, including setting their own goals, deciding what is important to them, and connecting the person to non-paid social support in the community.	Peer Worker sees their primary role as solving the person's problems and connecting them to other professional services.
Peer worker prioritizes the relationship with the person they are working with. Other issues are secondary. For example, the Peer worker starts the session together with a check in as to how things are going, including a short honest update on their own recovery before moving on to other issues and paperwork.	Peer worker is all business and struggles to build an authentic relationship with the person. Their focus is on checking off everything they need to get done with the person that day.

Conclusion

This narrative presented five components of evidence-based peer services: 1) the Helper Therapy Principle; 2) Peer Listening and Disclosing; 3) Recovery Planning; 4) Self-help Support Groups; and 5) Peer Bridging. Each of the five components of peer services was followed by Key Questions for supervisors to ask and also included signs of a highly skilled peer worker or performance that needs to be improved.

More Information

SHARE! 2020 Conference on Supervision Presentation: Evidence-based Peer Practices for Supervisors—Ruth Hollman, Chief Executive Officer,

306

SHARE!, Los Angeles, California. Recordings are available: https://share selfhelp.org/conferences/2020peer-supervision-workforce-conference/

SHARE! 2022 Conference on Supervision recordings are available: https://shareselfhelp.org/conferences/2022-peer-supervision-workforce-conference-video-powerpoints/

WRAP® has demonstrated effectiveness in three Randomized Controlled Trial (RCT) research studies:

- Cook, J., et al. (2009). Initial outcomes of a mental illness self-management program based on Wellness Recovery Action Planning, Psychiatric Services, 60:2, 246–249.
- Cook, J., et al. (2013). Impact of Wellness Recovery Action Planning on service utilization and need in a randomized controlled trial, Psychiatric Rehabilitation Journal, 36:4, 250–257.
- Jonikas, J., et al. (2012). Improving propensity for patient self-advocacy through Wellness Recovery Action Planning: Results of a randomized controlled trial, Community Mental Health Journal, 49, 260–269.

References

Copeland, M.E. (2002). Wellness Recovery Action Plan (WRAP). Peach Press, Dummerston, VT. https://www.wellnessrecoveryactionplan.com/

Hartigan E, Hollman R, Robison J. Peer Bridgers: A Distinctive Kind of Peer Provider Connecting Homeless People to Collaborative Housing ad Self-Help Support Groups at SHARE! The Community Psychologist, 2019 52(2) Spring. https://www.scra27.org/publications/tcp/tcp-past-issues/tcpspring2019/

Luks A. Helper's High Volunteering makes people feel good, physically and emotionally. Psych Today 1988 Oct:38-39
The New York Association of Psychiatric Rehabilitation Services evaluation, 2009. https://www.nyaprs.org/peer-bridger

Pagano ME, Post SG, Johnson SM. Alcoholics Anonymous-Related Helping and the Helper Therapy Principle. Alcohol Treat Q. 2010;29(1):23-34. doi:10.1080/07347324.2011.538320

Reissman F. The "helper" therapy principle. Social Work. 1965; 10:27–32.

Rogeness GA, Bednar RA. Teenage Helper: A Role in Community Mental Health. Amer Journal of Psychiatry, 1973 Aug:933-936. https://doi.org/10.1176/ajp.130.8.933

Roman LA, Lindsay JK, Moore JS, Shoemaker AL. Community health workers: examining the Helper Therapy principle. Public Health Nursing. 1999 Apr;16(2):87-95. doi: 10.1046/j.1525-1446.1999.00087. x. PMID: 10319658.

SAMHSA (2017). Value of Peers (Infographic). https://www.samhsa.gov/sites/default/files/programs_campaigns/brss_tacs/value-of-peers-2017.pdf

Self-Help And Recovery Exchange! (SHARE!) References: https://share selfhelp.org/about-share-the-self-help-and-recovery-exchange/research-shows-self-help-works/

Sledge WH, Lawless M, Sells D, Wieland M, O'Connell MJ, Davidson L. Effectiveness of peer support in reducing readmissions of persons with multiple psychiatric hospitalizations. Psychiatric Serv. 2011;62(5):541–544. doi: 10.1176/ps.62.5. pss6205_0541

What is WRAP® (n.d.) Advocates for Human Potential website. https://www.wellnessrecoveryactionplan.com/what-is-wrap/

Wiggins, G., & McTighe, J. (1998). Understanding by design. Alexandria, VA: Association for Supervision & Curriculum Development.

SECTION 3: SUPERVISION AND SUCCESSFUL EMPLOYMENT: OVERVIEW OF THE NATIONAL PEER WORKER SUPERVISION SURVEY

Dana Foglesong, MSW, NCPS, CRPS
Magellan Health

Jessica Wolf, PhD
Decision Solutions Consulting and Yale Department of Psychiatry

This is an overview of a national survey, conducted in 2017 by Dana Foglesong at Magellan Health of supervisors of PSW (peer support workers). The overview focuses on the quantitative information provided by supervisors to the survey with a brief summary of the answers to open-ended questions (qualitative data) that were published in a subsequent paper, Perceptions of Supervisors of Peer Support Workers (PSW) in Behavioral Health: Results from a National Survey.

Discussion

"Peer Support Supervision occurs when a supervisor and peer support worker (PSW) supervisee(s) formally meet to discuss and review the work and experience of the peer provider, with the aim of supporting the peer in their professional role (Daniels, et al., 2014)."

Research and professional literature about peer support services frequently address the importance of supervision to the quality of peer support services, such as the Pillars of Peer Support-VI Summit in 2015 that was convened specifically to address supervision. Yet there had not been a U.S. national survey of the perspectives of supervisors of peer support workers (PSW).

In 2017, Dana Foglesong at Magellan Health developed a 16-item survey disseminated through the National Association of Peer Supporters (N.A.P.S.) and several peer and professional networks to gather information from those providing supervision to PSW. A total of 1,238 people responded. 724 indicated they were currently supervising PSW with an additional 218 indicated they were currently supervising PSW have also worked as a PSW in the past. Figure 1 shows the respondents by state:

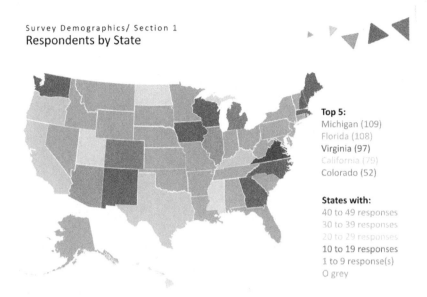

Survey Demographics/ Section 1
Respondents by State

Top 5:
Michigan (109)
Florida (108)
Virginia (97)
California (79)
Colorado (52)

States with:
40 to 49 responses
30 to 39 responses
20 to 29 responses
10 to 19 responses
1 to 9 response(s)
0 grey

A TOTAL of 937 supervisors responded to the following questions:

1. How often are you providing one-on-one supervision to PSWs? The top three chosen answers were:

- Once a week: 517
- Twice a month: 164
- Once a month: 135

Other answers: Less than once a week (62); More than once a month (59).

1. Typically, how long are your supervision sessions with PSWs? The top three chosen answers were:

- One hour: 376
- 30 minutes: 238
- 45 minutes: 166

Other answers: 15 minutes (87); More than one hour (51); Less than 15 minutes (19).

1. How long have you been in your current position? The top three chosen answers were:

- Between 2-5 years: 320
- Less than 2 years: 269
- Between 5-10 years: 200

OTHER ANSWER: More than 10 years (148)

1. How long have you supervised PSW? The top three chosen answers were:

- Between 2-5 years: 331
- More than 5 years: 278
- Between 1-2 years: 192

Other answer: Less than 1 year (136)

1. What is your professional credential? The top three rated credentials were:

- Social worker: 300
- Certified peer provider: 271
- Other: 153

Note: Respondents were able to report more than one license or credential on this question so the response total was more than 937. Those who chose a pre-assigned credential indicated: Licensed mental health counselor (134); Psychologist (91); No credential (85); Certified or licensed addictions counselor (71). The 153 respondents who indicated their credential was in the "Other" category indicated their credential as: Ph.D, Master's degree, Bachelor's degree, Nurse, Qualified Mental Health Professional, Physician, Behavioral Health Technician, Juris Doctor (J.D.), Pharmaceutical Chemist, Certified Therapeutic Recreational Specialist, Certified Peer Specialist Supervisor.

1. What is the job category that best describes your current position? The top three rated sites were:

- Manager: 390
- Administrator/Director: 290
- Direct Professional Service Provider: 76

Other job categories included: Peer provider (70), Supervisor (55), Coordinator (21), Direct Service Provider (20), and Other (20). The 20 respondents who indicated their credential was in the "Other" category indicated their credential as: Clinical Supervisor, Certified Peer Specialist Supervisor, Office Manager, Executive Director.

1. What is the best description of your work site type? The top three rated sites were:

- Outpatient-Community BH Center: 307
- Dept. of Veterans Affairs (VA) Medical/Outpatient: 134
- Outpatient-Peer-run Organization: 129

Other work site types included: Outpatient-recovery community organization (71), Outpatient-community mental health clinic (48), Intensive-outpatient treatment program (43), Inpatient-specialized behavioral health hospital (40), Shelter-residential support/housing services (35), Peer-run crisis alternative (33), State government inpatient/outpatient clinic (28), Outpatient-managed care plan (22), Inpatient-general hospital (18), Outpatient-private clinic or doctor's office (11), Partial Hospitalization day treatment program (10), Outpatient-vocational/employment agency (8).

Questions related to Supervisor Attitudes and Practices
A total of 798 supervisors responded to questions related to their attitudes and practices by indicating the degree to which they agreed or disagreed with the following statements:

1. PSWs are at a risk of relapse when they work in behavioral health settings: Agree (20%), Neutral (27%), Disagree (53%).
2. PSWs perform essentially the same duties as non-peer workers: Agree (24%), Neutral (9%), Disagree (67%).
3. Non-clinical tasks such as driving, running errands, and filing paperwork are appropriate roles for PSWs: Agree (22%), Neutral (27%), Disagree (51%).
4. Stigmatizing attitudes and policies toward PSWs is not an issue in my workplace: Agree (58%), Neutral (15%), Disagree (27%).

5. There is little relation between the integration of PSWs and an organization's recovery orientation: Agree (6%), Neutral (10%), Disagree (84%).
6. Supervisors of PSWs are responsible to advocate for the integration of PSW within the organization and the work team: Agree (93%), Neutral (2%), Disagree (5%).
7. PSWs should have different standards in regard to confidential information: Agree (6%), Neutral (7%), Disagree (70%).
8. A supervisor should not self-disclose with a PSW: Agree (10%), Neutral (26%), Disagree (48%).
9. Supervision of PSWs requires knowledge of the peer support roles, peer responsibilities, and recovery principles: Agree (97%), Neutral (1%), Disagree (2%).
10. To become a PSW, a person should no longer be using any behavioral health services: Agree (92%), Neutral (4%), Disagree (4%).
11. All staff need training about peer support and the PSWs' role for successful integration of PSW: Agree (95%), Neutral (3%), Disagree (2%).
12. PSW need specialized training to do their jobs well: Agree (88%), Neutral (7%), Disagree (5%).
13. Supervisors are responsible for monitoring the job performance of the people they supervise: Agree (98%), Neutral (1%), Disagree (1%).
14. Supervisors should model and support self-care practices: Agree (98%), Neutral (1%), Disagree (1%).
15. PSW should have access to workplace accommodations: Agree (91%), Neutral (7%), Disagree (2%).

Open-Ended Responses

A study of 837 supervisors who responded to the four open-ended questions on the survey was conducted in 2020 and published in the Community Mental Health Journal in 2021 (Foglesong, et al, 2021). Responses between supervisors who indicated that they also had work experience as a PSW (PS) were compared to supervisors who did not have work experience as a PSW (NPS). This is a brief summary of findings from this qualitative analysis:

The four open ended questions were:

1. In what ways, if any, are supervising PSWs different from other staff?
2. Responses: NPS (n=524), PS (n=163)

3. What qualities are important for a supervisor of peer support workers to have?
4. Responses: NPS (n=531), PS (n=167)
5. What are the different roles you play when supervising a peer support worker?
6. Responses: NPS (n=533), PS (n=167)
7. What questions or concerns do you have about the PSW in your organization?
8. Reponses: NPS (130), PS (n=59).

The analysis of supervisor open-ended answers to these questions illustrated different perceptions about supervision based on whether the supervisor did or did not have prior work experience as a PSW and highlighted this difference in three major themes:

- Knowledge Required of Supervisors
- Understanding of the role of the PSW
- Beliefs About What a PSW Needs to Do the Job

Conclusion

The key findings include:

1. There was a wide range of experience, with 65% of supervisors having 2 or more years
2. Questions related to supervisor attitudes and practices highlighted issues with stigma, disclosure and leadership
3. Growth in the number of states employing peers, as well as the work type sites and the number of supervisors
4. The survey did not specifically cover supervision training or, for those who did not have experience as a PSW, they identified as having lived experience of their own.
5. A subsequent study of the survey data led to conclusions about differences in attitudes between supervisors who had personal/work experience as a PSW and those supervisors who did not (Foglesong, 2021).

References

Daniels, A. S., Tunner, T. P., Powell, I., Fricks, L., Ashenden, P., (2015) Pillars

314

of Peer Support – VI: Peer Specialist Supervision. Pillars of Peer Support
Summit, Atlanta, GA. www.pillarsofpeersupport.org; March 2015.

Foglesong, D. & Wolf, J. (2018) Supervision and Successful Employment:
Overview of the National Peer Worker Supervision Survey [presentation],
National Peer Specialist Conference, Orlando, FL.

Foglesong, D., Spagnolo, A., Cronise, R., Forbes, J., Swarbrick, P., Edwards, J.,
& Pratt, C. (2021, June 1). Perceptions of Supervisors of Peer Support
Workers (PSW) in Behavioral Health: Results from a National Survey.
Community Mental Health Journal. Published online 2021. https://doi.org/10.
1007/s10597-021-00837-2

SECTION 4: YOU DO WHAT, HOW WELL? INTEGRATING THE PEER'S
VOICE IN SUPERVISION

George S. Braucht; LPC, CPCS,
CARES & Level II PCOMS Trainer, Brauchtworks Consulting

Performance support, vital for promoting the immediately experienced and
cumulative career growth of service providers, for peer service providers is
more different than like clinical supervision. The Partners for Change
Outcome Management System (PCOMS) is a routine outcome monitoring
process that informs service effectiveness using and privileging the service
recipient's voice. Eight randomized controlled trials (so far), a cohort study
and three benchmarking investigations unequivocally show that PCOMS
adds value to existing services while increasing efficiencies and improving
retention rates and outcomes including in public behavioral health systems.

This narrative illustrates how to integrate PCOMS' data into performance
support leading to a mastery level of peer service provider (PSP) competence
and confidence.

Bernard & Goodyear (2019, p. 9) define clinical supervision, "as an intervention provided by a more senior member of a profession to a more junior
colleague or colleagues who typically (but not always) are members of that
same profession. This relationship is evaluative, extends over time and has the
simultaneous purposes of enhancing the professional functioning of the more
junior person(s); monitoring the quality of professional services offered to the
clients that she, he or they see; and serving as a gatekeeper for the particular

profession the supervisee seeks to enter." Clinical supervision is alleged to be the signature pedagogy for preparing all mental health professionals however, recent studies call into question the fundamental differences in the clinician's focus on assessment, diagnosis and treatment and the peer service provider's (PSP) use of their lived experience credentials based on "regaining wellness and achieving a self-defined recovery despite a psychiatric and/or substance use condition." (Forbes, Pratt & Cronise, 2021) Extensive reports exist on PSP supervision including a consensus-based set of values (National Association of Peer Supporters, 2019), a fidelity measure (Chinman et al, 2016) and "new" learning collaboratives (Cronise, 2016). This narrative addresses a missing vital element – privileging the service recipient's voice.

Discussion

However beautiful the strategy, you should occasionally look at the results.

— SIR WINSTON CHURCHILL

Despite overall efficacy, meaning that service recipients are better off than similar others who do not access services, many peers (and clients!) do not benefit from professional services and dropouts are a problem. Providers vary significantly in success rates, are poor judges of negative outcomes, and often do not have a clue about their documented effectiveness. The "what's wrong with you" mindset that is pervasive in the behavioral health field (and others) does not fit the scientific research about change.

"Change, in truth, is far more about what's right with the people attempting it – their strengths, resources, ideas and relational supports – than the labels they are branded with or even the methods the therapist uses." (Duncan, 2005, p. xii) So beyond the usual monthly process and outcome metrics, e.g., the number of people seen individually and in groups, the duration of engagement, and how many "successfully discharged" vs didn't, the Partners for Change Outcome Management System (PCOMS) feedback intervention uses two, four-item scales to solicit essential service recipient feedback on the two factors proven to predict success regardless of your intervention model: 1) early progress, measured with the Outcome Rating Scale (ORS) and 2) the quality of the alliance using the Relationship Rating Scale (RRS) or for clinicians, the Session Rating Scale (SRS). Just add 5-10 minutes to the beginning and end of interactions.

PCOMS has been shown to be effective across many presenting concerns - substance use, mental health, carceral, etc. – and ecosystem involvements.

Furthermore, PCOMS identifies who is at risk for negative outcome before dropout or service failure; provides objective, quantifiable data on the effectiveness of providers and systems of care; uses reliable and valid but feasible measures for each interaction; and provides a mechanism for consumer preferences to guide intervention choice. This data is vital for performance support for prompting service providers' continuous progress toward mastery levels of competence and confidence.

The handout from the conference presentation (see More Information at the end of this article) provides three research-based key performance indicators used during appreciative performance support. That is followed by a Four Step Appreciative PCOMS Performance Support process that promotes the service providers' currently experienced and cumulative career growth. Service recipient feedback increases in value exponentially and consumer privilege becomes a reality when ORS scores extend past the immediate interaction into supervision to proactively address those who are not responding. The four-step supervisory process (Duncan, 2014; Duncan & Sparks, 2010) focuses first on ORS-identified at-risk service recipients, and then on individual service provider effectiveness and development. Based on outcome data instead of theoretical explanations or pontifications about why people are not changing, performance support identifies who is not benefiting so that services can be modified in the *next* interaction. This type of supervision departs from tradition because rather than the supervisee choosing who is discussed, the service recipients identify themselves by virtue of the change, or lack thereof, in their ORS scores. So, the ORS brings the service recipient's voice into supervision as well.

An important initial step in using PCOMS data is building a culture that values numbers and data. Helping supervisees become comfortable with simple statistics and to "love their data" encourages further exploration and reflection. Building a culture of trust and comfort about the data includes helping providers see that the numbers represent the service recipients' own progress assessments. Numbers on the measures are concrete representations of service recipient's perspectives that offer a direct way to describe service recipient benefit at the service provider and agency levels. The six-item Appreciative PCOMS Performance Support Conversation Regarding At-risk Peers/Clients illustrates how this conversation informs and empowers the peer and service provider with the last item focusing on how to "fail successfully."

Conclusion

The only man I know who behaves sensibly is my tailor; he takes my measurements anew each time he sees me. The rest go on with their old measurements and expect me to fit them.

— GEORGE BERNARD SHAW

Duncan & Reese (2016) suggest that using service recipient feedback data in supervision is an efficient and effective way to address the lack of focus on outcomes both in practice and research. Lambert and Hawkins (2001) first suggested that supervision could use outcome data to discuss service recipient progress and to inform future interactions and interventions. They also assert that outcome data can shape how time is spent in supervision, providing vital information to both facilitate training and ensure that service recipients are benefitting from interactions. From the supervisor perspective, using outcome and alliance data makes more efficient use of supervision time. Accurately assessing a supervisee's peer/caseload can be challenging and time-consuming when dealing with multiple supervisees. PCOMS data provides a quick "dashboard indicator" that can quickly identify who warrants more attention. Not only can using outcome and alliance data provide key information for assisting service providers who are struggling with specific service recipients, it can also highlight and reinforce the growth of supervisees with those who are faring well in the provided services. Ideally, service providers work themselves out of the central role in service recipients' recovery-oriented systems of care.

Outcome data also provides supervisors more direct access to supervisees' performance. For example, in some settings, supervisees may not be allowed to or are afraid to ask permission to record interactions. Supervisors then must rely on the supervisee's perspective. Research consistently shows that service providers, regardless of their experience level, have difficulty judging whether their service recipients are deteriorating (e.g., Hannan et al., 2005). This difficulty is perhaps exacerbated by any evaluative context where supervisees may tend to present their performance in a positive light and be reluctant to discuss challenges or mistakes.

Another advantage for supervisors is that PCOMS provides data-based feedback to supervisees. Effective supervision is generally assumed to require both positive and challenging feedback (Falender & Shafranske, 2004). Worthen and Lambert (2007) see using outcome data as a way to foster specific supervisory feedback that is "value neutral" because it was derived from the service recipient. This subtle shift may allow supervisor responses to seem more collaborative than evaluative, and perhaps better heard given that it arises from service recipients rather than a product of just the supervisor's opinion.

In summary, PCOMS fosters partnering with service recipients while identifying those who aren't responding and addressing the lack of progress in a positive, proactive way to keep them engaged while new directions and warm handoffs to new service providers are collaboratively sought. It also identifies who can be celebrated based on first-person evidence of progress.

PCOMS embraces two known predictors of ultimate intervention outcome. First, service recipients experience most of the change in the first eight visits (e.g., Baldwin, et al, 2009). People who report little or no progress in the first several interactions are unlikely to show improvement over the entire course of interactions and are prime candidates for the drop-out list. Monitoring change, or the lack thereof, identifies those who are not responding so that a new course can be charted. Secondly, a large body of research (Crits-Christoph, et al, 2013) shows a second robust predictor of change - the quality of the therapeutic or helping alliance from the view of the service recipient. In contrast to the service providers' view, service recipients who highly rate their partnership with the service provider are more apt to remain engaged and benefit from services.

PCOMS's light-touch, checking-in process usually takes 5-10 minutes to administer, score, and integrate into the beginning and toward the end of interactions. PCOMS also provides a gentle guide for selecting models and techniques that are congruent with the service recipient's worldview and theory of change, with a focus on outcomes. Besides the brevity of its measures and therefore its feasibility for everyday use given the demanding schedules of front-line service providers, PCOMS is distinguished by its routine involvement of service recipients in all aspects; scores on the progress and alliance instruments are openly shared and discussed at each administration. Their views of progress serve as a basis for beginning conversations, and their assessments of the quality of the alliance mark nearing the end of interactions. With this transparency, the measures provide a mutually understood reference point for discussing the reason(s) for seeking service, one's progress and level of engagement.

More Information

The 2020 SHARE Peer Supervision Workforce Conference session handout associated with this narrative is available at https://shareselfhelp. org/wp-content/uploads/2020/03/Braucht-You-do-what-how-well-Integrat ing-the-peers-voice-and-data-in-supervision-200225-Handout.pdf and the

recording is at https://www.youtube.com/watch?v=mogdyH-mng8&list=
PLO6ADB9wBqtaQ1WHOPswT4_D0QNoIIWPU&index=10.

In addition to the PCOMS tools, the Self-Completed Overview of
Recovery Experience (SCORE) Board (http://brauchtworks.com/
yahoo_site_admin/assets/docs/SCORE_Board_WHAM_160417.
62153815.pdf or page 4 of the handout) is useful for tracking progress on key
metrics that matter to the service recipient.

Copies of the PCOMS family of instruments in 33 languages are provided
free-of-charge to individual practitioners at https://betteroutcomesnow.
com/about-pcoms/pcoms-measures/. An affordable one-time group
license is required for agency or organizational use. Note that the bottom row
contains the peer measures and oral scripts for tele-health interactions.
Contact Dr. Barry L. Duncan via https://betteroutcomesnow.com/contact-
us/ to explore the state-of-the art Better Outcomes Now (BON) web application of the PCOMS created by Dr. Duncan, the developer of the clinical
process of PCOMS, and the organization that conducted the randomized
clinical trials that led to its evidence-based practice designation.

References

Baldwin, S., Berkeljon, A., Atkins, D., Olsen, L., & Nielsen, S. (2009). Rates of
change in naturalistic psychotherapy: Contrasting dose-effect and good-
enough level models of change. *Journal of Consulting and Clinical Psychology*,
77, 203-211.

Bernard, J. M. & Goodyear, R. K. (2019, 6th ed.). *Fundamentals of clinical supervision*. New York: Pearson.
Chinman, M., McCarthy, S., Mitchell-Miland, C, Daniels, K., Youk, A, &
Edelen, M. 2016). Early stages of development of a peer specialist fidelity
measure. *Psychiatric Rehabilitation Journal*, 39 (3), 256-265.

Cronise, R. (2016). Collaborative learning: A next step in the training of peer
support providers. *Psychiatric Rehabilitation Journal*, 39 (3), 292-294.

Duncan, B. (2005). *What's right with you: Debunking dysfunction and changing
your life*. Deerfield Beach, FL: Health Communication.

Duncan, B. (2014, 2nd ed.). *On becoming a better therapist: Evidence-based practice one client at a time*. Washington, DC: American Psychological Association.

Duncan, B. & Sparks, J. (2010, 2nd ed.). *Heroic clients, heroic agencies: Partners for change.* Jensen Beach, FL: Author.

Duncan, B. L., & Reese, R. J. (2016). Using PCOMS technology to improve outcomes and accelerate counselor development. In T. Rousmaniere & E. Renfro-Michel (Eds.), *Using technology to enhance clinical supervision* (pp. 135–156). American Counseling Association.

Falender, C. A., & Shafranske, E. P. (2004). *Clinical supervision: A competency-based approach.* Washington, DC: American Psychological Association.

Forbes, J., Pratt, C. & Cronise, R. (2021). Experiences of peer support specialists supervised by nonpeer supervisors. *Psychiatric Rehabilitation Journal,* 45 (1), 54-60.

Hannan, C., Lambert, M. J., Harmon, C., Nielsen, S. L., Smart, D. W., & Shimokawa, K. (2005). A lab test and algorithms for identifying clients at risk for treatment failure. *Journal of Clinical Psychology: in Session, 61,* 1-9.

Lambert, M. J., & Hawkins, E. J. (2001). Using information about patient progress in supervision: Are outcomes enhanced? *Australian Psychologist,* 36, 131–138.

National Association of Peer Supporters (2019). *National Practice Guidelines for Peer Specialists and Supervisors.* Washington, DC: N.A.P.S. https://www.peersupportworks.org/wp-content/uploads/2021/07/National-Practice-Guidelines-for-Peer-Specialists-and-Supervisors-1.pdf

Worthen, V. E., & Lambert, M. J. (2007). Outcome-oriented supervision: Advantages of adding systematic client tracking to supportive consultations. *Counselling and Psychotherapy Research, 7,* 48–53.

CHAPTER 12
DEVELOPING PRACTICE GUIDELINES FOR SUPERVISION

CHAPTER INTRODUCTION BY THE EDITORS

IN THIS CHAPTER, THE N.A.P.S. WORKFORCE AND SUPERVISION WORKGROUP, describes the purpose and process behind revising the original National Practice Guidelines for Peer Supporters to include guidance for supervisors. The chapter starts with an article by Steve Harrington on organizational change, which highlights many of the issues peer specialists face when working in traditional treatment settings that have not yet adopted, or are in the early stages of adopting recovery-oriented approaches. Organizational change can be daunting, but the National Practice Guidelines for Peer Specialists and Supervisors now offer supervisors a tool and an approach for helping to make the shift toward a recovery philosophy and a work environment that respects the perspectives of the peer specialists. Following Steve's article, the next reading includes excerpts from an Open Source article on the development and verification of the supervision guidelines by Dana Foglesong, Kelsey Stang Knowles, Rita Cronise, Jessica Wolf, and Jonathan P. Edward who are key members of the N.A.P.S. Workforce and Supervision Workgroup. As stated in the article that was published in Psychiatric Services here are some of the highlights:

- A taskforce within the National Association of Peer Supporters (N.A.P.S.) developed and released the National Practice Guidelines for Peer Supporters (NPG) in 2013 with a 98.8% approval rating among 1000 peer support providers nationwide.

- A workforce workgroup within N.A.P.S. revised the NPG to include supervision guidelines and released the National Practice Guidelines for Peer Specialists and Supervisors (NPG-S) in 2019, to strengthen supervisors' skills in upholding the core values of peer support.
- The main purpose of the NPG-S is to assist supervisors and peer support specialists as they embark together on a mutual learning process about peer support values and how best to put them into practice.

Finally, the third reading in this chapter contains elements of the 2019 release of the NPG-S for reference. Because the guidelines are subject to change, be sure to visit the N.A.P.S. website for the latest.

SECTION 1: ORGANIZATIONAL CULTURE CHANGE CAN HELP MENTAL HEALTH ORGANIZATIONS THRIVE

Steve Harrington, M.P.A., J.D., CPS
Founder, National Association of Peer Specialists (N.A.P.S.)

Recovery is not about programs—it is about people.

WE CAN ADMINISTER and implement the best mental health programs known, yet they are doomed to mediocrity—if not outright failure--if all involved do not reflect a recovery culture. Organizations that do the fundamental work to develop a recovery culture find programs and practices are adopted more readily and yield better results more quickly.

A recovery culture is founded on basic respect for individuals served by mental health systems and self-respect on the part of clients themselves. Such a culture involves full embracement of the strengths perspective, consumer involvement in treatment and policy formation, and inspiration of hope and courage.

Organizations typically fear adoption of a recovery culture because it means a true paradigm shift, which means change. Change is always fearful, but history shows thriving organizations are dynamic and learn to change when environmental factors require it. As those served by mental health systems recover, they are requiring change in the way treatment is designed and implemented.

Organizational cultures are characterized by "artifacts," espoused values, and basic assumptions. Such cultures are fundamental to the way organizations operate and have a profound effect on effectiveness and efficiency.

Artifacts include the language used by people in the organization, publications, organizational structure, and even the physical layout of offices. These artifacts reflect the way business is done and can either foster or impede a recovery culture.

Espoused values are important because they help organization's measure fidelity to those values. Strategic planning often produces impressive mission statements but, too often, those mission statements are more for public consumption than a reflection of true organizational values. For example, nearly every mental health system expresses recovery orientation but very few can pass the litmus test of meaningful consumer involvement.

Basic assumptions are the foundation of organizational culture and are often based on the collective values of workers, although effective leaders can have great influence on such assumptions. For example, social workers may say they embrace the recovery paradigm (espoused value) but, in practice, rely on traditional benefactor roles when counseling clients. The basic assumption remains that persons with psychiatric disorders cannot recover and will continually require assistance to secure housing, employment, health care, transportation and other basic needs.

When clinicians interact with those they serve based on such erroneous assumptions, the philosophy is self-fulfilling. Clients will not recover because services and organizations providing them are structured in a manner that reinforces these basic assumptions on an individual level.

Unfortunately, there are many powerful factors impeding the adoption of a recovery culture. Many public and non-profit mental health organizations have evolved from a government-based, bureaucratic structure and management style. Such organizations are ill-equipped to incorporate many recovery facets, including meaningful consumer input on treatment and policy.

Another impediment to recovery culture development is ambiguity. Recovery is unique to the individual and, as such, can have many definitions. The question many organizations ask is: How can we develop a recovery orientation when we don't know what recovery is?

Organizational fear is also a barrier to recovery cultures. Change is frightening at a personal level and the same is true for organizations. Because we do not know how change will affect control—at both personal and organization levels—we are inclined to maintain the status quo. As a result, organizational inertia ("We've always done it that way so there's no need to change now.") often prevails.

In addition to these most obvious recovery culture impediments, there are more subtle barriers. Politics, client mindsets, state and federal regulations, existing organizational structure, functions, organizational inertia, geographic and cultural diversity, physical layout of offices, communication styles, and leadership voids can have profound effects on an organization's ability to develop a recovery culture.

Organizational culture change can distinguish managers from leaders. Managers see a problem and seek a solution. Leaders, on the other hand, see problems as potential system failures and examine ways to change such systems so similar problems do not arise in the future.

Although the value of culture change has long been recognized in the for-profit sector, few government and non-profit organizations have undertaken a process to examine and analyze existing cultures and develop a plan for culture change. The array of culture-change barriers can be formidable and even unpopular initially.

One must also appreciate that culture change involves personal and organizational values that have been formed over long periods and are the result of experience. Culture change often takes much time (sometimes years) and prolonged effort. It is not an endeavor for the squeamish or those looking for a "quick fix."

In some mental health systems, there are some who advocate complete dissolution of existing entities in favor of starting over as a way to create recovery cultures. Indeed, this may be one reason peer case management agencies are emerging. But leaders of existing mental health treatment providers can undertake effective culture-change initiatives if they possess adequate courage to face the fear change brings and replace it with the passion to serve clients in the best ways possible.

These leaders must beware, however, of organizational development experts who bring with them pre-designed, "cookie cutter" approaches. Culture change requires in-depth understanding of the existing culture and the array of potential change barriers, which are unique to each organization.

While there is a tendency to look for easy answers to complex problems, such an approach is not practical or possible when it comes to organizational cultural change. Because of the host of external and internal factors affecting organizational structure, function, operation and management, each organization, regardless of level, must examine its own culture and devise plans to adopt or enhance recovery cultures.

If this task appears daunting, it is with good reason. Organizational cultural changes often take years to accomplish, and a "true and complete" recovery culture may be more of an ideal than a reality. But the many for-profit business organizations that have engaged in this ambitious endeavor have reaped great successes. Workers and managers are happier in their jobs, which leads to less turnover, innovation, motivation, higher quality, and satisfied customers. These same attributes can apply to mental health organizations.

Even though it is impractical and impossible to develop a model plan for culture change in mental health organizations, there is a place to start that can help administrators understand where they are and where they should be when it comes to recovery cultures. Consumers of mental health services are the best ones to identify and describe organizational cultural artifacts. Qualitative data obtained through interviews and focus groups can help administrators determine the need and extent of culture change.

The challenge of culture change brings with it a wealth of opportunities. True recovery cultures are innovative, effective, and result in a satisfied workforce and clientele. Instead of new programs that begin with a flair and fanfare and then die an agonizing death when grant funds expire, meaningful recovery initiatives are integrated into everyday operations and are fueled by the passion of workers and those they serve.

The ranks of peer specialists—persons with experience with a psychiatric disorder who help others with such disorders—are growing rapidly. The question only time will answer is whether peer support delivered by the peer specialist model is merely a faddish program or a recovery culture artifact.

The answer will be found in endurance. If, twenty years from now, peer specialists continue to be employed by mental health organizations and serve meaningful roles by inspiring hope in those they serve, then they are a recovery culture artifact. The orientation of an organization could be gauged —at least to some extent—by the quantity of peer specialists employed and the quality (meaningfulness) of their work.

Peer specialists can have profound effects on organizational culture. They can become agents of change through interaction with staff and community.

Recovery is not about programs. The best programs known will be mediocre at best unless the people who administer, manage and implement them are infused with a recovery culture.

STEVE HARRINGTON, B.S., M.P.A., J.D., received mental health services and was a recovery advocate from Grand Rapids, Mich.
Article used with permission.

Section 2: Development of the National Practice
Guidelines for Peer Specialists and Supervisors

*This section contains excerpts from an article by Dana Foglesong, Kelsey Knowles,
Rita Cronise, Jessica Wolf, and Jonathan Edwards that was published in Psychiatric
Services in 2021 on the development of the Supervision Guidelines. It provides an
inside look at how the guidelines were revised and verified by practicing supervisors.*

"In 2013, the National Association of Peer Supporters (N.A.P.S.) issued
practice guidelines based on the work of a task force that conducted an extensive literature search to identify the most common values, principles, and use
of language by peer support workers. The original National Practice Guidelines for Peer Supporters (NPG) identified 12 core values of peer support
including a short description of each value in practice. Unlike earlier rules
largely about trying to help peer support workers fit into traditional roles in
clinical cultures with a focus on deficits (what's wrong) and rules about what
peer workers can't do (don't overshare), these guidelines focused on strengths
and what peer workers can do. For each of the 12 core values there were
statements (competencies) about what that value looks like in practice. The
core values were reviewed by a peer leadership panel at SAMHSA and
endorsed with a 98.5% approval by over 1,000 peer supporters in the U.S., the
NPG were issued by the National Association of Peer Supporters1 (N.A.P.S.)
in 2013 and have been recognized in all 50 states and the World Health Organization (WHO) for training and guiding peer workers on respecting and
protecting the rights of people with mental disabilities worldwide (NAPS,
2013)."

"By 2017, N.A.P.S. leadership became increasingly aware of concerns
within the peer support workforce community about supervision practices
contradicting or conflicting with core peer support values. Peer support
specialists were frequently assigned menial tasks unrelated to direct peer
support practice, which focuses on voluntary engagement, instilling hope,
disclosing strategically, and creating opportunities for constructive dialogue
and meaningful activities that facilitate recovery and goal fulfillment."

Discussion

"Because the peer support worker role and approaches are unfamiliar to
many supervisors (in clinical treatment settings), peer specialists often found
themselves in situations where they were minimized, stigmatized, marginal-

ized, undermined, exploited, and retraumatized. In some cases, peer support workers experienced moral injury when directed to perform a job task that would cause to others the same harm the peer supporters had previously experienced as service users.

"To respond to these concerns, a work group composed of seven nationally recognized N.A.P.S. members and board members (six of whom were current or former peer support specialists or supervisors) was convened and met regularly over 18 months. The work group first sought to determine what guidance existed on the supervision of peer support workers. Although the supervision of peer support workers by a mental health professional had been an established requirement for Medicaid funding for more than a decade, 'the empirical literature offered little guidance to address the purpose, content, or process of supervision of the non-clinical peer support worker role (Forbes, 2021). Figure 1 shows a timeline of the activities of the workgroup.

N.A.P.S. National Practice Guidelines for Peer Specialists and Supervisors (NPG-S) Timeline

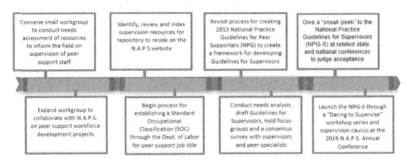

Figure 1: Timeline of the Development of the NPG-S.

"SOME OF THE research literature offered supervision as an avenue toward role clarity but without specific guidance on supervision based on recovery-oriented practices or on the values of peer support. After a review of both empirical and gray literature, the work group determined a gap existed in supervision specific to the peer support workforce (in clinical treatment settings). Any relevant public domain information was categorized by the work group and made publicly available on the N.A.P.S. website in a repository of supervision resources (https://www.peersupportworks.org/resources/supervision-resources)."

"Next, the work group drafted practical tips and guidance on the role of the supervisor to strengthen, integrate, and uphold peer support values. This revision to the NPG became known as the National Practice Guidelines for Peer Specialists and Supervisors (NPG-S). The NPG-S followed a development and consensus process similar to the original National Practice Guidelines (NPG).

"The work group reviewed the 12 core values from the existing NPG. Each new guideline focused on ways in which supervisors could help peer specialists uphold the core values and practices of peer support.

"During the development of the NPG-S, work group members used their real-world experiences in receiving supervision, in supervising peer support staff, or both. After the first draft was written, N.A.P.S. members were invited to complete targeted surveys to refine the supervision guidelines. The work group incorporated feedback received from 151 peer support specialists and 109 supervisors.

"The work group then arranged four online feedback sessions to determine how supervisors and peer support specialists might use the guidelines. Twenty of the 44 invited N.A.P.S. members participated in a feedback session. The work group analyzed notes from the feedback sessions, incorporated suggestions on content changes, and noted recommendations for future projects. A final draft was then circulated to the peer support workforce via e-mail through the N.A.P.S. listserv and affiliated peer organizations. In 2013, it was relatively easy to solicit feedback from 1,000 working peer specialists regarding the original NPG. However, the work group faced challenges identifying a large number of supervisors when soliciting feedback for the NPG-S. The N.A.P.S. membership and mailing lists for affiliated organizations are targeted to the interests of people with lived experience, which many supervisors may not consider to be relevant. Further efforts to locate and engage supervisors in ongoing education remain a priority for N.A.P.S.

"The results of the consensus process showed that 91% of respondents (N=213 of 234 responses) endorsed the NPG-S. On the basis of the approval rating and positive responses to the questions, the work group determined that the original intent of the NPG-S, to provide guidance on the role of supervisors in supporting peer specialists in practicing the core values as outlined in the NPG, had been achieved.

"In October 2019, N.A.P.S. and the supervision work group finalized the NPG-S, launched the guidelines at the N.A.P.S. annual conference in San Diego and posted them on the N.A.P.S. website. After further dissemination of the NPG-S through webinars and learning communities, it became evident that these guidelines apply to all supervisors, whether or not they had experienced a personal journey of recovery from mental health or substance use or had previously worked as a peer support specialist.

"Participants in educational workshops and webinars about the NPG-S indicated that the guidelines were 'straightforward and helpful' and could be used to help supervisors 'better understand how the boundaries and ethics of peer support differ from those observed in clinical practice.' The guidelines can be used as a tool by supervisors to gauge their understanding of peer support practices and by peer support staff to provide feedback to their supervisor to improve the supervision experience. Participants in many of these settings have also suggested that the NPG-S could be used as a fidelity tool for peer support specialists to reflect on how well their own performance aligns in practice with the principles of peer support. These guidelines could also be used to increase management and executive leadership awareness of peer support and as an advocacy tool for increased application and implementation of peer support values in organizational culture.

"The NPG-S provide additional opportunities to increase interdisciplinary team members' understanding of the peer role and core peer support values in practice. Clinical supervisors may struggle to understand the equally challenging complexities of the nonclinical peer support role. Role clarity is a predictor of job satisfaction for peer support workers. As the peer support workforce has grown, noticeable increases in role confusion and role drift have occurred. These issues are far more likely to occur when a supervisor unfamiliar with the core values of peer support attempts to act as a mentor or role model for these values and peer support competencies. For example, strategic or judicious self-disclosure is frequently outside a licensed practitioner's professional scope of practice; yet licensed practitioners are the most frequent supervisors for the peer support workforce in traditional service settings. Standard clinical approaches to providing supervision are therefore antithetical to peer support values when the supervisor's opportunities to effectively model peer roles are restricted.

"Perhaps most importantly, the NPG-S can assist supervisors in realigning peer support specialists' job descriptions and duties to match the underlying core value of mutual support, such as sharing relevant lived experience and reciprocal interpersonal relationships to build hope and trust, to foster identification, and to support choice. The NPG-S contain practical tips and new ideas for supervisors to consider when the supervisor's own professional training or code of ethics limits or prohibits them from being able to model how to draw on their own personal recovery experiences with individuals whom they support (Foglesong, 2021)."

Conclusion

This extended excerpt from a Psychiatric Services article by members of the N.A.P.S. Workforce and Supervision Workgroup described the purpose and process for revising the National Practice Guidelines to include guidance for supervisors, with ways in which these guidelines can be used by supervisors as a self-assessment tool toward improved supervision that is peer-informed and aligned with the core values of peer support.

References

Chappell D, Statz-Hill M: Job satisfaction of peers employed in mental health centers: a systematic review. Soc Work Ment Health 2016; 14:564–582

Chinman M, George P, Dougherty RH, et al.: Peer support services for individuals with serious mental illnesses: assessing the evidence. Psychiatr Serv 2014; 65:429–441. doi: 10.1176/appi.ps.201300244

Cronise R, Teixeira C, Rogers ES, et al.: The peer support workforce: results of a national survey. Psychiatr Rehabil J 2016; 39:211–221

Forbes J, Pratt C, Cronise R: Experiences of peer support specialists supervised by nonpeer supervisors. Psychiatr Rehabil J (Epub Apr 1, 2021) 33793288

Kaufman L, Kuhn WB, Manser SS: Peer Specialist Training and Certification Programs: National Overview 2016. Austin, TX, Texas Institute for Excellence in Mental Health, School of Social Work, University of Texas at Austin, 2017. https://sites.utexas.edu/mental-health-institute/files/2017/01/Peer-Specialist-Training-and-Certification-Programs-A-National-Overview-2016-Update-1.5.17.pdf

National Practice Guidelines for Peer Specialists and Supervisors. Washington, DC, National Association of Peer Supporters, 2019. https://www.peer supportworks.org/wp-content/uploads/2020/08/National-Practice-Guidelines-for-Peer-Specialists-and-Supervisors.pdf

National Practice Guidelines for Peer Supporters. Washington, DC, National Association of Peer Supporters, 2013. https://www.peersupportworks.org/wp-content/uploads/2021/02/nationalguidelines_updated.pdf

One-to-One Peer Support by and for People With Lived Experience: WHO QualityRights Guidance Module. Geneva, World Health Organization, 2019. https://apps.who.int/iris/bitstream/handle/10665/329591/9789241516785-eng.pdf

Smith DG: Letter by the Director of the Centers for Medicare and Medicaid Services (CMS) to State Medicaid Directors Regarding Guidance for Peer Support Services Under the Medicaid Program. Baltimore, Centers for Medicare and Medicaid Services, 2007. https://downloads.cms.gov/cmsgov/archived-downloads/SMDL/downloads/SMD081507A.pdfGoogle Scholar

Solomon P: Peer support/peer provided services underlying processes, benefits, and critical ingredients. Psychiatr Rehabil J 2004; 27:392–401

Walker G, Bryant W: Peer support in adult mental health services: a metasynthesis of qualitative findings. Psychiatr Rehabil J 2013; 36:28–34

Wolf J: National trends in peer specialist certification. Psychiatr Serv 2018; 69:1049

Wolf J, Lawrence LH, Ryan PM, et al.: Emerging practices in employment of persons in recovery in the mental health workforce. Am J Psychiatr Rehabil 2010; 133:189–207. oi: 10.1080/15487768.2010.501294

SECTION 3: REVISED NATIONAL PRACTICE GUIDELINES FOR PEER SPECIALISTS AND SUPERVISORS

This section contains the National Practice Guidelines for Peer Specialists and Supervisors by the National Association of Peer Supporters (N.A.P.S.).

Please note: This book is a publication of the National Association of Peer Supporters (N.A.P.S.). The National Practice Guidelines for Peer Specialists and

Supervisors (NPG-S) are included for the convenience of the reader who may not have access to the Internet while reading this book.

Use of the NPG-S from the book or directly from the link on the N.A.P.S website is encouraged in any work related to the practice of peer support and supervision. However, reprinting the NPG-S in other books or publications without the permission of N.A.P.S. is prohibited.

"The belief that recovery is possible for all who experience a psychiatric, traumatic, or substance use challenges is fundamental to the practice of peer support. The likelihood of long-term recovery is increased with effective support. Peer support has been demonstrated through research and practice to be highly effective. The original National Practice Guidelines for Peer Supporters (NPG) identified 12 core values of peer support including a short description of each value in practice. Unlike earlier rules trying to fit peer support workers into traditional roles and settings with a focus on deficits (avoiding relapse) and rules about what peer workers can't do, these guidelines focused on strengths and what peer workers can do in alignment with these 12 core values. Reviewed by a peer leadership panel at SAMHSA and endorsed with a 98.5% approval by over 1,000 peer supporters in the U.S., the NPG were issued by the National Association of Peer Supporters (N.A.P.S.) in 2013 and have been recognized in all 50 states and the World Health Organization (WHO) for training and guiding peer workers on respecting and protecting the rights of people with mental disabilities worldwide.

"With the continued growth of the peer workforce since 2013, increased attention has turned to supervision of peer support workers (also known as peer support specialists) (N.A.P.S., 2019)."

Guidelines for Supervisors

"Recognizing concerns about supervision, in 2018 N.A.P.S. convened a National Supervision Workgroup to review issues, existing research reports, curricula, and webinars related to the supervision of peer support specialists. A Supervision Resource page was created on the N.A.P.S. website. N.A.P.S. offered online discussions open to all peer support specialists and an additional monthly online discussion for supervisors. The Supervision Workgroup drafted National Practice Guidelines for Peer Specialists and Supervisors (NPG-S), identifying supervisors' roles in helping peer staff uphold the core values of the 2013 National Practice Guidelines for Peer Supporters. The Workgroup then sought national input through surveys and focus groups from both peer support specialists and supervisors. The NPS-G received an approval rating of 91.8% from 232 responses to a national survey (N.A.P.S., 2019)."

Purpose and Scope

"The purpose of the added guidelines for supervisors is to educate supervisors about the core peer support values as applied in supervisory relationships. The NPG-S describe the supervisor's role and offer practical tips about how supervisors can help peer support specialists remain true to the values outlined in the original NPG. The NPG-S are written for all supervisors, whether or not they have previously worked as peer support specialists. The NPG-S may be used to educate and/or advocate. They may be used as a self-assessment for supervisors to improve the supervision experience. The NPG-S can be used to educate management and executive leadership about the values of peer support and to advocate for increased promotion of these values in practice.

"These guidelines do not address general topics in supervision beyond the values of peer support. While some tips in the NPG-S apply to all staff, their purpose is to educate (or remind) supervisors and peer support specialists of peer support values (N.A.P.S., 2019)."

Peer and Non-Peer Supervision

"Ideally, all peer support specialists are supervised by people who have lived experience with recovery and peer support. However, with the rapid growth and continuing evolution of peer support in behavioral health care, integrated care, and related non-peer-run workplace settings, the number of experienced and interested peer support practitioners credentialed for funder-required supervisor eligibility is limited. Both lived experience and role-specific training are required to practice as a peer support specialist.

"Traditional academic education is not a substitute for the training and life experience of a peer support specialist who practices from the perspective of having lived experience.

"Whether or not a supervisor has lived experience as a peer supporter, the NPG-S offer important information to assist in delivering services in alignment with the fundamental values of peer support (N.A.P.S., 2019)."

Mutual Respect in Supervision

"The N.A.P.S. National Supervision Workgroup recognizes the importance of mutual respect in supervision. The NPG-S recognize that circumstances arise in traditionally-structured agencies in which liability may influence decisions including supervisors' use of authority. In these challenging situations, supervisors and supervisees can continue a mutually respectful relationship and open communication.

The focus of this document is the role of the supervisor in helping peer specialists practice the values in the N.A.P.S. NPG. Other recognized models for supervision of peer specialists may also be considered (N.A.P.S., 2019)."

National Practice Guidelines

The pages that follow contain the revised core values and their definitions, practice guidelines and examples of what they look like in practice, and the role of the supervisor in helping peer support staff to uphold the core values. The version contained in the following pages launched in 2019. The guidelines are subject to change, so be sure to check the N.A.P.S. website for the latest version.

National Practice
Guidelines for Peer
Specialists and
Supervisors

N.A.P.S.
NATIONAL ASSOCIATION OF PEER SUPPORTERS

Recovery is a process of change through which individuals improve their health and wellness, live a self-directed life, and strive to reach their full potential.

—SAMHSA's Working Definition of Recovery

National Practice Guidelines for Peer Specialists and Supervisors

N.A.P.S.

NATIONAL ASSOCIATION OF PEER SUPPORTERS

Recommended citation:
National Association of Peer Supporters (2019). *National Practice Guidelines for Peer Specialists and Supervisors*. Washington, DC: N.A.P.S.

National Association of Peer Supporters (N.A.P.S.) www.peersupportworks.org

Acknowledgements

This document was developed through the National Association of Peer Supporters (N.A.P.S.) Workforce Development Committee from 2017 through 2019. N.A.P.S. recognizes workgroup members Dana Foglesong, Kelsey Stang, Jessica Wolf, Jonathan P. Edwards, Martha Barbone, Mike Weaver, and Rita Cronise.

The workgroup further acknowledges the following seminal publications that directly influenced the development of the original (2013) National Practice Guidelines for Peer Supporters (NPG), upon which this revision is based.

Blanch, A., Filson, B., Penney, D. & Cave, C. (2012). Engaging Women in Trauma-Informed Peer Support: A Guidebook. Center for Mental Health Services, National Center for Trauma-Informed Care. Funded by the Substance Abuse and Mental Health Services Administration (SAMHSA) and the National Association of State Mental Health Program Directors (NASMHP).

Copeland, M.E. (n.d.). The Values and Ethics of WRAP. The Copeland Center for Wellness and Recovery.

Daniels, A. S., Tunner, T. P., Bergeson, S., Ashenden, P., Fricks, L. & Powell, I. (2013). Pillars of Peer Support Summit IV: Establishing Standards of Excellence. Funded by the Substance Abuse and Mental Health Services Administration (SAMHSA) and the National Association of State Mental Health Program Directors (NASMHP).

Van Tosh, L, & del Vecchio, P. (2000). Consumer-Operated Self-Help Programs: A Technical Report. U.S. Center for Mental Health Services, Rockville, MD.

World Health Organization (WHO). (2012) WHO QualityRights tool kit to assess and improve quality and human rights in mental health and social care facilities. World Health Organization, Geneva.

CONTENTS

BACKGROUND

The belief that recovery is possible for all who experience a psychiatric, traumatic, or substance use challenges is fundamental to the practice of peer support. The likelihood of long-term recovery is increased with effective support. Peer support has been demonstrated through research and practice to be highly effective.

The original *National Practice Guidelines for Peer Supporters* (NPG) identified 12 core values of peer support including a short description of each value in practice. Unlike earlier rules trying to fit peer support workers into traditional roles and settings with a focus on deficits (avoiding relapse) and rules about what peer workers can't do, these guidelines focused on strengths and what peer workers can do in alignment with these 12 core values.

Reviewed by a peer leadership panel at SAMHSA and endorsed with a 98.5% approval by over 1,000 peer supporters in the U.S., the NPG were issued by the National Association of Peer Supporters[1] (N.A.P.S.) in 2013 and have been recognized in all 50 states and the World Health Organization (WHO) for training and guiding peer workers on respecting and protecting the rights of people with mental disabilities worldwide.[2]

Guidelines for Supervisors

With the continued growth of the peer workforce since 2013, increased attention has turned to supervision of peer support workers (also known as peer support specialists).

Many states funded peer support worker positions through Medicaid reimbursement (Smith, 2007), which required supervision by a licensed (qualified) mental health professional as defined by each state. While this led to substantial growth in the peer support specialist workforce, it also resulted in peer support worker supervisors with no direct knowledge of peer support values; the supervisors' ethical codes often prevented practice of essential aspects of peer support such as self-disclosure (sharing relevant elements of one's own personal story to connect with someone else).

---

1. The organization changed its name from International Association of Peer Supporters to National Association of Peer Supporters in 2020.
2. The development of the original U.S. *National Practice Guidelines for Peer Supporters* is fully described in the original National Practice Guidelines for Peer Supporters (NAPS, 2013)

Recognizing concerns about supervision, in 2018 N.A.P.S. convened a National Supervision Workgroup to review issues, existing research reports, curricula, and webinars related to the supervision of peer support specialists. A Supervision Resource page was created on the N.A.P.S. website. N.A.P.S. continues to offer a monthly online discussion open to all peer support specialists and an additional monthly online discussion for supervisors.

The Supervision Workgroup drafted *National Practice Guidelines for Peer Specialists and Supervisors* (NPG-S), identifying supervisors' roles in helping peer staff uphold the core values of the 2013 National Practice Guidelines for Peer Supporters. The Workgroup sought national input through surveys and focus groups from both peer support specialists and supervisors. The NPS-G received an approval rating of 91.8% from 232 responses to a national survey.

Purpose and Scope
The purpose of the added guidelines for supervisors is to educate supervisors about the core peer support values as applied in supervisory relationships. The NPG-S describe the supervisor's role and offer practical tips about how supervisors can help peer support specialists remain true to the values outlined in the original NPG.

The NPG-S are written for all supervisors, whether or not they have previously worked as peer support specialists. The NPG-S may be used to educate and/or advocate. They may be used as a self-assessment for supervisors to improve the supervision experience. The NPG-S can be used to educate management and executive leadership about the values of peer support and to advocate for increased promotion of these values in practice.

These guidelines **do not address** general topics in supervision beyond the values of peer support. While some tips in the NPG-S apply to all staff, their purpose is to educate (or remind) supervisors and peer support specialists of peer support values.

Peer and Non-Peer Supervision
Ideally, all peer support specialists are supervised by people who have lived experience with recovery and peer support. However, with the rapid growth and continuing evolution of peer support in behavioral health care, integrated care, and related non-peer-run workplace settings, the number of experienced and interested peer support practitioners credentialed for funder-required supervisor eligibility is limited. Both lived experience and role-specific training are required to practice as a peer support specialist.

Traditional academic education is not a substitute for the training and life experience of a peer support specialist who practices from the perspective of having lived experience.

Whether or not a supervisor has lived experience as a peer supporter, the NPG-S offer important information to assist in delivering services in alignment with the fundamental values of peer support.

Mutual Respect in Supervision

The N.A.P.S. National Supervision Workgroup recognizes the importance of mutual respect in supervision. The NPG-S recognize that circumstances arise in traditionally-structured agencies in which liability may influence decisions including supervisors' use of authority. In these challenging situations, supervisors and supervisees can continue a mutually respectful relationship and open communication.

The focus of this document is the role of the supervisor in helping peer specialists practice the values in the N.A.P.S. NPG. Other recognized models for supervision of peer specialists may also be considered.

CORE VALUES

In addition to SAMHSA's Working Definition and Guiding Principles of Recovery, core values have been ratified by peer supporters across the U.S. as the core ethical values for peer support practice. With 98% agreement among nearly 1,000 peer supporters responding to surveys and participating in focus groups, the following 12 core values were identified and validated as a basis for this work:

1. Peer support is voluntary
2. Peer supporters are hopeful
3. Peer supporters are open minded
4. Peer supporters are empathetic
5. Peer supporters are respectful
6. Peer supporters facilitate change
7. Peer supporters are honest and direct
8. Peer support is mutual and reciprocal
9. Peer support is equally shared power
10. Peer support is strengths-focused
11. Peer support is transparent
12. Peer support is person-drive

344

CORE VALUE 1

Peer Support Is Voluntary

Recovery is a personal choice. The most basic value of peer support is that people freely choose to give or receive support. Being coerced, forced or pressured is against the nature of genuine peer support.

The voluntary nature of peer support makes it easier to build trust and connections with another.

PEER SUPPORTER GUIDELINES	SUPERVISOR GUIDELINES
Practice: **Support Choice**	The supervisor role is to:
· Peer supporters do not force or coerce others to participate in peer support services or any other service. · Peer supporters respect the rights of those they support to choose or cease support services or use the peer support services from a different peer supporter. · Peer supporters also have the right to choose not to work with individuals with a particular background if the peer supporter's personal issues or lack of expertise could interfere with the ability to provide effective support to these individuals. In these situations, the peer supporter would refer the individuals to other peer supporters or other service providers to provide assistance with the individuals' interests and desires. · Peer supporters advocate for choice when they observe coercion in any mental health or substance use service setting.	· Encourage peer support specialists in promoting individuals' choices including becoming more knowledgeable about trauma-informed approaches that reduce or eliminate force and coercion to create a safer environment for all. · Explore peer support specialists' choices about how they might or might not choose to work with certain individuals, especially if there are issues related to dual relationships or trauma. · Provide guidance to peer support specialists when they are advocating for choice or speaking up when coercion occurs, especially when it is subtle or systemic.

CORE VALUE 2

Peer Supporters Are Hopeful

The belief that recovery is possible brings hope to those feeling hopeless. Hope is the catalyst of recovery for many people.

Peer supporters demonstrate that recovery is real—they are the evidence that people can and do overcome the internal and external challenges that confront people with mental health, traumatic or substance use challenges. As role models, most peer supporters make a commitment to continue to grow and thrive as they "walk the walk" in their own pathway of recovery. By authentically living recovery, peer supporters inspire real hope that recovery is possible for others.

PEER SUPPORTER GUIDELINES	SUPERVISOR GUIDELINES
Practice: **Share Hope**	The supervisor role is to:
• Peer supporters tell strategic stories of their personal recovery in relation to current struggles faced by those who are being supported. • Peer supporters model recovery behaviors at work and act as ambassadors of recovery in all aspects of their work. • Peer supporters help others reframe life challenges as opportunities for personal growth.	• Demonstrate confidence in peer specialists' ability to share a hopeful message. • Provide a way to further develop skills for disclosing personal experience with the goals of inspiring hope, developing trust and rapport, and fostering strengths. • Model self-care, appropriate boundaries, and an authentic belief in recovery through language, attitude, and actions.

346

CORE VALUE 3

Peer Supporters Are Open Minded

Being judged can be emotionally distressing and harmful. Peer supporters "meet people where they are at" in their recovery experience even when the other person's beliefs, attitudes or ways of approaching recovery are far different from their own.

Being nonjudgmental means holding others in unconditional positive regard, with an open mind, a compassionate heart and full acceptance of each person as a unique individual.

PEER SUPPORTER GUIDELINES	SUPERVISOR GUIDELINES
Practice: **Withhold Judgment About Others**	The supervisor role is to:
• Peer supporters embrace differences of those they support as potential learning opportunities. • Peer supporters respect an individual's right to choose the pathways to recovery individuals believe will work best for them. • Peer supporters connect with others where and as they are. • Peer supporters do not evaluate or assess others.	• View differences as an opportunity for learning. Refrain from seeing differences as pathology (symptoms); consider "what happened?" rather than "what's wrong?" • Learn with and from peer support specialists about different pathways to recovery and alternate perspectives about individuals. • Respect peer support specialists' individual recovery journeys and knowledge of recovery approaches.

CORE VALUE 4

Peer Supporters Are Empathetic

Empathy is an emotional connection that is created by "putting yourself in the other person's shoes."

Peer supporters do not assume they know exactly what the other person is feeling even if they have experienced similar challenges.

They ask thoughtful questions and listen with sensitivity to be able to respond emotionally or spiritually to what the other person is feeling.

PEER SUPPORTER GUIDELINES	SUPERVISOR GUIDELINES
Practice: **Listen With Emotional Sensitivity**	The supervisor role is to:
• Peer supporters practice effective listening skills that are non-judgmental. • Peer supporters understand that even though others may share similar life experiences, the range of responses may vary considerably.	• Practice effective listening that is non-judgmental and empathic while balancing the need to hold peer support specialists accountable for their job duties.. • Provide adequate time and space, with coaching and feedback, for peer specialists to become proficient in this critical skill.

348

CORE VALUE 5

Peer Supporters Are Respectful

Each person is valued and seen as having something important and unique to contribute to the world. Peer supporters treat people with kindness, warmth, and dignity.

Peer supporters accept and are open to differences, encouraging people to share the gifts and strengths that come from human diversity.

Peer supporters honor and make room for everyone's ideas and opinions and believe every person is equally capable of contributing to the whole.

PEER SUPPORTER GUIDELINES	SUPERVISOR GUIDELINES
Practice: Be Curious and Embrace Diversity	The supervisor role is to:
· Peer supporters embrace the diversity of culture and thought as a means of personal growth for those they support and themselves. · Peer supporters encourage others to explore how differences can contribute to their lives and the lives of those around them. · Peer supporters practice patience, kindness, warmth, and dignity with the people they support. · Peer supporters treat each person they encounter with dignity and see them as worthy of all basic human rights. · Peer supporters embrace the full range of cultural experiences, strengths, and approaches to recovery for those they support and themselves.	· See peer support as different from traditional service, one that does not start with the assumption that there is a problem. Instead, peer support is a way of relating to many different world views. · Gain awareness of one's own world view including personal stigmas, stereotypes and bias that can interfere with the ability to treat all employees, including peer support specialists, with respect and fairness. · Take training themselves and support offering all agency employees, including supervisees, training on cultural humility, which is a process of openness and self-awareness that incorporates self-reflection and self-critique while willingly interacting with individuals from diverse cultures, ethnicities and gender orientations. · Invite ongoing feedback on personal and staff practice of cultural humility.

CORE VALUE 6

Peer Supporters Facilitate Change

Some of the worst human rights violations are experienced by people with psychiatric, trauma or substance use challenges. They are frequently seen as "objects of treatment" rather than human beings with the same fundamental rights to life, liberty and the pursuit of happiness as everyone else.

People may be survivors of violence (including physical, emotional, spiritual and mental abuse or neglect). Those with certain behaviors that make others uncomfortable may find themselves stereotyped, stigmatized and outcast by society.

Internalized oppression is common among people who have been rejected by society. Peer supporters treat people as human beings and remain alert to any practice (including the way people treat themselves) that is dehumanizing, demoralizing or degrading and will use their personal story and/or advocacy to be an agent for positive change.

PEER SUPPORTER GUIDELINES	SUPERVISOR GUIDELINES
Practice: **Educate and Advocate**	The supervisor role is to:
• Peer supporters recognize injustices peers face in all contexts, act as advocates, and facilitate change where appropriate.	• Define and model advocacy for peer support specialists, including advocating for organizational changes.
• Peer supporters strive to understand how injustices may affect people.	• Coach peer support specialists on how to respect the rights of individuals while helping individuals challenge and overcome injustice.
• Peer supporters encourage, coach and inspire those they support to challenge and overcome injustices.	• Build on lived experience, model recovery and advocate for peer support workers.
• Peer supporters use language that is supportive, encouraging, inspiring, motivating and respectful.	• Assist colleagues with understanding the peer specialist role and the perspective and experience of peer support specialists.
• Peer supporters help those they support explore areas in need of change for themselves and others.	• Identify situations in which the supervisor has responsibility to address agency liability and maintain respectful communication with peer support specialists when differences of opinion occur.
• Peer supporters recognize injustices peers face in all contexts and act as advocates and facilitate change where appropriate.	• Provide time and support for peer support specialists to connect with and participate in the greater peer movement and the peer workforce profession.

350

CORE VALUE 7

Peer Supporters Are Honest And Direct

Clear and thoughtful communication is fundamental to effective peer support.

Difficult issues are addressed with those who are directly involved. Privacy and confidentiality build trust.

Honest communication moves beyond the fear of conflict or hurting other people to the ability to respectfully work together to resolve challenging issues with caring and compassion, including issues related to stigma, abuse, oppression, crisis or safety.

PEER SUPPORTER GUIDELINES	SUPERVISOR GUIDELINES
Practice: **Address Difficult Issues with Caring and Compassion**	The supervisor role is to:
• Peer supporters respect privacy and confidentiality. • Peer supporters engage when desired by those they support, in candid, honest discussions about stigma, abuse, oppression, crisis or safety. • Peer supporters exercise compassion and caring in peer support relationships. • Peer supporters strive to build peer relationships based on integrity, honesty, respect, and trust.	• Establish clear boundaries, set reasonable and mutually agreed- on expectations. • Promote responsibility and accountability. • Build trust and develop the integrity of the supervisory relationship with peer support specialists through honest and respectful communication about strengths and areas that need improvement.

CORE VALUE 8
Peer Support Is Mutual And Reciprocal

In a peer support relationship, each person gives and receives in a fluid, constantly changing manner.

This is very different from what most people experience in treatment programs, where people are seen as needing help and staff is seen as providing that help.

In peer support relationships, each person has things to teach and learn. This is true whether you are a paid or volunteer peer supporter.

PEER SUPPORTER GUIDELINES	SUPERVISOR GUIDELINES
Practice: **Encourage Peers to Give and Receive**	The supervisor role is to:
• Peer supporters learn from those they support and those supported learn from peer supporters.	• Ask peer support specialists how they best receive feedback and direction.
• Peer supporters encourage peers to fulfill a fundamental human need — to be able to give as well as receive.	• Encourage co-learning (collaborative learning) and welcome peer support specialists' input in decision-making wherever possible.
• Peer supporters respect and honor a relationship with peers that evokes power-sharing and mutuality, wherever possible.	• Welcome feedback from peer support specialists during supervision sessions to develop supervisory relationships based on mutuality.

352

CORE VALUE 9

Peer Support Is Equally Shared Power

By definition, peers are equal.

Sharing power in a peer support relationship means equal opportunity for each person to express ideas and opinions, offer choices and contribute. Each person speaks and listens to what is said.

Abuse of power is avoided when peer support is a true collaboration.

PEER SUPPORTER GUIDELINES	SUPERVISOR GUIDELINES
Practice: **Embody Equality**	The supervisor role is to:
• Peer supporters use language that reflects a mutual relationship with those they support. • Peer supporters behave in ways that reflect respect and mutuality with those they support. • Peer supporters do not express or exercise power over those they support. • Peer supporters do not diagnose or offer medical services but do offer a complimentary service.	• Educate peer support specialists on the concept of power and the potential for inadvertently reinforcing power differentials in the peer support relationship. • Reinforce the non-clinical nature of the peer support role with peer support specialists and other organizational colleagues to avoid 'peer drift' or co-optation, and role ambiguity. • Consider how power in relationships, including the relationship between the supervisor and peer support specialist, affects those with histories of trauma, to create a safe work environment. • Support peer support specialist values and scope of non-clinical practice, especially in situations in which the peer support specialist is called upon to endorse or enforce a form of treatment or clinical practice.

CORE VALUE 10

Peer Support Is Strengths-Focused

Each person has skills, gifts and talents they can use to better their own life. Peer support focuses on what's strong, not what's wrong in another's life. Peer supporters share their own experiences to encourage people to see the "silver lining" or the positive things they have gained through adversity.

Through peer support, people get in touch with their strengths (the things they have going for them). They rediscover childhood dreams and long-lost passions that can be used to fuel recovery.

PEER SUPPORTER GUIDELINES	SUPERVISOR GUIDELINES
Practice: **See What's Strong, Not What's Wrong**	The supervisor role is to:
• Peer supporters encourage others to identify their strengths and use them to improve their lives. • Peer supporters focus on the strengths of those they support. • Peer supporters use their own experiences to demonstrate the use of one's strengths and to encourage and inspire those they support. • Peer supporters operate from a strength-based perspective and acknowledge the strengths, informed choices and decisions of peers as a foundation of recovery. • Peer supporters encourage others to explore dreams and goals meaningful to those they support. • Peer supporters don't fix or do for others what they can do for themselves.	• Model a focus on strengths rather than deficits with all employees. • Encourage peer support specialists to develop meaningful personal, career, and leadership development goals and suggest they use a similar process with those they support. • Encourage peer support specialists to use a strength-based approach to evaluate their own progress and performance; invite them to provide a similar strength-based approach when working with others.

354

CORE VALUE 11

Peer Support Is Transparent

Peer support is the process of giving and receiving non-clinical assistance to achieve long-term recovery from severe psychiatric, traumatic or substance use challenges.

Peer supporters are experientially credentialed to assist others in this process.

Transparency refers to set expectations with each person about what can and cannot be offered in a peer support relationship, including privacy and confidentiality.

Peer supporters communicate in plain language so people can readily understand and they "put a face on recovery" by sharing personal recovery experiences to inspire hope and the belief that recovery is real.

PEER SUPPORTER GUIDELINES	SUPERVISOR GUIDELINES
Practice: **Set Clear Expectations and Use Plain Language**	The supervisor role is to:
• Peer supporters clearly explain what can or cannot be expected of the peer support relationship. • Peer supporters use language that is clear, understandable and value and judgment-free. • Peer supporters use language that is supportive and respectful. • Peer supporters provide support in a professional yet humanistic manner. • Peer supporter roles are distinct from the roles of other behavioral health service professionals. • Peer supporters make only promises they can keep and use accurate statements. • Peer supporters do not diagnose nor do they prescribe or recommend medications or monitor their use.	• Use the job description to orient peer support specialists to job duties and requirements, including the type of documentation a peer support specialist is expected to keep, and to guide understanding of the performance review process. • Explain the supervisor's role, including connecting peer support specialists to other colleagues with additional expertise, as needed. • Describe the benefits and expectations of the supervisory relationship, including frequency and duration of supervision meetings. • Use plain, person-first language in all interactions with peer support specialists. • Reinforce the non-clinical nature of the peer support role with peer support specialists and colleagues, including documentation which is consistent with the peer support role.

CORE VALUE 12

Peer Support Is Person-Driven

All people have a fundamental right to make decisions about things related to their lives. Peer supporters inform people about options, provide information about choices and respect their decisions.

Peer supporters encourage people to move beyond their comfort zones, learn from their mistakes and grow from dependence on the system toward their chosen level of freedom and inclusion in the community of their choice.

PEER SUPPORTER GUIDELINES	SUPERVISOR GUIDELINES
Practice: **Focus on the Person, Not the Problems**	The supervisor role is to:
• Peer supporters encourage those they support to make their own decisions. • Peer supporters, when appropriate, offer options to those they serve. • Peer supporters encourage those they serve to try new things. • Peer supporters help others learn from mistakes. • Peer supporters encourage resilience. • Peer supporters encourage personal growth in others. • Peer supporters encourage and coach those they support to decide what they want in life and how to achieve it without judgment.	• Provide an environment where peer support specialists are empowered to move beyond comfort zones and learn from their mistakes. • Reframe unexpected outcomes as opportunities for personal growth, recovery, and resilience. • Assist peer support specialists in identifying areas for personal growth and creating professional development plans. • Recognize when the issues a peer support specialist brings up in supervision are beyond the supervisor's role; and suggest constructive ways to obtain help for these issues.

356

Glossary

In addition to identifying values upon which practice standards can be developed, it was necessary to define "peer support," "peer supporter," "peer," "peer support relationship" and "practice standards." Using surveys, literature reviews and consultations with the advisory group, the following definitions were developed:

Advocacy
Mental health advocacy includes a variety of different actions aimed at changing the major structural and attitudinal barriers to achieving positive mental health outcomes in populations. The concept, which is relatively new, was initially developed to reduce stigma and discrimination and to promote the human rights of persons with mental disorders (WHO 2019, WHO 2021).

Co-Learning
Co-learning (collaborative learning) is a situation in which two or more people attempt to learn something together. Unlike individual learning, people engaged in collaborative learning capitalize on one another's resources and skills (asking one another for information, evaluating one another's ideas, monitoring one another's work, etc.). More specifically, collaborative learning is based on the model that knowledge can be created within a population where members actively interact by sharing experiences (Cronise, 2016). Put differently, collaborative learning refers to methodologies and environments in which learners engage in a common task where each individual depends on and is accountable to each other (Randstad, 2019; Cornell, 2020). These include both face-to-face conversations and computer discussions (online forums, chat rooms, etc.).

Co-Optation/Peer Drift
Peer Specialists are an emerging workforce in behavioral health. Many Peer Specialists work side-by-side with clinicians on ACT teams, psychiatric rehabilitation programs, Common Ground Decision Support Centers, inpatient units, first episode psychosis teams, integrated health/behavioral health teams, etc. There is no doubt that Peer Specialists have many unique skills that enrich the entire team. However, within these traditional clinical settings, it's not unusual for Peer Specialists to begin to adopt the language and practices associated with the

clinical worldview. **In other words, over time the work of many Peer Specialists begins to resemble the work of clinicians on the team, taking on quasi-clinical roles rather than practicing as peer supporters according to peer support guidelines and standards** (Alberta & Ploski, 2014; Deegan, 2017)**.**

Peer support specialists working in treatment organizations are subject to processes of acculturation into professional cultures that peer support specialists working in peer organizations are not. Effective implementation should include specific efforts to minimize the cooptation of peer support specialists.

Cultural Humility

In a multicultural world where power imbalances exist, cultural humility is a process of openness, self-awareness, being egoless, and incorporating self-reflection and critique after willingly interacting with diverse individuals (Foronda, et al., 2015; Hogg Foundation, 2019; ATTC, 2020). The results of achieving cultural humility are mutual empowerment, respect, partnerships, optimal care, and lifelong learning. Cultural humility involves a change in the overall perspective and way of life. Cultural humility is a way of being. Employing cultural humility means being aware of power imbalances and being humble in every interaction with every individual. This process will not happen immediately, but it is speculated that with time, education, reflection, and effort, progress can be made.

Peer Support

Peer support is the process of giving and receiving non-clinical assistance to achieve long-term recovery from severe psychiatric, traumatic or substance use challenges. This support is provided by peer supporters - people who have "lived experience" and have been trained to assist others in initiating and maintaining long-term recovery and enhancing the quality of life for individuals and their families. Peer support services are inherently designed, developed, delivered, evaluated and supervised by peers in long-term recovery (White, 2009).

Peer Support Specialist (PSS)

An individual or multiple individuals employed in peer support roles. Job titles may include peer specialist, peer support worker, etc.

Peer Supporter

A peer supporter is someone who has experienced the healing process of recovery from psychiatric, traumatic and/or substance use challenges and, as a result, can offer assistance and support to promote another peer's own personal recovery journey. The peer supporter volunteers to share portions of his or her recovery experience in an appropriate and effective manner. Peer support specialists are typically trained, supervised, and paid to be peer supporters.

Peer

In the context of peer support, a peer is a person experiencing a psychiatric, traumatic, or substance use challenge who may benefit from peer support.

Peer Support Relationship

The qualities that make an effective peer supporter are best defined by the individual receiving support, rather than by an organization or provider of care. Matching peer supporters with peers often encompasses shared cultural characteristics, such as age, gender, ethnicity, language, sexual orientation, co-occurring challenges, experience in the military or with the criminal justice system or other identity-shaping life experiences that increase common language, mutual understanding, trust, confidence, and safety.

Practice Standards

Practice standards are rules or guidelines used as the basis for informed decision-making about acceptable work performance and practices. They are established by an authoritative entity through a collaborative process with input from a wide range of people who perform the work. Standards are based on values, ethics, principles, and competencies. Having a core set of standards is one important way to legitimize a field of practice (Townsend, 2012).

Transparent

Effective supervisors recognize that each individual they supervise will bring prior experiences, beliefs, ideas, and associations around supervision to the supervisory relationship. Supervisors bring their own past experiences, beliefs, and assumptions into the supervisory relationship, as well. It is therefore important to begin the supervisory relationship by sharing these experiences, expectations, hopes, and fears to build trust and pave the way for a shared understanding of what the current supervisory relationship will look like. A supervisor's willingness to be open, appropriately transparent, and attentive to the peer support specialist's ideas, concerns, and needs will help shape the supervisory relationship. It is important that both supervisor and supervisee view the supervisory relationship as a safe space for the supervisee to receive support, perform honest introspection, candidly share difficulties, and expose vulnerabilities. To that end, an important task of the supervisor is to intentionally foster trust. Supervisors are also often in an ideal position to facilitate meaningful conversations between clinical and peer support specialist that can help to identify and address or prevent these issues from taking root in the organizational culture. These conversations can normalize experiences, promote transparent conversations, and provide opportunities for staff of multiple disciplines to be a part of shaping new organizational norms (Philadelphia DBHIDS & Achara Consulting Inc., 2017).

Trauma-Informed Approach

Trauma-informed care is an approach to engaging people with histories of trauma that recognizes the presence of trauma symptoms and acknowledges the role that trauma has played in their lives. It seeks to change the paradigm from one that asks, "What's wrong with you?" to one that asks, "What has happened to you?" A trauma-informed approach reflects adherence to six key principles that apply across multiple types of settings: safety; trustworthiness and transparency; peer support; collaboration and mutuality; empowerment, voice and choice; and cultural, historical, and gender issues (Blanch, et al., 2012; CDC, 2020).

360

References

Alberta, A., & Ploski, R. (2014). Cooptation of Peer Support Staff: Quantitative Evidence. Rehabilitation Process and Outcome, 2014:3, 25-29. doi:10.4137/RPO.S12343. https://journals.sagepub.com/doi/pdf/10.4137/RPO.S12343

Blanch, A., Filson, B., Penney, D., Cave, C. (2012). Engaging Women in Trauma-Informed Peer Support: A Guidebook. Center for Mental Health Services (CMHS), National Center for Trauma-Informed Care (NCTIC), and Substance Abuse and Mental Health Services Administration (SAMHSA). https://www.nasmhpd.org/sites/default/files/PeerEngagementGuide_Color_REVISED_10_2012.pdf

Centers for Disease Control (CDC). (2020). Six Guiding Principles to a Trauma-Informed Approach. https://www.cdc.gov/cpr/infographics/6_principles_trauma_info.htm

Cornell University (2020). Collaborative Learning: Engaging Students. https://teaching.cornell.edu/teaching-resources/engaging-students/collaborative-learning

Cronise, R. (2016). Collaborative Learning: A Next Step in the Training of Peer Support Providers. Psychiatric rehabilitation journal, Vol.39 (3), p.292-294. https://pubmed.ncbi.nlm.nih.gov/27618465/

Deegan, P. (June 21, 2017). Peer Specialists are not Clinicians. https://www.commonground-program.com/blog/peer-specialists-are-not-clinicians

Foronda, C., Baptiste, D., & Reinholdt, M. (2015). Cultural Humility: A Concept Analysis. Journal of Transcultural Nursing. doi:10.1177/1043659615592677

Hogg Foundation (2019). 3 Things to Know: Cultural Humility. https://hogg.utexas.edu/3-things-to-know-cultural-humility

National Association of Peer Supporters. (2013). National Practice Guidelines for Peer Supporters. https://www.peersupportworks.org/wp-content/uploads/2021/02/nationalguidelines_updated.pdf

National Association of Peer Supporters. (2019). National Practice Guidelines for Peer Specialists and Supervisors. https://www.peersupportworks.org/wp-content/uploads/2021/07/National-Practice-Guidelines-for-Peer-Specialists-and-Supervisors.pdf

Peer Cultural Cooperative (2020). Cultural Humility Primer. Northwest Addiction Technology Transfer Center (ATTC), Seattle, WA, USA https://attcnetwork.org/sites/default/files/2020-11/Peer%20Primer%20FINAL.pdf

National Practice Guidelines for Peer Specialists and Supervisors : 21

Philadelphia Dept. of Behavioral Health and Intellectual Disabilities Services and Achara Consulting Inc. (2017). Peer Support Toolkit. Philadelphia, PA: DBHIDS., pp. 117 and 120: https://dbhids.org/wp-content/uploads/1970/01/PCCI_Peer-Support-Toolkit.pdf

Randstad (2019). Collaborative learning versus peer-to-peer learning. https://www.randstad.co.uk/career-advice/career-guidance/collaborative-learning-versus-peer-to-peer-learning/

Smith, D. (August 15, 2007). Letter to State Medicaid Directors with Guidance to States interested in peer support services under the Medicaid Program. https://downloads.cms.gov/cmsgov/archived-downloads/SMDL/downloads/smd081507a.pdf

Substance Abuse and Mental Health Services Administration (SAMHSA). (2012). SAMHSA'S Working Definition of Recovery and 10 Guiding Principles of Recovery. https://store.samhsa.gov/sites/default/files/d7/priv/pep12-recdef.pdf

Townsend, W. (Sept. 24, 2012). Pillars of Peer Support Summit Panel 1: Establishing National Credentials/Standards. https://www.pillarsofpeersupport.org/original-toolkits

White, W. (2009). Peer-Based Addiction Recovery Support: History, Theory, Practice and Scientific Evaluation. Counselor, 10(5), 54-59. http://www.williamwhitepapers.com/pr/2009Peer-RecoverySupportMonographExecutiveSummary.pdf

World Health Organization (WHO). (2019). One-to-one peer support by and for people with lived experience. WHO QualityRights guidance module. https://apps.who.int/iris/bitstream/handle/10665/329591/9789241516785-eng.pdf

World Health Organization (WHO). (2021). New WHO Guidance Seeks to Put an End to Human Rights Violations in Mental Health Care. https://www.who.int/news/item/10-06-2021-new-who-guidance-seeks-to-put-an-end-to-human-rights-violations-in-mental-health-care

More Information

Alberta, A., & Ploski, R. (2014). Cooptation of Peer Support Staff: Quantitative Evidence. Rehabilitation Process and Outcome, 2014:3, 25-29. doi:10.4137/RPO.S12343. https://journals. sagepub.com/doi/pdf/10.4137/RPO.S12343

Blanch, A., Filson, B., Penney, D. & Cave, C. (2012). Engaging Women in Trauma-Informed Peer Support: A Guidebook. Center for Mental Health Services, National Center for Trauma-Informed Care. Funded by the Substance Abuse and Mental Health Services Administration (SAMHSA) and the National Association of State Mental Health Program Directors (NASMHP).

Centers for Disease Control (CDC). (2020). Six Guiding Principles to a Trauma-Informed Approach. https://www.cdc.gov/cpr/infographics/6_principles_trauma_info.htm

Copeland, M.E. (n.d.). The Values and Ethics of WRAP. The Copeland Center for Wellness and Recovery.

Cornell University (2020). Collaborative Learning: Engaging Students. https://teaching.cornell. edu/teaching-resources/engaging-students/collaborative-learning

Cronise, R. (2016). Collaborative Learning: A Next Step in the Training of Peer Support Providers. Psychiatric rehabilitation journal, Vol.39 (3), p.292-294. https://pubmed.ncbi.nlm.nih. gov/27618465/

Daniels, A. S., Tunner, T. P., Bergeson, S., Ashenden, P., Fricks, L. & Powell, I. (2013). National Practice Guidelines for Peer Specialists and Supervisors... (2019). Retrieved January 3, 2022, from https://www.peersupportworks.org/wp-content/uploads/2021/07/National-Practice-Guidelines-for-Peer-Specialists-and-Supervisors-1.pdf

Deegan, P. (June 21, 2017). Peer Specialists are not Clinicians. Foglesong, D., Knowles, K., Cronise, R., Wolf, J. Edwards, J. (2021). National Practice Guidelines for Peer Support Specialists and Supervisors. Psychiatric Services. Published Online 13 July 2021. https://doi.org/10.1176/appi.ps.202000901

Foglesong, D., Spagnolo, A., Cronise, R., Forbes, J., Swarbrick, P., Edwards, J., & Pratt, C. (2021, June 1). Perceptions of Supervisors of Peer Support Workers (PSW) in Behavioral Health: Results from a National Survey. Community Mental Health Journal. Published online 2021. https://doi.org/10. 1007/s10597-021-00837-2https://www.commongroundprogram.com/blog/peer-specialists-are-not-clinicians

Forbes, J., Pratt, C., & Cronise, R. (2021, April 1). Experiences of peer support specialists supervised by nonpeer supervisors. *Psychiatric rehabilitation journal.* Published online 2021. http://dx.doi.org/10.1037/prj0000475

Foronda, C., Baptiste, D., & Reinholdt, M. (2015). Cultural Humility: A Concept Analysis. Journal of Transcultural Nursing. doi:10.1177/1043659615592677

Hogg Foundation (2019). 3 Things to Know: Cultural Humility. https://hogg. utexas. edu/3-things-to-know-cultural-humility

National Association of Peer Supporters. (2013). National Practice Guidelines for Peer Supporters. https://www.peersupportworks.org/wp-content/ uploads/2021/02/nationalguidelines_updated.pdf National Association of Peer Supporters. (2019).

National Practice Guidelines for Peer Specialists and Supervisors. https:// www.peersupportworks.org/wp-content/uploads/2021/07/ National-Prac- tice-Guidelines-for-Peer-Specialists-and-Supervisors.pdf

Peer Cultural Cooperative (2020). Cultural Humility Primer. Northwest Addiction Technology Transfer Center (ATTC), Seattle, WA, USA https://attc network.org/sites/default/ files/2020-11/Peer%20Primer%20FINAL.pdfRef- erences

Philadelphia Dept. of Behavioral Health and Intellectual Disabilities Services and Achara Consulting Inc. (2017). Peer Support Toolkit. Philadelphia, PA: DBHIDS., pp. 117 and 120: https://dbhids.org/wp-content/uploads/1970/ 01/PCCI_Peer-Support-Toolkit.pdf Randstad (2019). Collaborative learning versus peer-to-peer learning. https://www.randstad. co.uk/career-advice/ca- reer-guidance/collaborative-learning-versus-peer-to-peer-learning/

Smith, D. (August 15, 2007). Letter to State Medicaid Directors with Guid- ance to States interested in peer support services under the Medicaid Program. https://downloads.cms.gov/ cmsgov/archived-down- loads/SMDL/downloads/smd081507a.pdf Substance Abuse and Mental Health Services Administration (SAMHSA). (2012).

SAMHSA'S Working Definition of Recovery and 10 Guiding Principles of Recovery. https://store.samhsa.gov/sites/default/files/d7/priv/pep12-recde f.pdf Townsend, W. (Sept. 24, 2012).

Pillars of Peer Support Summit Panel 1: Establishing National Creden- tials/Standards. https://www.pillarsofpeersupport.org/original-toolkits

Pillars of Peer Support Summit IV: Establishing Standards of Excellence. Funded by the Substance Abuse and Mental Health Services Administration (SAMHSA) and the National Association of State Mental Health Program Directors (NASMHP). https://www.pillarsofpeersupport.org/original- toolkits

Pillars of Peer Support Summit VI: Peer Specialist Supervision. Funded by the Substance Abuse and Mental Health Services Administration (SAMHSA) and the National Association of State Mental Health Program Directors (NASMHP). https://www.pillarsofpeersupport.org/original-toolkits

Van Tosh, L, & del Vecchio, P. (2000). Consumer-Operated Self-Help Programs: A Technical Report. U.S. Center for Mental Health Services, Rockville, MD.

White, W. (2009). Peer-Based Addiction Recovery Support: History, Theory, Practice and Scientific Evaluation. Counselor, 10(5), 54-59. http://www.williamwhitepapers.com/pr/2009PeerRecoverySupportMonographExecutiveSummary.pdf

World Health Organization (WHO). (2021). New WHO Guidance Seeks to Put an End to Human Rights Violations in Mental Health Care. https://www.who.int/news/item/10-06-2021-newwho-guidance-seeks-to-put-an-end-to-human-rights-violations-in-mental-health-care

World Health Organization (WHO). (2019). One-to-one peer support by and for people with lived experience. WHO QualityRights guidance module. https://apps.who.int/iris/bitstream/handle/10665/329591/9789241516785-eng.pdf

World Health Organization (WHO). (2012) WHO QualityRights tool kit to assess and improve quality and human rights in mental health and social care facilities. World Health Organization, Geneva

Part 5: Special Interests

Chapter 13: Inclusion and Collaboration

- Chapter Introduction by the Editors
- Section 1: Peer Support During the Pandemic: Changes, Challenges, and Silver Linings
- Section 2: Peer Support Research Questions from the Perspective of Peers
- Section 3: Peer Support in Youth Residential Treatment Centers
- Section 4: Transforming Lives with the Arts

CHAPTER 13

INCLUSION AND COLLABORATION

CHAPTER INTRODUCTION BY THE EDITORS

PEER SUPPORT IS A RAPIDLY EVOLVING BEST PRACTICE. PEER SUPPORTERS ARE inherently adaptive, resilient, and empathetic. During the Covid- 19 pandemic, peers adapted to changing job roles. They also transitioned from traditional self-help practices to incorporating case management responsibilities. Also, through art peers have the ability to advocate and inspire allowing color to shine where it was once faded. Mental health programs created by people without lived experience have viewed peer support, which is a privilege to provide, as potentially harmful. Historically, research around peer support has been conducted by non-peers. However, having a peer support voice present in research and program development is integral for the collaboration and implementation of empirical peer support programs.

In the first reading Adams, Rogers, and Edwards examine the effects that the Covid-19 pandemic had on peer support specialists. This reading reports the positive impacts that the peer support work force experienced from the challenges of Covid-19. The next reading by Salzer and Thomas discusses incorporating a peers' perspective in research regarding peer support. Conversations from the 2016 N.A.P.S conference showed the enthusiasm from attendees and the importance of having peer voices heard in research on peer support. The third reading by Dettmer and Winter explores peer support in youth residential treatment centers by using first person narratives. The narratives from a former resident and a former staff member illustrated the need for peer support in youth residential treatment centers. Finally, Gayle Bluebird illustrates the importance of art in recovery. Through the holistic and societal benefits peers create through their trauma, settings such as hospitals have begun to embrace the values of peer support.

SECTION 1: PEER SUPPORT DURING THE PANDEMIC: CHANGES, CHALLENGES, AND SILVER LININGS

Wallis E. Adams, PhD,
Department of Sociology, California State University East Bay

E. Sally Rogers, ScD,
Center for Psychiatric Rehabilitation, Boston University

Jonathan P. Edwards, Ph.D., LCSW, ACSW, NYCPS
Workforce Development Consultant, Facilitator and Researcher
Former Board Member, National Association of Peer Supporters (N.A.P.S.)

We conducted two online surveys (May and December 2020) assessing the impact of COVID-19 on peer specialists in the US. Peer support specialists experienced modest job loss early in the pandemic, although full time employment returned to pre-pandemic levels by December 2020. Job tasks changed substantially, with an early decrease in individual and group support provision that partially rebounded, and increasing use of technology and work tasks related to the pandemic itself. Peer specialists reported experiencing high levels of isolation and communication challenges, and the individuals they supported faced substantial challenges related to isolation, mental health symptoms, substance use, housing instability, and violence. Despite the devastation of the pandemic, findings from both surveys also revealed a number of pandemic "silver linings". Most (73%) of peer specialists reported that they witnessed positive impacts from their work during the pandemic. These positive impacts benefited peer specialists themselves, individuals receiving peer support, and the broader peer support field. Our study showed that the peer support workforce drew on resources from colleagues, supervisors and organizations to effectively adapt to the pandemic. Peer specialists and colleagues navigated the difficult first year of the pandemic with resilience and creativity; the future of peer support could benefit from these lessons.

In the early weeks of the COVID-19 pandemic in the US, unprecedented lockdowns and isolation merged with skyrocketing unemployment and uncertainty. Among the many questions emerging from the uncertainty, an important one for us, as researchers, was: "How is the pandemic impacting peer support and supporters?" Researchers at Boston University's Center for Psychiatric Rehabilitations (CPR) partnered with representatives at the National Association of Peer Supporters (NAPS) to develop and conduct two national online surveys of US-based peer workers in May and December of 2020 to answer this question. While we have reported some of our findings from the first survey elsewhere (Adams et al., 2022), here we present a summary of findings from the two surveys. We emphasize pandemic "silver linings", or benefits, for peer support specialists (PSS), those supported, and the broader field of peer support.

Discussion

Individuals at CPR and NAPS developed, tested, and refined two online surveys assessing the impact of the COVID-19 pandemic on PSS employment, work tasks, challenges, benefits, technology use, and support. We launched the first online survey in May 2020, sending it to over 6,000 individuals on the NAPS listserv. Adults who were working or volunteering in peer support roles for at least 5 hours per week prior to the pandemic (February 2020) were eligible to complete the survey. We sent the second survey out in December 2020 to individuals who had completed the first survey. 1,280 US-based peer support specialists completed the first survey, and 496 completed the second survey. Most of the individuals who responded to the survey were female (69%), white (73%), and working full time prior to the pandemic (68%). About 31% worked in peer-run organizations, 44% worked in non-peer run mental health or social service agencies, and 25% worked in government agencies. We will focus on what we found in this chapter, but additional methodological details can be found elsewhere (Adams et al. 2022).

Job Loss & Job Tasks: Some PSS were laid off or lost a job early in the pandemic, although at rates less than national averages at the time (8.5% of survey 1 respondents reported job loss). The percent of individuals working full time or volunteering had returned to pre-pandemic levels by the end of 2020, while part time work did not return to pre-COVID levels. In May 2020, at the start of the pandemic, peer workers reported spending less time engaging in "traditional" peer support tasks than they had pre-COVID, including providing individual support and group facilitation. Although time spent providing individual support and group facilitation did not return to pre-COVID levels by the end of 2020, it increased significantly from earlier in the pandemic. PSS also reported engaging in a number of new tasks, including those related to technology (81%), connecting individuals to resources (47%) like food and housing, and tasks specific to the pandemic (54%) such as PPE provision and education.

Challenges & Benefits: Unfortunately, respondents reported that they themselves, as well as the individuals they were supporting, faced multiple challenges during the pandemic. PSS reported high levels of isolation and communication challenges. While this decreased slightly from survey 1 to survey 2, it remained very high. PSS reported that the individuals they serve faced high levels of these and additional challenges (including job loss and food insecurity). Of particular concern is that some of these challenges worsened over the course of the pandemic. Respondents reported greater housing instability, mental health symptoms, substance use, and interpersonal/family violence among the individuals they supported in December 2020 compared to the beginning of the pandemic, May 2020.

Despite these significant challenges, we were excited and surprised by how many individuals reported positive impacts related to their work during the pandemic. When asked in May 2020 whether there had been any positive impacts or benefits to peer support roles due to the pandemic, 73% of respondents indicated that there were. As one respondent wrote, "we are able to experience this unique situation together and really facilitate mutuality and strengthen the relationship" (ID 284).

The positive impacts seemed to remain, or even grow. When we asked about similar positive impacts or benefits seven months later, in our second survey, 74% of respondents again reported similar benefits. This time we asked who experienced these positive impacts, and respondents indicated benefits to the individuals being supported (80%), peer supporters themselves (68%), and the peer support field in general (61%).

PSS highlighted the way that their increased use of technology was allowing more individuals to participate in and benefit from peer support. As one PSS said, "I have been able to reach more people across the state that would normally never be able to come in." (ID 062). This includes those with mobility or transportation challenges, youth, and individuals living in rural areas. Respondent ID 1404 noted that the benefits of technology use should continue after the pandemic subsides: "I have learned telehealth and Zoom for virtual engagement, which is wonderful for the future after COVID-19 as well." Some respondents also reported personally benefiting from this, noting that they were happy to avoid stressful rush-hour commutes by working from home.

In addition to the individual benefits, some PSS noted that the pandemic had created the opportunity to shine more light on the importance of mental health and the broader importance of peer support. One respondent said that the pandemic had changed the perception of peer support and what it could bring to organization and the individuals served: "More staff now see for themselves the value and comfort peers can bring to anyone. Staff here at work have felt the impact of peers for themselves. Peers see that and the staff connect with peers in a more positive light." (ID 505).

Satisfaction with Support: Peer supporters were able to respond and adapt to the COVID crisis with innovation and resiliency, perhaps due (in part) to the support that they themselves received. So, despite reporting challenges in carrying out their work during the pandemic, and seeing significant distress among those they support, PSS reported a high level of satisfaction with the assistance made available to them by their organization, their supervisor, and their colleagues. In both of the surveys we conducted, on a 5-point scale (ranging from very satisfied (1.0) to very unsatisfied (5.0), individuals reported levels of satisfaction with support that were highest for their coworkers (Mean=1.87), their supervisor (Mean=1.97), and their organization (Mean=2.12).

When asked about specific types of support (social-emotional, training-educational, or material), average responses suggested a good level of satisfaction with scores ranging from 2.13 to 2.21. One individual poignantly reported very meaningful social-emotional support by stating: "I am told daily how the peer support that I provide has a positive impact on the lives of others. I am told that I am appreciated." (ID 477). Of their organizational support, one survey respondent said: "There have been several topical trainings and seminars related to peer support made available online that has helped me understand what I need to do and how to cope, find ways to cope and connect to others." (ID 288). As an example of the interconnectedness that can arise from organizational support, one respondent said: "Through offering increased support to all staff (peer and non-peer), I feel that our facility has gained a more cohesive bond and an environment that enables everyone to feel freer to communicate challenges and not hold those negative feelings in." (ID 34). Clearly, some organizations providing peer support services rose to the challenges of the pandemic by offering training and additional support specifically geared to the unusual circumstances in which PSS found themselves.

Conclusion

We were heartened by the responses we received from these two surveys of peer support specialists and their work. We were pleasantly surprised to learn that PSS did not lose employment in the large proportions that were reported in the general public. They also report high levels of organizational and workplace support. Still, PSS did report significant levels of financial strain, owing in part to their low salaries. Their job tasks continued to evolve and to rely heavily on technology and on meeting the basic needs (housing, food) of those they serve. PSS reported somewhat decreasing adverse effects of working during the pandemic for themselves personally, but continued high levels of social isolation, mental health symptoms and substance use among those they serve.

Responses allowed us to understand and document the creative ways in which PSS filled critical gaps in mental health services during the pandemic. We believe that the innovation that occurred during the pandemic must continue in order to maximize the benefit of peer support and to complement and supplement the work of other mental health providers. During the pandemic organizational rules and role boundaries were relaxed, allowing PSS to undertake job tasks that were needed, but that prior to the pandemic may not have been part of their day-to-day work. For example, making sure that the individuals they supported who were safely physically isolated, had food, shelter, and other basic necessities. PSS also helped to address the extreme sense of social isolation that was a devastating aspect of the early phases of the pandemic. Further, the use of telehealth approaches was an essential part of addressing that isolation. Telehealth approaches will continue to be useful for individuals unable to travel for support, or who may be unable because of illness or disability to do so. Maintaining telehealth as an option for PSS is critical going forward. Furthermore, having telehealth options appears to improve job satisfaction among some PSS, similar to reports in the general population. Taken together, hybrid services that combine and allow for in-person and telehealth support along with allowing maximum creativity in filling the needs of individuals served seems to be the optimal way to continue the greatest advantages of peer support we witnessed during the pandemic.

In conclusion, PSS reported creative and innovative approaches to addressing the increased isolation, lack of accessibility of programs and services, and other adverse effects of the pandemic. As one individual told us, "Hearing the words 'I gave up but your call made the difference in wanting to live' shows how providing support in a time of uncertainty is a positive impact" (ID 653) of peer support during the COVID-19 pandemic and beyond.

References

Adams, W.E., Rogers, E.S., Edwards, J.P., Lord, E.M., McKnight, L., & Barbone, M. (2022) Impact of COVID-19 on peer support specialists in the United States: Findings from a cross-sectional online survey. *Psychiatric Services, 71*(1), 9-17. https://doi.org/10.1176/appi.ps.202000915

SECTION 2: PEER SUPPORT RESEARCH QUESTIONS FROM THE PERSPECTIVE OF PEERS

Mark S. Salzer, PhD
Professor of Social and Behavioral Sciences, Temple University

Elizabeth Thomas
Assistant Professor of Social and Behavioral Sciences, Temple University

Research on peer support continues to expand in terms of research funding and numbers of publications. However, while it is recognized that the perspectives of those being studied can enhance research relevance, it is unclear how much current research on peer support incorporates the point of view of those with lived experience of mental health issues, including peer specialists themselves. This article offers such viewpoints.

There is a growing interest in research on peer support interventions in mental health services. Studies document numerous positive benefits for those who participate in these services, including peer providers themselves (Salzer & Shear, 2002). In fact, peer support has long been regarded as best practice (Salzer & MHASP, 2002) and as an evidence-based model of care (Davidson, et al., 2018 & CMS, 2016). Peer providers are employed in a variety of settings and in a number of capacities, often working to affect self-determination, health and wellness, hope, communication with providers, illness management, and stigma (Salzer, et al. 2010). Yet, the published literature on peer provided services is still in its infancy, and there are clear opportunities for additional research. That research should be driven by the interests and perspectives of peer specialists and others involved in peer relationships themselves. Recognizing the central role that those involved in the practice of peer support should have in establishing future research directions, the authors convened a group of individuals (more than 50 attended the session!) at the 2016 International Association of Peer Specialists (iNAPS) conference held in Philadelphia and asked what they perceived as the most important questions for the field.

Results

The themes and questions identified at this event are presented in Table 1.

Table 1. Peer Support Research Themes and Questions Derived by Peers

Research Theme	Research Questions
The Researchers	Who is doing the research and what are their potential biases? To what extent are policymakers involved in the research process? How serious are researchers about doing research on peer support? How many people driving the research agenda are peers themselves? How does disclosure of being a peer influence the peer support research process?
Research	Who is funding the research? Who is doing the peer review of peer

Process	support studies that are reviewed by journals? Whose agenda is driving the research?
Research Designs and Methods	What research designs might be most effective in doing peer support research? Who are researchers researching – peers, peer support, agencies, etc.? Which type of research design might be most appropriate to study peer support? RCTs may not be the right type of design to use; Can we even measure the benefits of peer support using the designs we are using? How or can we research online peer support? How can we do it most effectively? Does the research process and timeline respect (or is it consistent with) the recovery process? Research questions should look at combined peer support with other modalities;
Peer Support Process	How can we define mutuality in a peer support relationship? How do current service/structural factors affect mutuality in the peer relationship?
	How does power work in the peer support relationship and how does that affect outcomes? What are successful interventions/strategies for assuring that the person has the power? What is the practice of "therapy" compared to the practice of "peer support" and what is the difference? How do we explore the process of peer support? How does culture and language (i.e., non-English) or ethnicity affect a person's receptivity to peer support?
Peer Support Outcomes	What are the outcomes of peer support? Are there differences in process and outcome between peer support interventions that are integrated into traditional agencies and programs versus those that are stand alone? At what point in the service delivery process might peer support be most effective (e.g., early engagement/entry versus later in the process)? Are there some types of support services (e.g., use of music, art, drama, dance, poetry, storytelling, arts, etc.) that are better provided by peers? How long does it take to achieve what outcomes? What are the different types of peer support online interventions that can be used and are effective? What is the end goal for peer support? What are the outcomes that we should be
	looking at? What is the impact of peer support on suicide prevention, particularly in the VA?
Peer Support Workforce	How do we best support peer supporters? What are the "right" requirements for being a peer supporter in addition to having lived
	experience? What role does the supervisor play in supporting peer specialists in maintaining peer values in their work? How do regulations like background checks affect the employment of peer supporters? How do expectations about productivity and other stressful aspects of the job affect the health and wellness of peer supporters?

DISCUSSION AND CONCLUSION

A number of conclusions can be drawn from this conversation. First, the sheer number of people in attendance and number of questions generated by this group reflects the enthusiasm for research on peer support from key stakeholders. Second, the variety of questions, from those pertaining to the research process to the process and outcomes of peer support, demonstrates novel directions for further study. Third, while some of the questions produced by this group are similar to those asked by academic researchers, many are qualitatively different, highlighting the need to involve peers and other key stakeholders in the design and implementation of future research in this area. We hope that by sharing the results of this conversation we can help to energize productive collaborations among individuals who seek to advance the field. There are a growing number of researchers who have disclosed their lived experience and positions at universities for faculty with lived experience that will achieve this goal, but seeking the input from NAPS constituents, regardless of whether they are researchers or academics, is critically important to enhancing the research base and advancing peer support.

Acknowledgements

This was developed with support from the National Institute on Disability, Independent Living, and Rehabilitation Research (NIDILRR grant number #90RT5021-02-00). The contents being reported do not necessarily represent the policy of NIDILRR, ACL, HHS, and you should not assume endorsement by the Federal Government.

The following individuals agreed to be recognized for their contributions of ideas reported here: James Gillon, Ren Kramon, Terry Cox, Ken Schuesselin, Eve Hause, Dana Foglesong, Chaz Longwell, Miranda Klicker, Lauren Gardener, David Son, David Ford, Justin Brown, Ameika Malcolm, David Gumpert, Salvatore Wise Sr., Barb Greene, Jerome Hag, Brittany Brest, Ingrid Arrigo-Grenon, Valeria Chambers, Julia Preufice, John Anglin, Faith Boersma, Sharon T Keuhn, Tim Connors, Alice Koumenis, Andrew Natalie, Antonio Munoz, Naasiha Siddiqui, Ayako Aikawa, Jason Robison, Wallis Adams, Anthony Stratford, Andy Bornstein, Lindsay Little, Jeff Zitofstoy, Carrie McManus, Dawn Shoffstall, Thomas Brown, Tracey Canney, Chuck Maukus, Eugene Greninger, Sue Shannon, Maryann D. Mason, Carol Eloian, Reginald Cintron, Wilfred Rodriguez, Ruth Carrion, Linda Meyer, Pedro Toscao, Elena Kravitz, Melody Dutch, and Bill Beverley-Blanco.

More Information

To view this on the Temple University website:
http://tucollaborative.org/wp-content/uploads/2017/04/Peer-Support-Research-Questions-from-the-Perspective-of-iNAPS-Attendees.pdf

References

Centers for Medicare and Medicaid Services. State Medicaid Director Letter, SMDL 07-011 Baltimore, MD2007 [September 20, 2016]. Available from: https://downloads.cms.gov/cmsgov/archiveddownloads/SMDL/downloads/SMD081507A.pdf.

Davidson, L., Bellamy, C., Chinman, M., Farkas, M., Ostrow, L., Cook, J.A., Jonikas, J.A., Rosenthal, H., Bergeson, S., Daniels, A.S., & Salzer, M. (June 29, 2018). Revisiting the Rationale and Evidence for Peer Support. *Psychiatric Times*, 36(6). http://www.psychiatrictimes.com/special-reports/revisiting-rationale-and-evidence-peer-support.

Salzer MS, Schwenk E, Brusilovskiy E. (2010). Certified Peer Specialist Roles and Activities: Results From a National Survey. *Psychiatric Services.* 2010;61(5):520-3. PubMed PMID: WOS:000277249200019.

Salzer MS, Shear SL. (2002). Identifying consumer-provider benefits in evaluations of consumer delivered services. *Psychiatric Rehabilitation Journal.* 2002;25(3):281-8. PubMed PMID: WOS:000175515900009.

Salzer, M.S., & Mental Health Association of Southeastern Pennsylvania Best Practices Team (2002). Consumer-Delivered Services as a Best Practice in Mental Health Care and the Development of Practice Guidelines. *Psychiatric Rehabilitation Skills, 6,* 355-382.

SECTION 3: PEER SUPPORT IN YOUTH RESIDENTIAL TREATMENT CENTERS

Amey Dettmer, CPS, The Copeland Center for Wellness and Recovery

Ian Winter, MHRT, CSP

Peer support is a mutual practice that supports the idea that every person can live a full and independent life. Behind the walls of most youth residential treatment centers (YRTC), the practice of peer support is almost completely muted and acknowledgment of recovery options is often devoid. This narrative focuses on the information shared in the 2021 N.A.P.S. Conference Workshop titled: *Peer Support in Youth Residential Treatment Centers.* It elaborates on the views and experiences of the authors and addresses some of the barriers and issues for peer support occurring in these settings, as well as suggestions for peer support implementation to take flight.

The authors have combined lived experience as a survivor of the "troubled teen industry" due to being a prior resident of YRTC services and as a staff member employed at a YRTC.

A 2019 National Analysis of Peer Support Providers from University of Michigan's Behavioral Health Workforce Research Center found that only an estimated 9% of all existing YRTC's have reported having peer support offered in their programs (University of Michigan, 2019). This finding recognized that YRTC's deployed peer services at the lowest rates compared to other mental health facilities. This alarming fact demonstrates the desperate need for peer support to be more accessible to youth being served within these settings.

A national survey of residential treatment facilities found that 88.0% of YRTC providers involved in a survey completed by 293 centers, reported that staff had not even heard of family-driven, youth-guided principles or required further training to implement them (Brown, et al. 2010).

Beginning in 2020, the authors engaged in many conversations with other peer supporters and peer support allies, including people from Pennsylvania, Texas, Maine, California, and Oregon, and of the people contacted, it was found that any YRTC that once was offering peer support no longer was. In the past, peer support was offered through advisory councils and peer-led (not peer-developed) support groups, however, programs failed through changed leadership and lack of overall support from organizations. It is problematic that identifying a model program where peer support exists in this setting has been challenging.

Even with this difficulty to locate a program that has a peer support program, resources exist to support the expansion of peer support in YRTC. A handbook from the Building Bridges Initiative covers a robust overview of Youth Peer Advocates in Residential Treatment Settings which includes YRTC embracing change and adopting core values to create the cultural and organizational change that is needed in these settings to accommodate space for peer support to exist (SAMHSA, 2020) Additionally, A document titled;

Operationalizing and Funding Youth and Parent Peer Support Roles in Residential Treatment Settings begin to address some of these strategies for implementation (Nikkel, F et al., 2020)

Discussion

Peer support should be offered through youth-led and youth-developed peer support groups. Peer advisory councils and committees should be ongoing to support program decisions that impact the youth receiving services there and should honor collaboration between both YRTC staff and program residents/students. Peer support needs to be an integral practice within these settings. Additionally, peer support specialists should be hired as staff members within these settings to demonstrate recovery practices, create hope and honor the self-direction of youth in services.

Preparing the workplace for peer support in these settings is also key for successful implementation. This requires training and strategic planning for peer support implementation that addresses not only the development of peer programs, but the organizational culture shifts that need to occur to create an environment for these programs to grow. The N.A.P.S. National Peer Support Practice Guidelines, The Pillars of Peer Support, and the SAMHSA Core Competencies for Peer Workers in Behavioral Health Settings can be utilized to assist in the implementation planning.

In 2020, SAMHSA released a document titled the 2020 Behavioral Health Workforce Report which estimates a total of 184,684 children getting services in YRTC's annually. It states that 4,735 treatment teams are needed to serve the youth in these settings and that at least one Peer Support Specialist (PSS) should be on each team. The document calls for 6,392 PSS to adequately meet this need (Annapolis Coalition, 2020). However, without peer support programs existing in these settings, there are no available jobs for PSS to serve this community.

Lived experience of a former YRTC resident, Amey Dettmer

When I think about the year, I spent sentenced to a Youth Residential Treatment Center against my own will, I am plagued with memories that still haunt me ten years later. The level of unjust treatment, lack of trauma-informed approach, and blatant morally wrong behaviors and practices that occur to children within these settings make me sick to my stomach. It is a primary reason for me pursuing a career in peer support, as I hope one day people do not have to experience those types of demeaning and unhelpful atmospheres.

I can remember the first time I was "consequenced" for not obeying the rules. It was because I neglected to inform the staff members that my roommate had confided in me that suicidal ideations were on her mind. As a survivor of suicidal thoughts, I know how important and relieving it can be for someone to just share about their thoughts, and I was thankful my roommate trusted me and was opening up since we were all told we were there to deal with our issues. When my roommate decided it was time to tell the staff members how she was feeling, I was "consequence" for what my roommate had confided to me. Consequences meant long hours in a chair faced at the corner and a loss of level on the level system that gave me a little more freedom than most of the kids there. I spent months earning the level that gave me privileges. One of the privileges I earned was to be a peer mentor. Months of hard work and compliance was lost, when I was doing what I thought I was supposed to be doing, ultimately providing peer support in a supervised and structured setting.

Today, when I think about peer support as an earned privilege in this type of setting it just doesn't sit well with me. Peer support should be a core of the programming within these settings. I have heard time and time again that YRTC is meant to be a last resort for children when all other options are exhausted. However, these settings are often privatized and have become an easy placement for youth involved in foster care, juvenile justice, and Departments of Children and Families. They are heavily utilized within children and youth systems, yet poorly monitored for quality of services.

It was almost 15 years ago since I was in this type of treatment setting, and with every new opportunity I get today to hear what is going on behind the walls of these settings, I continue to learn that very little has changed towards recovery approaches in the last 15 years. Very little exists for advocacy efforts for peer support in these settings. Peer Support implementation is met with resistance and a common misconception of "that will not work in this program". It has been easier for me to find organizations aiming to blow the whistle on what happens behind these closed doors and to access troubled teen industry survivor stories than it is to find peer support existing within them. Many suggest it is a better strategy to close down these programs altogether, rather than continue to be met with deep-seeded resistance to change. Within the peer support movements that exist, (consumer, ex-patient, mad pride, psychiatric survivor, etc.) the troubled teen industry is not one I hear commonly spoken of. Yet at this current moment, there is an underestimated, 185,000 youth going through forced treatment in these settings.

Lived experience of a former YRTC staff member, Ian Winter

In my experience, the use of punitive practices by authoritarian staff overshadowed most opportunities students and staff had to practice peer support.

Working as a Mental Health Technician in a youth residential treatment center (YRTC) comes with unique challenges and perspectives.Especially since I am a youth peer with my own lived mental health experience and trained in peer support. While recently working at a YRTC, the most frequent challenge I had was juggling between adhering to the mission and values of the organization while taking a student's perspective on a situation. Taking a student's perspective was very taboo; this was because the staff was in a position of authority not a position of support. During my time working at a YRTC I was spoken to, written up, and disrespected for emphasizing the idea that everyone can learn, grow, recover, and live their best life.

I remember my first hour on campus. Another staff member was giving me a tour and explaining the rules and basic expectations. While explaining the rules this staff told me that "you cannot share anything about yourself with the kids". I was extremely confused by this. When I had my phone interview, I explained my background and was told peer support is a service that was provided. Sadly, the rules on staff sharing any lived experience were strictly enforced. A few days after I ended my probationary period I was written up for oversharing.

The statement I made that resulted in me getting written up was simply "I don't talk to my sister. We don't get along." I was pulled from that conversation and brought into a cluttered office. The office had three chairs set up. Two of them were next to the desk and one chair was right in the middle of the floor. When I walked in, I was told to have a seat in the chair in the middle of the room which was in perfect sight of the students who passed by, including the student to whom I was talking. The conversation was dreadful and inaccurate. It was over ten minutes of me being berated saying "what you're doing is sabotaging their programs, sharing experiences causes more harm." I would continue to hear these gross misconceptions multiple more times before leaving.

The YRTC did not respond to crises well. There were a few times I was on campus when a student self-harmed. The reaction from managers and some staff was to quickly blame the staff that "allowed" it to happen. There was a student who was struggling immensely with thoughts of self-harm and suicide. In one of the first conversations, I had with this student I disclosed about my teenage years specifically how I used to deal with frequent thoughts of suicide and how I overcame them. A few days later this student self-harmed while I was with their group. They were ok but after the shift, I walked into the office for our debrief. The lead staff that day, had the audacity to say, "this event was your fault, and it wouldn't have happened if you did your job." I was almost speechless at their reaction. I told this staff "If you were doing your job, you wouldn't have a petition going around signed by an entire group of fourteen students and one staff member who wants to see you treat them better." The lead ended the meeting there.

A common way staff-maintained control over the campus was reflection. Reflec-

tion is removing students from the group and sending them to an area to be alone. The reflection area was made up of four separate gazebos. Only two of the gazebos had a fire pit despite the freezing temperatures. When I started, there was already snow on the ground. Seeing a student serve reflection for the first time shocked me. This student was bundled up in an orange puffer coat, thick mittens, and a ski mask. Even though this student was the only student out serving reflection they weren't allowed to be at a gazebo with a fire pit. When I asked, "why is the student at a pit without a fire?" I was told, "it's an incentive for them to meet expectations."

When I started, I told students "I wouldn't have you do anything I wouldn't do. Except eating the food." The first few months I never sent a kid to reflection. The idea of sending a student to sit in the freezing cold for not meeting a ridiculous expectation was outrageous to me. At my probationary review, one of my areas of focus was to be stricter and enforce reflection more often. I was furious and astonished that an area of focus at a YRTC was to be more punitive. My mindset on reflection did not change after this meeting. I still thought reflection was cruel and went against the values and principles I have learned and practiced in my training as a peer supporter.

Resilience was a concept I emphasized whenever I could. I celebrated my ten years of being in my own treatment while at the YRTC. I was thirteen years old when I was diagnosed with bipolar disorder. For ten years I climbed a metaphorical mountain. On the tenth anniversary of my diagnosis, I decided to find the hardest trail I could find and hike it. The trail was extremely icy, and I fell. I fell about forty feet and became stuck on the side of a mountain. My rescue took a few hours. While I was stuck on that ledge I could see the rescues below, the ocean, and the trees. For four hours all I could do was enjoy the view and reflect on the actions that got me to where I am.

The next few weeks at work were interesting. The story of my fall did not take long to circle around campus. A student who was serving their reflection time asked me if the story was true. I confirmed that the rumors were true. This student asked me "What did it feel like?" I smiled and told them it was like a reflection. In a nearby doorway, the owner of the YRTC overheard my comparison. The owner pulled me aside and began to question what I was making the comparison to. I told the owner my story and that "I put myself self on reflection". The owner looked at me and sternly told me "It is not appropriate to make fun of our program. It's proven to work." I questioned the owner asking where I could find the research and they walked away.

Walking away, music, drawing, and journaling are common wellness tools that weren't allowed. Anything that was a way to express your emotions or a way to escape for a few minutes was a privilege and needed to be earned. The idea that there were only a few acceptable coping skills created significant barriers to implementing wellness-based groups and activities. I advocated heavily for five months for the YRTC to implement Wellness Recovery Action Plan WRAP® groups, which is a widely recognized evidence-based practice. After being at the YRTC for eight months, I was given the opportunity to introduce WRAP® to the students. During one of the first WRAP® conversations, the students and I went to a garden on the upper campus. We worked on identifying wellness tools in the garden. That was one of my favorite days. I had never seen the students this calm or happy since I started my employment with this program.

Although the group of students I was with were used to constant authoritative direction from staff, that day in the garden, I offered an approach that aligned with peer support values instead. I emphasized that participation is encouraged and voluntary, not mandatory. The garden had vibrant flowers and ripe produce. Upon arrival at the garden that day, the group of students poured out of the van and circled around me waiting for detailed instructions on what to do next. To their surprise, my instructions weren't detailed. I explained that "Wellness is subjective and that I can't force you to do things to be well. During this time in the garden, do what will have the most positive impact for you." Looking around I saw students digging up potatoes, eating produce they just picked and making fantastic floral arrangements. The students ended that day creating and drying their own floral arrangement. For a brief time after this positive experience of the students taking charge of their own wellness, I was confident I was going to bring peer support to this YRTC.

Unfortunately, one of the managers read my written plans for the times I would be spending with the students sharing about WRAP®. This manager thought I was unqualified to go over a crisis plan. The manager told me that "a crisis plan is too clinical for you to teach." Shortly after this downgrading, I received from a supervisor, I was speaking to the administration about what qualifies someone to talk about trauma and crisis. I was told at the time that "I need to be trauma-informed with each student." Very confused, I made my case that I strongly believe that I am trauma-informed. The program director looked at me and completely seriously asked "If you are trauma-informed, then inform us of this student's trauma." I sat there stunned that the person in charge of developing the mental health program for this YRTC showed such little concern and empathy when asking someone to describe trauma.

Peer supporters are empathic and is a practice that should be offered in any care setting that offers a trauma-informed approach. Empathy is a tool I rarely saw used due to the authoritative structures built into the programming at this particular YRTC. Some staff behaved exclusively punitively. One day, a staff member forced a teenage boy to carry a twenty-five-pound bucket with them all day. To this day, I still don't see any therapeutic value in that. This boy was in a setting sub-program that was made up of fourteen boys ages thirteen to eighteen. One of the boys in that group *wrote up a petition to have this staff treat them with more respect. The fourteenth boy signed right after he was given the bucket. I, as a staff member, didn't hesitate to sign as the staff representative and student advocate when I was asked. Little did I know I would be written up again for this. When speaking to the manager, in my reprimand, I was told "We don't want to give the kids that kind of power." A program that once said it offered peer support, wouldn't allow students to practice any forms of self-advocacy, self-direction, be supportive to each other or be offered any notion of recovery principles.*

No matter how obscure the rules and expectations were, working with those students was one of the most rewarding experiences of my life. I introduced a few students to peer support and helped nurture healthy conversations that other staff strictly prohibited. I was told I sabotaged the students' programs by sharing lived experiences. I was told sharing lived experience causes more damage. I am familiar with mental health research and my own experience that would dispute that. I was told peer support is practiced. What I learned is this organization was far from person driven and the values of peer support are virtually nonexistent. Now that I am more aware of what occurs in these settings and after being witness to this environment, I have a moral and ethical interest to facilitate change in these types of places. I foresee a change that offers peer support that aligns with the practice standards and is a common and celebrated practice that actually supports today's youth to find resiliency and recovery in a trauma-informed setting.

Conclusion

If these types of programs are to continue operations, we strongly advise that peer support programs are offered and access to peer support exists in all YRTC settings. These programs need to offer peer support that aligns with the values of peer support. Implementation is possible through the billing of Medicaid dollars, as in some states peer support Medicaid billing meets eligibility for ages 14 and up. Peers should be hired at all levels of YRTC from direct care to leadership positions. Opportunities need to exist for those in services to serve boards and advisory councils that influence the policies of each program. Additionally, technical assistance centers exist to support the design and advise in the implementation of peer support programs that align with peer support practice guidelines. Peer support is the key that will transform these settings from places that cause harm to places that create healing.

Learn more

Presentation: Peer Support in Youth Residential Treatment Centers, Amey

Dettmer and Ian Winter. Copeland Center. https://drive.google.com/file/d/1dw_ZaGGJHc5iIFTAaxRVnZjRQgUom_Af/view?usp=sharing

References

National Practice Guidelines for Peer Specialists and Supervisors... (2019). Retrieved January 3, 2022, from https://www.peersupportworks.org/wp-content/uploads/2021/07/National-Practice-Guidelines-for-Peer-Special ists-and-Supervisors-1.pdf

Nikkel, F., Bergan, J. & Simons, Dayana.(2020). Operationalizing and Funding Youth and Parent Peer Support in Residential Treatment Settings. SAMHSA TA Network. https://youthmovenational.org/wp-content/uploads/2020/07/Operationalizing-Peer-Support-FINAL-electronic.pdf

Behavioral Health Workforce Report. (n.d.). Retrieved February 6th, 2022, from https://8767e61b-c26e-4b0f-b872-d9e03c702a01.filesusr.com/ugd/8b1e4a_3578676a37824c2fba834e8e170f3c39.pdf or https://annapoliscoalition.org/wp-content/uploads/2021/03/behavioral-health-workforce-report-SAMHSA-2.pdf

Peer Youth Advocates in Residential Programs: Handbook Appendices Appendix A: Acknowledgements and Contributors Appendix B: Glossary Appendix C: Contacts for More Information Appendix E: Training, Tips and Tools, and Youth Lead Advisory Councils Training. (n.d.). Retrieved February 6, 2022, from https://www.build ingbridges4youth.org/sites/default/files/BBI%20Peer%20Youth%20Advo cate%20Handbook%20Appendices%20FINAL.pd

University of Michigan Behavioral Health Workforce Research Center. *National Analysis of Peer Support Providers: Practice Settings, Requirements, Roles and Reimbursements: .* (n.d.). Retrieved February 6th, 2022, from https://www.behavioralhealthworkforce.org/wp-content/uploads/2019/10/BHWRC-Peer-Workforce-Full-Report.pdf

Jonathan D. Brown PhD MHS, Kirsten Barrett PhD, Henry T. Ireys PhD, Kamala Allen MHS, Sheila A. Pires MPA & Gary Blau PhD (2010) *Family-Driven Youth-Guided Practices in Residential Treatment: Findings from a National Survey of Residential Treatment Facilities, Residential Treatment for Children & Youth,* 27:3, 149-159, DOI: 10.1080/0886571X.2010.500137

SAMHSA Core competencies for peer workers in behavioral health ... (2015). Retrieved February 10, 2022, from https://www.samhsa.gov/sites/default/files/programs_campaigns/brss_tacs/core-competencies_508_12_13_18.pdf

The Copeland Center for Wellness and Recovery. (n.d.). *Home.* Navigating Pillars of Peer Support. Retrieved February 11, 2022, from https://www.pillarsofpeersupport.org/

SECTION 4: TRANSFORMING LIVES WITH THE ARTS

Gayle Bluebird, RN
Consumer/Survivor

Using the Arts and Peer Support to Advance Healing & Recovery

Presented by "Bluebird" & Deb Trueheart

Art: "Bee Here Now" by Amy Smith

Art has become widely accepted as a means for peers to tell their stories, as a way for them to express themselves, for its power to heal and transform lives and increasingly a means of self-sufficiency.

Many peers with traumatic life experiences report the importance of the use of art and creativity as integral components of their recovery. The arts can be whatever we usually think of as being creative: writing, music, painting, dance, sculpture, storytelling, performance and journaling. All of these are pleasurable activities but can also be used as a conduit for expression of parts of ourselves we have not been able to express in any other way. Art is a powerful healing tool to explore deep emotions, the sorrows, the struggles and joys. Art is a safe way for survivors of trauma to express themselves without judgment or censor.

Discussion

Art offers us the ability to transform us by awakening parts of ourselves to recover and heal from earlier traumatic memories. Peers starting an artistic journey may find memories they hadn't started out to reveal. Through artwork, people can develop their own personal vocabularies for a fuller identity. Images on paper, words in poetry, or use of other medium, reflect back- at- us as mirrors of ourselves providing us with new insights.

Many peers have found a place of belonging. No one is telling them what to do or judging them. There is no discrimination in art. Because our stories are so similar in nature, we often understand what psychiatric survivors are saying before others do. Many peers have in common the death and doom prediction of lifelong dysfunction given by medical-model well-meaning psychiatrists and other mental health professionals. Art can pave a way to the potential that lies within us to be greater than we imagined ourselves to be.

Audiences are important. We are our first audience, self-critics, self-analysts for meaning. We make decisions whether to share our talent with others. Some of us destroy our art, afraid to reveal painful memories that we have uncovered or we de-value the worth of our expressions. Valuing our art is another step in our healing. Letting ourselves speak, giving permission for ourselves to continue, and eventually to share with others, is a separate but equally important challenge.

Our survivor movement has done a lot to bring us out of isolation. While art has not yet been fully seated at the decision tables as policy makers it has influenced the means of how personal change takes place, not as mental health treatment but as transformation of our thoughts and feelings. It allows us to transcend negative realities into perfect understandings of ourselves thus freeing us to *be ourselves*. It has allowed us to find each other in peer-operated organizations, including, drop-in centers, wellness centers and in some states, independent peer operated centers focused entirely on the arts. Having a place to go gives us opportunities to meet each other and support each other. We discuss our art over cups of tea, in support groups, in workshops. We give each other confidence. National conferences offer yet another way for exposure as we perform in talent shows or to exhibit visually our artwork. Art is flourishing. It is being discovered as if it was something new, but in fact, art has always been an important means of alternative healing.

More artists have begun to make a living from their art. Prominent among them is Jerome Lawrence who has painted series of beautifully combined colors on a wide variety of subjects. Some of them feature nature scenes while others focus on dancers, prancing horses, and others. The Carter Center exhibits his work and has taken a special interest in his art using one of his paintings for their annual fundraising event. Another consumer, Mike Skinner, writes songs about his recovery from childhood sexual abuse and on hope and spirituality. He puts out a regular newsletter and performs at many mental health conferences. Meghan Caughey, also, has created a name for herself. One of her works, *Strip Searched on the Inpatient Unit,* was inspired after reading Pema Chodron, spiritual writer, who said, "We should take full measure of joy in the 'juicy, spicy, and brilliant craziness and confusion'". Meghan has contrasting artwork, some created while she was extremely depressed and lifeless; later, in her lotus series, she describes her images as "coming out of the mud."

Conclusion

Art is leading the way for culture change in mental health settings. Environments change, comfort rooms have been created, bright colors are painted on walls, and use of full names in art exhibits is common instead of the traditional hiding of names of the artists. Art exhibits are common both in community settings and in mental health treatment settings. Art therapists are now being trained in recovery principles and offer choices to people they work with. Peer Specialists are part of several curriculum in two states known at this time, in New York State's Academy of Peer Services, and the state of Delaware. There are a few peers who have trained to become art therapists. Art has- the- ability to break down communication and eliminate the need for criticism. Creativity and the arts can lead us to the answers we seek, heal our wounds, help us to transform ourselves to become the persons we want to be. Having fun while creating is an answer itself to mental illness, for when we are so engaged, we do not have time to ruminate or reminisce; we are just there.

References

Baltic Street's Resource and Wellness Center. (n.d.). Retrieved from https://bkwellnesscenter.wordpress.com/about

Bluebird, G. (2022). Transforming my life with the arts. Webinar. Broadcast, May 24, 2022. [Video 53.59 min.] Recording: https://youtu.be/_dwkCgHcQX0
Presentation slides: https://aps-community.org/wp-content/uploads/2022/06/Arts-Illustrating-History.pdf

Bluebird, G. (Ed.). (2000). Participatory dialogues: A guide to organizing interactive discussions on mental health issues among consumers, provides, and family members. Washington D.C.: U.S. Department of Health and Human Services, Substance and Mental Health Services Administration, Center for Mental Health Services.

Bluebird, G. (Ed.) (2001). Reaching across with the arts: A self-help manual for mental health consumers. Ft. Lauderdale, FL: Peer Print.

Campbell, J., Ostrow, L., & Croft, B. (2015). We are the evidence: Evaluation of peer programs. Webinar. Retrieved from https://power2u.org/wp-content/uploads/2017/09/We-Are-the-Evidence_webinar.pdf

Chery, K. (2019). How listening to music can have psychological benefits. Retrieved from https://www.verywellmind.com/surprising-psychological-benefits-of-music-4126866

Creativity and mental health. (2019, November 23). In Wikipedia. Retrieved from https://en.m.wikipedia.org/wiki/Creativity_and_mental_health

Dodson, L. (2018). Creativity and mental health. Retrieved from https://www.insider.com/the-link-between-creativity-and-mental-health-2018-7

Friedman, M. B. (2012). Creativity and madness: Are they inherently linked? Article in HuffPost. Retrieved from https://www.huffpost.com/entry/creativity-madness_b_1463887

The Icarus Project [Fireweed Collective]. (n.d.). Retrieved from https://fireweedcollective.org/our-history/
Instruments of Healing. (n.d.). Retrieved from http://www.instrumentsofhealing.org

Kaimal, G. (2019). How art therapy can reduce stress and support mental health—how researchers changed the world, Episode 5. Retrieved from https://www.howresearchers.com/episodes/episode-5/

Malchiodi, C. A. (2002). The soul's palette: Drawing on art's transformative powers for health and well-being. Boston: Shambhala.

Malchiodi, C. A. (2013). Art therapy and health care. New York: Guilford Publications.

Malchiodi, C. C. (2015). Creativity as wellness practice. Psychology Today. Retrieved from https://www.psychologytoday.com/us/blog/arts-and-health/201512/creativity-wellness-practice

McNiff, S. (1992). Art as medicine: Creating a therapy of the imagination. Boston: Shambhala.

Mcniff, S. (2004). Art heals: How creativity cures the soul. Boston and London: Shambala.

National Coalition for Mental Health Recovery. (2021). Alternatives 2021 (virtual) conference. https://www.alternatives-conference.org/art-exhibit

News12 Connecticut. (2018). BX residents paint to end mental health stigma [Video file]. Retrieved from http://connecticut.news12.com/story/38176234/bx-residents-paint-to-end-mental-health-stigma

NYC Mural Arts Project, Department of Health and Mental Hygiene. (2018). Retrieved from https://www.muralartsproject.cityofnewyork.us/about/

Pallazzolo, F. (2017). Laura Anne Walker at SVA [Video file]. Retrieved from https://www.youtube.com/watch?v=gB71gUX-LT0

Pattani, A. (2018). How creative arts can change the way people deal with mental illness. Retrieved from https://www.inquirer.com/philly/health/mental-health-mental-illness-creative-arts-therapy-20181105.html

Penney, D., & Stastny, P. (2008). The lives they left behind: Suitcases from a state hospital attic. New York: Bellevue Literary Press.

Poole, S. (2014). The Atlanta Journal-Constitution. Artist Jerome Lawrence says he is always evolving. Retrieved from https://www.ajc.com/lifestyles/artist-jerome-lawrence-says-always-evolving/VvJkaB6kMiulQbYIJnHsTN/

Samuels, M., & Lane, M. R. (2013). Healing with the arts: A 12-week program to heal yourself and your community. Atria/Beyond Words, ISBN 978-1-58270-393-0.

Sea Lemon. (2016). 4 easy art projects to help you relax & de-stress [Video file]. Retrieved from https://www.youtube.com/watch?v=FpGrtBx7Xy8&t=12s

SecondStepPlayers. (n.d.). The Second Step Players [YouTube Channel]. Retrieved from https://www.youtube.com/channel/UC28doOu2PbR33_xSDBBiqfQ

Spaniol, S. (1993). An exploratory study of the perceptions of artists who have experienced mental illness. Unpublished Doctoral Dissertation, Boston University, Boston, MA.

Spaniol, S. (2004). An arts-based approach to participatory action research. Journal of Pedagogy, Pluralism, and Practice, 3(1), Article 6. Retrieved from https://digitalcommons.lesley.edu/jppp/vol3/iss1/6

Spaniol, S., & Bluebird, G. (2001). Participatory dialogues: Action research for art therapists and people with psychiatric disabilities. Proceedings of the American Art Therapy Association 32nd Annual Conference. Mundelien, Il: American Art Association

Spaniol, S., & Bluebird, G. (2002). Report: Creative partnerships—people with psychiatric disabilities and art therapists in dialogue. The Arts in Psychotherapy, 29, 107-114.

Stand Up for Mental Health. (2009). David Granirer's take on stigma [Video file]. Retrieved from https://www.youtube.com/watch?time_continue=4&v=_TUCjBWV7IA

Stuckey, H. L., & Nobel, J. (2010). The connection between art, healing, and public health: a review of current literature. American Journal of Public

Health, 100(2), 254-263. Retrieved from https://ajph.aphapublications.org/doi/10.2105/AJPH.2008.156497

The Awakenings Project. (2009). Retrieved from http://www.awakeningsproject.org

thepaparazishow. (2010). Black butterfly [Video file]. Retrieved from https://www.youtube.com/watch?v=DDRnuKw0BFw

Trueheart, D. L. (2009). Healing power of creative arts. Alternatives Arts Pre-conference, St Louis, MO.

UF Health Shands Arts in Medicine. (2015). What is arts in medicine? [Video file]. Retrieved from https://www.youtube.com/watch?v=TPb4XaemRtQ

Valentin, B. (2019). Go inside the Living Museum at Creedmoor Psychiatric Center in Queens. Article in Untapped New York. Retrieved from https://untappedcities.com/2019/03/25/go-inside-the-living-museum-at-creedmoor-psychiatric-center-in-queens/

Walker, L. A. (2018). Laura Anne Walker. Retrieved from https://www.artsy.net/artist/laura-anne-walker

Well Being Programs, Inc. (n.d.). Altered State of the Arts: A national network of mad artists. Informational brochure, pgs 1&2.

Wikipedia Contributors. (2020). Creativity and mental health. Retrieved from https://en.m.wikipedia.org/wiki/Creativity_and_mental_health

APPENDIX A: BIOGRAPHIES

- N.A.P.S. Board Members
- N.A.P.S. Workforce and Supervision Workgroup & Book Editors
- Contributor Biographies

N.A.P.S. Board Members

Kathy Cash

Kathy Cash, CPSS, DDiv, is a Veteran of the United States Army, a Certified Peer Support Specialist, Founder/CEO of Strategies 4 Hope Peer Empowerment Center, and the Pastor/Founder of Determined to Know Christ Ministries.

Dr. Cash is a subject matter expert on the value of Peer Support in the care of Veterans and has been an invited participant of Veteran panel discussions and research projects across the country. She is also a Wellness Recovery Action Plan (WRAP) Facilitator wherein she supports Veterans in developing his/her own recovery plan. A strong advocate for Women Veterans, Dr. Cash facilitates Women Veteran support groups; mentors and coaches Veterans through Vet to Vet, a national peer support program that focuses on meeting the needs of Veterans and their families; and she strives to gather and disseminate as much information as is available in support of all Veterans.

Dr. Cash serves on the board of the National Association of Peer Supporters (N.A.P.S.) and other community boards, including the National Association of Black Military Women (NABMW), Community Unity Partnership (C.U.P.) of Empowerment Coalition, and Transition Housing Solutions (THS). She works with various other community organizations such as Women Vets on Point, the Los Angeles LGBT Center, and The Dream Center; and is 1st Vice Commander of the American Legion, Jackie Robinson Post 252. Dr. Cash has been a guest on "The Voice of the Veteran" podcast, hosts a segment biweekly segment on Operation Confidence: America's Invisible Heroes radio show, and hosts her own podcast, "Change Your Focus and Live Life."

Dr. Cash is a licensed and ordained Pastor/Teacher and received her Doctorate in 2017. She has over 30 years of servanthood in Los Angeles, surrounding communities, and across the country, teaching leadership skills and spiritual growth. She formerly served as a Chaplain with the Los Angeles

County Sheriff's Department, and currently serves as a volunteer with the Los Angeles Police Department Clergy Council, Volunteers, and the Community Police Advisory Board.

Dr. Cash continues to live in Los Angeles and is the mother of three adult children.

TIM SAUBERS

Tim Saubers, CPS, got his start as a Wisconsin Certified Peer Specialist in 2016, and has worked in direct support and supervisory roles. He previously managed Wisconsin's Certified Peer Specialist and Certified Parent Peer Specialist state certification programs, and co-authored the curriculum and exam currently used in Wisconsin Certified Peer Specialist certification processes. He has also participated in the development of certification curriculum used by the State of Texas and the National Association for Addiction Professionals (NAADAC). Currently, he serves as the Program Coordinator for Workforce Development at the Peer Recovery Center of Excellence while also providing consultation centered on curriculum and exam development, research, and programmatic design.

Additionally, Tim sits on a variety of state and national committees and workgroups including chairing Disability Rights Wisconsin's Protection and Advocacy for Individuals with Mental Illness Advisory Council (DRW PAIMI) and serving as Vice President of the board of the National Association of Peer Supporters (N.A.P.S.), serving on the executive committee of the Consent, Autonomy, and Dignity Collective Liberation Group (CAD). He also previously served as co-chair of the Wisconsin Certified Peer Specialist Advisory Committee (CPSAC), and N.A.P.S.' Youth and Young Adult Peer Supporters Committee (YAYAPS), and sat on the Wisconsin Recovery Implementation Task Force (RITF), as well as the Wisconsin Department of Corrections Oversight Committee for Certified Peer Specialists (DOC CPSOC).

Tim centers the principles of equity and justice in his work while moving not just to disrupt and reform systems, but to create new systems in their entirety. He is currently based in Madison, Wisconsin and in his spare time enjoys volunteering, cooking, and paleontology.

ELISE PADILLA

Elise Padilla, MSW, MBA, CPSW, is the founder and owner of Rebel Leadership Group, LLC an organization focused on supporting leaders and entrepreneurs in developing strategy and workplaces focused on whole health. It's through lived experience that Elise finds power in changing broken systems focused on profit over people and has worked in the field of behavioral health for over 20 years. She believes in the efficacy of peer support for lasting recovery, as she found on her own journey. As a certified peer support worker, Elise supports local and national organizations such as the New Mexico Women's Reentry Center, Psychosocial Rehabilitation Association of New Mexico and National Association of Peer Supporters, where she sees the power of hope and humility in creating community. She believes that we all have something to give, and by developing strategy and confidence, we can find our own version of success. As an Enneagram 3, she uses her Achiever mindset to encourage those she works with, bringing humor and compassion to her everyday work. She is proud of her two young daughters and the changemakers they are becoming, and lives in the beautiful Land of Enchantment with them, her husband and a menagerie of animal friends. Elise is always looking for a good book and can be found wandering in nature, finding her peace.

VINCENT F. CAIMANO, PH.D.

Vince Caimano, Ph.D. is the Co-Founder and CEO of Peer Support Solutions. In 2003, as a peer, he was one of the first instructors of Mindfulness-Based Cognitive Therapy for Depression in the United States. Shortly thereafter, Vince started a successful face-to-face support group in his community. In 2009, he pioneered the use of video-chat based meetings for peer support. PSS's Support Groups Central and HeyPeers platforms, now help individuals from over 160 countries. The platforms assist people with behavioral health, chronic illness and rare disease issues. They host over 1,300 monthly meetings that help thousands of individuals.

Vince has been an invited presenter at many conferences, including four times at the Alternatives Annual Conference and three SAMHSA Behavioral Health and Technology Summit meetings. He has held executive and leadership roles at global consulting firms such as Accenture, Watson Wyatt, Towers Perrin and Opinion Research Corporation. His practice areas have included strategy clarification / implementation, performance management and development, executive coaching, employee research and leadership development. Vince was also COO for Amor Ministries, an organization that at that time worked with 25,000 participants to build homes for 1,100 families a year.

Earlier in his career he served as an HR and IT executive in a $7 billion aerospace company and he also founded and led the HR Strategy Forum, a professional organization for HR executives in California.

Vince earned his PhD in Organizational Psychology from Washington University in St. Louis and his BA in Psychology with a Business minor at the University of South Florida. He lives with his wife, near his daughters and their families in Pasadena California.

JESSI DAVIS (THEY/SHE)

Jessi Davis (she/they) is a certified Peer Supporter from Texas, and has been in the field since 2013. They currently live in Austin, Texas with their family. Jessi has worked in a variety of settings providing peer support and has a passion for ensuring that young people have access to quality, affordable peer support. Through their efforts, Jessi has impacted state, regional, and national programming focused on adult, and youth and young adult, mental health and substance use recovery. They are currently the President of the Board of Directors for the National Association of Peer Supporters (N.A.P.S.), and a Senior Program Coordinator for the South Southwest Mental Health Technology Transfer Center (region 6). Jessi has been a part of ACCEPT Tx, Youth Peer Support consulting, the Houston Texas ROSC, multiple conference planning committees, and the wider peer support community.

KERIS MYRICK

Keris Jän Myrick is a leading mental health advocate and executive, known for her innovative and inclusive approach to mental health reform and the public disclosure of her personal story (as featured in the New York Times series: Lives Restored). Ms. Myrick has over 15 years of experience in mental health services innovations, transformation, and peer workforce development. She is known for her collaborative style and innovative "whole person" approach to mental health. Ms. Myrick is the policy liaison for The National Association of Peer Supporters (N.A.P.S.) and a co-director of the Mental Health Strategic Impact Imitative (S2i). She is the developer and host of the podcast "Unapologetically Black Unicorns" focusing on mental health, race equity and lived experience. Ms. Myrick was formerly the Chief of Peer and Allied Health Professions for the Los Angeles County Department of Mental Health, and has served as the Director of the Office of Consumer Affairs for the Center for Mental Health Services (CMHS) of the United States Health and Human Services' Substance Abuse and Mental Health Services Administration (SAMHSA) and was the Board President of the National Alliance on Mental Illness (NAMI). Myrick is a Co-Editor of the Journal of Psychiatric Services "Lived Experience and Leadership" column and has authored numerous peer reviewed journal articles and book chapters. Ms. Myrick has a MS in organizational psychology from the California School of Professional Psychology of Alliant International University and an MBA from Case Western University's Weatherhead School of Management.

DANA FOGLESONG

Dana Foglesong, MSW, NCPS, CRPS, is the immediate-past president of the National Association of Peer Supporters. She also serves as the national senior director of recovery and resiliency (R&R) services for Magellan Health where she works to expand access to peer support and other recovery support services and improve the behavioral health system's capacity to provide recovery-oriented and trauma-informed care. She joined Magellan in 2015 as a director for a Medicaid mental illness specialty plan in Florida where she increased access to billable and non-billable peer support services and led a 1115 housing waiver pilot to expand availability of housing support services. Prior to Magellan, Dana served in a lived experience leadership role for the Florida Department of Children and Families in the Office of Substance Abuse and Mental Health where she developed the state's guide-lines on peer support services and spearheaded the state's recovery-oriented system of care (ROSC) transformation effort. Prior to working in state government, Dana founded the Peer Support Coalition of Florida, a statewide peer network, to ensure people served and their families were active partici-pants in the design, implementation and evaluation of systems and service delivery practices. She has over twenty years of board service including as an executive committee board member for the National Alliance on Mental Illness. Dana's work has shaped policy and practice related to peer support, including leading the group that developed the National Practice Guidelines for Peer Support Supervisors and the proposed standard occupational classi-fication definition for peer support specialists. She is a published author and co-author of peer and non-peer reviewed publications with a specific research interest in peer delivered and whole health approaches within inte-grated health settings. Dana is a nationally certified peer specialist and holds a master's degree in social work from the University of Central Florida.

N.A.P.S. Workforce and Supervision Workgroup & Book Editors

Rita Cronise

Rita Cronise, MS, ALWF, holds a distance faculty position with Rutgers University's Academy of Peer Services. She has lived experience of a major mental health diagnosis, and is certified as an advanced level WRAP facilitator, a peer specialist and peer specialist trainer in the VA and led the development of an advanced peer specialist training for the SAMHSA-funded Recovery to Practice program. In 2012, Rita coordinated the development of the National Practice Guidelines for the peer workforce through the National Association of Peer Supporters (N.A.P.S.). Rita continues to serve on a N.A.P.S. workgroup, developing guidance for the supervision of peer specialists and other related peer workforce issues. She is a frequent lecturer on peer support values, practice, and supervision.

Jonathan P. Edwards

Dr. Jonathan P. Edwards, Ph.D. , LCSW, ACSW, NYCPS, consults nationally advancing peer support workforce development including supervision and certification in mental health and substance use treatment settings. He has held numerous leadership positions, including director of peer support services for a large city hospital where he supervised nearly 30 peer specialists working across five different service settings; developed and facilitated support groups for family members; and contributed to various organization transformation projects. He received his M.Phil. and Ph.D. in Social Welfare from CUNY Graduate Center, his Master's in Social Work from Silberman School of Social Work at Hunter College and is a licensed clinical social worker. He is also an adjunct professor at Columbia School of Social Work, a member of the Academy of Certified Social Workers, a New York Certified Peer Specialist, and a Certified Personal Medicine Coach. Jonathan served on the National Association of Peer Supporters (N.A.P.S.) Board for four years,

New York Peer Specialist Certification Board since 2014, and Mental Health News Education Board since 2012. Jonathan identifies as a person in long-term recovery, which is the driving force behind his worldview, advocacy, scholarship, and professional direction. Dr. Edwards' research explores factors associated with job satisfaction among peer support workers in mental health treatment and recovery-oriented service settings.

GITA ENDERS

Gita Enders, LMSW, MA, NYCPS has worked in peer support, training, and supervision for over 20 years, with expertise in both mental health and substance use recovery. She has held leadership positions in Arizona and New York, primarily in public health facilities including peer-run agencies and traditional provider systems. Gita consults locally and nationally on peer programming and supervision, as well as on the development of training curricula. She received her MSW in Organizational Management and Leadership from Silberman School of Social Work at Hunter College, her MA in English from New York University, and is a licensed master social worker and New York Certified Peer Specialist. Gita is supervisor at the Peer Advisor Program at the Public Psychiatry Fellowship of Columbia University and New York State Psychiatric Institute. She has been a member of the Arizona Behavioral Health Planning Council, and serves on the Board of Baltic Street AEH, Inc.

JOANNE FORBES

Ms. Forbes PhD consults nationally on mental health system transformation and peer support service delivery, implementation, training, and supervision. She earned her PhD from Rutgers University's Department of Psychiatric Rehabilitation. She has years of experience in the field of mental health as an advocate, educator, administrator, and peer supporter. Her published research on peer supervision is considered a seminal work in the field. She is a frequent presenter at conferences and is the author of the book, *Madness: Heroes Returning from the Front Lines.* In the 1980's she started a peer run Customer Service Department in a large metropolitan psychiatric hospital which evolved into Baltic Street AEH, Inc., one of the largest national peer-run agencies. She is a national trainer and expert not only in peer services but also transforming mental health systems to a recovery orientation. She has been widely recognized by state and national organizations as a visionary and advocate for those facing mental health challenges

Contributor Biographies

Wallis Adams

Wallis Adams is an Assistant Professor of Sociology at California State University, East Bay. Prior to this position, she was a Postdoctoral Fellow at the Center for Psychiatric Rehabilitation at Boston University. Much of her research centers on the peer workforce, including this current project assessing the impact of the COVID-19 pandemic on peer specialists in the US.

Lori Ashcraft

Lori Ashcraft, PhD. During her 40-year behavioral health career, Lori has had a strong interest in the therapeutic effects of self-determination, choice, and personal freedom. She did her dissertation on freedom, spending a month in Russia at the time the Soviet Union collapsed, and focused her inquiry in Soviet mental hospitals where the lack of freedom and choice was pervasive. Lori's vision for the future is to continue teaching recovery principles and practices, assuring people that they can recover. She has developed numerous curricula designed to help individuals with psychiatric experiences move beyond recovery and build resilience by finding their purpose, making their own unique contribution, and using their experiences to help others grow and recover. Her own passion for recovery stems from personal experience having lived with severe depression most of her life. Early in 2015, Lori created a new company, Resilience, Inc. with her husband Gene Johnson. The vision of Resilience is a legacy of recovery and resilience through innovation that will be self-sustaining by creating a world filled with hope, love and healing. Resilience is now merged with Crestwood and together we are building a strong peer workforce within Crestwood programs. We are also passionate about training peers to work in all other peer friendly programs, and this will continue to change the world of behavioral health.

Andy Bernstein

Andy Bernstein, PhD, CPRP, is a psychologist and a psychiatric rehabilitation practitioner who has long been involved in the consumer movement and in peer support as a helping paradigm and an evolving discipline. His doctoral dissertation in 1989 was on the development of self-help groups, and he has been closely involved with N.A.P.S. since attending its first conference in 2006 with NJ peer colleagues. Andy provided technical support to the NJ Consumer-Provider Association for 10 years until he moved to Arizona, where he serves as Clinical Director of Camp Wellness, a SAMHSA award-winning recovery-oriented adult education program which employs peers as Health Mentors.

Dan Berstein

Dan Berstein, MHS, is the founder of MH Mediate, the Co-Founder at the CUNY Dispute Resolution Center's Dispute Resolution in Mental Health Initiative, and the Co-Chair of the Diversity Committee at the American Bar Association Section of Dispute Resolution. He is the author of the book, *Mental Health and Conflicts: A Handbook for Empowerment* (available at https://www.americanbar.org/products/inv/book/420367133/) and his TEDx Talk "How to Talk About Mental Health Without Offending Everyone" can be viewed at https://youtu.be/nstRHTVv0Aw. Visit the Dispute Resolution in Mental Health Initiative to access more resources, by visiting www.mhmediate.com/drmh.

Gayle Bluebird

Gayle Bluebird, AKA Bluebird, has been a pioneer working to change the culture of the mental health system for many years in different parts of the country. She is known for promoting the arts to heal from trauma and emotional abuse and has formed national networks of artists, writers, and performers, who tell their mental health stories through art. She has received many awards, including the prestigious Voice Award from the Substance Abuse and Mental Health Administration (SAMHSA) in 2010. In her last position, she was the director of peer services in the state of Delaware, where she helped to develop and implement several peer programs, including a successful arts center, The Creative Vision Factory. Now retired, she spends much of her time writing daily poems on Facebook. She has written a book called *Tootles' Tails*, that contains stories written in the voice of her dog,

Tootles, soon to be published. You can find her on Facebook or email her at
gaylebluebird1943@gmail.com.

PATRICIA BLUM

Patricia Blum, PhD, is passionate about bringing peer support services and
peer leadership to traditional psychiatric programs throughout California for
over 30 years. She introduced the peer support role to Crestwood in the
1990s and by 2003 we had a Peer Advocate in the organizational executive
leadership team. Patricia has a master's in art therapy and a PhD in Psychology, publishing her dissertation on Stigma in 2006. Patricia presented at the
Alternative conference in the early 2000's, supported the county and
statewide Recovery task force groups, supported California Anti- Stigma
campaign and continues to champion peer led services throughout California.
Today with Recovery and Resilience Solutions, Patricia promotes the person
served as the expert in their care and this approach as the future of behavioral
health. From the 1990's, I had the belief that anyone with lived experience,
regardless of discipline, could use their recovery story to support others. We
can create a support system at all levels of care, a nurse will be a more
compassionate nurse, a housekeeper will be kinder and a cook more
thoughtful with the background of shared experience. For almost 30 years we
have hired and promoted people with lived experience to support and grow
recovery and resilience. In 2008 Crestwood and the Resilience Inc leaders
first partnered to begin the formal education of staff that have become our
peer support specialist and in 2015 through statewide grants we started the
journey of training our staff at all positions on the competencies of peer
support specialist. In 2019 we partnered Resilience Inc creating Recovery and
Resilience Solutions. This has propelled Crestwood peer support training and
recovery leadership. Crestwood has many opportunities for growth. The
support and expertise of the Resilience team has allowed us to do organizational analysis and create the scaffolding and supports needed to sustain
growth emerging towards recovery as an organization and for eth people we
serve. In 2021, completing the Peer Specialist training, I gained a solid understanding of recovery and resilience as a provider, as an organizational leader
and as an individual. This brings a unique perspective with family member
experience, living with a mental health challenge and maintaining hope, spiritual alignment, respect, compassion, flexibility, trust and love all leading to
sustained recovery.

Thomasina Borkman

Thomasina Borkman, PhD, has a doctoral degree in sociology from Columbia University, studies and publishes about peer-run groups (e.g., Alcoholics Anonymous, Recovery International, Family Survivors of Suicide, or mental health consumer-run organizations) as Professor of Sociology Emerita at George Mason University and as Affiliate Scientist at Alcohol Research Group. She has participated in feminist consciousness-raising, cancer support and bereavement support groups. For 44 years she has been a member of 12-step/12 tradition anonymous groups. This combination of researcher and participant gives her both insider and outsider perspectives.

George S. Braucht

George S. Braucht, LPC, CPCS & CARES. Mr. Braucht's 14,000+ hours of psychotherapy, supervision, and applied community psychology experience focuses on professional and peer workforce development that emphasizes continuous service quality and program outcome improvement. In peer services, George co-founded the Certified Addiction Recovery Empowerment Specialist Academy, a peer recovery coach training that is operational in several states, and the Forensic Peer Mentor Ready4Reentry training. Clinical programs he led include a statewide recovery counseling program for people on parole, opening Georgia's first two in-prison therapeutic community programs and the first five-day reporting centers, and initiating several statewide reentry initiatives. In addition to teaching psychology, curricula George developed include an Enhanced Supervision Program training for correctional and reentry staff, certification trainings for Recovery Residence Managers and for REC CAP, a recovery capital scale and data management system. George is a Charter Board Member of the National Alliance for Recovery Residences and a Recovery Consultant for SAMHSA's Opioid Response Network.

Rita Cronise

Rita Cronise, MS, ALWF, holds a distance faculty position with Rutgers University's Academy of Peer Services. She has lived experience of a major mental health diagnosis, and is certified as an advanced level WRAP facilitator, a peer specialist and peer specialist trainer in the VA and led the development of an advanced peer specialist training for the SAMHSA-funded Recovery to Practice program. In 2012, Rita coordinated the development of the National Practice Guidelines for the peer workforce through the National Association of Peer Supporters (N.A.P.S.). Rita continues to serve on a N.A.P.S. workgroup, developing guidance for the supervision of peer specialists and other related peer workforce issues. She is a frequent lecturer on peer support values, practice, and supervision.

AMEY DETTMER

Amey Dettmer, CPS, is a Certified Peer Specialist who has been building a career in peer support since 2011. She has experience with direct service, supervision, training and technical assistance. Her work with the Copeland Center for Wellness and Recovery has taken her all over the United States offering wellness, recovery and peer support education. She currently is the Program Manager of the SAMHSA-funded Doors to Wellbeing National Consumer Technical Assistance Center. In 2018 she was recognized for her leadership by N.A.P.S. with the Disruptive Innovator Award honoring her for outstanding contributions to peer support. Amey has a passion for expanding access to peer support and is a national leader in the peer support movement.

JONATHAN P. EDWARDS

Dr. Jonathan P. Edwards, Ph.D. , LCSW, ACSW, NYCPS, consults nationally advancing peer support workforce development including supervision and certification in mental health and substance use treatment settings. He has held numerous leadership positions, including director of peer support services for a large city hospital where he supervised nearly 30 peer specialists working across five different service settings; developed and facilitated support groups for family members; and contributed to various organization transformation projects. He received his M.Phil. and Ph.D. in Social Welfare from CUNY Graduate Center, his Master's in Social Work from Silberman School of Social Work at Hunter College and is a licensed clinical social worker. He is also an adjunct professor at Columbia School of Social Work, a member of the Academy of Certified Social Workers, a New York Certified Peer Specialist, and a Certified Personal Medicine Coach. Jonathan served on the National Association of Peer Supporters (N.A.P.S.) Board for four years, New York Peer Specialist Certification Board since 2014, and Mental Health News Education Board since 2012. Jonathan identifies as a person in long-term recovery, which is the driving force behind his worldview, advocacy, scholarship, and professional direction. Dr. Edwards' research explores factors associated with job satisfaction among peer support workers in mental health treatment and recovery-oriented service settings.

GITA ENDERS

Gita Enders, LMSW, MA, NYCPS has worked in peer support, training, and supervision for over 20 years, with expertise in both mental health and substance use recovery. She has held leadership positions in Arizona and New York, primarily in public health facilities including peer-run agencies and traditional provider systems. Gita consults locally and nationally on peer programming and supervision, as well as on the development of training curricula. She received her MSW in Organizational Management and Leadership from Silberman School of Social Work at Hunter College, her MA in English from New York University, and is a licensed master social worker and New York Certified Peer Specialist. Gita is supervisor at the Peer Advisor Program at the Public Psychiatry Fellowship of Columbia University and New York State Psychiatric Institute. She has been a member of the Arizona Behavioral Health Planning Council, and serves on the Board of Baltic Street AEH, Inc.

DANA FOGLESONG

Dana Foglesong, MSW, NCPS, CRPS, has held national leadership positions in the private and nonprofit sectors and within state government. In these roles, Dana utilizes her professional experience and lived/living experience of recovery to transform policy and practice, deliver data-driven innovation, and work for the meaningful inclusion of people served and their families in the design, implementation, and evaluation of systems and service delivery practices. Her work has been instrumental in shaping federal and state policy and practice related to peer support.

JOANNE FORBES

Ms. Forbes, PhD, consults nationally on mental health system transformation and peer support service delivery, implementation, training, and supervision. She earned her PhD from Rutgers University's Department of Psychiatric Rehabilitation. She has years of experience in the field of mental health as an advocate, educator, administrator, and peer supporter. Her published research on peer supervision is considered a seminal work in the field. She is a frequent presenter at conferences and is the author of the book, *Madness:*

Heroes Returning from the Front Lines. In the 1980's she started a peer run Customer Service Department in a large metropolitan psychiatric hospital which evolved into Baltic Street AEH, Inc., one of the largest national peer-run agencies. She is a national trainer and expert not only in peer services but also transforming mental health systems to a recovery orientation. She has been widely recognized by state and national organizations as a visionary and advocate for those facing mental health challenges.

PHYLLIS FOXWORTH

Phyllis Foxworth is the Advocacy Vice President at the Depression and Bipolar Support Alliance, the leading peer-directed organization for people living with mood disorders. After being diagnosed with a mental health condition in early adulthood, Ms. Foxworth continues to live in wellness and facilitates a weekly DBSA Family & Friends Support Group.

Ms. Foxworth is a contributor to the first medical textbook on The Diagnosis and Management of Agitation providing a chapter titled: *Patient Rights, Patient, and Family Perspectives on Agitation* and is a co-principal investigator on two PCORI projects. Ms. Foxworth has served as a patient representative panelist at several FDA public meetings and directed DBSA in hosting the first externally led patient focused drug development meeting that has focused on mental health.

CHERYL GAGNE

Cheryl Gagne, Sc.D., is a senior associate at C4 Innovations. Her areas of interests and expertise are workforce training and development (including peer workers), transforming behavioral health programs and systems to promote recovery and person-centered practices, using evidence-based practices in programs, and evaluating recovery-oriented services. She has a passion for increasing the involvement of people with lived experience of recovery in the development, delivery, and evaluation of behavioral health and social services. Cheryl is a person in recovery from mental illness and addiction. She is an advocate for others who are in recovery and are striving for their rights to participate in communities of their choice.

RUTH HOLLMAN

Ruth Hollman is the Founder/Chief Executive Officer of SHARE! the Self-help And Recovery Exchange in Los Angeles (www.shareselfhelp.org). She is a cultural anthropologist by training and did her PhD dissertation research in Thailand. She received the American Psychological Association SCRA Award for Distinguished Contribution to Practice in Community Psychology in 2016 for the innovative peer programs she has designed to facilitate recovery for mental health consumers. She combines the latest research on what works with her 28 years of experience at SHARE!

Yumiko L. Ikuta

Yumiko Ikuta, MBA, is a consumer and the Director of the Office of Rehabilitation in the Bureau of Mental Health at the NYC Dept. of Health & Mental Hygiene. Her Office oversees over 80 non-clinical treatment, rehabilitation programs including supported employment, education support services, clubhouses, psychosocial clubs, peer support, respite, self-help, advocacy and outreach as well as peer specialist training programs. Her experience in peer specialist education is extensive as the former Deputy Director of Howie the Harp Peer Advocacy Center and the former Program Manager of the Academy of Peer Services. Yumiko also worked closely with the NYS Office of Mental Health to develop Medicaid billable Home and Community Based Services and its delivery system. She worked for over 15 years in the corporate sector and for the US Agency for International Development at the Dept. of State as an economic development officer in several developing countries. She also started up and operated her own wholesale and retail fine jewelry business on Madison Avenue in NYC. Yumiko holds a BA in Economics and East Asian Studies and an MBA in Marketing and International Business both from Columbia University.

Clarence Jordan

Clarence Jordan, MBA, is Vice President of Wellness & Recovery for Beacon Health Options. In this role, he provides strategic direction and leadership for the company's national Wellness & Recovery program. He is responsible for various initiatives to operationalize Beacon Health Options' commitment to recovery-based principles in the delivery of behavioral health services. Jordan is a former naval officer, and his recovery journey is chronicled in National Council Magazine's "50 Years, 50 Stories of Recovery" special issue to commemorate the 50th anniversary of the Community Mental Health Act. Clarence has a Master's in Business Administration (MBA) from Naval Post Graduate School, Monterey, CA.

Clarence Jordan has deep roots in the National Alliance on Mental Illness

(NAMI) and has served multiple terms on its National Board of Directors. Prior to that, as the NAMI Tennessee state office Director of Multicultural Outreach Initiative, he developed and wrote "A Family Guide to Mental Health: What You Need to Know." His work led to NAMI Tennessee receiving the coveted National Multicultural Outreach Award. In 2009 he conducted a press conference at the National Press Club in Washington, D.C. sponsored by NAMI on the experience of military families involved in the Afghanistan and Iraq wars. In 2010, he provided testimony before the U.S. Senate Committee on Veterans' Affairs on the mental health needs of veterans and their families.

Clarence Jordan received the Consumer Leadership Award at the Substance Abuse and Mental Health Service Administration (SAMHSA) 2010 National Voice Awards, as well as its 2012 VOICE Awards Fellowship. In 2014, the National Council for Behavioral Health named him its Peer Specialist of the Year.

In 2015 Clarence served on the National Academies of Sciences, Engineering and Medicine's Committee on the Science of Changing Behavioral Health Social Norms Board on Behavioral, Cognitive, and Sensory Sciences Division of Behavioral and Social Sciences Education. The Committee conducted a yearlong study on these behaviors as they occur Nationally and several western societies. The results of the study were published in 2016, "Ending Discrimination Against People with Mental and Substance Use Disorders."

KELSEY KNOWLES

Kelsey's own recovery journey began in 2012 and launched her career in substance use and mental health services. Her experience includes providing direct services, leading state-wide programs, and consulting and presenting nationally on best practices. Kelsey received an MSW from Florida State University and is a RCSWI, Certified Recovery Peer Specialist, Certified Community Health Worker, and Certified Recovery Support Specialist. Along with a group of dedicated leaders in the field, she co-authored the "National Practice Guidelines for Peer Specialists and Supervisors", published by Psychiatric Services in 2021.

LISA KUGLER

Lisa Kugler, PsyD, is a licensed psychologist in the state of Pennsylvania. Dr. Kugler has been active in the field of substance abuse and mental health services providing direct care, executing administrative duties, and conducting research for over 25 years.

Currently, Dr. Kugler leads all clinical, operations, and development for the provider affiliate to Beacon Health Options, Beacon Care Services. In addition, she is leading the strategic vision for peer recovery services within the combined Beacon/Anthem organization. Previously she was the Vice President/ CEO of the Beacon Health Options Maryland Division. She led her team in the management of behavioral health Medicaid benefits for over 1 million covered lives in the state of Maryland. She worked with the state, counties, providers, and oversight to make certain that individuals are receiving the appropriate treatment to assist them in their recovery journeys. Dr. Kugler served as the Vice President of Clinical Services for Value Behavioral Health of Pennsylvania (VBH-PA) where Dr. Kugler oversaw all clinical operations. Prior to her position at Beacon Health Options, Dr. Kugler led for the Center for Treatment of Addictive Disorders at the Pittsburgh Veteran's Administration. Dr. Kugler has provided services to adults, veterans, inmates, adolescents, and children. She has been involved in research endeavors that focused on repetitive transcranial magnetic stimulation (rTMS) and Dr. Kugler completed a study that examined the impact of methadone maintenance therapy on executive functioning.

Dr. Kugler has presented locally, regionally, nationally, and internationally on topics focused on substance abuse concerns, motivational interviewing, peer supports, and recovery and resiliency.

Lyn Legere

Lyn has promoted her passion for workforce development for the past 25 years, knowing first-hand how work can be a powerful facilitator of recovery. She has worked across the board from policy to practice to implementation of peer support, supported employment and education, and Social Security work incentive education, all in the effort to promote an accessible path to vocational recovery for people with mental health challenges. Currently, Lyn is working at BU Center for Psychiatric Rehabilitation where she is Project Director for the CAPP Peer Coaching project and RiseUP Above Benefits for mental health practitioners.

Michelle Love

Michelle Love, CPS, is a human rights officer with Advocates Behavioral Health Residential Services.

Nicole MacAskill-Kaylie

Nicole MacAskill-Kaylie is a human rights officer with Advocates Behavioral Health Residential Services.

Chris Martin

Chris Martin has spent over 20 years developing, designing, and delivering peer support and recovery-oriented training programs. Chris's own lived recovery experience gives him a credential of "having been there" which he brings to all his writing and training programs. He has delivered trainings throughout the US as well as the UK, New Zealand. Canada, and Singapore. Chris has also provided peer support services in both hospital and community-based settings and served as a manager, supervisor, and coach for peer support specialist teams.

Debbie Nicolellis

Debbie's career has focused on understanding and promoting the career aspirations of people with lived experience. Debbie and Lyn Legere worked to bring the best of psychiatric rehabilitation and peer support together through Vocational Peer Support. At UMass Chan's Transitions to Adulthood Center for Research, Debbie currently trains providers to support young adults in their success in work and school through HYPE (Helping Youth on the Path to Employment), including FSST (Focused Skill and Strategy Training, an executive functioning curriculum).

Laysha Ostrow

Laysha Ostrow, PhD, is the CEO of Live & Learn, Inc. Her research agenda focuses on employment outcomes and working conditions for individuals with psychiatric disabilities. She is the PI on two NIDILRR-funded field-initiated grants: the Certified Peer Specialist Career Outcomes Study, and *Reclaiming Employment*. In addition to her duties at Live & Learn, Inc., Dr. Ostrow is an Adjunct Professor in the School of Community and Global Health at Claremont Graduate University. She completed a Postdoctoral Research Fellowship in the Department of Psychiatry at UCSF and holds a PhD from the Johns Hopkins School of Public Health and a Master of Public Policy from the Heller School for Social Policy and Management at Brandeis

University. Dr. Ostrow has first-hand lived experience of the special education, Social Security disability, and psychiatric systems.

SCOTT PALLUCK

Scott Palluck serves as the Director of Operations Process Analysis for Crestwood Recovery and Resilience Solutions, a training and consulting division of Crestwood Behavioral Health, Inc. He earned a master's degree in Sociology from Western Illinois University. Scott has had the honor of working alongside leaders in recovery for the past two decades. He has a passion for creating innovative ways to integrate recovery and resilience practices into organizational systems. In addition, Scott has had the opportunity to support the growth and development of peer workforces with numerous counties and community-based organizations throughout California.

TAMMI S. PAUL

Tammi is the Deputy Director, Oregon Family Support Network. Tammi came to OFSN with over 20 years of experience working in higher education and special education law. She is an educator by nature and couples that with her lived experience parenting 3 youth who experience mental health challenges and developmental disabilities. Tammi's work with OFSN is grounded in building a thriving Training and Workforce Development program which has included developing and writing a state approved curriculum to certify Family Support Specialists to work in Medicaid billing environments. She has also worked alongside the 9 recognized tribes in Oregon to support the development and delivery of a curriculum that prioritizes tribal values, culture and practices and meets Medicaid billing requirements. Tammi serves as a curriculum reviewer for State of Oregon peer training programs and provides consultation, training and workforce development convenings nationally.

HAYLEY PEEK

Hayley Peek is a Mental Health Consultant, focused on creating safe spaces and breaking open conversations around supporting mental health. She leads from a place of living experience with mental illness and recovery and weaves elements of her own story into her work for the purpose of connecting with others and providing insights and education on how we look and speak about mental health. She offers keynote presentations, workshops and peer support services across Canada. www.HayleyPeek.com

MORGAN PELOT

Morgan Pelot, BA, BS, is the Research Program Manager of Live & Learn Inc. a California-based social enterprise that connects lived experience with learned expertise in mental health services research. She graduated from University of California, Santa Cruz with a major in Psychology and Molecular, Cell, and Developmental Biology. She has worked on research and consulting projects related to medication decision-making, peer-run program evaluation, and peer specialist certification. Additionally, Ms. Pelot served as a peer counselor for almost three years. Her passion for research is fueled by wanting to make a difference and supporting change in the mental health system.

ANNA ROCKHILL

Anna Rockhill, MPP, is a Senior Research Associate at Portland State University where she works on projects having to do with child welfare, substance use disorder, domestic violence and homelessness. She has had the privilege of working on a number of studies focusing on peer services in a variety of settings including the child welfare system and re-entry (formerly incarcerated) programs.

E. SALLY ROGERS

E. Sally Rogers is the former Executive Director and Director of Research at the Center for Psychiatric Rehabilitation at Boston University. Since its founding, the Center has been a leader in the paradigm shift to a recovery focus for the mental health field. In her current capacity as Research Professor, Dr. Rogers conducts studies of innovative interventions, qualitative research and develops measures. She has focused significant attention on the peer specialist workforce, including a systematic review, a special journal issue on peer-delivered services, surveys of the peer specialist workforce, and currently, a clinical trial of a coaching intervention for peer specialists experiencing role stress. Dr. Rogers is the author/co-author of numerous scholarly publications on topics related to the health and recovery of individuals with mental health conditions.

MARK SALZER

Mark Salzer, PhD, is a psychologist and Professor of Social and Behavioral Sciences in the College of Public Health at Temple University. He is also the Director of the Temple University Collaborative on Community Inclusion (www.tucollaborative.org). Dr. Salzer has been a peer support ally since 1988 when he began supporting an international mutual-aid organization for people in recovery. He has since partnered with peer support leaders on research and evaluation, developing and understanding the certified peer specialist workforce, and educating the non-peer behavioral health workforce about peer support and the authentic integration of peer support in behavioral healthcare.

DIANN SCHUTTER

Diann Schutter, CPSS, lives with a major mental health diagnosis. She is a Certified Peer Support Specialist and a WRAP facilitator in Grand Rapids, Michigan. Diann is one of the founding members of NAPS. She served on the board of directors for more than a decade. She was one of the friendly people at the registration desk checking in for the national peer support conferences and she attended more than 10 national conferences in different states. Diann loves being a Certified Peer Support Specialist because she has a lot of passion for assisting others on their journey of recovery and instills hope in the people she meets. She states, "One day as a CPSS is more rewarding than 20+ years at Mijer, Inc.," which is a retail store in Grand Rapids. Since 2018 Diann has been a caregiver through an agency. She works with the geriatric population. All of her clients have a diagnosis of a mental illness. Most of them also suffer from Dementia, Alzheimer's, and/or physical disabilities.

ASHLEY SPROUL

Ashley Sproul (she/her/hers), is a Certified Peer Specialist and the Peer Support Coordinator of The Living Room, a Peer-run crisis alternative drop-in center in Framingham, MA. Ashley is a psychiatric survivor who is deeply passionate about Peer Support and racial justice work, as these areas have been an instrumental part of her own recovery. She is dedicated to supporting others as they navigate their own wellness in times of emotional distress and spends much of her time creating and facilitating trainings regarding Peer Support, human rights, racial equity, and anti-oppression. Some of her other passions include spending time with family, playing music and finding ways to incorporate artistic creativity into Peer Support spaces.

KIM SUNDERLAND

Kim Sunderland has promoted the development of peer support across Canada as author of the Mental Health Commission of Canada's Peer Support Guidelines, and the inaugural Executive Director of Peer Support Accreditation and Certification Canada (currently known as Peer Support Canada). Kim continues to facilitate peer support workshops and consult around the development of workplace peer support programs. Kim is currently involved in bringing supportive communication skills to a broader audience as co-author of the 'Supporting Through Struggle' workshop. Kim's book *"It's All Gonna Be Okay – From Mad and Sad to Calm and Confident"* is forthcoming. www.KimSunderland.ca

CARINA TEIXEIRA

Carina Teixeira, PhD, is an academic, psychologist, and music artist. Her interest in peer support started years ago when she was doing a post-doctoral fellowship at Boston University Center for Psychiatric Rehabilitation. Nowadays, Carina teaches psychology and neuroscience at King's College London and supervises MSc projects in the area of personal recovery and peer support. Recently, Carina has been interested in peer support for refugees with experience of psychosis, peer support for suicide survivors, and peer support for victims of domestic violence. Carina addresses these same topics in her songs and uses her music as a vehicle for mental health advocacy.

ELIZABETH THOMAS

Elizabeth Thomas, PhD, is an Assistant Professor in the Department of Social and Behavioral Sciences in the College of Public Health at Temple University. As a psychologist, she is a longstanding admirer, ally, and researcher of peer support. Her research has focused on understanding how the peer-to-peer relationship impacts mental health service outcomes, how peers can support self-determination, decision-making, and engagement in services, and what can be done to support the peer workforce, particularly youth/young adult peer supporters. She partners with peer specialists in the research process whenever possible, benefitting significantly from the enriching effects of lived experience perspectives.

Linda May Wacker

Linda May Wacker, MEd, QMHP, CADC, is Program Director of Morrison Child & Family Services' Parent Mentor Program, which provides peer recovery support to Child-Welfare involved parents in six counties in Oregon. She has been a peer mentor trainer and supervisor for the past 10 years. Wacker co-authored Morrison's Oregon Health Authority-accredited Parent Mentor/CRM Training Curriculum and contributed as an editor to Substance Use Disorder Peer Delivered Services Child Welfare Best Practices Curriculum. Smith, K. Debban, C. Sanden, S. Martin, E. Wurscher, J. Wacker, L M. Klapperich, M. Paul, J. (2017). Wacker holds a Master's degree in Counseling, but learned everything she knows about addiction, recovery, and peer supervision from parents in recovery over the past 10 years.

Victoria (Vic) Welle

Vic Welle (no pronouns or they/them) is an activist, psychiatric survivor, and once-aspiring minister who remains passionate about creating trauma-informed, culturally sensitive spiritual support for people experiencing emotional distress. Vic is a trainer and consultant for non-coercive crisis alternatives such as peer run respites, and co-founded Monarch House Peer Run Respite in Wisconsin. Vic's education includes graduate level theology studies and many years of direct experience living and working in community with other survivors.

Ian Winter

Ian works as a Crisis Support Professional with Crisis & Counseling Centers. Ian graduated from Rutgers School of Health Professionals with an A.S in Psycho-Social Rehabilitation. Diagnosed eleven years ago with bipolar disorder he struggled with thoughts of being alone and abnormal. He always thought his life would be dark. After a few years Ian became a member of the Doors to Wellbeing National Youth Advisory Council as well as The Young Adult Youth Association of Peer Support. Working on local, state, and national levels Ian hopes to be a pioneer in changing mental health programs in youth systems. He likes to say he lives in the brightest colors because he defied expectations to become the optimistic and passionate voice for change, he always wanted to be!

JESSICA WOLF

Jessica Wolf, PhD, is Principal of Decision Solutions Consulting, Assistant Clinical Professor in the Yale Department of Psychiatry, Senior Consultant to the Annapolis Coalition on the Behavioral Health Workforce and former member of the National Association of Peer Supporters (iNAPS) Workforce Development Committee. She served as a Connecticut Department of Mental Health Regional Administrator, developed the Department's Education and Training Division, and founded and coordinated the MERGE Mental Health Certificate Program at Housatonic Community College in Bridgeport, CT. Jessica's lived experience of mental health conditions, trauma, and recovery informs her workforce consulting and commitment to strengthen the peer workforce.

ROBYN WOODHOUSE

Robyn Woodhouse was a Human Rights Coordinator with Advocates Behavioral Health Residential Services at the time of her submission.

MX. YAFFA

Mx. Yaffa, also known as Ahmad Abojaradeh (they/them), is an award-winning disabled, mad, trans, queer, Muslim, Indigenous Palestinian. Mx. Yaffa conducts transformative work around displacement, decolonization, equity, and centering lived experiences of individuals most impacted by injustice. Mx. Yaffa is a storyteller and an equity and transformation consultant, having shared their story with over 100,000 audience members at speaking events globally specializing in global and community vision building. Mx. Yaffa is an engineer, with a specialty in sustainability and social engineering, a peer support specialist, and an equity and transformation consultant. Mx. Yaffa utilizes peer support as a foundation for all their work, supporting peer-run spaces in organizational capacity building, equity, and sustainment. Mx. Yaffa brings together engineering, peer support, and trauma to support their vision of more equitable and accountable communities that lead to individuals' self-actualization. In their free time, Mx. Yaffa is a world traveler and novelist, having visited over 70 countries and written over a dozen books.

APPENDIX B: HISTORY OF N.A.P.S.

HISTORY OF N.A.P.S.

THE FOLLOWING HISTORY OF THE NATIONAL ASSOCIATION OF PEER SUPPORTERS (N.A.P.S.) has been adapted from a few different sources: (1) a conversation with founder, Steve Harrington; (2) a presentation given at the 10th Annual Peer Specialist Conference in Philadelphia by former co-director Lori Ashcraft and long-time ally Andy Bernstein; (3) a conversation with charter N.A.P.S. members Diann Schutter and Mike Roaleen; (4) information provided by past N.A.P.S. director, Martha Barbone; and (5) input from 2022 N.A.P.S. board members, Jessi Davis and Cathy Cash.

A BRIEF HISTORY OF THE NATIONAL ASSOCIATION OF PEER SUPPORTERS (N.A.P.S.)

A compilation on the organization's history with contributions by Lori Ashcraft, Martha Barbone, Andy Bernstein, Rita Cronise, Steve Harrington, Mike Roaleen, and Diann Schutter, Kathy Cash, and Jessi Davis

"So why are you helping me, anyway?" The person was someone who had seemingly lost all hope of ever getting better, ever living a life that mattered, or ever even feeling like there was any point to living at all.

"I'm a peer support specialist," Steve replied gently, as he sat next to the person.

The person was used to answering the standard intake questions and waited for the pencil and checklist to come out. When it didn't appear, the person squinted at Steve's face, which showed an uncommon mix of respect and concern. With a puzzled expression the person asked, "what is a peer specialist?"

Steve Harrington was a peer support specialist (PSS) at Touchstone, an agency in Grand Rapids, Michigan. Because the job and title were new to the agency, Steve had answered that question, "what is a peer specialist?" countless times for the people receiving services. He was purposely not getting much direction from his supervisor, who knew Steve and the other PSS's needed to use their personal experiences to build trusting relationships first before they could be effective in offering peer to peer support. His supervisor knew that each person is different, living with different circumstances, and Steve and the others would find their own unique way to connect and then provide support. So instead of giving Steve direction on how to perform the role (because his supervisor had never performed the role himself), Steve's supervisor said, "use what you've learned about recovery in your own life, listen carefully, and do what comes naturally to you with each person, and then tell me what you did."

His supervisor's confidence in Steve and the others paid off. After two months, Steve and the others reported back to this supervisor, and their job descriptions were created. Each job description was tailored to include ways each of them had used their personal experiences and unique personal attributes, like a good sense of humor, to connect with and build relationships with people who, it seemed, nobody else could reach. Steve and five other PSS's at Touchstone went through a similar process of creating their own unique job description.

Steve met regularly with other PSSs at Touchstone and various agencies in Grand Rapids, Michigan to compare what they were doing and to learn how they could do their jobs better. The support they received from each other was not only important to doing their jobs well but to staying well themselves.

As he learned more about peer support services, Steve realized that he and his colleagues were not alone. There were other peers being hired in other parts of the country. They wondered what those other peers were experiencing; what problems they were facing and what solutions they were coming up with. This curiosity prompted Steve to take a trip to various places in different states visiting programs that hired peers. He soon became convinced of the need for a national association where peers could learn from each other and belong to something beyond their immediate jobs. This, he reasoned, would reduce the feeling of isolation and separation.

In 2004, Steve and founding members Mike Roaleen, Diann Schutter,

Karen Murphy, Joel Penney, Lynette Johnson-Bilski, and Sue Clossen met regularly at the Unlimited Alternatives Drop-in Center to form the National Association of Peer *Specialists* (NAPS). Artist Susan Meekoff joined shortly after they got started. The association was renamed a few years later to the National Association of Peer Supporters (N.A.P.S.) to be more inclusive of those providing peer support in any role or title, including those who provide volunteer services.

To help reduce the sense of isolation and to share helpful information, Steve began to send out newsletters. The group gathered at Steve's house for mailing parties. And through this simple newsletter outreach, he invited people to become members. He knew that peer specialists could not afford a lot, so he charged a low fee for an annual membership just to help cover printing and mailing costs. Steve spoke regularly with peer specialists across the country and shared what he was learning along the way. He used humor in his presentations and became a popular public speaker on the subject of peer support.

In 2007, the first National Conference was held in Denver. Andy Bernstein, a clinical psychologist who through the years became one of the most faithful allies joined at that time and has stayed active in the organization through the years. The National Conference has been held in different locations around the country ever since.

Year	Location	Theme	Keynote
2007	Denver	Climbing the Mountain Together	Gayle Bluebird
2008	Philadelphia	The Recovery Revolution: Peer Supports on the front line	Joseph Rogers
2009	Phoenix	Acquiring the Recovery Fire	Larry Fricks, Lori Ashcraft, and Mary Blake
2010	Chicago	Setting Sails in Windy Weather	Antonio Lambert
2011	Raleigh	Where Peer Support Meets Southern Charm	Peter Ashenden
2012	Philadelphia	The Recovery Revolution: Part 2	Wilma Townsend, Matthew Federici, Allen Doederlein
2013	Anaheim	Growing Bigger and Best through Sharing	Lyn Legere and Keris Myrick
2014	Atlanta	Changing Times, Changing Profession	Larry Davidson, Larry Fricks, Allen Daniels, Peter Ashenden, Steve Ford
2015	San Antonio	Advocacy, Poverty and Peer Support	Gayle Bluebird, Gitane Williams
2016	Philadelphia	Collaborating for Unity	Matthew Federici, Mark Salzer, Sharon Wise, Robyn Priest, Gina Calhoun, Gayathri Ramprasad
2017	Phoenix	Recovering and Sustaining Peer Support: Creating a Path for Our Future	Pat Deegan, Chacku Mathai, Sally Zinman, Lori Ashcraft
2018	Orlando	Reinforcing Our Roots: Designing Our Future	Keris Myrick, Azza Altiraifi Mark Salzer
2019	San Diego	Daring to Rise	Khatera Aslami, Dr. Nadia Richardson, Kelly Davis, Vesper Moore, and Amey Dettmer.
2020	No Conference		
2021	Virtual Online	Uniting the Peer Workforce	Miriam E. Delphin-Rittmon, Noah Abdenour, Juan Velez Court

In 2007, to better understand peer support services in the U.S., Steve conducted a national survey of satisfaction and compensation.

In 2010, SAMHSA awarded the Recovery to Practice (RTP) contract to six professional associations, including NAPS and the Depression and Bipolar Support Alliance (DBSA) to create a training program for peer specialists. Lisa Goodale, a social worker with DBSA joined and became another important ally. The RTP contract included a requirement for a situational analysis of the peer support workforce, which Steve created from his survey and input from peers he had connected with across the country.

In 2012, the association piloted a collaborative learning model for peer support specialists to develop their own communities of practice called Next Steps, which was well received by those who took the training. In 2013, the association issued National Practice Guidelines (NPG) for Peer *Supporters* based on a consensus process in which 1,000 peer support providers nationally gave a 98% approval rating for 12 core values and guidelines for what those values look like in practice.

In 2014, Steve partnered with Dan O'Brien-Mazza, National Director of Peer Support Services at the Department of Veteran Affairs VA to create an annual recognition day for peer specialists, "Global Peer Support Celebration Day", which is celebrated annually on the 3rd Thursday of October.

In 2015, Steve Harrington had a career-ending stroke, however in his retirement he found joy in the simple things like gardening and fishing. He was finally able to take his own advice on self-care and, although Steve passed away in November of 2021 his legacy carries on.

In 2016, after Steve's stroke, Rita Cronise and Lori Ashcraft stepped up as interim co-directors. Under their leadership, the 10th Annual National Peer Specialist Conference was held in Philadelphia with over 650 in attendance. In 2017, Beth Filson was named executive director. She was succeeded by Mike Weaver and Martha Barbone. Lisa St. George was the board president in 2017 and she was succeeded by Dana Foglesong in 2019 and Jessi Davis in 2021.

Accomplishments

The association has a worldwide mailing list of over 6,000 with a significant reach to the wider peer community through affiliated organizations like the National Mental Health Consumers' Self-Help Clearinghouse, the National Coalition on Mental Health Recovery, and the SAMHSA National Consumer Technical Assistance Centers, which respectively each have mailing lists in the tens of thousands.

In 2017, the association participated in a study by the U.S. Government Accounting Office (GAO) which gave a report to Congress on Leading Practices for State Programs to Certify Peer Specialists. The report was published in November 2018.

In 2018, the association participated in a series of educational programs through the Patient-Centered Outcomes Research Institute (PCORI). Following an 18-month consensus building process, a national workforce workgroup, led by Jonathan P. Edwards, and included Jessica Wolf, Rita Cronise, Kelsey (Stang) Knowles, Dana Foglesong, Gita Enders, Joanne Forbes, and (later) Ian Winter. The workgroup supplemented the existing National Practice Guidelines (NPG) with guidance for supervisors as agreed upon through focus groups, surveys, and a consensus process similar to the one used to confirm the original NPG. The enhanced guidelines, named the National Practice Guidelines for Peer Specialists and Supervisors (NPG-S) were introduced at the 2019 National Conference in San Diego. The workgroup continues to develop education and training for the workforce, with an emphasis on supervision.

In 2019, the association co-sponsored the International Initiative for Mental Health Leadership (IIMHL) Exchange and Peer Leadership Match which took place in September in New Haven, CT, and Washington DC. The association also played a key role in the Mental Health and Substance Use Disorders Forum at the National Academies of Science in Washington DC.

As of September 2020, the association had successfully offered 48 webinars, sponsored by Optum. With continued support of Optum the national workforce workgroup (joined by Ivanna Bond and Ian Winter) offered a five-month Supervision Learning Collaborative based, in part, on the National Practice Guidelines for Peer Specialists and Supervisors (NPG-S).

From 2006-2019, the association was best known for its annual National Conference for Peer Supporters. After a one-year break due to the uncertainty around the COVID pandemic, the association resumed its long tradition of offering an annual National Conference in 2021 through a virtual conference.

Benefits of Membership

There are many benefits of belonging to a membership organization. In addition to gaining the latest innovations in practices, as demonstrated by the narratives provided by conference presenters in this volume, there is greater visibility in numbers and more ways to advocate for change that will have an impact on issues that are directly related to peer support and services. If you are not already a member, visit the National Association of Peer Supporters website and join! You can join as a Professional, Ally, or Sustainer:

https://www.peersupportworks.org/register/professional/
https://www.peersupportworks.org/register/ally/
https://www.peersupportworks.org/register/sustainer/

Rita Cronise, MS, ALWF
Former Director of N.A.P.S., current member of the N.A.P.S. workforce and
supervision workgroup, and faculty, Rutgers University, Academy of Peer
Services.

Appendix C: Tributes to Fallen Leaders

Tributes to our Fallen Leaders

This book is dedicated to Steve Harrington, Founder of the National Association of Peer Supporters (N.A.P.S.) and champion of peer support until his passing in 2021.

Andy Bernstein, former N.A.P.S. board member and friend of Steve writes, "I first met Steve Harrington at the First Annual Peer Support Conference, in Denver, in 2007. Although I was not a peer, Steve welcomed me to this amazing project he had started, essentially taking the position that there was room in 'the movement' for many different kinds of supporters and collaborators. I think he was impressed that I had brought to the conference several peer colleagues from New Jersey, where for 20 years I was involved in the mental health consumer movement as an ally, never having my life interrupted by mental health challenges, or by behavioral health treatment that I'd received at numerous times since childhood. My role with peers—who at that time in our part of the world called themselves consumer-providers—had been as a colleague in starting self-help groups and consumer-run organizations, and I was learning as much or more from them as I ever learned from my graduate studies in psychology. Steve seemed to understand that collaboration among different kinds of actors was a healthy trait for an organization to have, and in this way, he was perhaps demonstrating an early awareness of what is now referred to as intersectionality, but from a strengths-based perspective.

And strengths are where it was at for Steve: he was an inveterate optimist, always finding the good in people and the opportunities which presented themselves whenever a challenge came his way. He would be singularly undaunted year after year as complexities and complications arose in the planning process for each new conference. It didn't matter whether it was a booked venue choosing to undergo renovations at the same time that we were supposed to be meeting there, presenters backing out at the last minute, or finances looking like they were going to sink the whole endeavor: Steve just refused to get rattled, and he used both his unlimited creativity and his ability to recruit helpers and support to make lemonade out of lemons.

He placed above all else people's capacity to learn from each other's stories, and in settings which ranged from formal workshops and plenary sessions to cigar breaks right outside of hotel main doors, he listened. He heard about peers' relationships with county and state authorities, about agencies mis-using peers to do work which was anathema to the core values of the profession, and about the heart-felt conflicts within the field about whether peer support needed to follow in the paths of more traditional disciplines such as psychology, counseling and social work to be regulated and more formally credentialed. He heard about salary disparities, continuing stigma from within the mental health field, and arguments between those who eschewed the use of medications and those who swore by it. And he heard about the successes and setbacks of countless individual conference attendees as they shared the long struggles they had with their own personal demons.

Regarding the former, Steve adamantly espoused a kind of community decision-making model, seeking viewpoints from as many stakeholders as possible, wanting to ensure that all voices were heard. And as for the latter, more than almost anyone else that I know, Steve managed to convey a sense of hope and empowerment to people who at the moment were not feeling it. His own story, one filled with ups and downs, is a rich source of inspiration and courage, and in one of his most popular books, *Trees of Hope: Planting Seeds for a Better Life* (Maritime Press, 2007), he gives myriad examples of ways to view and experience the often-unfair world that can help all of us find paths to success, along the way embracing kindness, forgiveness, understanding, and wholeness.

A word here about Steve's own wholeness. In addition to getting his law degree when a school of social work urged him to leave the program due to his psychiatric history, Steve worked at various times as a reporter, editor, photographer, teacher and rancher. He was the first and perhaps only post-doc without an advanced degree in the social sciences to be admitted to

Boston University's Center for Psychiatric Rehabilitation, and the two years that he and Zach spent in their 10th floor oceanside apartment in Revere gave him a constant view of the ocean which he loved so much, despite not being able to scuba dive in it as he'd done when much younger in Lake Michigan.

Steve was incredibly well read, and he brought his formal education in natural resources, biology and public administration to numerous projects and adventures in the wild, including a sometimes-harrowing barge trip with fellow peers down the Mississippi River that taught him and his fellow travelers an important lesson about race and prejudice. And in 2015, when his stroke essentially ended his ability to read and compromised his working memory, he handed off the most significant part of his life's work to people he knew and trusted, and made the best of yet another new situation, turning to gardening, farming, and being a good neighbor and partner.

Steve's loss is felt by so many of us in different ways. Some will remember his generosity, as for many years, he funded much of iNAPS' activity through his own money, and always made provisions for scholarships to the Annual Conference. Others will recall his visionary sense of inclusiveness: it was largely Steve's influence which led to the expansion of what initially was just NAPS--the National Association of Peer Specialists--into iNAPS--the International Association of Peer Supporters--thus allowing peer support from around the world to be included in our work, and encouraging supporters of peer support, like me and many other non-peers, to join in the work. Still others, especially his friends and colleagues from the early years, will remember his sense of adventure and his willingness to take risks and embrace uncertainty. But I think it is Steve's gentle wisdom, his openness, his sense of humor, and the acceptance he showed of his own and others' humanness by which he will be remembered most fondly by those of us who knew him through his work in peer support. Remembered, loved, respected, encouraged and inspired by...that's what I hope his legacy will be."

Andy Bernstein, PhD, CPRP
Former N.A.P.S. Board Member
Clinical Director, UA RISE Health and Wellness Center (Camp Wellness)
Clinical Professor, UA College of Medicine, Dept of Family and Community Medicine
May 22, 2022, Tucson, AZ

TRIBUTES TO OUR LEADERS AND ALLIES WHO RECENTLY PASSED

Steve Harrington – tribute compiled by Rita Cronise. https://aps-community.org/2021/12/14/remembering-steve/ (http://bit.ly/3UaQEAo)

Bill Anthony – tribute compiled by Lori Ashcraft. https://aps-community.org/2020/09/17/tributes-to-bill-anthony-compiled-by-lori-ashcraft/ (http://bit.ly/3iiAKGX)

George Ebert – tribute by Lauren Tenney. https://www.peergalaxy.com/event/george-ebert-tribute/ (http://bit.ly/3F3S9Mt) http://www.laurentenney.us/files/133946208.pdf (http://bit.ly/3Vbogja)

Ed Knight – tribute by Laura Van Tosh. https://www.nyaprs.org/e-news-bulletins/2019/1/30/lat-ed-knight-dont-give-up-your-delusions-of-grandeur-those-are-your-goals (http://bit.ly/3Vp8VuQ)

Darby Penney – tribute compiled by Harvey Rosenthal. https://aps-community.org/event/a-celebration-of-the-life-of-darby-penney/ (http://bit.ly/3U46D3m)

Jacki McKinney – tribute compiled by Celia Brown. https://aps-community.org/memories-of-jacki-mckinney/ (http://bit.ly/3EAwHgO)

Sally Zinman – tribute compiled by Harvey Rosenthal. https://aps-community.org/2022/08/29/in-everlasting-honor-and-memory-of-sally-zinman/ (http://bit.ly/3UdNmMS)

Printed in Great Britain
by Amazon

26957550R00245